Walt Whitman

D1043456

The Works of
Walt Whitman

*with an Introduction by David Rogers,
and Bibliography*

Wordsworth Poetry Library

This edition published 1995 by Wordsworth Editions Ltd,
Cumberland House, Crib Street, Ware, Hertfordshire SG12 9ET.

Copyright © Wordsworth Editions Ltd 1995.

All rights reserved. This publication may not be
reproduced, stored in a retrieval system,
or transmitted, in any form or by any means, electronic,
mechanical, photocopying, recording or otherwise,
without the prior permission of the publishers.

ISBN 1-85326-433-4

Printed and bound in Denmark by Nørhaven.

The paper in this book is produced from pure wood
pulp, without the use of chlorine or any other substance
harmful to the environment. The energy used in its
production consists almost entirely of hydroelectricity
and heat generated from waste materials, thereby
conserving fossil fuels and contributing little to the
greenhouse effect.

Introduction

Walt Whitman is, in the strictest sense of the word, the most original of all American poets, for with the publication of the first edition of *Leaves of Grass* in 1855 American poetry first assumes a distinct national voice. Other American poets had been content to borrow their language and their conventions from the British. Their verse displays little effort to come to terms with the unique vitality of the new nation and what America, both as an idea and an actual physical space, had begun to represent to most of its inhabitants and to the emerging modern world. Poets such as James Russell Lowell, John Greenleaf Whittier, and Henry Longfellow, the venerable author of the enormously popular 'Hiawatha', – the so-called fireside poets – continued to write decorous, 'respectable' verse, modelled on aristocratic British poetry. Their verse was rhymed; it was structured by conventional metrical feet; and it was, as they thought all poetry should be, suitable for reading aloud in mixed company.

By comparison, Whitman's verse – full of what one reviewer at the time called 'words usually banished from polite society' – fits into no previously defined category of genre, combining, as it does, autobiography with sociological tract and religious sermon with a lyricism of unabashed sensuality. Free-flowing and organic in form, it resembles prose rather than poetry, and experimentally punctuated prose at that. The individual it celebrates represents a new breed of American. Restless, egalitarian, and unafraid to contradict himself, Whitman's persona rejects the ethic of hard work he constantly admires. He prefers instead to 'loaf' on the summer grass and among the masses of his fellow citizens and to 'invite' his soul.

Like the universe with which he longs to merge, Whitman's representative American is more a process than a given, inherited form. So too, in a manner of speaking, was the poet. Born on Long Island, New York in 1819 to parents of modest means who were themselves barely literate, Whitman received little formal education. Before publishing his first edition, he worked variously as an itinerant schoolteacher, a journalist, and news-paper editor (quitting as editor of the *Brooklyn Daily Eagle* in 1847 over the paper's conservative position on slavery). That original edition, published anonymously and at Whitman's expense, contained twelve untitled poems and a preface blending what one critic has called a 'bumptious nationalism' with loosely developed notes for poems Whitman had already planned to write in the future. Whitman appeared on the front cover, self-assured, bearded, and informally dressed, in an engraving of a good Daguerreotype photograph. Only the place of publication, the poet's newly adopted home Brooklyn, adorned the title page. The reader had to wait twenty-nine more pages before being formally introduced to 'Walt Whitman, an American, one of the roughs, a kosmos'.

The 1855 edition included at least five of Whitman's finest poems, later known as 'The Sleepers', 'Song of Occupation', 'I Think of Time', 'There Was a Child Went Forth', and 'Song of Myself', the central poem of that and all subsequent editions. Each of the fifty-two sections or chants of the latter poem has its own appropriate shape and can be read separately as a self-contained poem. However, when read as a unified whole (and aloud), as it should be, the poem, which posits all existing things as equally and eternally good, leads the reader through an almost musical progression of symbols, thoughts, and emotional intensity, narrating the self's transcendental search for meaning in a cycle of birth, death, and rebirth. The 'I' of the poem (often punned with 'eye') starts his journey toward spiritual union with the observation of a simple spear of grass, the poem's central image of the miraculous divinity of average people and everyday things. He then observes the daily lives of individuals around Manhattan, before setting off across the continent, soaring into space and through time, travelling finally beyond death before returning, resurrected, to his starting point in the grass, having invited the reader to follow.

Here, as throughout most of Whitman's early poems, the vision has as much in common with Eastern philosophy as it does American nationalism. The basic unit of verse is, as Gay Wilson Allen has shown, the statement or, more specifically, the independent clause. Whitman worked hard to refine and transform everyday language and diction for his poetic purpose and vision. Typically, he organized his independent clauses in series, often linked by the rhetorical trope of anaphora, the appearance of the same word at the beginning of consecutive lines of verse. By using that device to introduce sequences of parallel clauses (clauses made up of almost exact syntactical units), Whitman not only created a rhythm of both sound and thought, but he also aligned form and content, highlighting the distinctiveness of the different objects or people he surveys while simultaneously implying their inherent connection.

A second edition followed quickly in 1856. With it, Whitman added twenty new poems, the most notable being 'Sun-Down Poem' (later 'Crossing Brooklyn Ferry'), and replaced the original preface with a letter from the transcendentalist Ralph Waldo Emerson (included without Emerson's permission) congratulating the younger poet at the start of a great career. A third appeared in 1860 with eighty-six additions, among them, 'Out of the Cradle Endlessly Rocking' and the forty-five that comprise the section entitled 'Calamus'. The poems in 'Calamus' are particularly interesting, for they represent some of the best poems of love between men ever written. It would be mistake, however, to call them homosexual love poems. The notion of homosexual or 'gay' love did not exist in the mid-nineteenth century in the same way that it does today. Men could and did express passionate affection without the sexual act defining their identity. Moreover, Whitman's doctrine of 'the manly love of comrades' does not only signify literally. Instead it connotes any open, sensual, unashamedly physical union, regardless of gender. (Such a forthright attitude toward sex distinguishes Whitman's representative American from other, generally more prudish and/or latent prototypes of the American male.)

With the fourth edition, published in 1868, Whitman began to see *Leaves of Grass* less as literature and more as a personal record. He modified some of his earlier techniques and concentrated chiefly on revising individual poems, changing titles and reorganizing the overall shape of the collection to make the meanings of the poems more interdependent and allegorical in plan. As a consequence, the form of the collection became more controlled, the symbolism generally more contrived. Whitman's version appears less mystical, and the soul is more closely identified with personality.

Critics and biographers have offered a number of reasons for this shift of emphasis and outlook. Yet part of the answer must lie in the increasingly evident loss of American innocence (and with it Whitman's) in the last third of the century. The country was at war with itself from 1861 to 1865, and for a time Whitman helped to nurse the wounded in hospitals around Washington, D.C. The experience, which he recorded in prose under the title *Specimen Days* and in the slightly disappointing cycle of poems originally published under the separate title of *Drum Taps*, left Whitman understandably disillusioned. So too did the assassination of President Abraham Lincoln in 1864, which led to one of Whitman's weakest but most recited poems, 'O Captain, My Captain!' and later one of his finest, the elegy 'When Lilacs Last in the Dooryard Bloom'd'. The latter follows the seven stages of traditional Greek elegies, achieving its final, conventional reconciliation with loss and consolation of the living in the convergence of its three central images – the lilac, the star, and the hermit thrush.

Perhaps a greater reason, however, lies in the co-option, into mainly economic terms, of the individualism Whitman had idealised in the early poetry and in the public debasement of the rugged frontier spirit he had often championed, most explicitly in 'Pioneers, O Pioneers'. As was typical for the nineteenth century, Whitman considered material advance a necessary adjunct to spiritual progress. The 'unseen', as he liked to say, was to be found in the 'seen', and in one of his best later poems, 'Passage to India', he attempted to humanise the discoveries and inventions of the period in a celebration of the opening of the Suez Canal, the expansion of the continent by railroad, and the completion of the Atlantic cable. For Whitman all three represent acts linking the entire world and signalling an age of universal peace.

As events in the last quarter of the century unfolded, however, Whitman himself must surely have appreciated some of the irony of his poem. For the post-war years, which Mark Twain called 'The Gilded Age', also saw the rise of a particularly irresponsible social destructiveness, always latent in Whitman's ideal pioneer. Industrialists (referred to as 'robber barons') ruthlessly exploited land and labour in a quest for monopolistic power and huge fortune. The federal government officially encouraged Western settlement by allowing a wholesale slaughter of buffalo certain to achieve the virtual genocide of native Americans.

Whitman suffered a paralytic stroke in 1873 and soon after retired to Camden, New Jersey. A sixth edition of *Leaves of Grass*, marking the centennial of American independence, nevertheless appeared in 1876, and a seventh, in which Whitman permanently fixed the order of his poems, in 1881. A final or 'Deathbed' edition, reproducing the 1881 edition, which Whitman had authorized as the edition from which all future ones should be derived, and including the two annexes printed in this current text, is dated 1891-92. Not long after, Whitman died, in Camden, on March 26, 1892, only five days short of his seventy-third birthday.

Time and events have shown how increasingly intractable the open, progressive self Whitman articulated in his early poetry has become and how potentially misguided American notions of innocence and exceptionalism may be. Democracy expressed as an ideal in which citizens act more like religious than political converts sounds now more naive than optimistic, and the legacy Whitman bestowed on future American poets looks more problematic. For all that, however, Whitman remains a monumental figure. *Leaves of Grass* continues to stand as one the most remarkable single volumes of poetry in the English language.

David Rogers
Kingston University

SELECTED READINGS

Carlisle, Fred E., *The Uncertain Self: Whitman's Drama of Identity* (Lansing: Michigan State University Press, 1973).
Erkkila Betsy, *Whitman the Political Poet* (New York and Oxford: Oxford University Press, 1989).
Kaplan, James, *Walt Whitman: A Life* (New York: Simon and Schuster, 1980).
Miller, Edwin Haviland, ed. *A Century of Whitman Criticism* (Bloomington and London: Indiana University Press, 1969).
Nathanson, Tenny, *Whitman's Presence: Body, Voice, and Writing in 'Leaves of Grass'* (New York and London: New York University Press, 1992).

PUBLISHER'S NOTE

Whitman revised and re-arranged his poetry a great deal. This edition helps the reader by giving the date of composition of each poem (if known, otherwise the date of its first known publication) below the last line of the poem, to the left. The date of its final revision and inclusion in *Leaves of Grass* is given at the right. The Biographical and Bibliographical Chronology will, it is hoped, prove an added help as a cross-reference index.

The text of the poetry is that of the Inclusive Edition, itself based upon the last edition which Whitman revised. Rejected or uncollected poems are added at the end.

Contents

xiii

SEA-DRIFT

BY THE ROADSIDE

Biographical and
Bibliographical Chronology

NOTE.—The purpose of this chronology is to assist the reader who wishes to read Whitman's poetry, prose and letters chronologically and together as a composite autobiography. It is not intended as a complete index to the material in the volume.

The record of publications is extended beyond the date of the poet's death in order to complete the list of Whitman's writings printed to date. An exhaustive bibliography (supplementing those by Frank Shay, Carolyn Wells and Alfred F. Goldsmith, and Emory Holloway and Henry S. Saunders) is about to go to the press of Houghton, Mifflin and Company, Boston, prepared by Clifton Joseph Furness and Henry S. Saunders in collaboration with the present editor.

1819. May 31, born on a farm at West Hills, near Huntington, Long Island.

1823. Moved to Brooklyn, living first in Front Street, near the ferry.

1825-30. Attended public school; office boy to a lawyer and a doctor.

1831-34. In Brooklyn printing offices, learning the trade.

1836. A compositor in New York.

1836-41. Taught schools, "boarding round" in various parts of Long Island.

1838. June 5, started a weekly newspaper, *The Long Islander*, at Huntington.

1839-40. At Jamaica, as compositor on *Long Island Democrat*, in which he published most of his earliest extant verse and prose, 1839-40.
Also electioneering for Van Buren.

1841. May, returned to New York. Worked as compositor and editor and began writing prose and verse for magazines.

1842. His poorly written *Franklin Evans*, a temperance tract, widely read.

1846-48. Edited Brooklyn *Daily Eagle*. Lost position because of liberal (free soil) political principles.

1848. March-May, in New Orleans as an editor of *Daily Crescent*. Accompanied on journey by his brother Jefferson.
June 15, back in Brooklyn. Active in "Barnburner" political campaign.
September, began editing Brooklyn *Freeman*.

1849. September, retired from *Freeman* and probably made a second trip to the South.

1850. March 22, publishes first free verse, "Blood Money", on slavery issue.
May-June, anonymously connected with Brooklyn *Daily Advertiser*.

1851-54. Contributor or correspondent for New York *Evening Post*.
Carpentering and house building with his father. At work on *Leaves of Grass*.

1855. July 4, First Edition, *Leaves of Grass*, Brooklyn, no publisher, 4to, 94 pp.
July 11, lost his father by death.
July 21, received Emerson's famous letter praising his book.
September 17, visited by Moncure D. Conway.
November 10, visited by Thoreau and Alcott.
November, published the first of a number of articles in *Life Illustrated*. Connection ended about August, 1856.

1856. Second Edition, *Leaves of Grass*, Brooklyn, printed and sold by Fowler and Wells, 16mo, 384 pp.
Interested in Republican presidential campaign.
Visited by Emerson.

1857-59. Edited Brooklyn *Daily Times*.

1860. Third Edition, *Leaves of Grass*, Boston, Thayer and Eldridge, 12 mo, 456 pp.
Leaves of Grass. Imprints, criticisms of Whitman's poetry.
March, in Boston, seeing his poems through the press.
Met William Douglas O'Connor and J. T. Trowbridge.
April, *Atlantic Monthly* published "Bardic Symbols".

1861. June 8, began series of twenty-five *Brooklynia* sketches for Brooklyn weekly *Standard*; ended November, 1862.
Fall, journeyed through Long Island.
Composed some of *Drum-Taps* poems, publishing some to stimulate recruiting.

1862. Wrote articles for New York *Leader*.
December 16, left for Virginia war front, where his brother George had been reported wounded.

1863. January, returned to Washington with the wounded and began volunteer missionary work in the hospitals. Wrote war correspondence of New York and Brooklyn papers and did copying to support himself and to supply funds for his ministrations. Distributed gifts from others to the wounded.
November, met John Burroughs.

1864. June 23, prostrated, returned home, for nearly a half-year in Brooklyn, where he continued to visit hospitals.
Planned publication of *Drum-Taps*.

1865. January 24, appointed to clerkship in Indian Bureau, Interior Department, where he worked a few hours a day. Salary, $1200.
May 11, promoted to a clerkship of the second class.
June 30, dismissed by James Harlan, Secretary of Interior.
August, appointed clerk in Attorney General's Office.
September, O'Connor gave Whitman his sobriquet by publishing *The Good Gray Poet*, protesting against his dismissal by Harlan for authorship "of an indecent book".
Walt Whitman's Drum-Taps, New York, 1865, no publisher. All but the first few copies contain the *Sequel to Drum-Taps*, which includes "When Lilacs Last in the Dooryard Bloom'd".

1866. Probably met Peter Doyle in this year.

1867. Fourth Edition, *Leaves of Grass*, New York, no publisher, 12mo, 338 pp.
Assisted John Burroughs in writing *Notes on Walt Whitman as Poet and Person*.

1867. October, regularly assigned as recording clerk. Salary, $1600 a year.

1868. William Michael Rossetti's selected *Poems by Walt Whitman*, J. C. Hotten, London.
October, visiting congressman Thomas Davis in Providence, Rhode Island.

1869. June-July, Mrs. Anne Gilchrist read the Rossetti selection and fell in love with the poet.
August-September, in Brooklyn on vacation.

1870. August-September, in Brooklyn on vacation, having his poems electrotyped for the 1871 Edition of *Leaves of Grass*.

1871. Summer in Brooklyn.
July, received cordial letter from Tennyson.
September 7, read "After All, Not to Create Only" at opening of American Institute in New York.
Fifth Edition, *Leaves of Grass*, Washington, no publisher, 8vo, 384 pp., and *Passage to India*, 120 pp., in one volume. Both also published separately.
After All Not to Create Only, Washington, no publisher.
Democratic Vistas, Washington, no publisher.

1872. February-April, July, in Brooklyn.
June, journeyed to Hanover, Vermont, to read "As a Strong Bird on Pinions Free" at the Dartmouth College Commencement, visiting his sister at Burlington on the return trip.
Democratic Vistas translated into Danish by Rudolph Schmidt.
Sixth Edition, *Leaves of Grass*, Washington, 8vo, no publisher. Little change from Fifth Edition.

1873. January 23, suffered an attack of paralysis.
February 19, lost his sister-in-law (Mrs. Jefferson Whitman) by death.
March 10, transferred to the office of the Solicitor of the Treasury.
May 20, started to sea coast in search of health, but got only as far as Camden, New Jersey, where he lived with his brother Col. George Whitman till 1884.

May 23, lost his mother, who died at Camden.

Wrote verse and prose for *Daily Graphic*.

Met Horace Traubel, who was to prove a devoted friend and voluminous biographer.

1874. January-March, wrote six articles on the war for the New York *Weekly Graphic*.

March, published "The Prayer of Columbus", swan song of his greatest poetry, in *Harper's*.

June, wrote "The Song of the Universal", read by proxy at the Tufts College Commencement.

July 1, dismissed from clerkship, which he had held by employing a substitute.

1875. November, visited by Lord Houghton. Visited Washington and Baltimore. Poor health.

Memoranda During the War, author's publication, Camden.

1876. Seventh Edition (Author's Centennial), *Leaves of Grass*, Camden, reprint of 1871 Edition.

Two Rivulets, Prose and Verse, Camden, containing *Democratic Vistas, Centennial Songs*, and *Passage to India*.

Robert Buchanan's letter about Whitman's need attracted wide attention in England and the new books brought substantial financial returns.

Summer, went, as often later, to Timber Creek, near Whitehorse, for sun and baths, gradually improving in health. Wrote nature notes, later included in *Specimen Days*. Mrs. Gilchrist moved to Philadelphia to be near him.

1877. February, visited J. H. Johnston in New York and John Burroughs in Ulster County.

May 1, visited by Edward Carpenter, and by Dr. R. M. Bucke, in 1883 to become his authorized biographer.

1878. June-July, visited J. H. Johnston and Burroughs.

1879. April 14, delivered the first of his Lincoln lectures at Steck Hall in New York. Afterwards he visited Burroughs at Esopus.

September-December, visited Jefferson Whitman in St. Louis and travelled as far west as Denver.

1880. June-September, visited Dr. Bucke at London, Ontario, and with him visited Montreal, Quebec and the Saguenay River, making notes, to be posthumously published in *Diary in Canada*.

1881. April, delivered Lincoln lecture in Boston; visited Longfellow.

May, visited J. H. Johnston for six weeks at Mott Haven.

July, returned to his birthplace.

August, in Boston, reading proofs for Osgood Edition of his poems. Visited Concord as guest of Frank B. Sanborn and was entertained at dinner by Emerson and his family.

Eighth Edition, *Leaves of Grass*, Boston, James R. Osgood and Co., 8vo, 382 pp. London editions issued by Bogue and by Trübner and Co.

1882. Osgood, threatened with prosecution, abandoned the publication of *Leaves of Grass*, and Whitman, with the same plates, issued the Ninth Edition in Camden, as an Author's Edition. Later in the year Rees, Welsh and Company, Philadelphia, published the book. David McKay published various editions from these plates.

Specimen Days and Collect, Rees, Welsh and Company, Philadelphia. Issued the next year in Glasgow by Wilson and McCormick.

1883. September, at Ocean Grove, New Jersey, with Burroughs.

1884. March, bought house at 328 Mickle Street, where he was to spend the remaining nine years of his life and where he was visited by a great number of foreign and American admirers.

1885. Too lame to get about; a subscription was taken to buy him a horse and buggy, Mark Twain, Richard Watson Gilder, Oliver Wendel Holmes, Whittier, and others contributing.

1886. Royalties very small, but Talcott Williams arranged for a Lincoln lecture at Chestnut Street Opera House in Philadelphia, which netted $692.

Summer, on a voyage to Montauk Point, Long Island.

December, *Pall Mall Gazette*, printing a rumour that Whitman was starving, raised £125.

An unsuccessful attempt was made to obtain for Whitman a pension for his hospital services.

The Poems of Walt Whitman, selection by Ernest Rhys, Walter Scott, London.

1887. April 15, delivered Lincoln lecture in Madison Square Theatre, New York, attended by Mark Twain, John Hay, Lowell, St. Gaudens, Edmund Clarence Stedman, and other prominent persons. Andrew Carnegie paid $350 for a box; proceeds, $600.

Friends in Boston donated $800 to poet.

Specimen Days in America, revised, Walter Scott, London.

1888. April, suffered new paralytic attack; near death in November.

November Boughs, David McKay, Philadelphia; English Edition, Alexander Gardner, Paisley and London, 1889.

Democratic Vistas and Other Papers, Walter Scott, London.

Complete Poems and Prose of Walt Whitman, Authenticated and Personal. (*Handled by Walt Whitman*), *Portraits from Life. Autograph, Containing Sands at Seventy and November Boughs.*

Regular contributor to New York *Herald*.

1889. May 31, birthday dinner given him by citizens of Camden.

Ninth Edition, *Leaves of Grass*, containing *Sands at Seventy* and "A Backward Glance O'er Travel'd Roads", issued as a birthday souvenir. Later issued by D. Appleton and Company, 1908, and by Mitchell Kennerley, 1914.

1890. April 15, Whitman delivered Lincoln lecture at Contemporary Club.

May 31, attended a public birthday dinner in Philadelphia.

October 21, Robert Ingersoll gave a benefit lecture on "Liberty in Literature" at Horticultural Hall, Philadelphia.

December, ill with pneumonia.

1891. *Good-Bye, My Fancy,* 2d Annex to *Leaves of Grass,*
David McKay, Philadelphia.
Tenth Edition, *Leaves of Grass,* containing *Sands at
Seventy, Good-Bye, My Fancy,* "A Backward Glance
O'er Travel'd Roads," and portrait from life, David
McKay, the so-called "Deathbed Edition".

1892. March 26, died at Camden.
March 30, buried in a tomb in Harleigh Cemetery
designed by himself.
Complete Prose Works, David McKay, Philadelphia.

1897. *Calamus,* letters to Peter Doyle, edited by Richard
Maurice Bucke, Laurens Maynard, Boston.
Eleventh Edition, *Leaves of Grass,* containing *Old Age
Echoes,* Small, Maynard, and Company, Boston. Later
reprinted by D. Appleton and Company, 1908; Mitchell
Kennerley, 1914, English imprint, G. P. Putnam's Sons.

1898. *Complete Prose Works, Specimen Days and Collect,
November Boughs* and *Good-Bye, My Fancy,* Small,
Maynard and Company, Boston. Later reprinted by
D. Appleton and Company, 1908; Mitchell Kennerley,
1914; and Doubleday, Page & Co.
The Wound Dresser, letters from Whitman to his mother
during the war, edited by Richard Maurice Bucke,
Small, Maynard and Company, Boston.

1899. *Notes and Fragments,* edited by Richard Maurice Bucke,
printed for private distribution.

1902. *The Complete Writings of Walt Whitman,* issued under
the editorial supervision of his Literary Executors,
Richard Maurice Bucke, Thomas B. Harned and
Horace L. Traubel, containing biographical and critical
material and Trigg's Variorum Readings, 10 volumes,
G. P. Putnam's Sons, New York and London. The three
volumes of verse were issued in one by Doubleday, Page
and Company, Garden City, in 1917.

1920. *The Gathering of the Forces,* Whitman writings in the
Brooklyn *Eagle,* edited by Cleveland Rodgers and John
Black, G. P. Putnam's Sons, New York and London, 2
volumes.

1921. *The Uncollected Poetry and Prose of Walt Whitman*, 2 volumes, edited by Emory Holloway, Doubleday, Page and Company, Garden City, and William Heinemann, London (1922).

1924. Inclusive Edition, *Leaves of Grass*, including variorum readings, prefaces and rejected poems, edited by Emory Holloway, Doubleday, Page and Company, Garden City.

Walt Whitman

COME, said my soul,
Such verses for my body let us write, (for we are one,)
That should I after death invisibly return,
Or, long, long hence, in other spheres,
There to some group of mates the chants resuming,
(Tallying earth's soil, trees, winds, tumultuous waves,)
Ever with pleas'd smile I may keep on,
Ever and ever yet the verses owning—as, first, I here and now,
Signing for soul and body, set to them my name,

Walt Whitman

Leaves of Grass

Inscriptions

ONE'S-SELF I SING

One's-self I sing, a simple separate person,
Yet utter the word Democratic, the word En-Masse.

Of physiology from top to toe I sing,
Not physiognomy alone nor brain alone is worthy for the
    Muse, I say the Form complete is worthier far,
The Female equally with the Male I sing.

Of Life immense in passion, pulse, and power,
Cheerful, for freest action form'd under the laws divine,
The Modern Man I sing.
1867   1871

AS I PONDER'D IN SILENCE

As I ponder'd in silence,
Returning upon my poems, considering, lingering long,
A Phantom arose before me with distrustful aspect,
Terrible in beauty, age, and power,
The genius of poets of old lands,
As to me directing like flame its eyes,
With finger pointing to many immortal songs,
And menacing voice, *What singest thou?* it said,
Know'st thou not there is but one theme for ever-enduring bards?
And that is the theme of War, the fortune of battles,
The making of perfect soldiers.

Be it so, then I answer'd,
I too haughty Shade also sing war, and a longer and greater one
    than any,
Waged in my book with varying fortune, with flight, advance
    and retreat, victory deferr'd and wavering,

(Yet methinks certain, or as good as certain, at the last,) the
        field the world,
For life and death, for the Body and for the eternal Soul,
Lo, I too am come, chanting the chant of battles,
I above all promote brave soldiers.
1871   1871

IN CABIN'D SHIPS AT SEA

IN cabin'd ships at sea,
The boundless blue on every side expanding,
With whistling winds and music of the waves, the large im-
        perious waves,
Or some lone bark buoy'd on the dense marine,
Where joyous full of faith, spreading white sails,
She cleaves the ether mid the sparkle and the foam of day, or
        under many a star at night,
By sailors young and old haply will I, a reminiscence of the
        land, be read,
In full rapport at last.

Here are our thoughts, voyagers' thoughts,
Here not the land, firm land, alone appears, may then by them
        be said,
The sky o'erarches here, we feel the undulating deck beneath
        our feet,
We feel the long pulsation, ebb and flow of endless motion.
The tones of unseen mystery, the vague and vast suggestions of
        the briny world, the liquid-flowing syllables,
The perfume, the faint creaking of the cordage, the melancholy
        rhythm,
The boundless vista and the horizon far and dim are all here,
And this is ocean's poem.

Then falter not O book, fulfil your destiny,
You not a reminiscence of the land alone,
You too as a lone bark cleaving the ether, purpos'd I know
        not whither, yet ever full of faith,
Consort to every ship that sails, sail you!
Bear forth to them folded my love, (dear mariners, for you
        I fold it here in every leaf;)

Speed on my book! spread your white sails my little bark
    athwart the imperious waves,
Chant on, sail on, bear o'er the boundless blue from me to
    every sea,
This song for mariners and all their ships.
1871   1881

TO FOREIGN LANDS

I HEARD that you ask'd for something to prove this puzzle the
    New World,
And to define America, her athletic Democracy,
Therefore I send you my poems that you behold in them
    what you wanted.
1860   1871

TO A HISTORIAN

You who celebrate bygones,
Who have explored the outward, the surfaces of the races,
    the life that has exhibited itself,
Who have treated of man as the creature of politics, aggre-
    gates, rulers and priests,
I, habitan of the Alleghanies, treating of him as he is in him-
    self in his own rights,
Pressing the pulse of the life that has seldom exhibited itself,
    (the great pride of man in himself),
Chanter of Personality, outlining what is yet to be,
I project the history of the future.
1860   1871

TO THEE OLD CAUSE

To thee old cause!
Thou peerless, passionate, good cause,
Thou stern, remorseless, sweet idea,
Deathless throughout the ages, races, lands,
After a strange sad war, great war for thee,
(I think all war through time was really fought, and ever will
    be really fought, for thee,)
These chants for thee, the eternal march of thee.

(A war O soldiers not for itself alone,
Far, far more stood silently waiting behind, now to advance
    in this book.)

Thou orb of many orbs!
Thou seething principle! thou well-kept, latent germ! thou
    centre!
Around the idea of thee the war revolving,
With all its angry and vehement play of causes,
(With vast results to come for thrice a thousand years,)
These recitatives for thee,—my book and the war are one,
Merged in its spirit I and mine, as the contest hinged on thee,
As a wheel on its axis turns, this book unwitting to itself,
Around the idea of thee.
1871   1881

EIDÓLONS

I met a seer,
Passing the hues and objects of the world,
The fields of art and learning, pleasure, sense,
        To glean eidólons.

Put in thy chants said he,
No more the puzzling hour nor day, nor segments, parts, put
    in,
Put first before the rest as light for all and entrance-song of all,
        That of eidólons.

Ever the dim beginning,
Ever the growth, the rounding of the circle,
Ever the summit and the merge at last, (to surely start again,)
        Eidólons! eidólons!

Ever the mutable,
Ever materials, changing, crumbling, re-cohering,
Ever the ateliers, the factories divine,
        Issuing eidólons.

Lo, I or you,
Or woman, man, or state, known or unknown,
We seeming solid wealth, strength, beauty build,
        But really build eidólons.

The ostent evanescent,
The substance of an artist's mood or savan's studies long,
Or warrior's, martyr's, hero's toils,
    To fashion his eidólon.

    Of every human life,
(The units gather'd, posted, not a thought, emotion, deed,
    left out,)
The whole or large or small summ'd, added up,
    In its eidólon.

    The old, old urge,
Based on the ancient pinnacles, lo, newer, higher pinnacles,
From science and the modern still impell'd,
    The old, old urge, cidólons.

    The present now and here,
America's busy, teeming, intricate whirl,
Of aggregate and segregate for only thence releasing,
    To-day's eidólons.

    These with the past,
Of vanish'd lands, of all the reigns of kings across the sea,
Old conquerors, old campaigns, old sailor's voyages,
    Joining eidólons.

    Densities, growth, façades,
Strata of mountains, soils, rocks, giant trees,
Far-born, far-dying, living long, to leave,
    Eidólons everlasting.

    Exaltè, rapt, ecstatic,
The visible but their womb of birth,
Of orbic tendencies to shape and shape and shape,
    The mighty earth-eidólon.

    All space, all time,
(The stars, the terrible perturbations of the suns,
Swelling, collapsing, ending, serving their longer, shorter
    use,)
    Fill'd with eidólons only.

The noiseless myriads,
The infinite oceans where the rivers empty,
The separate countless free identities, like eyesight,
      The true realities, eidólons.

Not this the world,
Nor these the universes, they the universes,
Purport and end, ever the permanent life of life,
      Eidólons, eidólons.

Beyond thy lectures learn'd professor,
Beyond thy telescope or spectroscope observer keen, beyond
   all mathematics,
Beyond the doctor's surgery, anatomy, beyond the chemist
   with his chemistry,
      The entities of entities, eidólons.

Unfixed yet fix'd,
Ever shall be, ever have been and are,
Sweeping the present to the infinite future,
      Eidólons, eidólons, eidólons.

The prophet and the bard,
Shall yet maintain themselves, in higher stages yet,
Shall mediate to the Modern, to Democracy, interpret yet to
   them,
      God and eidólons.

And thee my soul,
Joys, ceaseless exercises, exaltations,
Thy yearning amply fed at last, prepared to meet,
      Thy mates, eidólons.

Thy body permanent,
The body lurking there within thy body,
The only purport of the form thou art, the real I myself,
      An image, an eidólon.

Thy very songs not in thy songs,
No special strains to sing, none for itself,
But from the whole resulting, rising at last and floating,
      A round full-orb'd eidólon.

1876   1876

FOR HIM I SING

For him I sing,
I raise the present on the past,
(As some perennial tree out of its roots, the present on the past,)
With time and space I him dilate and fuse the immortal laws,
To make himself by them the law unto himself.
1871   1871

WHEN I READ THE BOOK

When I read the book, the biography famous,
And is this then (said I) what the author calls a man's life?
And so will some one when I am dead and gone write my life?
(As if any man really knew aught of my life,
Why even I myself I often think know little or nothing of my
    real life,
Only a few hints, a few diffused faint clews and indirections
I seek for my own use to trace out here.)
1867   1871

BEGINNING MY STUDIES

Beginning my studies the first step pleas'd me so much,
The mere fact consciousness, these forms, the power of motion,
The least insect or animal, the senses, eyesight, love,
The first step I say awed me and pleas'd me so much,
I have hardly gone and hardly wish'd to go any farther,
But stop and loiter all the time to sing it in ecstatic songs.
1867   1871

BEGINNERS

How they are provided for upon the earth, (appearing at
    intervals,)
How dear and dreadful they are to the earth,
How they inure to themselves as much as to any—what a
    paradox appears their age,
How people respond to them, yet know them not,
How there is something relentless in their fate all times,
How all times mischoose the objects of their adulation and
    reward,
And how the same inexorable price must still be paid for the
    same great purchase.
1860   1860

TO THE STATES

To the States or any one of them, or any city of the States,
 Resist much, obey little,
Once unquestioning obedience, once fully enslaved,
Once fully enslaved, no nation, state, city, of this earth, ever
 afterward resumes its liberty.
1860   1881

ON JOURNEYS THROUGH THE STATES

On journeys through the States we start,
(Ay through the world, urged by these songs,
Sailing henceforth to every land, to every sea,)
We willing learners of all, teachers of all, and lovers of all.

We have watch'd the seasons dispensing themselves and
 passing on,
And have said, Why should not a man or woman do as much
 as the seasons, and effuse as much?

We dwell a while in every city and town,
We pass through Kanada, the North-east, the vast valley of
 the Mississippi, and the Southern States,
We confer on equal terms with each of the States,
We make trial of ourselves and invite men and women to hear,
We say to ourselves, Remember, fear not, be candid, pro-
 mulge the body and the soul,
Dwell a while and pass on, be copious, temperate, chaste,
 magnetic,
And what you effuse may then return as the seasons return,
And may be just as much as the seasons.
1860   1871

TO A CERTAIN CANTATRICE

Here, take this gift,
I was reserving it for some hero, speaker, or general;
One who should serve the good old cause, the great idea, the
 progress and freedom of the race,
Some brave confronter of despots, some daring rebel;
But I see that what I was reserving belongs to you just as
 much as to any.
1860   1871

ME IMPERTURBE

Me imperturbe, standing at ease in Nature,
Master of all or mistress of all, aplomb in the midst of irrational things,
Imbued as they, passive, receptive, silent as they,
Finding my occupation, poverty, notoriety, foibles, crimes, less important than I thought,
Me toward the Mexican sea, or in the Mannahatta or the Tennessee, or far north or inland,
A river man, or a man of the woods or of any farm-life of these States or of the coast, or the lakes or Kanada,
Me wherever my life is lived, O to be self-balanced for contingencies,
To confront night, storms, hunger, ridicule, accidents, rebuffs, as the trees and animals do.
1860   1881

SAVANTISM

Thither as I look I see each result and glory retracing itself and nestling close, always obligated,
Thither hours, months, years—thither trades, compacts, establishments, even the most minute,
Thither every-day life, speech, utensils, politics, persons, estates;
Thither we also, I with my leaves and songs, trustful, admirant,
As a father to his father going takes his children along with him.
1860   1860

THE SHIP STARTING

Lo, the unbounded sea,
On its breast a ship starting, spreading all sails, carrying even her moonsails,
The pennant is flying aloft as she speeds she speeds so stately
    —below emulous waves press forward,
They surround the ship with shining curving motions and foam.
1865   1881

I HEAR AMERICA SINGING

I HEAR America singing, the varied carols I hear,
Those of mechanics, each one singing his as it should be
blithe and strong,
The carpenter singing his as he measures his plank or beam,
The mason singing his as he makes ready for work, or leaves
off work,
The boatman singing what belongs to him in his boat, the
deck-hand singing on the steamboat deck,
The shoemaker singing as he sits on his bench, the hatter
singing as he stands,
The wood-cutter's song, the ploughboy's on his way in the
morning, or at noon intermission or at sundown,
The delicious singing of the mother, or of the young wife at
work, or of the girl sewing or washing,
Each singing what belongs to him or her and to none else,
The day what belongs to the day—at night the party of young
fellows, robust, friendly,
Singing with open mouths their strong melodious songs.
1860   1867

WHAT PLACE IS BESIEGED?

WHAT place is besieged, and vainly tries to raise the siege?
Lo, I send to that place a commander, swift, brave, immortal,
And with him horse and foot, and parks of artillery,
And artillery-men, the deadliest that ever fired gun.
1860   1867

STILL THOUGH THE ONE I SING

STILL though the one I sing,
(One, yet of contradictions made,) I dedicate to Nationality,
I leave in him revolt, (O latent right of insurrection! O
quenchless, indispensable fire!)
1871   1871

SHUT NOT YOUR DOORS

SHUT not your doors to me proud libraries,
For that which was lacking on all your well-fill'd shelves, yet
needed most, I bring,
Forth from the war emerging, a book I have made,

The words of my book nothing, the drift of it every thing,
A book separate, not link'd with the rest nor felt by the in-
tellect,
But you ye untold latencies will thrill to every page.
1865   1881

POETS TO COME

POETS to come! orators, singers, musicians to come!
Not to-day is to justify me and answer what I am for,
But you, a new brood, native, athletic, continental, greater
than before known,
Arouse! for you must justify me.

I myself but write one or two indicative words for the future,
I but advance a moment only to wheel and hurry back in the
darkness.

I am a man who, sauntering along without fully stopping,
turns a casual look upon you and then averts his face,
Leaving it to you to prove and define it,
Expecting the main things from you.
1860   1867

TO YOU

STRANGER, if you passing meet me and desire to speak to me,
why should you not speak to me?
And why should I not speak to you?
1860   1860

THOU READER

THOU reader throbbest life and pride and love the same as I,
Therefore for thee the following chants.
1881   1881

Starting from Paumanok

1

STARTING from fish-shape Paumanok where I was born,
Well-begotten, and rais'd by a perfect mother,
After roaming many lands, lover of populous pavements,
Dweller in Mannahatta my city, or on southern savannas,
Or a soldier camp'd or carrying my knapsack and gun, or a
    miner in California,
Or rude in my home in Dakota's woods, my diet meat, my
    drink from the spring,
Or withdrawn to muse and meditate in some deep recess,
Far from the clank of crowds intervals passing rapt and
    happy,
Aware of the fresh free giver the flowing Missouri, aware of
    mighty Niagara,
Aware of the buffalo herds grazing the plains, the hirsute and
    strong-breasted bull,
Of earth, rocks, Fifth-month flowers experienced, stars, rain,
    snow, my amaze,
Having studied the mocking-bird's tones and the flight of the
    mountain-hawk,
And heard at dawn the unrivall'd one, the hermit thrush
    from the swamp-cedars,
Solitary, singing in the West, I strike up for a New World.

2

Victory, union, faith, identity, time,
The indissoluble compacts, riches, mystery,
Eternal progress, the kosmos, and the modern reports.

This then is life,
Here is what has come to the surface after so many throes
    and convulsions.

How curious! how real!
Underfoot the divine soil, overhead the sun.

See revolving the globe,
The ancestor-continents away group'd together,
The present and future continents north and south, with the
    isthmus between.

See, vast trackless spaces,
As in a dream they change, they swiftly fill,
Countless masses debouch upon them,
They are now cover'd with the foremost people, arts, institu-
    tions, known.

See, projected through time,
For me an audience interminable.

With firm and regular step they wend, they never stop,
Successions of men, Americanos, a hundred millions,
One generation playing its part and passing on,
Another generation playing its part and passing on in its turn,
With faces turn'd sideways or backward towards me to listen,
With eyes retrospective towards me.

3

Americanos! conquerors! marches humanitarian!
Foremost! century marches! Libertad! masses!
For you a programme of chants.

Chants of the prairies,
Chants of the long-running Mississippi, and down to the
    Mexican sea,
Chants of Ohio, Indiana, Illinois, Iowa, Wisconsin and Min-
    nesota,
Chants going forth from the centre from Kansas, and thence
    equidistant,
Shooting in pulses of fire ceaseless to vivify all.

4

Take my leaves America, take them South and take them
    North,

Make welcome for them everywhere, for they are your own
    offspring,
Surround them East and West, for they would surround you,
And you precedents, connect lovingly with them, for they
    connect lovingly with you.

I conn'd old times,
I sat studying at the feet of the great masters,
Now if eligible O that the great masters might return and
    study me.

In the name of these States shall I scorn the antique?
Why these are the children of the antique to justify it.

5

Dead poets, philosophs, priests,
Martyrs, artists, inventors, governments long since,
Language-shapers on other shores,
Nations once powerful, now reduced, withdrawn, or desolate,
I dare not proceed till I respectfully credit what you have left
    wafted hither,
I have perused it, own it is admirable, (moving awhile among
    it,)
Think nothing can ever be greater, nothing can ever deserve
    more than it deserves,
Regarding it all intently a long while, then dismissing it,
I stand in my place with my own day here.

Here lands female and male,
Here the heir-ship and heiress-ship of the world, here the
    flame of materials,
Here spirituality the translatress, the openly-avow'd,
The ever-tending, the finalè of visible forms,
The satisfier, after due long-waiting now advancing,
Yes here comes my mistress the soul.

6

The soul,
Forever and forever—longer than soil is brown and solid--
    longer than water ebbs and flows.

I will make the poems of materials, for I think they are to be
the most spiritual poems,
And I will make the poems of my body and of mortality,
For I think I shall then supply myself with the poems of my
soul and of immortality.

I will make a song for these States that no one State may
under any circumstances be subjected to another State,
And I will make a song that there shall be comity by day and
by night between all the States, and between any two of
them,
And I will make a song for the ears of the President, full of
weapons with menacing points,
And behind the weapons countless dissatisfied faces;
And a song make I of the One form'd out of all,
The fang'd and glittering One whose head is over all,
Resolute warlike One including and over all,
(However high the head of any else that head is over all.)

I will acknowledge contemporary lands,
I will trail the whole geography of the globe and salute cour-
teously every city large and small,
And employments! I will put in my poems that with you is
heroism upon land and sea,
And I will report all heroism from an American point of
view.

I will sing the song of companionship,
I will show what alone must finally compact these,
I believe these are to found their own ideal of manly love,
indicating it in me,
I will therefore let flame from me the burning fires that were
threatening to consume me,
I will lift what has too long kept down those smouldering
fires,
I will give them complete abandonment,
I will write the evangel-poem of comrades and of love,
For who but I should understand love with all its sorrow and
joy?
And who but I should be the poet of comrades?

7

I am the credulous man of qualities, ages, races,
I advance from the people in their own spirit,
Here is what sings unrestricted faith.

Omnes! omnes! let others ignore what they may,
I make the poem of evil also, I commemorate that part also,
I am myself just as much evil as good, and my nation is—and
    I say there is in fact no evil,
(Or if there is I say it is just as important to you, to the land
    or to me, as any thing else.)

I too, following many and follow'd by many, inaugurate a
    religion, I descend into the arena,
(It may be I am destin'd to utter the loudest cries there, the
    winner's pealing shouts,
Who knows? they may rise from me yet, and soar above
    every thing.)

Each is not for its own sake,
I say the whole earth and all the stars in the sky are for reli-
    gion's sake.

I say no man has ever yet been half devout enough,
None has ever yet adored or worship'd half enough,
None has begun to think how divine he himself is, and how
    certain the future is.

I say that the real and permanent grandeur of these States
    must be their religion,
Otherwise there is no real and permanent grandeur;
(Nor character nor life worthy the name without religion,
Nor land nor man or woman without religion.)

8

What are you doing young man?
Are you so earnest, so given up to literature, science, art,
    amours?
These ostensible realities, politics, points?
Your ambition or business whatever it may be?

It is well—against such I say not a word, I am their poet also,
But behold! such swiftly subside, burnt up for religion's sake,
For not all matter is fuel to heat, impalpable flame, the essential life of the earth,
Any more than such are to religion.

9

What do you seek so pensive and silent?
What do you need camerado?
Dear son do you think it is love?

Listen dear son—listen America, daughter or son,
It is a painful thing to love a man or woman to excess, and yet it satisfies, it is great,
But there is something else very great, it makes the whole coincide,
It, magnificent, beyond materials, with continuous hands sweeps and provides for all.

10

Know you, solely to drop in the earth the germs of a greater religion,
The following chants each for its kind I sing.

My comrade!
For you to share with me two greatnesses, and a third one rising inclusive and more resplendent,
The greatness of Love and Democracy, and the greatness of Religion.

Melange mine own, the unseen and the seen,
Mysterious ocean where the streams empty,
Prophetic spirit of material shifting and flickering around me,
Living beings, identities now doubtless near us in the air that we know not of,
Contact daily and hourly that will not release me,
These selecting, these in hints demanded of me.

Not he with a daily kiss onward from childhood kissing me,

Has winded and twisted around me that which holds me to
    him,
Any more than I am held to the heavens and all the spiritual
    world,
After what they have done to me, suggesting themes.

O such themes—equalities! O divine average!
Warblings under the sun, usher'd as now, or at noon, or
    setting,
Strains musical flowing through ages, now reaching hither,
I take to your reckless and composite chords, add to them,
    and cheerfully pass them forward.

11

As I have walk'd in Alabama my morning walk,
I have seen where the she-bird the mocking-bird sat on her
    nest in the briers hatching her brood.

I have seen the he-bird also,
I have paus'd to hear him near at hand inflating his throat
    and joyfully singing.

And while I paus'd it came to me that what he really sang for
    was not there only,
Nor for his mate nor himself only, nor all sent back by the
    echoes,
But subtle, clandestine, away beyond,
A charge transmitted and gift occult for those being born.

12

Democracy! near at hand to you a throat is now inflating
    itself and joyfully singing.

Ma femme! for the brood beyond us and of us,
For those who belong here and those to come,
I exultant to be ready for them will now shake out carols
    stronger and haughtier than have ever yet been heard
    upon earth.
I will make the songs of passion to give them their way,
And your songs outlaw'd offenders, for I scan you with kin-
    dred eyes, and carry you with me the same as any.

I will make the true poem of riches,
To earn for the body and the mind whatever adheres and
  goes forward and is not dropt by death;
I will effuse egotism and show it underlying all, and I will be
  the bard of personality,
And I will show of male and female that either is but the
  equal of the other,
And sexual organs and acts! do you concentrate in me, for I
  am determin'd to tell you with courageous clear voice to
  prove you illustrious,
And I will show that there is no imperfection in the present,
  and can be none in the future,
And I will show that whatever happens to anybody it may be
  turn'd to beautiful results,
And I will show that nothing can happen more beautiful than
  death,
And I will thread a thread through my poems that time and
  events are compact,
And that all the things of the universe are perfect miracles,
  each as profound as any.

I will not make poems with reference to parts,
But I will make poems, songs, thoughts, with reference to
  ensemble,
And I will not sing with reference to a day, but with reference
  to all days,
And I will not make a poem nor the least part of a poem but
  has reference to the soul,
Because having look'd at the objects of the universe, I find
  there is no one nor any particle of one but has reference
  to the soul.

13

Was somebody asking to see the soul?
See, your own shape and countenance, persons, substances,
  beasts, the trees, the running rivers, the rocks and sands.

All hold spiritual joys and afterwards loosen them;
How can the real body ever die and be buried?

Of your real body and any man's or woman's real body,
Item for item it will elude the hands of the corpse-cleaners
    and pass to fitting spheres,
Carrying what has accrued to it from the moment of birth to
    the moment of death.

Not the types set up by the printer return their impression,
    the meaning, the main concern,
Any more than a man's substance and life or a woman's sub-
    stance and life return in the body and the soul,
Indifferently before death and after death.

Behold, the body includes and is the meaning, the main con-
    cern, and includes and is the soul;
Whoever you are, how superb and how divine is your body,
    or any part of it!

14

Whoever you are, to you endless announcements!

Daughter of the lands did you wait for your poet?
Did you wait for one with a flowing mouth and indicative
    hand?
Toward the male of the States, and toward the female of the
    States,
Exulting words, words to Democracy's lands.

Interlink'd, food-yielding lands!
Land of coal and iron! land of gold! land of cotton, sugar,
    rice!
Land of wheat, beef, pork! land of wool and hemp! land of
    the apple and the grape!
Land of the pastoral plains, the grass-fields of the world! land
    of those sweet-air'd interminable plateaus!
Land of the herd, the garden, the healthy house of adobie!
Lands where the north-west Columbia winds, and where the
    south-west Colorado winds!
Land of the eastern Chesapeake! land of the Delaware!
Land of Ontario, Erie, Huron, Michigan!
Land of the Old Thirteen! Massachusetts land! land of Ver-
    mont and Connecticut!

Land of the ocean shores! land of sierras and peaks!

Land of boatmen and sailors! fishermen's land!

Inextricable lands! the clutch'd together! the passionate
    ones!

The side by side! the elder and younger brothers! the bony-
    limb'd!

The great women's land! the feminine! the experienced sisters
    and the inexperienced sisters!

Far breath'd land! Arctic braced! Mexican breez'd! the di-
    verse! the compact!

The Pennsylvanian! the Virginian! the double Carolinian!

O all and each well-loved by me! my intrepid nations! O I at
    any rate include you all with perfect love!

I cannot be discharged from you! not from one any sooner
    than another!

O death! O for all that, I am yet of you unseen this hour with
    irrepressible love,

Walking New England, a friend, a traveler,

Splashing my bare feet in the edge of the summer ripples on
    Paumanok's sands,

Crossing the prairies, dwelling again in Chicago, dwelling in
    every town,

Observing shows, births, improvements, structures, arts,

Listening to orators and oratresses in public halls,

Of and through the States as during life, each man and
    woman my neighbor,

The Louisianian, the Georgian, as near to me, and I as near
    to him and her,

The Mississippian and Arkansian yet with me, and I yet with
    any of them,

Yet upon the plains west of the spinal river, yet in my house
    of adobie,

Yet returning eastward, yet in the Seaside State or in Mary-
    land,

Yet Kanadian cheerily braving the winter, the snow and ice
    welcome to me,

Yet a true son either of Maine or of the Granite State, or the
    Narragansett Bay State, or the Empire State,

Yet sailing to other shores to annex the same, yet welcoming
    every new brother,

Hereby applying these leaves to the new ones from the hour
they unite with the old ones,
Coming among the new ones myself to be their companion
and equal, coming personally to you now,
Enjoining you to acts, characters, spectacles, with me.

15

With me with firm holding, yet haste, haste on.

For your life adhere to me,
(I may have to be persuaded many times before I consent to
give myself really to you, but what of that?
Must not Nature be persuaded many times?)

No dainty dolce affettuoso I,
Bearded, sun-burnt, gray-neck'd, forbidding, I have arrived,
To be wrestled with as I pass for the solid prizes of the uni-
verse,
For such I afford whoever can persevere to win them.

16

On my way a moment I pause,
Here for you! and here for America!
Still the present I raise aloft, still the future of the States I
harbinge glad and sublime,
And for the past I pronounce what the air holds of the red
aborigines.

The red aborigines,
Leaving natural breaths, sounds of rain and winds, calls as of
birds and animals in the woods, syllabled, to us for
names,
Okonee, Koosa, Ottawa, Monongahela, Sauk, Natchez,
Chattahoochee, Kaqueta, Oronoco,
Wabash, Miami, Saginaw, Chippewa, Oshkosh, Walla-
Walla,
Leaving such to the States they melt, they depart, charging
the water and the land with names.

17

Expanding and swift, henceforth,
Elements, breeds, adjustments, turbulent, quick and audacious,
A world primal again, vistas of glory incessant and branching,
A new race dominating previous ones and grander far, with new contests,
New politics, new literatures and religions, new inventions and arts.

These, my voice announcing—I will sleep no more but arise,
You oceans that have been calm within me! how I feel you, fathomless, stirring, preparing unprecedented waves and storms.

18

See, steamers steaming through my poems,
See, in my poems immigrants continually coming and landing,
See, in arriere, the wigwam, the trail, the hunter's hut, the flatboat, the maize-leaf, the claim, the rude fence, and the backwoods village,
See, on the one side the Western Sea and on the other the Eastern Sea, how they advance and retreat upon my poems as upon their own shores,
See, pastures and forests in my poems—see, animals wild and tame—see, beyond the Kaw, countless herds of buffalo feeding on short curly grass,
See, in my poems, cities, solid, vast, inland, with paved streets, with iron and stone edifices, ceaseless vehicles, and commerce,
See, the many-cylinder'd steam printing-press—see, the electric telegraph stretching across the continent,
See, through Atlantica's depths pulses American Europe reaching, pulses of Europe duly return'd,
See, the strong and quick locomotive as it departs, panting, blowing the steam-whistle,
See, ploughmen ploughing farms—see, miners digging mines —see, the numberless factories,

See, mechanics busy at their benches with tools—see from
    among them superior judges, philosophs, Presidents,
    emerge, drest in working dresses,
See, lounging through the shops and fields of the States, me
    well-belov'd, close-held by day and night,
Hear the loud echoes of my songs there—read the hints come
    at last.

19

O camerado close! O you and me at last, and us two only.
O a word to clear one's path ahead endlessly!
O something ecstatic and undemonstrable! O music wild!
O now I triumph—and you shall also;
O hand in hand—O wholesome pleasure—O one more de-
    sirer and lover!
O to haste firm holding—to haste, haste on with me.
1860   1881

Song of Myself

1

I CELEBRATE myself, and sing myself,
And what I assume you shall assume,
For every atom belonging to me as good belongs to you.

I loafe and invite my soul,
I lean and loafe at my ease observing a spear of summer grass.

My tongue, every atom of my blood, form'd from this soil,
    this air,
Born here of parents born here from parents the same, and
    their parents the same,
I, now thirty-seven years old in perfect health begin,
Hoping to cease not till death.

Creeds and schools in abeyance,
Retiring back a while sufficed at what they are, but never for-
    gotten,

I harbor for good or bad, I permit to speak at every hazard,
Nature without check with original energy.

2

Houses and rooms are full of perfumes, the shelves are
    crowded with perfumes,
I breathe the fragrance myself and know it and like it,
The distillation would intoxicate me also, but I shall not let it.

The atmosphere is not a perfume, it has no taste of the dis-
    tillation, it is odorless,
It is for my mouth forever, I am in love with it,
I will go to the bank by the wood and become undisguised
    and naked,
I am mad for it to be in contact with me.

The smoke of my own breath,
Echoes, ripples, buzz'd whispers, love-root, silk-thread,
    crotch and vine,
My respiration and inspiration, the beating of my heart, the
    passing of blood and air through my lungs,
The sniff of green leaves and dry leaves, and of the shore and
    dark-color'd sea-rocks, and of hay in the barn,
The sound of the belch'd words of my voice loos'd to the
    eddies of the wind,
A few light kisses, a few embraces, a reaching around of arms,
The play of shine and shade on the trees as the supple boughs
    wag,
The delight alone or in the rush of the streets, or along the
    fields and hill-sides,
The feeling of health, the full-noon trill, the song of me rising
    from bed and meeting the sun.

Have you reckon'd a thousand acres much? have you rec-
    kon'd the earth much?
Have you practis'd so long to learn to read?
Have you felt so proud to get at the meaning of poems?

Stop this day and night with me and you shall possess the
    origin of all poems,

You shall possess the good of the earth and sun, (there are
    millions of suns left,)
You shall no longer take things at second or third hand, nor
    look through the eyes of the dead, nor feed on the
    spectres in books,
You shall not look through my eyes either, nor take things
    from me,
You shall listen to all sides and filter them from your self.

3

I have heard what the talkers were talking, the talk of the
    beginning and the end,
But I do not talk of the beginning or the end.

There was never any more inception than there is now,
Nor any more youth or age than there is now,
And will never be any more perfection than there is now,
Nor any more heaven or hell than there is now.

Urge and urge and urge,
Always the procreant urge of the world.
Out of the dimness opposite equals advance, always sub-
    stance and increase, always sex,
Always a knit of identity, always distinction, always a breed
    of life.

To elaborate is no avail, learn'd and unlearn'd feel that it is so.

Sure as the most certain sure, plumb in the uprights, well
    entretied, braced in the beams,
Stout as a horse, affectionate, haughty, electrical,
I and this mystery here we stand.

Clear and sweet is my soul, and clear and sweet is all that is
    not my soul.

Lack one lacks both, and the unseen is proved by the seen,
Till that becomes unseen and receives proof in its turn.

Showing the best and dividing it from the worst age vexes age,
Knowing the perfect fitness and equanimity of things, while
    they discuss I am silent, and go bathe and admire myself.

Welcome is every organ and attribute of me, and of any man
 hearty and clean,
Not an inch nor a particle of an inch is vile, and none shall be
 less familiar than the rest.

I am satisfied—I see, dance, laugh, sing;
As the hugging and loving bed-fellow sleeps at my side
 through the night, and withdraws at the peep of the day
 with stealthy tread,
Leaving me baskets cover'd with white towels swelling the
 house with their plenty,
Shall I postpone my acceptation and realization and scream
 at my eyes,
That they turn from gazing after and down the road,
And forthwith cipher and show me to a cent,
Exactly the value of one and exactly the value of two, and
 which is ahead?

4

Trippers and askers surround me,
People I meet, the effect upon me of my early life or the ward
 and city I live in, or the nation,
The latest dates, discoveries, inventions, societies, authors
 old and new,
My dinner, dress, associates, looks, compliments, dues,
The real or fancied indifference of some man or woman I
 love,
The sickness of one of my folks or of myself, or ill-doing or
 loss or lack of money, or depressions or exaltations,
Battles, the horrors of fratricidal war, the fever of doubtful
 news, the fitful events;
These come to me days and nights and go from me again,
But they are not the Me myself.
Apart from the pulling and hauling stands what I am,
Stands amused, complacent, compassionating, idle, uni-
 tary,
Looks down, is erect, or bends an arm on an impalpable cer-
 tain rest,
Looking with side-curved head curious what will come next,

Both in and out of the game and watching and wondering
at it.

Backward I see in my own days where I sweated through fog
with linguists and contenders,
I have no mockings or arguments, I witness and wait.

5

I believe in you my soul, the other I am must not abase itself
to you,
And you must not be abased to the other.

Loafe with me on the grass, loose the stop from your throat,
Not words, not music or rhyme I want, not custom or lecture,
not even the best,
Only the lull I like, the hum of your valvèd voice.

I mind how once we lay such a transparent summer morn-
ing,
How you settled your head athwart my hips and gently turn'd
over upon me,
And parted the shirt from my bosom-bone, and plunged your
tongue to my bare-stript heart,
And reach'd till you felt my beard, and reach'd till you held
my feet.

Swiftly arose and spread around me the peace and knowledge
that pass all the argument of the earth,
And I know that the hand of God is the promise of my
own,
And I know that the spirit of God is the brother of my own,
And that all the men ever born are also my brothers, and the
women my sisters and lovers,

And that a kelson of the creation is love,
And limitless are leaves stiff or drooping in the fields,
And brown ants in the little wells beneath them,
And mossy scabs of the worm fence, heap'd stones, elder,
mullein and poke-weed.

6

A child said *What is the grass?* fetching it to me with full
    hands,
How could I answer the child? I do not know what it is any
    more than he.

I guess it must be the flag of my disposition, out of hopeful
    green stuff woven.

Or I guess it is the handkerchief of the Lord,
A scented gift and remembrancer designedly dropt,
Bearing the owner's name someway in the corners, that we
    may see and remark, and say *Whose?*

Or I guess the grass is itself a child, the produced babe of the
    vegetation.

Or I guess it is a uniform hieroglyphic,
And it means, Sprouting alike in broad zones and narrow
    zones,
Growing among black folks as among white,
Kanuck, Tuckahoe, Congressman, Cuff, I give them the
    same, I receive them the same.

And now it seems to me the beautiful uncut hair of graves.

Tenderly will I use you curling grass,
It may be you transpire from the breasts of young men,
It may be if I had known them I would have loved them,
It may be you are from old people, or from offspring taken
    soon out of their mothers' laps,
And here you are the mothers' laps.

This grass is very dark to be from the white heads of old
    mothers,
Darker than the colourless beards of old men,
Dark to come from under the faint red roofs of mouths.

O I perceive after all so many uttering tongues,
And I perceive they do not come from the roofs of mouths
    for nothing.

I wish I could translate the hints about the dead young men
    and women,
And the hints about old men and mothers, and the offspring
    taken soon out of their laps.

What do you think has become of the young and old men?
And what do you think has become of the women and chil-
    dren?

They are alive and well somewhere,
The smallest sprout shows there is really no death,
And if ever there was it led forward life, and does not wait at
    the end to arrest it,
And ceas'd the moment life appear'd.

All goes onward and outward, nothing collapses,
And to die is different from what any one supposed, and
    luckier.

7

Has any one supposed it lucky to be born?
I hasten to inform him or her it is just as lucky to die, and I
    know it.

I pass death with the dying and birth with the new-wash'd
    babe, and am not contain'd between my hat and boots,
And peruse manifold objects, no two alike and every one
    good,
The earth good and the stars good, and their adjuncts all
    good.

I am not an earth nor an adjunct of an earth,
I am the mate and companion of people, all just as immortal
    and fathomless as myself,
(They do not know how immortal, but I know.)

Every kind for itself and its own, for me mine male and fe-
    male,
For me those that have been boys and that love women,
For me the man that is proud and feels how it stings to be
    slighted,

For me the sweet-heart and the old maid, for me mothers and
    the mothers of mothers,
For me lips that have smiled, eyes that have shed tears,
For me children and the begetters of children.

Undrape! you are not guilty to me, nor stale nor discarded,
I see through the broadcloth and gingham whether or no,
And am around, tenacious, acquisitive, tireless, and cannot
    be shaken away.

8

The little one sleeps in its cradle,
I lift the gauze and look a long time, and silently brush away
    flies with my hand.

The youngster and the red-faced girl turn aside up the bushy
    hill,
I peeringly view them from the top.

The suicide sprawls on the bloody floor of the bedroom,
I witness the corpse with its dabbled hair, I note where the
    pistol has fallen.

The blab of the pave, tires of carts, sluff of boot-soles, talk of
    the promenaders,
The heavy omnibus, the driver with his interrogating thumb,
    the clank of the shod horses on the granite floor,
The snow-sleighs, clinking, shouted jokes, pelts of snow-balls,
The hurrahs for popular favorites, the fury of rous'd mobs,
The flap of the curtain'd litter, a sick man inside borne to the
    hospital,
The meeting of enemies, the sudden oath, the blows and fall,
The excited crowd, the policeman with his star quickly work-
    ing his passage to the centre of the crowd,
The impassive stones that receive and return so many echoes,
What groans of over-fed or half-starv'd who fall sunstruck or
    in fits,
What exclamations of women taken suddenly who hurry
    home and give birth to babes,

B   H.W.

What living and buried speech is always vibrating here, what
    howls restrain'd by decorum,
Arrests of criminals, slights, adulterous offers made, accept-
    ances, rejections with convex lips,
I mind them or the show or resonance of them—I come and I
    depart.

9

The big doors of the country barn stand open and ready,
The dried grass of the harvest-time loads the slow-drawn
    wagon,
The clear light plays on the brown gray and green inter-
    tinged,
The armfuls are pack'd to the sagging mow.

I am there, I help, I came stretch'd atop of the load,
I felt its soft jolts, one leg reclined on the other,
I jump from the cross-beams and seize the clover and
    timothy,
And roll head over heels and tangle my hair full of wisps.

10

Alone far in the wilds and mountains I hunt,
Wandering amazed at my own lightness and glee,
In the late afternoon choosing a safe spot to pass the night,
Kindling a fire and broiling the fresh-kill'd game,
Falling asleep on the gather'd leaves with my dog and gun by
    my side.

The Yankee clipper is under her sky-sails, she cuts the sparkle
    and scud,
My eyes settle the land, I bend at her prow or shout joyously
    from the deck.

The boatmen and clam-diggers arose early and stopt for
    me,
I tuck'd my trowser-ends in my boots and went and had a
    good time;
You should have been with us that day round the chowder-
    kettle.

I saw the marriage of the trapper in the open air in the far
 west, the bride was a red girl,
Her father and his friends sat near cross-legged and dumbly
 smoking, they had moccasins to their feet and large
 thick blankets hanging from their shoulders,
On a bank lounged the trapper, he was drest mostly in skins,
 his luxuriant beard and curls protected his neck, he held
 his bride by the hand,
She had long eyelashes, her head was bare, her coarse straight
 locks descended upon her voluptuous limbs and reach'd
 to her feet.

The runaway slave came to my house and stopt outside,
I heard his motions crackling the twigs of the woodpile,
Through the swung half-door of the kitchen I saw him limpsy
 and weak,
And went where he sat on a log and led him in and assured
 him,
And brought water and fill'd a tub for his sweated body and
 bruis'd feet,
And gave him a room that enter'd from my own, and gave
 him some coarse clean clothes,
And remember perfectly well his revolving eyes and his awk-
 wardness,
And remember putting plasters on the galls of his neck and
 ankles;
He staid with me a week before he was recuperated and
 pass'd north,
I had him sit next me at table, my fire-lock lean'd in the
 corner.

11

Twenty-eight young men bathe by the shore,
Twenty-eight young men and all so friendly;
Twenty-eight years of womanly life and all so lonesome.

She owns the fine house by the rise of the bank,
She hides handsome and richly drest aft the blinds of the
 window.

Which of the young men does she like the best?
Ah the homeliest of them is beautiful to her.

Where are you off to, lady? for I see you,
You splash in the water there, yet stay stock still in your room.

Dancing and laughing along the beach came the twenty-
ninth bather,
The rest did not see her, but she saw them and loved them.

The beards of the young men glisten'd with wet, it ran from
their long hair,
Little streams pass'd all over their bodies.

An unseen hand also pass'd over their bodies,
It descended tremblingly from their temples and ribs.

The young men float on their backs, their white bellies bulge
to the sun, they do not ask who seizes fast to them,
They do not know who puffs and declines with pendant and
bending arch,
They do not think whom they souse with spray.

12

The butcher-boy puts off his killing-clothes, or sharpens his
knife at the stall in the market,
I loiter enjoying his repartee and his shuffle and break-
down.

Blacksmiths with grimed and hairy chests environ the anvil,
Each has his main-sledge, they are all out, there is a great
heat in the fire.

From the cinder-strew'd threshold I follow their movements,
The lithe sheer of their waists plays even with their massive
arms,
Overhand the hammers swing, overhand so slow, overhand
so sure,
They do not hasten, each man hits in his place.

13

The negro holds firmly the reins of his four horses, the block
    swags underneath on its tied-over chain,
The negro that drives the long dray of the stone-yard, steady
    and tall he stands pois'd on one leg on the string-
    piece,
His blue shirt exposes his ample neck and breast and loosens
    over his hip-band,
His glance is calm and commanding, he tosses the slouch of
    his hat away from his forehead,
The sun falls on his crispy hair and mustache, falls on the
    black of his polish'd and perfect limbs.

I behold the picturesque giant and love him, and I do not
    stop there,
I go with the team also.

In me the caresser of life wherever moving, backward as well
    as forward sluing,
To niches aside and junior bending, not a person or object
    missing,
Absorbing all to myself and for this song.

Oxen that rattle the yoke and chain or halt in the leafy shade,
    what is that you express in your eyes?
It seems to me more than all the print I have read in my life.

My tread scares the wood-drake and wood-duck on my dis-
    tant and day-long ramble,
They rise together, they slowly circle around.

I believe in those wing'd purposes,
And acknowledge red, yellow, white, playing within me,
And consider green and violet and the tufted crown inten-
    tional,
And do not call the tortoise unworthy because she is not
    something else,
And the jay in the woods never studied the gamut, yet trills
    pretty well to me,
And the look of the bay mare shames silliness out of me.

14

The wild gander leads his flock through the cool night,
Ya-honk he says, and sounds it down to me like an invitation,
The pert may suppose it meaningless, but I listening close,
Find its purpose and place up there toward the wintry sky.

The sharp-hoof'd moose of the north, the cat on the house-
    sill, the chickadee, the prairie-dog,
The litter of the grunting sow as they tug at her teats,
The brood of the turkey-hen and she with her half-spread
    wings,
I see in them and myself the same old law.

The press of my foot to the earth springs a hundred affec-
    tions,
They scorn the best I can do to relate them.

I am enamour'd of growing out-doors,
Of men that live among cattle or taste of the ocean or woods,
Of the builders and steerers of ships and the wielders of axes
    and mauls, and the drivers of horses,
I can eat and sleep with them week in and week out.

What is commonest, cheapest, nearest, easiest, is Me,
Me going in for my chances, spending for vast returns,
Adorning myself to bestow myself on the first that will take
    me,
Not asking the sky to come down to my good will,
Scattering it freely forever.

15

The pure contralto sings in the organ loft,
The carpenter dresses his plank, the tongue of his foreplane
    whistles its wild ascending lisp,
The married and unmarried children ride home to their
    Thanksgiving dinner,
The pilot seizes the king-pin, he heaves down with a strong
    arm,
The mate stands braced in the whale-boat, lance and harpoon
    are ready,

The duck-shooter walks by silent and cautious stretches,
The deacons are ordain'd with cross'd hands at the altar,
The spinning-girl retreats and advances to the hum of the big wheel,
The farmer stops by the bars as he walks on a First-day loafe and looks at the oats and rye,
The lunatic is carried at last to the asylum a confirm'd case,
(He will never sleep any more as he did in the cot in his mother's bedroom;)
The jour printer with gray head and gaunt jaws works at his case,
He turns his quid of tobacco while his eyes blurr with the manuscript;
The malform'd limbs are tied to the surgeon's table,
What is removed drops horribly in a pail;
The quadroon girl is sold at the auction-stand, the drunkard nods by the bar-room stove,
The machinist rolls up his sleeves, the policeman travels his beat, the gate-keeper marks who pass,
The young fellow drives the express-wagon, (I love him, though I do not know him;)
The half-breed straps on his light boots to compete in the race,
The western turkey-shooting draws old and young, some lean on their rifles, some sit on logs,
Out from the crowd steps the marksman, takes his position, levels his piece;
The groups of newly-come immigrants cover the wharf or levee,
As the woolly-pates hoe in the sugar-field, the overseer views them from his saddle,
The bugle calls in the ball-room, the gentlemen run for their partners, the dancers bow to each other,
The youth lies awake in the cedar-roof'd garret and harks to the musical rain,
The Wolverine sets traps on the creek that helps fill the Huron,
The squaw wrapt in her yellow-hemm'd cloth is offering moccasins and bead-bags for sale,
The connoisseur peers along the exhibition-gallery with half-shut eyes bent sideways,

As the deck-hands make fast the steamboat the plank is thrown for the shore-going passengers,

The young sister holds out the skein while the elder sister winds it off in a ball, and stops now and then for the knots,

The one-year wife is recovering and happy having a week ago borne her first child,

The clean-hair'd Yankee girl works with her sewing-machine or in the factory or mill,

The paving-man leans on his two-handed rammer, the reporter's lead flies swiftly over the note-book, the sign-painter is lettering with blue and gold,

The canal boy trots on the tow-path, the book-keeper counts at his desk, the shoemaker waxes his thread,

The conductor beats time for the band and all the performers follow him,

The child is baptized, the convert is making his first professions,

The regatta is spread on the bay, the race is begun, (how the white sails sparkle!)

The drover watching his drove sings out to them that would stray,

The pedler sweats with his pack on his back, (the purchaser higgling about the odd cent;)

The bride unrumples her white dress, the minute-hand of the clock moves slowly,

The opium-eater reclines with rigid head and just-open'd lips,

The prostitute draggles her shawl, her bonnet bobs on her tipsy and pimpled neck,

The crowd laugh at her blackguard oaths, the men jeer and wink to each other,

(Miserable! I do not laugh at your oaths nor jeer you;)

The President holding a cabinet council is surrounded by the great Secretaries,

On the piazza walk three matrons stately and friendly with twined arms,

The crew of the fish-smack pack repeated layers of halibut in the hold,

The Missourian crosses the plains toting his wares and his cattle,

As the fare-collector goes through the train he gives notice by
the jingling of loose change,
The floor-men are laying the floor, the tinners are tinning the
roof, the masons are calling for mortar,
In single file each shouldering his hod pass onward the
laborers;
Seasons pursuing each other the indescribable crowd is
gather'd, it is the fourth of Seventh-month, (what salutes
of cannon and small arms!)
Seasons pursuing each other the plougher ploughs, the
mower mows, and the winter-grain falls in the ground;
Off on the lakes the pike-fisher watches and waits by the hole
in the frozen surface,
The stumps stand thick round the clearing, the squatter
strikes deep with his axe,
Flatboatmen make fast towards dusk near the cotton-wood
or pecan-trees,
Coon-seekers go through the regions of the Red river or
through those drain'd by the Tennessee, or through
those of the Arkansas,
Torches shine in the dark that hangs on the Chattahooche or
Altamahaw,
Patriarchs sit at supper with sons and grandsons and great-
grandsons around them,
In walls of adobie, in canvas tents, rest hunters and trappers
after their day's sport,
The city sleeps and the country sleeps,
The living sleep for their time, the dead sleep for their time,
The old husband sleeps by his wife and the young husband
sleeps by his wife;
And these tend inward to me, and I tend outward to them,
And such as it is to be of these more or less I am,
And of these one and all I weave the song of myself.

16

I am of old and young, of the foolish as much as the wise,
Regardless of others, ever regardful of others,
Maternal as well as paternal, a child as well as a man,
Stuff'd with the stuff that is coarse and stuff'd with the stuff
that is fine,

One of the Nation of many nations, the smallest the same
     and the largest the same,
A Southerner soon as a Northerner, a planter nonchalant
     and hospitable down by the Oconee I live,
A Yankee bound my own way ready for trade, my joints the
     limberest joints on earth and the sternest joints on earth,
A Kentuckian walking the vale of the Elkhorn in my deer-
     skin leggings, a Louisianian or Georgian,
A boatman over lakes or bays or along coasts, a Hoosier,
     Badger, Buck-eye;
At home on Kanadian snow-shoes or up in the bush, or with
     fishermen off Newfoundland,
At home in the fleet of ice-boats, sailing with the rest and
     tacking,
At home on the hills of Vermont or in the woods of Maine,
     or the Texan ranch,
Comrade of Californians, comrade of free North-Westerners,
     (loving their big proportions,)
Comrade of raftsmen and coalmen, comrade of all who shake
     hands and welcome to drink and meat,
A learner with the simplest, a teacher of the thoughtfullest,
A novice beginning yet experient of myriads of seasons,
Of every hue and caste am I, of every rank and religion,
A farmer, mechanic, artist, gentleman, sailor, quaker,
Prisoner, fancy-man, rowdy, lawyer, physician, priest.

I resist any thing better than my own diversity,
Breathe the air but leave plenty after me,
And am not stuck up, and am in my place.

(The moth and the fish-eggs are in their place,
The bright suns I see and the dark suns I cannot see are in
     their place,
The palpable is in its place and the impalpable is in its place.)

17

These are really the thoughts of all men in all ages and lands,
     they are not original with me,
If they are not yours as much as mine they are nothing, or
     next to nothing,

If they are not the riddle and the untying of the riddle they
    are nothing,
If they are not just as close as they are distant they are
    nothing.

This is the grass that grows wherever the land is and the
    water is,
This the common air that bathes the globe.

18

With music strong I come, with my cornets and my drums,
I play not marches for accepted victors only, I play marches
    for conquer'd and slain persons.

Have you heard that it was good to gain the day?
I also say it is good to fall, battles are lost in the same spirit in
    which they are won.

I beat and pound for the dead,
I blow through my embouchures my loudest and gayest for
    them.

Vivas to those who have fail'd!
And to those whose war-vessels sank in the sea!
And to those themselves who sank in the sea!
And to all generals that lost engagements, and all overcome
    heroes!
And the numberless unknown heroes equal to the greatest
    heroes known!

19

This is the meal equally set, this the meat for natural hunger,
It is for the wicked just the same as the righteous, I make
    appointments with all,
I will not have a single person slighted or left away,
The kept-woman, sponger, thief, are hereby invited,
The heavy-lipp'd slave is invited, the venerealee is invited;
There shall be no difference between them and the rest.

This is the press of a bashful hand, this the float and odor of
    hair,

This the touch of my lips to yours, this the murmur of yearning,
This the far-off depth and height reflecting my own face,
This the thoughtful merge of myself, and the outlet again.

Do you guess I have some intricate purpose?
Well I have, for the Fourth-month showers have, and the
    mica on the side of a rock has.

Do you take it I would astonish?
Does the daylight astonish? does the early redstart twittering
    through the woods?
Do I astonish more than they?

This hour I tell things in confidence,
I might not tell everybody, but I will tell you.

20

Who goes there? hankering, gross, mystical, nude;
How is it I extract strength from the beef I eat?

What is a man anyhow? what am I? what are you?

All I mark as my own you shall offset it with your own,
Else it were time lost listening to me.

I do not snivel that snivel the world over,
That months are vacuums and the ground but wallow and filth.

Whimpering and truckling fold with powders for invalids,
    conformity goes to the fourth-remov'd,
I wear my hat as I please indoors or out.

Why should I pray? why should I venerate and be ceremoni-
    ous?

Having pried through the strata, analyzed to a hair, counsel'd
    with doctors and calculated close,
I find no sweeter fat than sticks to my own bones.

In all people I see myself, none more and not one a barley-
    corn less,
And the good or bad I say of myself I say of them.

I know I am solid and sound,
To me the converging objects of the universe perpetually flow,
All are written to me, and I must get what the writing means.

I know I am deathless,
I know this orbit of mine cannot be swept by a carpenter's
    compass,
I know I shall not pass like a child's carlacue cut with a burnt
    stick at night.

I know I am august,
I do not trouble my spirit to vindicate itself or be understood,
I see that the elementary laws never apologize,
(I reckon I behave no prouder than the level I plant my house
    by, after all.)

I exist as I am, that is enough,
If no other in the world be aware I sit content,
And if each and all be aware I sit content.

One world is aware and by far the largest to me, and that is
    myself,
And whether I come to my own to-day or in ten thousand or
    ten million years,
I can cheerfully take it now, or with equal cheerfulness I can
    wait.

My foothold is tenon'd and mortis'd in granite,
I laugh at what you call dissolution,
And I know the amplitude of time.

21

I am the poet of the Body and I am the poet of the Soul,
The pleasures of heaven are with me and the pains of hell are
    with me,
The first I graft and increase upon myself, the latter I trans-
    late into a new tongue.

I am the poet of the woman the same as the man,
And I say it is as great to be a woman as to be a man,
And I say there is nothing greater than the mother of men.

I chant the chant of dilation or pride,
We have had ducking and deprecating about enough,
I show that size is only development.

Have you outstript the rest? are you the President?
It is a trifle, they will more than arrive there every one, and
    still pass on.

I am he that walks with the tender and growing night,
I call to the earth and sea half-held by the night.

Press close bare-bosom'd night—press close magnetic nour-
    ishing night!
Night of south winds—night of the large few stars!
Still nodding night—mad naked summer night.

Smile O voluptuous cool-breath'd earth!
Earth of the slumbering and liquid trees!
Earth of departed sunset—earth of the mountains misty-topt!
Earth of the vitreous pour of the full moon just tinged with
    blue!
Earth of shine and dark mottling the tide of the river!
Earth of the limpid gray of clouds brighter and clearer for
    my sake!
Far-swooping elbow'd earth—rich apple-blossom'd earth!
Smile, for your lover comes.

Prodigal, you have given me love—therefore I to you give
    love!
O unspeakable passionate love.

22

You sea! I resign myself to you also—I guess what you mean,
I behold from the beach your crooked inviting fingers,
I believe you refuse to go back without feeling of me,
We must have a turn together, I undress, hurry me out of
    sight of the land,
Cushion me soft, rock me in billowy drowse,
Dash me with amorous wet, I can repay you.

Sea of stretch'd ground-swells,
Sea breathing broad and convulsive breaths,
Sea of the brine of life and of unshovell'd yet always-ready
    graves,
Howler and scooper of storms, capricious and dainty sea,
I am integral with you, I too am of one phase and of all
    phases.

Partaker of influx and efflux, I, extoller of hate and concilia-
    tion,
Extoller of amies and those that sleep in each others' arms.

I am he attesting sympathy,
(Shall I make my list of things in the house and skip the house
    that supports them?)

I am not the poet of goodness only, I do not decline to be the
    poet of wickedness also.

What blurt is this about virtue and about vice?
Evil propels me and reform of evil propels me, I stand in-
    different,
My gait is no fault-finder's or rejecter's gait,
I moisten the roots of all that has grown.

Did you fear some scrofula out of the unflagging pregnancy?
Did you guess the celestial laws are yet to be work'd over and
    rectified?

I find one side a balance and the antipodal side a balance,
Soft doctrine as steady help as stable doctrine,
Thoughts and deeds of the present our rouse and early start.

This minute that comes to me over the past decillions,
There is no better than it and now.

What behaved well in the past or behaves well to-day is not
    such a wonder,
The wonder is always and always how there can be a mean
    man or an infidel.

23

Endless unfolding of words of ages!
And mine a word of the modern, the word En-Masse.

A word of the faith that never balks,
Here or henceforward it is all the same to me, I accept Time
    absolutely.

It alone is without flaw, it alone rounds and completes
    all,
That mystic baffling wonder alone completes all.

I accept Reality and dare not question it,
Materialism first and last imbuing.

Hurrah for positive science! long live exact demonstration!
Fetch stonecrop mixt with cedar and branches of lilac,
This is the lexicographer, this the chemist, this made a gram-
    mar of the old cartouches,
These mariners put the ship through dangerous unknown
    seas,
This is the geologist, this works with the scalpel, and this is a
    mathematician.

Gentlemen, to you the first honors always!
Your facts are useful, and yet they are not my dwelling,
I but enter by them to an area of my dwelling.

Less the reminders of properties told my words,
And more the reminders they of life untold, and of freedom
    and extrication,
And make short account of neuters and geldings, and favor
    men and women fully equipt,
And beat the gong of revolt, and stop with fugitives and
    them that plot and conspire.

24

Walt Whitman, a kosmos, of Manhattan the son,
Turbulent, fleshy, sensual, eating, drinking and breeding,

No sentimentalist, no stander above men and women or
    apart from them,
No more modest than immodest.

Unscrew the locks from the doors!
Unscrew the doors themselves from their jambs!

Whoever degrades another degrades me,
And whatever is done or said returns at last to me.

Through me the afflatus surging and surging, through me the
    current and index.

I speak the pass-word primeval, I give the sign of democracy,
By God! I will accept nothing which all cannot have their
    counterpart of on the same terms.

Through me many long dumb voices,
Voices of the interminable generation of prisoners and slaves,
Voices of the diseas'd and despairing and of thieves and
    dwarfs,
Voices of cycles of preparation and accretion,
And of the threads that connect the stars, and of wombs and
    of the father-stuff,
And of the rights of them the others are down upon,
Of the deform'd, trivial, flat, foolish, despised,
Fog in the air, beetles rolling balls of dung.

Through me forbidden voices,
Voices of sexes and lusts, voices veil'd and I remove the veil,
Voices indecent by me clarified and transfigur'd.

I do not press my fingers across my mouth,
I keep as delicate around the bowels as around the head and
    heart,
Copulation is no more rank to me than death is.

I believe in the flesh and the appetites,
Seeing, hearing, feeling, are miracles, and each part and tag
    of me is a miracle.

Divine am I inside and out, and I make holy whatever I touch
or am touch'd from,
The scent of these arm-pits aroma finer than prayer,
This head more than churches, bibles, and all the creeds.

If I worship one thing more than another it shall be the
spread of my own body, or any part of it,
Translucent mould of me it shall be you!
Shaded ledges and rests it shall be you!
Firm masculine colter it shall be you!
Whatever goes to the tilth of me it shall be you!
You my rich blood! your milky stream pale strippings of my
life!
Breast that presses against other breasts it shall be you!
My brain it shall be your occult convolutions!
Root of wash'd sweet-flag! timorous pond-snipe! nest of
guarded duplicate eggs! it shall be you!
Mix'd tussled hay of head, beard, brawn, it shall be you!
Trickling sap of maple, fibre of manly wheat, it shall be
you!
Sun so generous it shall be you!
Vapors lighting and shading my face it shall be you!
You sweaty brooks and dews it shall be you!
Winds whose soft-tickling genitals rub against me it shall be
you!
Broad muscular fields, branches of live oak, loving lounger in
my winding paths, it shall be you!
Hands I have taken, face I have kiss'd, mortal I have ever
touch'd, it shall be you.

I dote on myself, there is that lot of me and all so luscious,
Each moment and whatever happens thrills me with joy,
I cannot tell how my ankles bend, nor whence the cause of
my faintest wish,
Nor the cause of the friendship I emit, nor the cause of the
friendship I take again.

That I walk up my stoop, I pause to consider if it really be,
A morning-glory at my window satisfies me more than the
metaphysics of books.

To behold the day-break!
The little light fades the immense and diaphanous shadows,
The air tastes good to my palate.

Hefts of the moving world at innocent gambols silently rising,
    freshly exuding,
Scooting obliquely high and low.

Something I cannot see puts upward libidinous prongs,
Seas of bright juice suffuse heaven.

The earth by the sky staid with, the daily close of their junc-
    tion,
The heav'd challenge from the east that moment over my
    head,
The mocking taunt, See then whether you shall be master!

25

Dazzling and tremendous how quick the sun-rise would kill
    me,
If I could not now and always send sun-rise out of me.

We also ascend dazzling and tremendous as the sun,
We found our own O my soul in the calm and cool of the
    day-break.

My voice goes after what my eyes cannot reach,
With the twirl of my tongue I encompass worlds and volumes
    of worlds.

Speech is the twin of my vision, it is unequal to measure itself,
It provokes me forever, it says sarcastically,
Walt you contain enough, why don't you let it out then?

Come now I will not be tantalized, you conceive too much of
    articulation,
Do you not know O speech how the buds beneath you are
    folded?
Waiting in gloom, protected by frost,
The dirt receding before my prophetical screams,
I underlying causes to balance them at last,

My knowledge my live parts, it keeping tally with the mean-
   ing of all things,
Happiness, (which whoever hears me let him or her set out in
   search of this day.)

My final merit I refuse you, I refuse putting from me what I
   really am,
Encompass worlds, but never try to encompass me,
I crowd your sleekest and best by simply looking toward
   you.

Writing and talk do not prove me,
I carry the plenum of proof and every thing else in my face,
With the hush of my lips I wholly confound the skeptic.

26

Now I will do nothing but listen,
To accrue what I hear into this song, to let sounds contribute
   toward it.

I hear bravuras of birds, bustle of growing wheat, gossip of
   flames, clack of sticks cooking my meals.
I hear the sound I love, the sound of the human voice,
I hear all sounds running together, combined, fused or
   following,
Sounds of the city and sounds out of the city, sounds of the
   day and night,
Talkative young ones to those that like them, the loud laugh
   of work-people at their meals,
The angry base of disjointed friendship, the faint tones of the
   sick,
The judge with hands tight to the desk, his pallid lips pro-
   nouncing a death-sentence,
The heave'e'yo of stevedores unlading ships by the wharves,
   the refrain of the anchor-lifters,
The ring of alarm-bells, the cry of fire, the whirr of swift-
   streaking engines and hose-carts with premonitory
   tinkles and color'd lights,
The steam-whistle, the solid roll of the train of approaching
   cars,

The slow march play'd at the head of the association march-
ing two and two,
(They go to guard some corpse, the flag-tops are draped with
black muslin.)

I hear the violoncello, ('tis the young man's heart's com-
plaint,)
I hear the key'd cornet, it glides quickly in through my ears,
It shakes mad-sweet pangs through my belly and breast.

I hear the chorus, it is a grand opera,
Ah this indeed is music—this suits me.

A tenor large and fresh as the creation fills me,
The orbic flex of his mouth is pouring and filling me full.

I hear the train'd soprano (what work with hers is this?)
The orchestra whirls me wider than Uranus flies,
It wrenches such ardors from me I did not know I possess'd
them,
It sails me, I dab with bare feet, they are lick'd by the indolent
waves,
I am cut by bitter and angry hail, I lose my breath,
Steep'd amid honey'd morphine, my windpipe throttled in
fakes of death,
At length let up again to feel the puzzle of puzzles,
And that we call Being.

27

To be in any form, what is that?
(Round and round we go, all of us, and ever come back
thither,)
If nothing lay more develop'd the quahaug in its callous shell
were enough.

Mine is no callous shell,
I have instant conductors all over me whether I pass or stop,
They seize every object and lead it harmlessly through me.

I merely stir, press, feel with my fingers, and am happy,
To touch my person to some one else's is about as much as I
can stand.

28

Is this then a touch? quivering me to a new identity,
Flames and ether making a rush for my veins,
Treacherous tip of me reaching and crowding to help them,
My flesh and blood playing out lightning to strike what is
    hardly different from myself,
On all sides prurient provokers stiffening my limbs,
Straining the udder of my heart for its withheld drip,
Behaving licentious toward me, taking no denial,
Depriving me of my best as for a purpose,
Unbuttoning my clothes, holding me by the bare waist,
Deluding my confusion with the calm of the sunlight and
    pasture-fields,
Immodestly sliding the fellow-senses away,
They bribed to swap off with touch and go and graze at the
    edges of me,
No consideration, no regard for my draining strength or my
    anger,
Fetching the rest of the herd around to enjoy them a while,
Then all uniting to stand on a headland and worry me.

The sentries desert every other part of me,
They have left me helpless to a red marauder,
They all come to the headland to witness and assist against
    me.

I am given up by traitors,
I talk wildly, I have lost my wits, I and nobody else am the
    greatest traitor,
I went myself first to the headland, my own hands carried me
    there.

You villain touch! what are you doing? my breath is tight in
    its throat,
Unclench your floodgates, you are too much for me.

29

Blind loving wrestling touch, sheath'd hooded sharp-tooth'd
    touch!
Did it make you ache so, leaving me?

Parting track'd by arriving, perpetual payment of perpetual
    loan,
Rich showering rain, and recompense richer afterward.

Sprouts take and accumulate, stand by the curb prolific and
    vital,
Landscapes projected masculine, full-sized and golden.

30

All truths wait in all things,
They neither hasten their own delivery nor resist it,
They do not need the obstetric forceps of the surgeon,
The insignificant is as big to me as any,
(What is less or more than a touch?)

Logic and sermons never convince,
The damp of the night drives deeper into my soul.

(Only what proves itself to every man and woman is so,
Only what nobody denies is so.)

A minute and a drop of me settle my brain,
I believe the soggy clods shall become lovers and lamps,
And a compend of compends is the meat of a man or woman,
And a summit and flower there is the feeling they have for
    each other,
And they are to branch boundlessly out of that lesson until it
    becomes omnific,
And until one and all shall delight us, and we them.

31

I believe a leaf of grass is no less than the journey-work of
    the stars,
And the pismire is equally perfect, and a grain of sand, and
    the egg of the wren,
And the tree-toad is a chef-d'œuvre for the highest,
And the running blackberry would adorn the parlors of
    heaven,
And the narrowest hinge in my hand puts to scorn all
    machinery,

And the cow crunching with depress'd head surpasses any
  statue,
And a mouse is miracle enough to stagger sextillions of
  infidels.

I find I incorporate gneiss, coal, long-threaded moss, fruits,
  grains, esculent roots,
And am stucco'd with quadrupeds and birds all over,
And have distanced what is behind me for good reasons,
But call any thing back again when I desire it.

In vain the speeding or shyness,
In vain the plutonic rocks send their old heat against my
  approach,
In vain the mastodon retreats beneath its own powder'd
  bones,
In vain objects stand leagues off and assume manifold shapes,
In vain the ocean setting in hollows and the great monsters
  lying low,
In vain the buzzard houses herself with the sky,
In vain the snake slides through the creepers and logs,
In vain the elk takes to the inner passes of the woods,
In vain the razor-bill'd auk sails far north to Labrador,
I follow quickly, I ascend to the nest in the fissure of the
  cliff.

32

I think I could turn and live with animals, they're so placid
  and self-contain'd,
I stand and look at them long and long.

They do not sweat and whine about their condition,
They do not lie awake in the dark and weep for their sins,
They do not make me sick discussing their duty to God,
Not one is dissatisfied, not one is demented with the mania of
  owning things,
Not one kneels to another, nor to his kind that lived thou-
  sands of years ago,
Not one is respectable or unhappy over the whole earth.

So they show their relations to me and I accept them,
They bring me tokens of myself, they evince them plainly in
their possession.

I wonder where they get those tokens,
Did I pass that way huge times ago and negligently drop
them?

Myself moving forward then and now and forever,
Gathering and showing more always and with velocity,
Infinite and omnigenous, and the like of these among them,
Not too exclusive toward the reachers of my remembrancers,
Picking out here one that I love, and now go with him on
brotherly terms.

A gigantic beauty of a stallion, fresh and responsive to my
caresses,
Head high in the forehead, wide between the ears,
Limbs glossy and supple, tail dusting the ground,
Eyes full of sparkling wickedness, ears finely cut, flexibly
moving.

His nostrils dilate as my heels embrace him,
His well-built limbs tremble with pleasure as we race around
and return.
I but use you a minute, then I resign you, stallion,
Why do I need your paces when I myself out-gallop them?
Even as I stand or sit passing faster than you.

33

Space and Time! now I see it is true, what I guess'd at,
What I guess'd when I loaf'd on the grass,
What I guess'd while I lay alone in my bed,
And again as I walk'd the beach under the paling stars of the
morning.

My ties and ballasts leave me, my elbows rest in sea-gaps,
I skirt sierras, my palms cover continents,
I am afoot with my vision.

By the city's quadrangular houses—in log huts, camping
with lumbermen,

Along the ruts of the turnpike, along the dry gulch and rivu-
let bed,

Weeding my onion-patch or hoeing rows of carrots and par-
snips, crossing savannas, trailing in forests,

Prospecting, gold-digging, girdling the trees of a new pur-
chase,

Scorch'd ankle-deep by the hot sand, hauling my boat down
the shallow river,

Where the panther walks to and fro on a limb overhead,
where the buck turns furiously at the hunter,

Where the rattlesnake suns his flabby length on a rock, where
the otter is feeding on fish,

Where the alligator in his tough pimples sleeps by the
bayou,

Where the black bear is searching for roots or honey, where
the beaver pats the mud with his paddle-shaped tail;

Over the growing sugar, over the yellow-flower'd cotton
plant, over the rice in its low moist field,

Over the sharp-peak'd farm house, with its scallop'd scum
and slender shoots from the gutters,

Over the western persimmon, over the long-leav'd corn, over
the delicate blue-flower flax,

Over the white and brown buckwheat, a hummer and buzzer
there with the rest,

Over the dusky green of the rye as it ripples and shades in the
breeze;

Scaling mountains, pulling myself cautiously up, holding on
by low scragged limbs,

Walking the path worn in the grass and beat through the
leaves of the brush,

Where the quail is whistling betwixt the woods and the wheat-
lot,

Where the bat flies in the Seventh-month eve, where the great
gold-bug drops through the dark,

Where the brook puts out of the roots of the old tree and
flows to the meadow,

Where cattle stand and shake away flies with the tremulous
shuddering of their hides,

Where the cheese-cloth hangs in the kitchen, where andirons
    straddle the hearth-slab, where cobwebs fall in festoons
    from the rafters;
Where trip-hammers crash, where the press is whirling its
    cylinders,
Where the human heart beats with terrible throes under its
    ribs,
Where the pear-shaped balloon is floating aloft, (floating in
    it myself and looking composedly down,)
Where the life-car is drawn on the slip-noose, where the heat
    hatches pale-green eggs in the dented sand,
Where the she-whale swims with her calf and never forsakes it,
Where the steam-ship trails hind-ways its long pennant of
    smoke,
Where the fin of the shark cuts like a black chip out of the
    water,
Where the half-burn'd brig is riding on unknown currents,
Where shells grow to her slimy deck, where the dead are
    corrupting below;
Where the dense-starr'd flag is borne at the head of the regi-
    ments,
Approaching Manhattan up by the long-stretching island,
Under Niagara, the cataract falling like a veil over my coun-
    tenance,
Upon a door-step, upon the horse-block of hard wood out-
    side,
Upon the race-course, or enjoying picnics or jigs or a good
    game of base-ball,
At he-festivals, with blackguard gibes, ironical license, bull-
    dances, drinking, laughter,
At the cider-mill tasting the sweets of the brown mash, suck-
    ing the juice through a straw,
At apple-peelings wanting kisses for all the red fruit I find,
At musters, beach-parties, friendly bees, huskings, house-
    raisings;
Where the mocking-bird sounds his delicious gurgles, cackles,
    screams, weeps,
Where the hay-rick stands in the barn-yard, where the dry-
    stalks are scatter'd, where the brood-cow waits in the
    hovel,

Where the bull advances to do his masculine work, where the
stud to the mare, where the cock is treading the hen,
Where the heifers browse, where geese nip their food with
short jerks,
Where sun-down shadows lengthen over the limitless and
lonesome prairie,
Where herds of buffalo make a crawling spread of the square
miles far and near,
Where the humming-bird shimmers, where the neck of the
long-lived swan is curving and winding,
Where the laughing-gull scoots by the shore, where she laughs
her near-human laugh,
Where bee-hives range on a gray bench in the garden half hid
by the high weeds,
Where band-neck'd partridges roost in a ring on the ground
with their heads out,
Where burial coaches enter the arch'd gates of a cemetery,
Where winter wolves bark amid wastes of snow and icicled
trees,
Where the yellow-crown'd heron comes to the edge of the
marsh at night and feeds upon small crabs,
Where the splash of swimmers and divers cools the warm
noon,
Where the katy-did works her chromatic reed on the walnut-
tree over the wall,
Through patches of citrons and cucumbers with silver-wired
leaves,
Through the salt-lick or orange glade, or under conical firs,
Through the gymnasium, through the curtain'd saloon,
through the office or public hall;
Pleas'd with the native and pleas'd with the foreign, pleas'd
with the new and old,
Pleas'd with the homely woman as well as the handsome,
Pleas'd with the quakeress as she puts off her bonnet and
talks melodiously,
Pleas'd with the tune of the choir of the whitewash'd church,
Pleas'd with the earnest words of the sweating Methodist
preacher, impress'd seriously at the camp-meeting;
Looking in at the shop-windows of Broadway the whole fore-
noon, flatting the flesh of my nose on the thick plate glass,

Wandering the same afternoon with my face turn'd up to the
    clouds, or down a lane or along the beach,
My right and left arms round the sides of two friends, and I
    in the middle;
Coming home with the silent and dark-cheek'd bush-boy,
    (behind me he rides at the drape of the day,)
Far from the settlements studying the print of animals' feet,
    or the moccasin print,
By the cot in the hospital reaching lemonade to a feverish
    patient,
Nigh the coffin'd corpse when all is still, examining with a
    candle;
Voyaging to every port to dicker and adventure,
Hurrying with the modern crowd as eager and flickle as any,
Hot toward one I hate, ready in my madness to knife him,
Solitary at midnight in my back yard, my thoughts gone from
    me a long while,
Walking the old hills of Judæa with the beautiful gentle God
    by my side,
Speeding through space, speeding through heaven and the
    stars,
Speeding amid the seven satellites and the broad ring, and
    the diameter of eighty thousand miles,
Speeding with tail'd meteors, throwing fire-balls like the
    rest,
Carrying the crescent child that carries its own full mother in
    its belly,
Storming, enjoying, planning, loving, cautioning,
Backing and filling, appearing and disappearing,
I tread day and night such roads.

I visit the orchards of spheres and look at the product,
And look at quintillions ripen'd and look at quintillions
    green.

I fly those flights of a fluid and swallowing soul,
My course runs below the soundings of plummets.

I help myself to material and immaterial,
No guard can shut me off, no law prevent me.

I anchor my ship for a little while only,
My messengers continually cruise away or bring their returns
to me.

I go hunting polar furs and the seal, leaping chasms with a
pike-pointed staff, clinging to topples of brittle and blue.

I ascend to the foretruck,
I take my place late at night in the crow's-nest,
We sail the arctic sea, it is plenty light enough,
Through the clear atmosphere I stretch around on the won-
derful beauty,
The enormous masses of ice pass me and I pass them, the
scenery is plain in all directions,
The white-topt mountains show in the distance, I fling out
my fancies toward them,
We are approaching some great battle-field in which we are
soon to be engaged,
We pass the colossal outposts of the encampment, we pass
with still feet and caution,
Or we are entering by the suburbs some vast and ruin'd city,
The blocks and fallen architecture more than all the living
cities of the globe.

I am a free companion, I bivouac by invading watchfires,
I turn the bridegroom out of bed and stay with the bride
myself,
I tighten her all night to my thighs and lips.

My voice is the wife's voice, the screech by the rail of the stairs,
They fetch my man's body up dripping and drown'd.

I understand the large hearts of heroes,
The courage of present times and all times,
How the skipper saw the crowded and rudderless wreck of
the steamship, and Death chasing it up and down the
storm,
How he knuckled tight and gave not back an inch, and was
faithful of days and faithful of nights,
And chalk'd in large letters on a board, *Be of good cheer, we
will not desert you;*

How he follow'd with them and tack'd with them three days
    and would not give it up,
How he saved the drifting company at last,
How the lank loose-gown'd women look'd when boated
    from the side of their prepared graves,
How the silent old-faced infants and the lifted sick, and the
    sharp-lipp'd unshaved men;
All this I swallow, it tastes good, I like it well, it becomes
    mine,
I am the man, I suffer'd, I was there.

The disdain and calmness of martyrs,
The mother of old, condemn'd for a witch, burnt with dry
    wood, her children gazing on,
The hounded slave that flags in the race, leans by the fence,
    blowing, cover'd with sweat,
The twinges that sting like needles his legs and neck, the
    murderous buckshot and the bullets,
All these I feel or am.

I am the hounded slave, I wince at the bite of the dogs,
Hell and despair are upon me, crack and again crack the
    marksmen,
I clutch the rails of the fence, my gore dribs, thinn'd with the
    ooze of my skin,
I fall on the weeds and stones,
The riders spur their unwilling horses, haul close,
Taunt my dizzy ears and beat me violently over the head with
    whip-stocks.

Agonies are one of my changes of garments,
I do not ask the wounded person how he feels, I myself be-
    come the wounded person,
My hurts turn livid upon me as I lean on a cane and observe.

I am the mash'd fireman with breast-bone broken,
Tumbling walls buried me in their debris,
Heat and smoke I inspired, I heard the yelling shouts of my
    comrades,
I heard the distant click of their picks and shovels,
They have clear'd the beams away, they tenderly lift me forth.

I lie in the night air in my red shirt, the pervading hush is for
    my sake,
Painless after all I lie exhausted but not so unhappy,
White and beautiful are the faces around me, the heads are
    bared of their fire-caps,
The kneeling crowd fades with the light of the torches.

Distant and dead resuscitate,
They show as the dial or move as the hands of me, I am the
    clock myself.

I am an old artillerist, I tell of my fort's bombardment,
I am there again.

Again the long roll of the drummers,
Again the attacking cannon, mortars,
Again to my listening ears the cannon responsive.

I take part, I see and hear the whole,
The cries, curses, roar, the plaudits for well-aim'd shots,
The ambulanza slowly passing trailing its red drip,
Workmen searching after damages, making indispensable
    repairs,
The fall of grenades through the rent roof, the fan-shaped
    explosion,
The whizz of limbs, heads, stone, wood, iron, high in the
    air.

Again gurgles the mouth of my dying general, he furiously
    waves with his hand,
He gasps through the clot *Mind not me—mind—the entrench-
ments.*

34

Now I tell what I knew in Texas in my early youth,
(I tell not the fall of Alamo,
Not one escaped to tell the fall of Alamo,
The hundred and fifty are dumb yet at Alamo,)
'Tis the tale of the murder in cold blood of four hundred and
    twelve young men.

Retreating they had form'd in a hollow square with their bag-
gage for breastworks,
Nine hundred lives out of the surrounding enemy's, nine
times their number, was the price they took in ad-
vance,
Their colonel was wounded and their ammunition gone,
They treated for an honorable capitulation, receiv'd writing
and seal, gave up their arms and march'd back prisoners
of war.

They were the glory of the race of rangers,
Matchless with horse, rifle, song, supper, courtship,
Large, turbulent, generous, handsome, proud, and affection-
ate,
Bearded, sunburnt, drest in the free costume of hunters,
Not a single one over thirty years of age.

The second First-day morning they were brought out in
squads and massacred, it was beautiful early summer,
The work commenced about five o'clock and was over by
eight.

None obey'd the command to kneel,
Some made a mad and helpless rush, some stood stark and
straight,
A few fell at once, shot in the temple or heart, the living and
dead lay together,
The maim'd and mangled dug in the dirt, the new-comers saw
them there,
Some half-kill'd attempted to crawl away,
These were despatch'd with bayonets or batter'd with the
blunts of muskets.
A youth not seventeen years old seiz'd his assassin till two
more came to release him,
The three were all torn and cover'd with the boy's blood.

At eleven o'clock began the burning of the bodies;
That is the tale of the murder of the four hundred and twelve
young men.

35

Would you hear of an old-time sea-fight?
Would you learn who won by the light of the moon and stars?
List to the yarn, as my grandmother's father the sailor told it
        to me.

Our foe was no skulk in his ship I tell you, (said he,)
His was the surly English pluck, and there is no tougher or
        truer, and never was, and never will be;
Along the lower'd eve he came horribly raking us.

We closed with him, the yards entangled, the cannon touch'd,
My captain lash'd fast with his own hands.

We had receiv'd some eighteen pound shots under the water,
On our lower-gun-deck two large pieces had burst at the first
        fire, killing all around and blowing up overhead.

Fighting at sun-down, fighting at dark,
Ten o'clock at night, the full moon well up, our leaks on the
        gain, and five feet of water reported,
The master-at-arms loosing the prisoners confined in the
        after-hold to give them a chance for themselves.

The transit to and from the magazine is now stopt by the
        sentinels,
They see so many strange faces they do not know whom to trust.

Our frigate takes fire,
The other asks if we demand quarter?
If our colors are struck and the fighting done?

Now I laugh content, for I hear the voice of my little captain,
We have not struck, he composedly cries, *we have just begun
        our part of the fighting*.

Only three guns are in use,
One is directed by the captain himself against the enemy's
        main-mast,
Two well serv'd with grape and canister silence his musketry
        and clear his decks.

The tops alone second the fire of this little battery, especially
    the main-top,
They hold out bravely during the whole of the action.

Not a moment's cease,
The leaks gain fast on the pumps, the fire eats toward the
    powder-magazine.

One of the pumps has been shot away, it is generally thought
    we are sinking.

Serene stands the little captain,
He is not hurried, his voice is neither high nor low,
His eyes give more light to us than our battle-lanterns.

Toward twelve there in the beams of the moon they surrender
    to us.

36

Stretch'd and still lies the midnight,
Two great hulls motionless on the breast of the darkness,
Our vessel riddled and slowly sinking, preparations to pass
    to the one we have conquer'd,
The captain on the quarter-deck coldly giving his orders
    through a countenance white as a sheet,
Near by the corpse of the child that serv'd in the cabin,
The dead face of an old salt with long white hair and care-
    fully curl'd whiskers,
The flames spite of all that can be done flickering aloft and
    below,
The husky voices of the two or three officers yet fit for duty,
Formless stacks of bodies and bodies by themselves, dabs of
    flesh upon the masts and spars,
Cut of cordage, dangle of rigging, slight shock of the soothe
    of waves,
Black and impassive guns, litter of powder-parcels, strong
    scent,
A few large stars overhead, silent and mournful shining,
Delicate sniffs of sea-breeze, smells of sedgy grass and fields
    by the shore, death-messages given in charge to sur-
    vivors,

The hiss of the surgeon's knife, the gnawing teeth of his
    saw,
Wheeze, cluck, swash of falling blood, short wild scream, and
    long, dull, tapering groan,
These so, these irretrievable.

37

You laggards there on guard! look to your arms!
In at the conquer'd doors they crowd! I am possess'd!
Embody all presences outlaw'd or suffering,
See myself in prison shaped like another man,
And feel the dull unintermitted pain,
For me the keepers of convicts shoulder their carbines and
    keep watch,
It is I let out in the morning and barr'd at night.

Not a mutineer walks handcuff'd to jail but I am handcuff'd
    to him and walk by his side,
(I am less the jolly one there, and more the silent one with
    sweat on my twitching lips.)

Not a youngster is taken for larceny but I go up too, and am
    tried and sentenced.

Not a cholera patient lies at the last gasp but I also lie at the
    last gasp,
My face is ash-color'd, my sinews gnarl, away from me
    people retreat.

Askers embody themselves in me and I am embodied in
    them,
I project my hat, sit shame-faced, and beg.

38

Enough! enough! enough!
Somehow I have been stunn'd. Stand back!
Give me a little time beyond my cuff'd head, slumbers,
    dreams, gaping,
I discover myself on the verge of a usual mistake.

That I could forget the mockers and insults!
That I could forget the trickling tears and the blows of the
    bludgeons and hammers! ·
That I could look with a separate look on my own crucifixion
    and bloody crowning!

I remember now,
I resume the overstaid fraction,
The grave of rock multiplies what has been confided to it, or
    to any graves,
Corpses rise, gashes heal, fastenings roll from me.

I troop forth replenish'd with supreme power, one of an
    average unending procession,
Inland and sea-coast we go, and pass all boundary lines,
Our swift ordinances on their way over the whole earth,
The blossoms we wear in our hats the growth of thousands of
    years.

Eleves, I salute you! come forward!
Continue your annotations, continue your questionings.

39

The friendly and flowing savage, who is he?
Is he waiting for civilization, or past it and mastering it?

Is he some Southwesterner rais'd out-doors? is he Kanadian?
Is he from the Mississippi country? Iowa, Oregon, Califor-
    nia?
The mountains? prairie-life, bush-life? or sailor from the sea?

Wherever he goes men and women accept and desire him,
They desire he should like them, touch them, speak to them,
    stay with them.

Behavior lawless as snow-flakes, words simple as grass, un-
    comb'd head, laughter, and naivetè,
Slow-stepping feet, common features, common modes and
    emanations,
They descend in new forms from the tips of his fingers,

They are wafted with the odor of his body or breath, they fly
    out of the glance of his eyes.

40

Flaunt of the sunshine I need not your bask—lie over!
You light surfaces only, I force surfaces and depths also.

Earth! you seem to look for something at my hands,
Say, old top-knot, what do you want?

Man or woman, I might tell how I like you, but cannot,
And might tell what it is in me and what it is in you, but
    cannot,
And might tell that pining I have, that pulse of my nights and
    days.

Behold, I do not give lectures or a little charity,
When I give I give myself.

You there, impotent, loose in the knees,
Open your scarf'd chops till I blow grit within you,
Spread your palms and lift the flaps of your pockets,
I am not to be denied, I compel, I have stores plenty and to
    spare,
And any thing I have I bestow.

I do not ask who you are, that is not important to me,
You can do nothing and be nothing but what I will infold
    you.

To cotton-field drudge or cleaner of privies I lean,
On his right cheek I put the family kiss,
And in my soul I swear I never will deny him.

On women fit for conception I start bigger and nimbler
    babes,
(This day I am jetting the stuff of far more arrogant repub-
    lics.)

To any one dying, thither I speed and twist the knob of the
    door,

Turn the bed-clothes toward the foot of the bed,
Let the physician and the priest go home.

I seize the descending man and raise him with resistless will,
O despairer, here is my neck,
By God, you shall not go down! hang your whole weight
    upon me.

I dilate you with tremendous breath, I buoy you up,
Every room of the house do I fill with an arm'd force,
Lovers of me, bafflers of graves.

Sleep—I and they keep guard all night,
Not doubt, not disease shall dare to lay finger upon you,
I have embraced you, and henceforth possess you to myself,
And when you rise in the morning you will find what I tell
    you is so.

41

I am he bringing help for the sick as they pant on their backs,
And for strong upright men I bring yet more needed help.

I heard what was said of the universe,
Heard it and heard it of several thousand years;
It is middling well as far as it goes—but is that all?

Magnifying and applying come I,
Outbidding at the start the old cautious hucksters,
Taking myself the exact dimensions of Jehovah,
Lithographing Kronos, Zeus his son, and Hercules his
    grandson,
Buying drafts of Osiris, Isis, Belus, Brahma, Buddha,
In my portfolio placing Manito loose, Allah on a leaf, the
    crucifix engraved,
With Odin and the hideous-faced Mexitli and every idol and
    image,
Taking them all for what they are worth and not a cent more,
Admitting they were alive and did the work of their days,
(They bore mites as for unfledg'd birds who have now to rise
    and fly and sing for themselves,)

Accepting the rough deific sketches to fill out better in myself,
    bestowing them freely on each man and woman I see,
Discovering as much or more in a framer framing a house,
Putting higher claims for him there with his roll'd-up sleeves
    driving the mallet and chisel,
Not objecting to special revelations, considering a curl of
    smoke or a hair on the back of my hand just as curious
    as any revelation,
Lads ahold of fire-engines and hook-and-ladder ropes no less
    to me than the gods of the antique wars,
Minding their voices peal through the crash of destruction,
Their brawny limbs passing safe over charr'd laths, their
    white foreheads whole and unhurt out of the flames;
By the mechanic's wife with her babe at her nipple interced-
    ing for every person born,
Three scythes at harvest whizzing in a row from three lusty
    angels with shirts bagg'd out at their waists,
The snag-tooth'd hostler with red hair redeeming sins past
    and to come,
Selling all he possesses, traveling on foot to fee lawyers for
    his brother and sit by him while he is tried for forgery;
What was strewn in the amplest strewing the square rod
    about me, and not filling the square rod then,
The bull and the bug never worshipp'd half enough,
Dung and dirt more admirable than was dream'd,
The supernatural of no account, myself waiting my time to
    be one of the supremes,
The day getting ready for me when I shall do as much good
    as the best, and be as prodigious;
By my life-lumps! becoming already a creator,
Putting myself here and now to the ambush'd womb of the
    shadows.

42

A call in the midst of the crowd,
My own voice, orotund sweeping and final.

Come my children,
Come my boys and girls, my women, household and inti-
    mates,

Now the performer launches his nerve, he has pass'd his pre-
lude on the reeds within.

Easily written loose-finger'd chords—I feel the thrum of your
climax and close.

My head slues round on my neck,
Music rolls, but not from the organ,
Folks are around me, but they are no household of mine.

Ever the hard unsunk ground,
Ever the eaters and drinkers, ever the upward and downward
sun, ever the air and the ceaseless tides,
Ever myself and my neighbors, refreshing, wicked, real,
Ever the old inexplicable query, ever that thorn'd thumb,
that breath of itches and thirsts,
Ever the vexer's *hoot! hoot!* till we find where the sly one
hides and bring him forth,
Ever love, ever the sobbing liquid of life,
Ever the bandage under the chin, ever the trestles of death.

Here and there with dimes on the eyes walking,
To feed the greed of the belly the brains liberally spooning,
Tickets buying, taking, selling, but in to the feast never once
going,
Many sweating, ploughing, thrashing, and then the chaff for
payment receiving,
A few idly owning, and they the wheat continually claiming.

This is the city and I am one of the citizens,
Whatever interests the rest interests me, politics, wars, mar-
kets, newspapers, schools,
The mayor and councils, banks, tariffs, steamships, factories,
stocks, stores, real estate and personal estate.

The little plentiful manikins skipping around in collars and
tail'd coats,
I am aware who they are, (they are positively not worms or
fleas,)
I acknowledge the duplicates of myself, the weakest and
shallowest is deathless with me,

What I do and say the same waits for them,
Every thought that flounders in me the same flounders in
them.

I know perfectly well my own egotism,
Know my omnivorous lines and must not write any less,
And would fetch you whoever you are flush with myself.

Not words of routine this song of mine,
But abruptly to question, to leap beyond yet nearer bring;
This printed and bound book—but the printer and the
printing-office boy?
The well-taken photographs—but your wife or friend close
and solid in your arms?
The black ship mail'd with iron, her mighty guns in her
turrets— but the pluck of the captain and engineers?
In the houses the dishes and fare and furniture—but the host
and hostess, and the look out of their eyes?
The sky up there—yet here or next door, or across the way?
The saints and sages in history—but you yourself?
Sermons, creeds, theology—but the fathomless human
brain,
And what is reason? and what is love? and what is life?

43

I do not despise you priests, all time, the world over,
My faith is the greatest of faiths and the least of faiths,
Enclosing worship ancient and modern and all between
ancient and modern,
Believing I shall come again upon the earth after five thou-
sand years,
Waiting responses from oracles, honoring the gods, saluting
the sun,
Making a fetich of the first rock or stump, powowing with
sticks in the circle of obis,
Helping the llama or brahmin as he trims the lamps of the
idols,
Dancing yet through the streets in a phallic procession, rapt
and austere in the woods a gymnosophist,
Drinking mead from the skull-cup, to Shastas and Vedas
admirant, minding the Koran,

Walking the teokallis, spotted with gore from the stone and
    knife, beating the serpent-skin drum,
Accepting the Gospels, accepting him that was crucified,
    knowing assuredly that he is divine,
To the mass kneeling or the puritan's prayer rising, or sitting
    patiently in a pew,
Ranting and frothing in my insane crisis, or waiting dead-like
    till my spirit arouses me,
Looking forth on pavement and land, or outside of pavement
    and land,
Belonging to the winders of the circuit of circuits.

One of that centripetal and centrifugal gang I turn and talk
    like a man leaving charges before a journey.

Down-hearted doubters dull and excluded,
Frivolous, sullen, moping, angry, affected, dishearten'd,
    atheistical,
I know every one of you, I know the sea of torment, doubt,
    despair and unbelief.

How the flukes splash!
How they contort rapid as lightning, with spasms and spouts
    of blood!

Be at peace bloody flukes of doubters and sullen mopers,
I take my place among you as much as among any,
The past is the push of you, me, all, precisely the same,
And what is yet untried and afterward is for you, me, all
    precisely the same.

I do not know what is untried and afterward,
But I know it will in its turn prove sufficient, and cannot fail.

Each who passes is consider'd, each who stops is consider'd,
    not a single one can it fail.

It cannot fail the young man who died and was buried,
Nor the young woman who died and was put by his side,
Nor the little child that peep'd in at the door, and then drew
    back and was never seen again,

Nor the old man who has lived without purpose, and feels it
 with bitterness worse than gall,
Nor him in the poor house tubercled by rum and the bad
 disorder,
Nor the numberless slaughter'd and wreck'd, nor the brutish
 koboo call'd the ordure of humanity,
Nor the sacs merely floating with open mouths for food to
 slip in,
Nor any thing in the earth, or down in the oldest graves of
 the earth,
Nor any thing in the myriads of spheres, nor the myriads of
 myriads that inhabit them,
Nor the present, nor the least wisp that is known.

44

It is time to explain myself—let us stand up.

What is known I strip away,
I launch all men and women forward with me into the Un-
 known.

The clock indicates the moment—but what does eternity
 indicate?

We have thus far exhausted trillions of winters and summers,
There are trillions ahead, and trillions ahead of them.

Births have brought us richness and variety,
And other births will bring us richness and variety.

I do not call one greater and one smaller,
That which fills its period and place is equal to any.

Were mankind murderous or jealous upon you, my brother,
 my sister?
I am sorry for you, they are not murderous or jealous upon
 me,
All has been gentle with me, I keep no account with lamenta-
 tion,
(What have I to do with lamentation?)

I am an acme of things accomplish'd, and I an encloser of
   things to be.

My feet strike an apex of the apices of the stairs,
On every step bunches of ages, and larger bunches between
   the steps,
All below duly travel'd, and still I mount and mount.

Rise after rise bow the phantoms behind me,
Afar down I see the huge first Nothing, I know I was even
   there,
I waited unseen and always, and slept through the lethargic
   mist,
And took my time, and took no hurt from the fetid carbon.

Long I was hugg'd close—long and long.

Immense have been the preparations for me,
Faithful and friendly the arms that have help'd me.

Cycles ferried my cradle, rowing and rowing like cheerful
   boatmen,
For room to me stars kept aside in their own rings,
They sent influences to look after what was to hold me.

Before I was born out of my mother generations guided me,
My embryo has never been torpid, nothing could overlay it.

For it the nebula cohered to an orb,
The long slow strata piled to rest it on,
Vast vegetables gave it sustenance,
Monstrous sauroids transported it in their mouths and de-
   posited it with care.

All forces have been steadily employ'd to complete and de-
   light me,
Now on this spot I stand with my robust soul.

45

O span of youth! ever-push'd elasticity!
O manhood, balanced, florid and full.

My lovers suffocate me,
Crowding my lips, thick in the pores of my skin,
Jostling me through streets and public halls, coming naked to
me at night,
Crying by day *Ahoy!* from the rocks of the river, swinging
and chirping over my head,
Calling my name from flower-beds, vines, tangled under-
brush,
Lighting on every moment of my life,
Bussing my body with soft balsamic busses,
Noiselessly passing handfuls out of their hearts and giving
them to be mine.

Old age superbly rising! O welcome, ineffable grace of dying
days!

Every condition promulges not only itself, it promulges what
grows after and out of itself,
And the dark hush promulges as much as any.

I open my scuttle at night and see the far-sprinkled systems,
And all I see multiplied as high as I can cipher edge but the
rim of the farther systems.

Wider and wider they spread, expanding, always expanding,
Outward and outward and forever outward.

My sun has his sun and round him obediently wheels,
He joins with his partners a group of superior circuit,
And greater sets follow, making specks of the greatest inside
them.

There is no stoppage and never can be stoppage,
If I, you, and the worlds, and all beneath or upon their sur-
faces, were this moment reduced back to a pallid float,
it would not avail in the long run,
We should surely bring up again where we now stand,
And surely go as much farther, and then farther and farther.

A few quadrillions of eras, a few octillions of cubic leagues,
do not hazard the span or make it impatient,
They are but parts, any thing is but a part.

See ever so far, there is limitless space outside of that,
Count ever so much, there is limitless time around that.

My rendezvous is appointed, it is certain,
The Lord will be there and wait till I come on perfect terms,
The great Camerado, the lover true for whom I pine will be
    there.

46

I know I have the best of time and space, and was never
    measured and never will be measured.

I tramp a perpetual journey, (come listen all!)
My signs are a rain-proof coat, good shoes, and a staff cut
    from the woods,
No friend of mine takes his ease in my chair,
I have no chair, no church, no philosophy,
I lead no man to a dinner-table, library, exchange,
But each man and each woman of you I lead upon a knoll,
My left hand hooking you round the waist,
My right hand pointing to landscapes of continents and the
    public road.

Not I, not any one else can travel that road for you,
You must travel it for yourself.

It is not far, it is within reach,
Perhaps you have been on it since you were born and did not
    know,
Perhaps it is everywhere on water and on land.

Shoulder your duds dear son, and I will mine, and let us
    hasten forth,
Wonderful cities and free nations we shall fetch as we go.

If you tire, give me both burdens, and rest the chuff of your
    hand on my hip,
And in due time you shall repay the same service to me,
For after we start we never lie by again.

This day before dawn I ascended a hill and look'd at the
    crowded heaven,
And I said to my spirit *When we become the enfolders of those
    orbs, and the pleasure and knowledge of every thing in
    them, shall we be fill'd and satisfied then?*
And my spirit said *No, we but level that lift to pass and con-
    tinue beyond.*

You are also asking me questions and I hear you,
I answer that I cannot answer, you must find out for yourself.

Sit a while dear son,
Here are biscuits to eat and here is milk to drink,
But as soon as you sleep and renew yourself in sweet clothes,
    I kiss you with a good-by kiss and open the gate for your
    egress hence.

Long enough have you dream'd contemptible dreams,
Now I wash the gum from your eyes,
You must habit yourself to the dazzle of the light and of
    every moment of your life.

Long have you timidly waded holding a plank by the shore,
Now I will you to be a bold swimmer,
To jump off in the midst of the sea, rise again, nod to me,
    shout, and laughingly dash with your hair.

47

I am the teacher of athletes,
He that by me spreads a wider breast than my own proves
    the width of my own,
He most honors my style who learns under it to destroy the
    teacher.

The boy I love, the same becomes a man not through derived
    power, but in his own right,
Wicked rather than virtuous out of conformity or fear,
Fond of his sweetheart, relishing well his steak,
Unrequited love or a slight cutting him worse than sharp
    steel cuts,

First-rate to ride, to fight, to hit the bull's eye, to sail a skiff,
  to sing a song or play on the banjo,
Preferring scars and the beard and faces pitted with small-
  pox over all latherers,
And those well-tann'd to those that keep out of the sun.

I teach straying from me, yet who can stray from me?
I follow you whoever you are from the present hour,
My words itch at your ears till you understand them.

I do not say these things for a dollar or to fill up the time
  while I wait for a boat,
(It is you talking just as much as myself, I act as the tongue of
  you,
Tied in your mouth, in mine it begins to be loosen'd.)

I swear I will never again mention love or death inside a
  house,
And I swear I will never translate myself at all, only to him or
  her who privately stays with me in the open air.

If you would understand me go to the heights or water-
  shore,
The nearest gnat is an explanation, and a drop or motion of
  waves a key,
The maul, the oar, the hand-saw, second my words.

No shutter'd room or school can commune with me,
But roughs and little children better than they.

The young mechanic is closest to me, he knows me well,
The woodman that takes his axe and jug with him shall take
  me with him all day,
The farm-boy ploughing in the field feels good at the sound
  of my voice,
In vessels that sail my words sail, I go with fishermen and
  seamen and love them.

The soldier camp'd or upon the march is mine,
On the night ere the pending battle many seek me, and I do
  not fail them,

On that solemn night (it may be their last) those that know
     me seek me.

My face rubs to the hunter's face when he lies down alone in
     his blanket,
The driver thinking of me does not mind the jolt of his
     wagon,
The young mother and old mother comprehend me,
The girl and the wife rest the needle a moment and forget
     where they are,
They and all would resume what I have told them.

48

I have said that the soul is not more than the body,
And I have said that the body is not more than the soul,
And nothing, not God, is greater to one than one's self is,
And whoever walks a furlong without sympathy walks to his
     own funeral drest in his shroud,
And I or you pocketless of a dime may purchase the pick of
     the earth,
And to glance with an eye or show a bean in its pod con-
     founds the learning of all times,
And there is no trade or employment but the young man fol-
     lowing it may become a hero,
And there is no object so soft but it makes a hub for the
     wheel'd universe,
And I say to any man or woman, Let your soul stand cool
     and composed before a million universes.

And I say to mankind, Be not curious about God,
For I who am curious about each am not curious about
     God,
(No array of terms can say how much I am at peace about
     God and about death.)

I hear and behold God in every object, yet understand God
     not in the least,
Nor do I understand who there can be more wonderful than
     myself.

Why should I wish to see God better than this day?
I see something of God each hour of the twenty-four, and
each moment then,
In the faces of men and women I see God, and in my own
face in the glass,
I find letters from God dropt in the street, and every one is
sign'd by God's name,
And I leave them where they are, for I know that wheresoe'er
I go,
Others will punctually come for ever and ever.

49

And as to you Death, and you bitter hug of mortality, it is
idle to try to alarm me.

To his work without flinching the accoucheur comes,
I see the elder-hand pressing receiving supporting,
I recline by the sills of the exquisite flexible doors,
And mark the outlet, and mark the relief and escape.

And as to you Corpse I think you are good manure, but that
does not offend me,
I smell the white roses sweet-scented and growing,
I reach to the leafy lips, I reach to the polish'd breasts of
melons.

And as to you Life I reckon you are the leavings of many
deaths,
(No doubt I have died myself ten thousand times before.)

I hear you whispering there O stars of heaven,
O suns—O grass of graves—O perpetual transfers and pro-
motions,
If you do not say any thing how can I say any thing?

Of the turbid pool that lies in the autumn forest,
Of the moon that descends the steeps of the soughing twi-
light,
Toss, sparkles of day and dusk—toss on the black stems that
decay in the muck,
Toss to the moaning gibberish of the dry limbs.

I ascend from the moon, I ascend from the night,
I perceive that the ghastly glimmer is noonday sunbeams
     reflected,
And debouch to the steady and central from the offspring
     great or small.

50

There is that in me—I do not know what it is—but I know it
     is in me.

Wrench'd and sweaty—calm and cool then my body be-
     comes,
I sleep—I sleep long.

I do not know it—it is without name—it is a word unsaid,
It is not in any dictionary, utterance, symbol.

Something it swings on more than the earth I swing on,
To it the creation is the friend whose embracing awakes me.

Perhaps I might tell more. Outlines! I plead for my brothers
     and sisters.

Do you see O my brothers and sisters?
It is not chaos or death—it is form, union, plan—it is eternal
     life—it is Happiness.

51

The past and present wilt—I have fill'd them, emptied them,
And proceed to fill my next fold of the future.

Listener up there! what have you to confide to me?
Look in my face while I snuff the sidle of evening,
(Talk honestly, no one else hears you, and I stay only a
     minute longer.)

Do I contradict myself?
Very well then I contradict myself,
(I am large, I contain multitudes.)

I concentrate toward them that are nigh, I wait on the door-
     slab.

Who has done his day's work? who will soonest be through
    with his supper?
Who wishes to walk with me?

Will you speak before I am gone? will you prove already too
    late?

52

The spotted hawk swoops by and accuses me, he complains
    of my gab and my loitering.

I too am not a bit tamed, I too am untranslatable,
I sound my barbaric yawp over the roofs of the world.

The last scud of day holds back for me,
It flings my likeness after the rest and true as any on the
    shadow'd wilds,
It coaxes me to the vapor and the dusk.

I depart as air, I shake my white locks at the runaway sun,
I effuse my flesh in eddies, and drift it in lacy jags.

I bequeath myself to the dirt to grow from the grass I love,
If you want me again look for me under your boot-soles.

You will hardly know who I am or what I mean,
But I shall be good health to you nevertheless,
And filter and fibre your blood.

Failing to fetch me at first keep encouraged,
Missing me one place search another,
I stop somewhere waiting for you.
1855   1881

Children of Adam

TO THE GARDEN THE WORLD

To the garden the world anew ascending,
Potent mates, daughters, sons, preluding,
The love, the life of their bodies, meaning and being,
Curious here behold my resurrection after slumber,
The revolving cycles in their wide sweep having brought me
    again,
Amorous, mature, all beautiful to me, all wondrous,
My limbs and the quivering fire that ever plays through them,
    for reasons, most wondrous,
Existing I peer and penetrate still,
Content with the present, content with the past,
By my side or back of me Eve following,
Or in front, and I following her just the same.
1860   1867

FROM PENT-UP ACHING RIVERS

FROM pent-up aching rivers,
From that of myself without which I were nothing,
From what I am determin'd to make illustrious, even if I
    stand sole among men,
From my own voice resonant, singing the phallus,
Singing the song of procreation,
Singing the need of superb children and therein superb grown
    people,
Singing the muscular urge and the blending,
Singing the bedfellow's song, (O resistless yearning!
O for any and each the body correlative attracting!
O for you whoever you are your correlative body! O it,
    more than all else, you delighting!)
From the hungry gnaw that eats me night and day,

From native moments, from bashful pains, singing them,
Seeking something yet unfound though I have diligently
    sought it many a long year,
Singing the true song of the soul fitful at random,
Renascent with grossest Nature or among animals,
Of that, of them and what goes with them my poems in-
    forming,
Of the smell of apples and lemons, of the pairing of birds,
Of the wet of woods, of the lapping of waves,
Of the mad pushes of waves upon the land, I them chanting,
The overture lightly sounding, the strain anticipating,
The welcome nearness, the sight of the perfect body,
The swimmer swimming naked in the bath, or motionless on
    his back lying and floating,
The female form approaching, I pensive, love-flesh tremulous
    aching,
The divine list for myself or you or for any one making,
The face, the limbs, the index from head to foot, and what it
    arouses,
The mystic deliria, the madness amorous, the utter abandon-
    ment,
(Hark close and still what I now whisper to you,
I love you, O you entirely possess me,
O that you and I escape from the rest and go utterly off, free
    and lawless,
Two hawks in the air, two fishes swimming in the sea not
    more lawless than we;)
The furious storm through me careering, I passionately
    trembling,
The oath of the inseparableness of two together, of the
    woman that loves me and whom I love more than my
    life, that oath swearing,
(O I willingly stake all for you,
O let me be lost if it must be so!
O you and I! what is it to us what the rest do or think?
What is all else to us? only that we enjoy each other and ex-
    haust each other if it must be so;)
From the master, the pilot I yield the vessel to,
The general commanding me, commanding all, from him
    permission taking,

From time the programme hastening, (I have loiter'd too
    long as it is,)
From sex, from the warp and from the woof,
From privacy, from frequent repinings alone,
From plenty of persons near and yet the right person not
    near,
From the soft sliding of hands over me and thrusting of
    fingers through my hair and beard,
From the long sustain'd kiss upon the mouth or bosom,
From the close pressure that makes me or any man drunk,
    fainting with excess,
From what the divine husband knows, from the work of
    fatherhood,
From exultation, victory and relief from the bedfellow's
    embrace in the night,
From the act-poems of eyes, hands, hips and bosoms,
From the cling of the trembling arm,
From the bending curve and the clinch,
From side by side the pliant coverlet off-throwing,
From the one so unwilling to have me leave, and me just as
    unwilling to leave,
(Yet a moment O tender waiter, and I return,)
From the hour of shining stars and dropping dews,
From the night a moment I emerging flitting out,
Celebrate you act divine and you children prepared for,
And you stalwart loins.
1860   1881

I SING THE BODY ELECTRIC

1

I SING the body electric,
The armies of those I love engirth me and I engirth them,
They will not let me off till I go with them, respond to
    them,
And discorrupt them, and charge them full with the charge of
    the soul.

Was it doubted that those who corrupt their own bodies con-
    ceal themselves?

And if those who defile the living are as bad as they who de-
　　file the dead?
And if the body does not do fully as much as the soul?
And if the body were not the soul, what is the soul?

2

The love of the body of man or woman balks account, the
　　body itself balks account,
That of the male is perfect, and that of the female is perfect.

The expression of the face balks account,
But the expression of a well-made man appears not only in
　　his face,
It is in his limbs and joints also, it is curiously in the joints of
　　his hips and wrists,
It is in his walk, the carriage of his neck, the flex of his waist
　　and knees, dress does not hide him,
The strong sweet quality he has strikes through the cotton
　　and broad-cloth,
To see him pass conveys as much as the best poem, perhaps
　　more,
You linger to see his back, and the back of his neck and
　　shoulder-side.

The sprawl and fulness of babes, the bosoms and heads of
　　women, the folds of their dress, their style as we pass in
　　the street, the contour of their shape downwards,
The swimmer naked in the swimming-bath, seen as he
　　swims through the transparent green-shine, or lies with
　　his face up and rolls silently to and fro in the heave of
　　the water,
The bending forward and backward of rowers in row-boats,
　　the horseman in his saddle,
Girls, mothers, house-keepers, in all their performances,
The group of laborers seated at noon-time with their open
　　dinner kettles, and their wives waiting,
The female soothing a child, the farmer's daughter in the
　　garden or cow-yard,
The young fellow hoeing corn, the sleigh-driver driving his
　　six horses through the crowd,

The wrestle of wrestlers, two apprentice-boys, quite grown,
 lusty, good-natured, native-born, out on the vacant lot
 at sundown after work,
The coats and caps thrown down, the embrace of love and
 resistance,
The upper-hold and under-hold, the hair rumpled over and
 blinding the eyes;
The march of firemen in their own costumes, the play of
 masculine muscle through clean-setting trowsers and
 waist-straps,
The slow return from the fire, the pause when the bell strikes
 suddenly again, and the listening on the alert,
The natural, perfect, varied attitudes, the bent head, the
 curv'd neck and the counting;
Such-like I love—I loosen myself, pass freely, am at the
 mother's breast with the little child,
Swim with the swimmers, wrestle with wrestlers, march in
 line with the firemen, and pause, listen, count.

3

I knew a man, a common farmer, the father of five sons,
And in them the fathers of sons, and in them the fathers of
 sons.

This man was of wonderful vigor, calmness, beauty of person,
The shape of his head, the pale yellow and white of his hair
 and beard, the immeasurable meaning of his black eyes,
 the richness and breadth of his manners,
These I used to go and visit him to see, he was wise also,
He was six feet tall, he was over eighty years old, his sons
 were massive, clean, bearded, tan-faced, handsome,
They and his daughters loved him, all who saw him loved him,
They did not love him by allowance, they loved him with
 personal love,
He drank water only, the blood show'd like scarlet through
 the clear-brown skin of his face,
He was a frequent gunner and fisher, he sail'd his boat him-
 self, he had a fine one presented to him by a ship-joiner,
 he had fowling-pieces presented to him by men that
 loved him,

When he went with his five sons and many grand-sons to hunt or fish, you would pick him out as the most beautiful and vigorous of the gang,

You would wish long and long to be with him, you would wish to sit by him in the boat that you and he might touch each other.

4

I have perceiv'd that to be with those I like is enough,

To stop in company with the rest at evening is enough,

To be surrounded by beautiful, curious, breathing, laughing flesh is enough,

To pass among them or touch any one, or rest my arm ever so lightly round his or her neck for a moment, what is this then?

I do not ask any more delight, I swim in it as in a sea.

There is something in staying close to men and women and looking on them, and in the contact and odor of them, that pleases the soul well,

All things please the soul, but these please the soul well.

5

This is the female form,

A divine nimbus exhales from it from head to foot,

It attracts with fierce undeniable attraction,

I am drawn by its breath as if I were no more than a helpless vapor, all falls aside but myself and it,

Books, art, religion, time, the visible and solid earth, and what was expected of heaven or fear'd of hell, are now consumed,

Mad filaments, ungovernable shoots play out of it, the response likewise ungovernable,

Hair, bosom, hips, bend of legs, negligent falling hands all diffused, mine too diffused,

Ebb stung by the flow and flow stung by the ebb, love-flesh swelling and deliciously aching,

Limitless limpid jets of love hot and enormous, quivering jelly of love, white-blow and delirious juice,

Bridegroom night of love working surely and softly into the
    prostrate dawn,
Undulating into the willing and yielding day,
Lost in the cleave of the clasping and sweet-flesh'd day.

This the nucleus—after the child is born of woman, man is
    born of woman,
This the bath of birth, this the merge of small and large, and
    the outlet again.

Be not ashamed women, your privilege encloses the rest, and
    is the exit of the rest,
You are the gates of the body, and you are the gates of the soul.

The female contains all qualities and tempers them,
She is in her place and moves with perfect balance,
She is all things duly veil'd, she is both passive and active,
She is to conceive daughters as well as sons, and sons as well
    as daughters.

As I see my soul reflected in Nature,
As I see through a mist, One with inexpressible completeness,
    sanity, beauty,
See the bent head and arms folded over the breast, the Fe-
    male I see.

6

The male is not less the soul nor more, he too is in his place,
He too is all qualities, he is action and power,
The flush of the known universe is in him,
Scorn becomes him well, and appetite and defiance become
    him well,
The wildest largest passions, bliss that is utmost, sorrow that
    is utmost become him well, pride is for him,
The full-spread pride of man is calming and excellent to the
    soul,
Knowledge becomes him, he likes it always, he brings every
    thing to the test of himself,
Whatever the survey, whatever the sea and the sail he strikes
    soundings at last only here,
(Where else does he strike soundings except here?)

The man's body is sacred and the woman's body is sacred,
No matter who it is, it is sacred—is it the meanest one in the
laborer's gang?
Is it one of the dull-faced immigrants just landed on the
wharf?
Each belongs here or anywhere just as much as the well-off,
just as much as you,
Each has his or her place in the procession.

(All is a procession,
The universe is a procession with measured and perfect
motion.)

Do you know so much yourself that you call the meanest
ignorant?
Do you suppose you have a right to a good sight, and he or
she has no right to a sight?
Do you think matter has cohered together from its diffuse
float, and the soil is on the surface, and water runs and
vegetation sprouts,
For you only, and not for him and her?

7

A man's body at auction,
(For before the war I often go to the slave-mart and watch
the sale,)
I help the auctioneer, the sloven does not half know his
business.

Gentlemen look on this wonder,
Whatever the bids of the bidders they cannot be high enough
for it,
For it the globe lay preparing quintillions of years without
one animal or plant,
For it the revolving cycles truly and steadily roll'd.

In this head the all-baffling brain,
In it and below it the makings of heroes.

Examine these limbs, red, black, or white, they are cunning in
tendon and nerve,
They shall be stript that you may see them.

Exquisite senses, life-lit eyes, pluck, volition,
Flakes of breast-muscle, pliant backbone and neck, flesh not
flabby, good-sized arms and legs,
And wonders within there yet.

Within there runs blood,
The same old blood! the same red-running blood!
There swells and jets a heart, there all passions, desires,
reachings, aspirations,
(Do you think they are not there because they are not ex-
press'd in parlors and lecture-rooms?)

This is not only one man, this the father of those who shall
be fathers in their turns,
In him the start of populous states and rich republics,
Of him countless immortal lives with countless embodiments
and enjoyments.

How do you know who shall come from the offspring of his
offspring through the centuries?
(Who might you find you have come from yourself, if you
could trace back through the centuries?)

8

A woman's body at auction,
She too is not only herself, she is the teeming mother of
mothers,
She is the bearer of them that shall grow and be mates to the
mothers.

Have you ever loved the body of a woman?
Have you ever loved the body of a man?
Do you not see that these are exactly the same to all in all
nations and times all over the earth?

If any thing is sacred the human body is sacred,
And the glory and sweat of a man is the token of manhood
untainted,
And in man or woman a clean, strong, firm-fibred body, is
more beautiful than the most beautiful face.

Have you seen the fool that corrupted his own live body? or
the fool that corrupted her own live body?
For they do not conceal themselves, and cannot conceal
themselves.

9

O my body! I dare not desert the likes of you in other men
and women, nor the likes of the parts of you,
I believe the likes of you are to stand or fall with the likes of
the soul, (and that they are the soul,)
I believe the likes of you shall stand or fall with my poems,
and that they are my poems,
Man's, woman's, child's, youth's, wife's, husband's, mother's,
father's, young man's, young woman's poems,
Head, neck, hair, ears, drop and tympan of the ears,
Eyes, eye-fringes, iris of the eye, eyebrows, and the waking or
sleeping of the lids,
Mouth, tongue, lips, teeth, roof of the mouth, jaws, and the
jaw-hinges,
Nose, nostrils of the nose, and the partition,
Cheeks, temples, forehead, chin, throat, back of the neck,
neck-slue,
Strong shoulders, manly beard, scapula, hind-shoulders, and
the ample side-round of the chest,
Upper-arm, armpit, elbow-socket, lower-arm, arm-sinews,
arm-bones,
Wrist and wrist-joints, hand, palm, knuckles, thumb, fore-
finger, finger-joints, finger-nails,
Broad breast-front, curling hair of the breast, breast-bone,
breast-side,
Ribs, belly, backbone, joints of the backbone,
Hips, hip-sockets, hip-strength, inward and outward round,
man-balls, man-root,
Strong set of thighs, well carrying the trunk above,
Leg-fibres, knee, knee-pan, upper-leg, under-leg,
Ankles, instep, foot-ball, toes, toe-joints, the heel;
All attitudes, all the shapeliness, all the belongings of my or
your body or of any one's body, male or female,
The lung-sponges, the stomach-sac, the bowels sweet and
clean,

The brain in its folds inside the skull-frame,
Sympathies, heart-valves, palate-valves, sexuality, maternity,
Womanhood and all that is a woman, and the man that
　　comes from woman,
The womb, the teats, nipples, breast-milk, tears, laughter,
　　weeping, love-looks, love-perturbations and risings,
The voice, articulation, language, whispering, shouting aloud,
Food, drink, pulse, digestion, sweat, sleep, walking, swim-
　　ming,
Poise on the hips, leaping, reclining, embracing, arm-curving
　　and tightening,
The continual changes of the flex of the mouth, and around
　　the eyes,
The skin, the sunburnt shade, freckles, hair,
The curious sympathy one feels when feeling with the hand
　　the naked meat of the body,
The circling rivers the breath, and breathing it in and out,
The beauty of the waist, and thence of the hips, and thence
　　downward toward the knees,
The thin red jellies within you or within me, the bones and
　　the marrow in the bones,
The exquisite realization of health;
O I say these are not the parts and poems of the body only,
　　but of the soul,
O I say now these are the soul!
1855　　　　　　　　　　　　　　　　　　　　1881

A WOMAN WAITS FOR ME

A WOMAN waits for me, she contains all, nothing is lacking,
Yet all were lacking if sex were lacking, or if the moisture of
　　the right man were lacking.
Sex contains all, bodies, souls,
Meanings, proofs, purities, delicacies, results, promulgations,
Songs, commands, health, pride, the maternal mystery, the
　　seminal milk,
All hopes, benefactions, bestowals, all the passions, loves,
　　beauties, delights of the earth,
All the governments, judges, gods, follow'd persons of the
　　earth,

These are contain'd in sex as parts of itself and justifications
    of itself.

Without shame the man I like knows and avows the deli-
    ciousness of his sex,
Without shame the woman I like knows and avows hers.

Now I will dismiss myself from impassive women,
I will go stay with her who waits for me, and with those
    women that are warm-blooded and sufficient for me,
I see that they understand me and do not deny me,
I see that they are worthy of me, I will be the robust husband
    of those women.

They are not one jot less than I am,
They are tann'd in the face by shining suns and blowing
    winds,
Their flesh has the old divine suppleness and strength,
They know how to swim, row, ride, wrestle, shoot, run,
    strike, retreat, advance, resist, defend themselves,
They are ultimate in their own right—they are calm, clear,
    well-possess'd of themselves.

I draw you close to me, you women,
I cannot let you go, I would do you good,
I am for you, and you are for me, not only for our own sake,
    but for others' sakes,
Envelop'd in you sleep greater heroes and bards,
They refuse to awake at the touch of any man but me.

It is I, you women, I make my way,
I am stern, acrid, large, undissuadable, but I love you,
I do not hurt you any more than is necessary for you,
I pour the stuff to start sons and daughters fit for these States,
    I press with slow rude muscle,
I brace myself effectually, I listen to no entreaties,
I dare not withdraw till I deposit what has so long accumu-
    lated within me.

Through you I drain the pent-up rivers of myself,
In you I wrap a thousand onward years,

On you I graft the grafts of the best-beloved of me and
    America,
The drops I distil upon you shall grow fierce and athletic
    girls, new artists, musicians, and singers,
The babes I beget upon you are to beget babes in their turn,
I shall demand perfect men and women out of my love-
    spendings,
I shall expect them to interpenetrate with others, as I and you
    interpenetrate now,
I shall count on the fruits of the gushing showers of them, as
    I count on the fruits of the gushing showers I give now,
I shall look for loving crops from the birth, life, death, im-
    mortality, I plant so lovingly now.

1856   1871

SPONTANEOUS ME

Spontaneous me, Nature,
The loving day, the mounting sun, the friend I am happy
    with,
The arm of my friend hanging idly over my shoulder,
The hillside whiten'd with blossoms of the mountain ash,
The same late in autumn, the hues of red, yellow, drab,
    purple, and light and dark green,
The rich coverlet of the grass, animals and birds, the private
    untrimm'd bank, the primitive apples, the pebble-stones,
Beautiful dripping fragments, the negligent list of one after
    another as I happen to call them to me or think of them,
The real poems, (what we call poems being merely pictures,)
The poems of the privacy of the night, and of men like me,
This poem drooping shy and unseen that I always carry, and
    that all men carry,
(Know once for all, avow'd on purpose, wherever are men like
    me, are our lusty lurking masculine poems,)
Love-thoughts, love-juice, love-odor, love-yielding, love-
    climbers, and the climbing sap,
Arms and hands of love, lips of love, phallic thumb of love,
    breasts of love, bellies press'd and glued together with
    love,
Earth of chaste love, life that is only life after love,

The body of my love, the body of the woman I love, the body
    of the man, the body of the earth,
Soft forenoon airs that blow from the south-west,
The hairy wild-bee that murmurs and hankers up and down,
    that gripes the full-grown lady-flower, curves upon her
    with amorous firm legs, takes his will of her, and holds
    himself tremulous and tight till he is satisfied;
The wet of woods through the early hours,
Two sleepers at night lying close together as they sleep, one
    with an arm slanting down across and below the waist of
    the other,
The smell of apples, aromas from crush'd sage-plant, mint,
    birch-bark,
The boy's longings, the glow and pressure as he confides to
    me what he was dreaming,
The dead leaf whirling its spiral whirl and falling still and
    content to the ground,
The no-form'd stings that sights, people, objects, sting me
    with,
The hubb'd sting of myself, stinging me as much as it ever
    can any one,
The sensitive, orbic, underlapp'd brothers, that only privi-
    leged feelers may be intimate where they are,
The curious roamer the hand roaming all over the body, the
    bashful withdrawing of flesh where the fingers soothingly
    pause and edge themselves,
The limpid liquid within the young man,
The vex'd corrosion so pensive and so painful,
The torment, the irritable tide that will not be at rest,
The like of the same I feel, the like of the same in others,
The young man that flushes and flushes, and the young
    woman that flushes and flushes,
The young man that wakes deep at night, the hot hand seek-
    ing to repress what would master him,
The mystic amorous night, the strange half-welcome pangs,
    visions, sweats,
The pulse pounding through palms and trembling encircling
    fingers, the young man all color'd, red, ashamed, angry;
The souse upon me of my lover the sea, as I lie willing and
    naked,

The merriment of the twin babies that crawl over the grass in
the sun, the mother never turning her vigilant eyes from
them,
The walnut-trunk, the walnut-husks, and the ripening or
ripen'd long-round walnuts,
The continence of vegetables, birds, animals,
The consequent meanness of me should I skulk or find myself
indecent, while birds and animals never once skulk or
find themselves indecent,
The great chastity of paternity, to match the great chastity of
maternity,
The oath of procreation I have sworn, my Adamic and fresh
daughters,
The greed that eats me day and night with hungry gnaw, till
I saturate what shall produce boys to fill my place when
I am through,
The wholesome relief, repose, content,
And this bunch pluck'd at random from myself,
It has done its work—I toss it carelessly to fall where it may.
1856   1867

ONE HOUR TO MADNESS AND JOY

ONE hour to madness and joy! O furious! O confine me not!
(What is this that frees me so in storms?
What do my shouts amid lightnings and raging winds mean?)

O to drink the mystic deliria deeper than any other man!
O savage and tender achings! (I bequeath them to you, my
children,
I tell them to you, for reasons, O bridegroom and bride.)

O to be yielded to you whoever you are, and you to be yielded
to me in defiance of the world!
O to return to Paradise! O bashful and feminine!
O to draw you to me, to plant on you for the first time the
lips of a determin'd man.

O the puzzle, the thrice-tied knot, the deep and dark pool, all
untied and illumin'd!

O to speed where there is space enough and air enough at
        last!
To be absolv'd from previous ties and conventions, I from
        mine and you from yours!
To find a new unthought-of nonchalance with the best of
        Nature!
To have the gag remov'd from one's mouth!
To have the feeling to-day or any day I am sufficient as I am.

O something unprov'd! something in a trance!
To escape utterly from others' anchors and holds!
To drive free! to love free! to dash reckless and dangerous!
To court destruction with taunts, with invitations!
To ascend, to leap to the heavens of the love indicated to me!
To rise thither with my inebriate soul!
To be lost if it must be so!
To feed the remainder of life with one hour of fulness and
        freedom!
With one brief hour of madness and joy.
1860   1881

OUT OF THE ROLLING OCEAN THE CROWD

OUT of the rolling ocean the crowd came a drop gently to me,
Whispering *I love you, before long I die,*
I have travel'd a long way merely to look on you to touch you,
For I could not die till I once look'd on you,
For I fear'd I might afterward lose you.

Now we have met, we have look'd, we are safe,
Return in peace to the ocean my love,
I too am part of that ocean my love, we are not so much
        separated,
Behold the great rondure, the cohesion of all, how perfect!
But as for me, for you, the irresistible sea is to separate us,
As for an hour carrying us diverse, yet cannot carry us di-
        verse forever;
Be not impatient—a little space— know you I salute the air,
        the ocean and the land,
Every day at sundown for your dear sake my love.
1865   1867

AGES AND AGES RETURNING AT INTERVALS

AGES and ages returning at intervals,
Undestroy'd, wandering immortal,
Lusty, phallic, with the potent original loins, perfectly sweet,
I, chanter of Adamic songs,
Through the new garden the West, the great cities calling,
Deliriate, thus prelude what is generated, offering these,
     offering myself,
Bathing myself, bathing my songs in Sex,
Offspring of my loins.
1860   1867

WE TWO, HOW LONG WE WERE FOOL'D

WE two, how long we were fool'd,
Now transmuted, we swiftly escape as Nature escapes,
We are Nature, long have we been absent, but now we return,
We become plants, trunks, foliage, roots, bark,
We are bedded in the ground, we are rocks,
We are oaks, we grow in the openings side by side,
We browse, we are two among the wild herds spontaneous as
     any,
We are two fishes swimming in the sea together,
We are what locust blossoms are, we drop scent around lanes
     mornings and evenings,
We are also the coarse smut of beasts, vegetables, minerals,
We are two predatory hawks, we soar above and look down,
We are two resplendent suns, we it is who balance ourselves
     orbic and stellar, we are as two comets,
We prowl fang'd and four-footed in the woods, we spring on
     prey,
We are two clouds forenoons and afternoons driving over-
     head,
We are seas mingling, we are two of those cheerful waves
     rolling over each other and interwetting each other,
We are what the atmosphere is, transparent, receptive, per-
     vious, impervious,
We are snow, rain, cold, darkness, we are each product and
     influence of the globe,

We have circled and circled till we have arrived home again,
 we two,
We have voided all but freedom and all but our own joy.
1860   1881

O HYMEN! O HYMENEE!

O HYMEN! O hymenee! why do you tantalize me thus?
O why sting me for a swift moment only?
Why can you not continue? O why do you now cease?
Is it because if you continued beyond the swift moment you
 would soon certainly kill me?
1860   1867

I AM HE THAT ACHES WITH LOVE

I AM he that aches with amorous love;
Does the earth gravitate? does not all matter, aching, attract
 all matter?
So the body of me to all I meet or know.
1860   1867

NATIVE MOMENTS

NATIVE moments—when you come upon me—ah you are
 here now,
Give me now libidinous joys only,
Give me the drench of my passions, give me life coarse and
 rank,
To-day I go consort with Nature's darlings, to-night too,
I am for those who believe in loose delights, I share the mid-
 night orgies of young men,
I dance with the dancers and drink with the drinkers,
The echoes ring with our indecent calls, I pick out some low
 person for my dearest friend,
He shall be lawless, rude, illiterate, he shall be one con-
 demned by others for deeds done,
I will play a part no longer, why should I exile myself from
 my companions?
O you shunn'd persons, I at least do not shun you,
I come forthwith in your midst, I will be your poet,
I will be more to you than to any of the rest.
1860   1881

ONCE I PASS'D THROUGH A POPULOUS CITY

ONCE I pass'd through a populous city imprinting my brain
    for future use with its shows, architecture, customs,
    traditions,
Yet now of all that city I remember only a woman I casually
    met there who detain'd me for love of me,
Day by day and night by night we were together—all else has
    long been forgotten by me,
I remember I say only that woman who passionately clung to
    me,
Again we wander, we love, we separate again,
Again she holds me by the hand, I must not go,
I see her close beside me with silent lips sad and tremulous.
1860   1867

I HEARD YOU SOLEMN-SWEET PIPES OF THE ORGAN

I HEARD you solemn-sweet pipes of the organ as last Sunday
    morn I pass'd the church,
Winds of autumn, as I walk'd the woods at dusk I heard your
    long-stretch'd sighs up above so mournful,
I heard the perfect Italian tenor singing at the opera, I heard
    the soprano in the midst of the quartet singing;
Heart of my love! you too I heard murmuring low through
    one of the wrists around my head,
Heard the pulse of you when all was still ringing little bells
    last night under my ear.
1861   1867

FACING WEST FROM CALIFORNIA'S SHORES

FACING west from California's shores,
Inquiring, tireless, seeking what is yet unfound,
I, a child, very old, over waves, towards the house of mater-
    nity, the land of migrations, look afar,
Look off the shores of my Western sea, the circle almost
    circled;
For starting westward from Hindustan, from the vales of
    Kashmere,

From Asia, from the north, from the God, the sage, and the
  hero,
From the south, from the flowery peninsulas and the spice
  islands,
Long having wander'd since, round the earth having wan-
  der'd,
Now I face home again, very pleas'd and joyous,
(But where is what I started for so long ago?
And why is it yet unfound?)
1860   1867

AS ADAM EARLY IN THE MORNING

As Adam early in the morning,
Walking forth from the bower refresh'd with sleep,
Behold me where I pass, hear my voice, approach,
Touch me, touch the palm of your hand to my body as I pass,
Be not afraid of my body.
1860   1867

Calamus

IN PATHS UNTRODDEN

In paths untrodden,
In the growths by margins of pond-waters,
Escaped from the life that exhibits itself,
From all the standards hitherto publish'd, from the pleasures,
    profits, conformities,
Which too long I was offering to feed my soul,
Clear to me now standards not yet publish'd, clear to me that
    my soul,
That the soul of the man I speak for rejoices in comrades,
Here by myself away from the clank of the world,
Tallying and talk'd to here by tongues aromatic,
No longer abash'd, (for in this secluded spot I can respond as
    I would not dare elsewhere,)
Strong upon me the life that does not exhibit itself, yet con-
    tains all the rest,
Resolv'd to sing no songs to-day but those of manly attach-
    ment,
Projecting them along that substantial life,
Bequeathing hence types of athletic love,
Afternoon this delicious Ninth-month in my forty-first year,
I proceed for all who are or have been young men,
To tell the secret of my nights and days,
To celebrate the need of comrades.
1860   1867

SCENTED HERBAGE OF MY BREAST

Scented herbage of my breast,
Leaves from you I glean, I write, to be perused best after-
    wards,
Tomb-leaves, body-leaves growing up above me above death.

Perennial roots, tall leaves, O the winter shall not freeze you
delicate leaves,

Every year shall you bloom again, out from where you retired
you shall emerge again;

O I do not know whether many passing by will discover you
or inhale your faint odor, but I believe a few will;

O slender leaves! O blossoms of my blood! I permit you to
tell in your own way of the heart that is under you,

O I do not know what you mean there underneath yourselves,
you are not happiness,

You are often more bitter than I can bear, you burn and sting
me,

Yet you are beautiful to me you faint-tinged roots, you make
me think of death,

Death is beautiful from you, (what indeed is finally beautiful
except death and love?)

O I think it is not for life I am chanting here my chant of
lovers, I think it must be for death,

For how calm, how solemn it grows to ascend to the atmo-
sphere of lovers,

Death or life I am then indifferent, my soul declines to prefer,

(I am not sure but the high soul of lovers welcomes death
most,)

Indeed O death, I think now these leaves mean precisely the
same as you mean,

Grow up taller sweet leaves that I may see! grow up out of
my breast!

Spring away from the conceal'd heart there!

Do not fold yourself so in your pink-tinged roots timid leaves!

Do not remain down there so ashamed, herbage of my breast!

Come I am determin'd to unbare this broad breast of mine, I
have long enough stifled and choked;

Emblematic and capricious blades I leave you, now you serve
me not,

I will say what I have to say by itself,

I will sound myself and comrades only, I will never again
utter a call only their call,

I will raise with it immortal reverberations through the States,

I will give an example to lovers to take permanent shape and
will through the States,

Through me shall the words be said to make death exhilarat-
　　ing.
Give me your tone therefore O death, that I may accord with
　　it,
Give me yourself, for I see that you belong to me now above
　　all, and are folded inseparably together, you love and
　　death are,
Nor will I allow you to balk me any more with what I was
　　calling life,
For now it is convey'd to me that you are the purports essen-
　　tial,
That you hide in these shifting forms of life, for reasons, and
　　that they are mainly for you,
That you beyond them come forth to remain, the real reality,
That behind the mask of materials you patiently wait, no
　　matter how long,
That you will one day perhaps take control of all,
That you will perhaps dissipate this entire show of appear-
　　ance,
That may-be you are what it is all for, but it does not last so
　　very long,
But you will last very long.
1860　　　　　　　　　　　　　　　　　　　　　　　1881

WHOEVER YOU ARE HOLDING ME NOW IN HAND

WHOEVER you are holding me now in hand,
Without one thing all will be useless,
I give you fair warning before you attempt me further,
I am not what you supposed, but far different.

Who is he that would become my follower?
Who would sign himself a candidate for my affections?

The way is suspicious, the result uncertain, perhaps destruc-
　　tive,
You would have to give up all else, I alone would expect to
　　be your sole and exclusive standard,
Your novitiate would even then be long and exhausting,

The whole past theory of your life and all conformity to the
    lives around you would have to be abandon'd,
Therefore release me now before troubling yourself any fur-
    ther, let go your hand from my shoulders,
Put me down and depart on your way.

Or else by stealth in some wood for trial,
Or back of a rock in the open air,
(For in any roof'd room of a house I emerge not, nor in com-
    pany,
And in libraries I lie as one dumb, a gawk, or unborn, or
    dead,)
But just possibly with you on a high hill, first watching lest
    any person for miles around approach unawares,
Or possibly with you sailing at sea, or on the beach of the sea
    or some quiet island,
Here to put your lips upon mine I permit you,
With the comrade's long-dwelling kiss or the new husband's
    kiss,
For I am the new husband and I am the comrade.

Or if you will, thrusting me beneath your clothing,
Where I may feel the throbs of your heart or rest upon your
    hip,
Carry me when you go forth over land or sea;
For thus merely touching you is enough, is best,
And thus touching you would I silently sleep and be carried
    eternally.

But these leaves conning you con at peril,
For these leaves and me you will not understand,
They will elude you at first and still more afterward, I will
    certainly elude you,
Even while you should think you had unquestionably caught
    me, behold!
Already you see I have escaped from you.

For it is not for what I have put into it that I have written
    this book,
Nor is it by reading it you will acquire it,

Nor do those know me best who admire me and vauntingly
    praise me,
Nor will the candidates for my love (unless at most a very
    few) prove victorious,
Nor will my poems do good only, they will do just as much
    evil, perhaps more,
For all is useless without that which you may guess at many
    times and not hit, that which I hinted at;
Therefore release me and depart on your way.

1860   1881

FOR YOU O DEMOCRACY

COME, I will make the continent indissoluble,
I will make the most splendid race the sun ever shone upon,
I will make divine magnetic lands,
        With the love of comrades,
            With the life-long love of comrades.

I will plant companionship thick as trees along all the rivers
    of America, and along the shores of the great lakes, and
    all over the prairies,
I will make inseparable cities with their arms about each
    other's necks,
        By the love of comrades,
            By the manly love of comrades.

For you these from me, O Democracy, to serve you ma
    femme!
For you, for you I am trilling these songs.

1860   1881

THESE I SINGING IN SPRING

THESE I singing in spring collect for lovers,
(For who but I should understand lovers and all their sorrow
    and joy?
And who but I should be the poet of comrades?)
Collecting I traverse the garden the world, but soon I pass
    the gates,
Now along the pond-side, now wading in a little, fearing not
    the wet,

Now by the post-and-rail fences where the old stones thrown
    there, pick'd from the fields, have accumulated,
(Wild-flowers and vines and weeds come up through the
    stones and partly cover them, beyond these I pass,)
Far, far in the forest, or sauntering later in summer, before I
    think where I go,
Solitary, smelling the earthy smell, stopping now and then in
    the silence,
Alone I had thought, yet soon a troop gathers around me,
Some walk by my side and some behind, and some embrace
    my arms or neck,
They the spirits of dear friends dead or alive, thicker they
    come, a great crowd, and I in the middle,
Collecting, dispensing, singing, there I wander with them,
Plucking something for tokens, tossing toward whoever is
    near me,
Here, lilac, with a branch of pine,
Here, out of my pocket, some moss which I pull'd off a live-
    oak in Florida as it hung trailing down,
Here, some pinks and laurel leaves, and a handful of sage,
And here what I now draw from the water, wading in the
    pond-side,
(O here I last saw him that tenderly loves me, and returns
    again never to separate from me,
And this, O this shall henceforth be the token of comrades,
    this calamus-root shall,
Interchange it youths with each other! let none render it back!)
And twigs of maple and a bunch of wild orange and chestnut,
And stems of currants and plum-blows, and the aromatic
    cedar,
These I compass'd around by a thick cloud of spirits,
Wandering, point to or touch as I pass, or throw them loosely
    from me,
Indicating to each one what he shall have, giving something
    to each;
But what I drew from the water by the pond-side, that I
    reserve,
I will give of it, but only to them that love as I myself am
    capable of loving.

1860   1867

NOT HEAVING FROM MY RIBB'D BREAST ONLY

Not heaving from my ribb'd breast only,
Not in sighs at night in rage dissatisfied with myself,
Not in those long-drawn, ill-supprest sighs,
Not in many an oath and promise broken,
Not in my wilful and savage soul's volition,
Not in the subtle nourishment of the air,
Not in this beating and pounding at my temples and wrists,
Not in the curious systole and diastole within which will one
     day cease,
Not in many a hungry wish told to the skies only,
Not in cries, laughter, defiances, thrown from me when alone
     far in the wilds,
Not in husky pantings through clinch'd teeth,
Not in sounded and resounded words, chattering words,
     echoes, dead words,
Not in the murmurs of my dreams while I sleep,
Nor the other murmurs of these incredible dreams of every
     day,
Nor in the limbs and senses of my body that take you and
     dismiss you continually—not there,
Not in any or all of them O adhesiveness! O pulse of my life!
Need I that you exist and show yourself any more than in
     these songs.

1860   1867

OF THE TERRIBLE DOUBT OF APPEARANCES

Of the terrible doubt of appearances,
Of the uncertainty after all, that we may be deluded,
That may-be reliance and hope are but speculations after all,
That may-be identity beyond the grave is a beautiful fable
     only,
May-be the things I perceive, the animals, plants, men, hills,
     shining and flowing waters,
The skies of day and night, colors, densities, forms, may-be
     these are (as doubtless they are) only apparitions, and
     the real something has yet to be known,
(How often they dart out of themselves as if to confound me
     and mock me!

How often I think neither I know, nor any man knows, aught
   of them,)
May-be seeming to me what they are (as doubtless they in-
   deed but seem) as from my present point of view, and
   might prove (as of course they would) nought of what
   they appear, or nought anyhow, from entirely changed
   points of view;
To me these and the like of these are curiously answer'd by
   my lovers, my dear friends,
When he whom I love travels with me or sits a long while
   holding me by the hand,
When the subtle air, the impalpable, the sense that words and
   reason hold not, surround us and pervade us,
Then I am charged with untold and untellable wisdom, I am
   silent, I require nothing further,
I cannot answer the question of appearances or that of iden-
   tity beyond the grave,
But I walk or sit indifferent, I am satisfied,
He ahold of my hand has completely satisfied me.
1860   1867

THE BASE OF ALL METAPHYSICS

AND now gentlemen,
A word I give to remain in your memories and minds,
As base and finalè too for all metaphysics.

(So to the students the old professor,
At the close of his crowded course.)

Having studied the new and antique, the Greek and Ger-
   manic systems,
Kant having studied and stated, Fichte and Schelling and
   Hegel,
Stated the lore of Plato, and Socrates greater than Plato,
And greater than Socrates sought and stated, Christ divine
   having studied long,
I see reminiscent to-day those Greek and Germanic systems,
See the philosophies all, Christian churches and tenets see,
Yet underneath Socrates clearly see, and underneath Christ
   the divine I see,

The dear love of man for his comrade, the attraction of
    friend to friend,
Of the well-married husband and wife, of children and
    parents,
Of city for city and land for land.
1871   1871

RECORDERS AGES HENCE

RECORDERS ages hence,
Come, I will take you down underneath this impassive ex-
    terior, I will tell you what to say of me,
Publish my name and hang up my picture as that of the ten-
    derest lover,
The friend the lover's portrait, of whom his friend his lover
    was fondest,
Who was not proud of his songs, but of the measureless
    ocean of love within him, and freely pour'd it forth,
Who often walk'd lonesome walks thinking of his dear
    friends, his lovers,
Who pensive away from one he lov'd often lay sleepless and
    dissatisfied at night,
Who knew too well the sick, sick dread lest the one he lov'd
    might secretly be indifferent to him,
Whose happiest days were far away through fields, in woods,
    on hills, he and another wandering hand in hand, they
    twain apart from other men,
Who oft as he saunter'd the streets curv'd with his arm the
    shoulder of his friend, while the arm of his friend rested
    upon him also.
1860   1867

WHEN I HEARD AT THE CLOSE OF THE DAY

WHEN I heard at the close of the day how my name had been
    receiv'd with plaudits in the capitol, still it was not a
    happy night for me that follow'd,
And else when I carous'd, or when my plans were accom-
    plish'd, still I was not happy,
But the day when I rose at dawn from the bed of perfect
    health, refresh'd, singing, inhaling the ripe breath of
    autumn,

When I saw the full moon in the west grow pale and disap-
pear in the morning light,

When I wander'd alone over the beach, and undressing
bathed, laughing with the cool waters, and saw the sun
rise,

And when I thought how my dear friend my lover was on his
way coming, O then I was happy,

O then each breath tasted sweeter, and all that day my food
nourish'd me more, and the beautiful day pass'd well,

And the next came with equal joy, and with the next at even-
ing came my friend,

And that night while all was still I heard the waters roll slowly
continually up the shores,

I heard the hissing rustle of the liquid and sands as directed
to me whispering to congratulate me,

For the one I love most lay sleeping by me under the same
cover in the cool night,

In the stillness in the autumn moonbeams his face was in-
clined toward me,

And his arm lay lightly around my breast—and that night I
was happy.

1860   1867

ARE YOU THE NEW PERSON DRAWN
TOWARD ME?

ARE you the new person drawn toward me?

To begin with take warning, I am surely far different from
what you suppose;

Do you suppose you will find in me your ideal?

Do you think it is so easy to have me become your lover?

Do you think the friendship of me would be unalloy'd satis-
faction?

Do you think I am trusty and faithful?

Do you see no further than this façade, this smooth and
tolerant manner of me?

Do you suppose yourself advancing on real ground toward a
real heroic man?

Have you no thought O dreamer that it may be all maya,
illusion?

1860   1867

ROOTS AND LEAVES THEMSELVES ALONE

Roots and leaves themselves alone are these,
Scents brought to men and women from the wild woods and
pond-side,
Breast-sorrel and pinks of love, fingers that wind around
tighter than vines,
Gushes from the throats of birds hid in the foliage of trees as
the sun is risen,
Breezes of land and love set from living shores to you on the
living sea, to you O sailors!
Frost-mellow'd berries and Third-month twigs offer'd fresh
to young persons wandering out in the fields when the
winter breaks up,
Love-buds put before you and within you whoever you
are,
Buds to be unfolded on the old terms,
If you bring the warmth of the sun to them they will open
and bring form, color, perfume, to you,
If you become the aliment and the wet they will become
flowers, fruits, tall branches and trees.
1860   1867

NOT HEAT FLAMES UP AND CONSUMES

Not heat flames up and consumes,
Not sea-waves hurry in and out,
Not the air delicious and dry, the air of ripe summer, bears
lightly along white down-balls of myriads of seeds,
Wafted, sailing gracefully, to drop where they may;
Not these, O none of these more than the flames of me, con-
suming, burning for his love whom I love,
O none more than I hurrying in and out;
Does the tide hurry, seeking something, and never give up?
O I the same,
O nor down-balls nor perfumes, nor the high rain-emitting
clouds, are borne through the open air,
Any more than my soul is borne through the open air,
Wafted in all directions O love, for friendship, for you.
1860   1867

TRICKLE DROPS

TRICKLE drops! my blue veins leaving!
O drops of me! trickle, slow drops,
Candid from me falling, drip, bleeding drops,
From wounds made to free you whence you were prison'd,
From my face, from my forehead and lips,
From my breast, from within where I was conceal'd, press
    forth red drops, confession drops,
Stain every page, stain every song I sing, every word I say,
    bloody drops,
Let them know your scarlet heat, let them glisten,
Saturate them with yourself all ashamed and wet,
Glow upon all I have written or shall write, bleeding drops,
Let it all be seen in your light, blushing drops.
1860   1867

CITY OF ORGIES

CITY of orgies, walks and joys,
City whom that I have lived and sung in your midst will one
    day make you illustrious,
Not the pageants of you, not your shifting tableaus, your
    spectacles, repay me,
Not the interminable rows of your houses, nor the ships at
    the wharves,
Nor the processions in the streets, nor the bright windows
    with goods in them,
Nor to converse with learn'd persons, or bear my share in the
    soiree or feast;
Not those, but as I pass O Manhattan, your frequent and
    swift flash of eyes offering me love,
Offering response to my own—these repay me,
Lovers, continual lovers, only repay me.
1860   1867

BEHOLD THIS SWARTHY FACE

BEHOLD this swarthy face, these gray eyes,
This beard, the white wool unclipt upon my neck,
My brown hands and the silent manner of me without charm;

Yet comes one a Manhattanese and ever at parting kisses me
    lightly on the lips with robust love,
And I on the crossing of the street or on the ship's deck give a
    kiss in return,
We observe that salute of American comrades land and sea,
We are those two natural and nonchalant persons.
1860   1867

I SAW IN LOUISIANA A LIVE-OAK GROWING

I saw in Louisiana a live-oak growing,
All alone stood it and the moss hung down from the branches,
Without any companion it grew there uttering joyous leaves
    of dark green,
And its look, rude, unbending, lusty, made me think of my-
    self,
But I wonder'd how it could utter joyous leaves standing
    alone there without its friend near, for I knew I could
    not,
And I broke off a twig with a certain number of leaves upon
    it, and twined around it a little moss,
And brought it away, and I have placed it in sight, in my room,
It is not needed to remind me as of my own dear friends,
(For I believe lately I think of little else than of them,)
Yet it remains to me a curious token, it makes me think of
    manly love;
For all that, and though the live-oak glistens there in Louisi-
    ana solitary in a wide flat space,
Uttering joyous leaves all its life without a friend a lover near,
I know very well I could not.
1860   1867

TO A STRANGER

Passing stranger! you do not know how longingly I look
    upon you,
You must be he I was seeking, or she I was seeking, (it comes
    to me as of a dream,)
I have somewhere surely lived a life of joy with you,
All is recall'd as we flit by each other, fluid, affectionate,
    chaste, matured,

You grew up with me, were a boy with me or a girl with
    me,
I ate with you and slept with you, your body has become not
    yours only nor left my body mine only,
You give me the pleasure of your eyes, face, flesh, as we pass,
    you take of my beard, breast, hands, in return,
I am not to speak to you, I am to think of you when I sit
    alone or wake at night alone,
I am to wait, I do not doubt I am to meet you again,
I am to see to it that I do not lose you.
1860   1867

THIS MOMENT YEARNING AND THOUGHTFUL

THIS moment yearning and thoughtful sitting alone,
It seems to me there are other men in other lands yearning
    and thoughtful,
It seems to me I can look over and behold them in Germany,
    Italy, France, Spain,
Or far, far away, in China, or in Russia or Japan, talking
    other dialects,
And it seems to me if I could know those men I should become
    attached to them as I do to men in my own lands,
O I know we should be brethren and lovers,
I know I should be happy with them.
1860   1867

I HEAR IT WAS CHARGED AGAINST ME

I HEAR it was charged against me that I sought to destroy
    institutions,
But really I am neither for nor against institutions,
(What indeed have I in common with them? or what with the
    destruction of them?)
Only I will establish in the Mannahatta and in every city of
    these States inland and seaboard,
And in the fields and woods, and above every keel little or
    large that dents the water,
Without edifices or rules or trustees or any argument,
The institution of the dear love of comrades.
1860   1867

THE PRAIRIE-GRASS DIVIDING

THE prairie-grass dividing, its special odor breathing,
I demand of it the spiritual corresponding,
Demand the most copious and close companionship of men,
Demand the blades to rise of words, acts, beings,
Those of the open atmosphere, coarse, sunlit, fresh, nutri-
    tious,
Those that go their own gait, erect, stepping with freedom
    and command, leading not following,
Those with a never-quell'd audacity, those with sweet and
    lusty flesh clear of taint,
Those that look carelessly in the faces of Presidents and
    governors, as to say *Who are you?*
Those of earth-born passion, simple, never constrain'd, never
    obedient,
Those of inland America.
1860   1867

WHEN I PERUSE THE CONQUER'D FAME

WHEN I peruse the conquer'd fame of heroes and the victories
    of mighty generals, I do not envy the generals,
Nor the President in his Presidency, nor the rich in his great
    house,
But when I hear of the brotherhood of lovers, how it was
    with them,
How together through life, through dangers, odium, un-
    changing, long and long,
Through youth and through middle and old age, how un-
    faltering, how affectionate and faithful they were,
Then I am pensive—I hastily walk away fill'd with the bitter-
    est envy.
1860   1871

WE TWO BOYS TOGETHER CLINGING

WE two boys together clinging,
One the other never leaving,
Up and down the roads going, North and South excursions
    making,

Power enjoying, elbows stretching, fingers clutching,
Arm'd and fearless, eating, drinking, sleeping, loving,
No law less than ourselves owning, sailing, soldiering, thiev-
　　ing, threatening,
Misers, menials, priests alarming, air breathing, water drink-
　　ing, on the turf or the sea-beach dancing,
Cities wrenching, ease scorning, statutes mocking, feebleness
　　chasing,
Fulfilling our foray.
1860　　　　　　　　　　　　　　　　　　　　1867

A PROMISE TO CALIFORNIA

A PROMISE to California,
Or inland to the great pastoral Plains, and on to Puget sound
　　and Oregon;
Sojourning east a while longer, soon I travel toward you, to
　　remain, to teach robust American love,
For I know very well that I and robust love belong among
　　you, inland, and along the Western sea;
For these States tend inland and toward the Western sea, and
　　I will also.
1860　　　　　　　　　　　　　　　　　　　　1867

HERE THE FRAILEST LEAVES OF ME

HERE the frailest leaves of me and yet my strongest lasting,
Here I shade and hide my thoughts, I myself do not expose
　　them,
And yet they expose me more than all my other poems.
1860　　　　　　　　　　　　　　　　　　　　1871

NO LABOR-SAVING MACHINE

No labor-saving machine,
Nor discovery have I made,
Nor will I be able to leave behind me any wealthy bequest to
　　found a hospital or library,
Nor reminiscence of any deed of courage for America,
Nor literary success nor intellect, nor book for the book-shelf,
But a few carols vibrating through the air I leave,
For comrades and lovers.
1860　　　　　　　　　　　　　　　　　　　　1881

A GLIMPSE

A GLIMPSE through an interstice caught,
Of a crowd of workmen and drivers in a bar-room around
    the stove late of a winter night, and I unremark'd seated
    in a corner,
Of a youth who loves me and whom I love, silently approach-
    ing and seating himself near, that he may hold me by the
    hand,
A long while amid the noises of coming and going, of drink-
    ing and oath and smutty jest,
There we two, content, happy in being together, speaking
    little, perhaps not a word.
1860   1867

A LEAF FOR HAND IN HAND

A LEAF for hand in hand;
You natural persons old and young!
You on the Mississippi and on all the branches and bayous
    of the Mississippi!
You friendly boatmen and mechanics! you roughs!
You twain! and all processions moving along the streets!
I wish to infuse myself among you till I see it common for
    you to walk hand in hand.
1860   1867

EARTH, MY LIKENESS

EARTH, my likeness,
Though you look so impassive, ample and spheric there,
I now suspect that is not all;
I now suspect there is something fierce in you eligible to burst
    forth,
For an athlete is enamour'd of me, and I of him,
But toward him there is something fierce and terrible in me
    eligible to burst forth,
I dare not tell it in words, not even in these songs.
1860   1867

I DREAM'D IN A DREAM

I DREAM'D in a dream I saw a city invincible to the attacks of
    the whole of the rest of the earth,
I dream'd that was the new city of Friends,
Nothing was greater there than the quality of robust love, it
    led the rest,
It was seen every hour in the actions of the men of that city,
And in all their looks and words.
1860   1867

WHAT THINK YOU I TAKE MY PEN IN HAND?

WHAT think you I take my pen in hand to record?
The battle-ship, perfect-model'd, majestic, that I saw pass the
    offing to-day under full sail?
The splendors of the past day? or the splendor of the night
    that envelops me?
Or the vaunted glory and growth of the great city spread
    around me?—no ;
But merely of two simple men I saw to-day on the pier in the
    midst of the crowd, parting the parting of dear friends,
The one to remain hung on the other's neck and passionately
    kiss'd him,
While the one to depart tightly prest the one to remain in his
    arms.
1860   1867

TO THE EAST AND TO THE WEST

To the East and to the West,
To the man of the Seaside State and of Pennsylvania,
To the Kanadian of the north, to the Southerner I love,
These with perfect trust to depict you as myself, the germs
    are in all men,
I believe the main purport of these States is to found a superb
    friendship, exaltè, previously unknown,
Because I perceive it waits, and has been always waiting,
    latent in all men.
1860   1867

SOMETIMES WITH ONE I LOVE

SOMETIMES with one I love I fill myself with rage for fear I
    effuse unreturn'd love,
But now I think there is no unreturn'd love, the pay is certain
    one way or another,
(I loved a certain person ardently and my love was not re-
    turn'd,
Yet out of that I have written these songs.)
1860   1867

TO A WESTERN BOY

MANY things to absorb I teach to help you become eleve of
    mine;
Yet if blood like mine circle not in your veins,
If you be not silently selected by lovers and do not silently
    select lovers,
Of what use is it that you seek to become eleve of mine?
1860   1881

FAST-ANCHOR'D ETERNAL O LOVE!

FAST-ANCHOR'D eternal O love! O woman I love!
O bride! O wife! more resistless than I can tell, the thought
    of you!
Then separate, as disembodied or another born,
Ethereal, the last athletic reality, my consolation,
I ascend, I float in the regions of your love O man,
O sharer of my roving life.
1860   1867

AMONG THE MULTITUDE

AMONG the men and women the multitude,
I perceive one picking me out by secret and divine signs,
Acknowledging none else, not parent, wife, husband, bro-
    ther, child, any nearer than I am,
Some are baffled, but that one is not—that one knows me.

Ah lover and perfect equal,
I meant that you should discover me so by faint indirections,
And I when I meet you mean to discover you by the like in
    you.
1860   1881

O YOU WHOM I OFTEN AND SILENTLY COME

O YOU whom I often and silently come where you are that I
    may be with you,
As I walk by your side or sit near, or remain in the same
    room with you,
Little you know the subtle electric fire that for your sake is
    playing within me.
1860   1867

THAT SHADOW MY LIKENESS

THAT shadow my likeness that goes to and fro seeking a liveli-
    hood, chattering, chaffering,
How often I find myself standing and looking at it where it
    flits,
How often I question and doubt whether that is really me;
But among my lovers and caroling these songs,
O I never doubt whether that is really me.
(1859?)   1881

FULL OF LIFE NOW

FULL of life now, compact, visible,
I, forty years old the eighty-third year of the States,
To one a century hence or any number of centuries hence,
To you yet unborn these, seeking you.

When you read these I that was visible am become invisible,
Now it is you, compact, visible, realizing my poems, seeking
    me,
Fancying how happy you were if I could be with you and
    become your comrade;
Be it as if I were with you. (Be not too certain but I am now
    with you.)
1860   1871

Salut Au Monde!

1

O TAKE my hand Walt Whitman!
Such gliding wonders! such sights and sounds!
Such join'd unended links, each hook'd to the next,
Each answering all, each sharing the earth with all.

What widens within you Walt Whitman?
What waves and soils exuding?
What climes? what persons and cities are here?
Who are the infants, some playing, some slumbering?
Who are the girls? who are the married women?
Who are the groups of old men going slowly with their arms
    about each other's necks?
What rivers are these? what forests and fruits are these?
What are the mountains call'd that rise so high in the
    mists?
What myriads of dwellings are they fill'd with dwellers?

2

Within me latitude widens, longitude lengthens,
Asia, Africa, Europe, are to the east—America is provided
    for in the west,
Banding the bulge of the earth winds the hot equator,
Curiously north and south turn the axis-ends,
Within me is the longest day, the sun wheels in slanting rings,
    it does not set for months,
Stretch'd in due time within me the midnight sun just rises
    above the horizon and sinks again,
Within me zones, seas, cataracts, forests, volcanoes, groups,
Malaysia, Polynesia, and the great West Indian islands.

3

What do you hear Walt Whitman?

I hear the workman singing and the farmer's wife singing,
I hear in the distance the sounds of children and of animals
early in the day,
I hear emulous shouts of Australians pursuing the wild horse,
I hear the Spanish dance with castanets in the chestnut shade,
to the rebeck and guitar,
I hear continual echoes from the Thames,
I hear fierce French liberty songs,
I hear of the Italian boat-sculler the musical recitative of old
poems,
I hear the locusts in Syria as they strike the grain and grass
with the showers of their terrible clouds,
I hear the Coptic refrain toward sundown, pensively falling
on the breast of the black venerable vast mother the Nile,
I hear the chirp of the Mexican muleteer, and the bells of the
mule,
I hear the Arab muezzin calling from the top of the mosque,
I hear the Christian priests at the altars of their churches, I
hear the responsive base and soprano,
I hear the cry of the Cossack, and the sailor's voice putting to
sea at Okotsk,
I hear the wheeze of the slave-coffle as the slaves march on, as
the husky gangs pass on by twos and threes, fasten'd
together with wrist-chains and ankle-chains,
I hear the Hebrew reading his records and psalms,
I hear the rhythmic myths of the Greeks, and the strong
legends of the Romans,
I hear the tale of the divine life and bloody death of the beau-
tiful God the Christ,
I hear the Hindoo teaching his favorite pupil the loves, wars,
adages, transmitted safely to this day from poets who
wrote three thousand years ago.

4

What do you see Walt Whitman?
Who are they you salute, and that one after another salute you?

I see a great round wonder rolling through space,
I see diminute farms, hamlets, ruins, graveyards, jails, fac-
tories, palaces, hovels, huts of barbarians, tents of
nomads upon the surface,
I see the shaded part on one side where the sleepers are sleep-
ing, and the sunlit part on the other side,
I see the curious rapid change of the light and shade,
I see distant lands, as real and near to the inhabitants of them
as my land is to me.

I see plenteous waters,
I see mountain peaks, I see the sierras of Andes where they
range,
I see plainly the Himalayas, Chian Shahs, Altays, Ghauts,
I see the giant pinnacles of Elbruz, Kazbek, Bazardjusi,
I see the Styrian Alps, and the Karnac Alps,
I see the Pyrenees, Balks, Carpathians, and to the north the
Dofrafields, and off at sea mount Hecla,
I see Vesuvius and Etna, the mountains of the Moon, and the
Red mountains of Madagascar,
I see the Lybian, Arabian, and Asiatic deserts,
I see huge dreadful Arctic and Antarctic icebergs,
I see the superior oceans and the interior ones, the Atlantic
and Pacific, the sea of Mexico, the Brazilian sea, and the
sea of Peru,
The waters of Hindustan, the China sea, and the gulf of
Guinea,
The Japan waters, the beautiful bay of Nagasaki land-lock'd
in its mountains,
The spread of the Baltic, Caspian, Bothnia, the British shores,
and the bay of Biscay,
The clear-sunn'd Mediterranean, and from one to another of
its islands,
The White sea, and the sea around Greenland.

I behold the mariners of the world,
Some are in storms, some in the night with the watch on the
lookout,
Some drifting helplessly, some with contagious diseases.

I behold the sail and steamships of the world, some in clusters in port, some on their voyages,

Some double the cape of Storms, some cape Verde, others capes Guardafui, Bon, or Bajadore,

Others Dondra head, others pass the straits of Sunda, others cape Lopatka, others Behring's straits,

Others cape Horn, others sail the gulf of Mexico or along Cuba or Hayti, others Hudson's bay or Baffin's bay,

Others pass the straits of Dover, others enter the Wash, others the firth of Solway, others round cape Clear, others the Land's End,

Others traverse the Zuyder Zee or the Scheld,

Others as comers and goers at Gibraltar or the Dardanelles,

Others sternly push their way through the northern winter-packs,

Others descend or ascend the Obi or the Lena,

Others the Niger or the Congo, others the Indus, the Burampooter and Cambodia,

Others wait steam'd up ready to start in the ports of Australia,

Wait at Liverpool, Glasgow, Dublin, Marseilles, Lisbon, Naples, Hamburg, Bremen, Bordeaux, the Hague, Copenhagen,

Wait at Valparaiso, Rio Janeiro, Panama.

5

I see the tracks of the railroads of the earth,
I see them in Great Britain, I see them in Europe,
I see them in Asia and in Africa.

I see the electric telegraphs of the earth,
I see the filaments of the news of the wars, deaths, losses, gains, passions, of my race.

I see the long river-stripes of the earth,
I see the Amazon and the Paraguay,
I see the four great rivers of China, the Amour, the Yellow River, the Yiang-tse, and the Pearl,
I see where the Seine flows, and where the Danube, the Loire, the Rhone, and the Guadalquiver flow,

I see the windings of the Volga, the Dnieper, the Oder,
I see the Tuscan going down the Arno, and the Venetian
    along the Po,
I see the Greek seaman sailing out of Egina bay.

6

I see the sight of the old empire of Assyria, and that of Per-
    sia, and that of India,
I see the falling of the Ganges over the high rim of Saukara.

I see the place of the idea of the Deity incarnated by avatars
    in human forms,
I see the spots of the successions of priests on the earth,
    oracles, sacrificers, brahmins, sabians, llamas, monks,
    muftis, exhorters,
I see where druids walk'd the groves of Mona, I see the
    mistletoe and vervain,
I see the temples of the deaths of the bodies of Gods, I see the
    old signifiers.

I see Christ eating the bread of his last supper in the midst of
    youths and old persons,
I see where the strong divine young man the Hercules toil'd
    faithfully and long and then died,
I see the place of the innocent rich life and hapless fate of the
    beautiful nocturnal son, the full-limb'd Bacchus,
I see Kneph, blooming, drest in blue, with the crown of
    feathers on his head,
I see Hermes, unsuspected, dying, well-belov'd, saying to the
    people *Do not weep for me*,
*This is not my true country, I have lived banish'd from my true
    country, I now go back there,*
I return to the celestial sphere where every one goes in his turn.

7

I see the battle-fields of the earth, grass grows upon them and
    blossoms and corn,
I see the tracks of ancient and modern expeditions.

I see the nameless masonries, venerable messages of the un-
known events, heroes, records of the earth.

I see the places of the sagas,
I see pine-trees and fir-trees torn by northern blasts,
I see granite bowlders and cliffs, I see green meadows and
lakes,
I see the burial-cairns of Scandinavian warriors,
I see them raised high with stones by the marge of restless
oceans, that the dead men's spirits when they wearied of
their quiet graves might rise up through the mounds and
gaze on the tossing billows, and be refresh'd by storms,
immensity, liberty, action.

I see the steppes of Asia,
I see the tumuli of Mongolia, I see the tents of Kalmucks
and Baskirs,
I see the nomadic tribes with herds of oxen and cows,
I see the table-lands notch'd with ravines, I see the jungles
and deserts,
I see the camel, the wild steed, the bustard, the fat-tail'd
sheep, the antelope, and the burrowing wolf.

I see the highlands of Abyssinia,
I see flocks of goats feeding, and see the fig-tree, tamarind,
date,
And see fields of teff-wheat and places of verdure and gold.

I see the Brazilian vaquero,
I see the Bolivian ascending mount Sorata,
I see the Wacho crossing the plains, I see the incomparable
rider of horses with his lasso on his arm,
I see over the pampas the pursuit of wild cattle for their hides.

8, [9]

I see the regions of snow and ice,
I see the sharp-eyed Samoiede and the Finn,
I see the seal-seeker in his boat poising his lance,
I see the Siberian on his slight-built sledge drawn by dogs,

I see the porpoise-hunters, I see the whale-crews of the south
  Pacific and the north Atlantic,
I see the cliffs, glaciers, torrents, valleys, of Switzerland—I
  mark the long winters and the isolation.

I see the cities of the earth and make myself at random a part
  of them,
I am a real Parisian,
I am a habitan of Vienna, St. Petersburg, Berlin, Constan-
  tinople,
I am of Adelaide, Sidney, Melbourne,
I am of London, Manchester, Bristol, Edinburgh, Limerick,
I am of Madrid, Cadiz, Barcelona, Oporto, Lyons, Brussels,
  Berne, Frankfort, Stuttgart, Turin, Florence,
I belong in Moscow, Cracow, Warsaw, or northward in
  Christiania or Stockholm, or in Siberian Irkutsk, or in
  some street in Iceland,
I descend upon all those cities, and rise from them again.

10

I see vapors exhaling from unexplored countries,
I see the savage types, the bow and arrow, the poison'd
  splint, the fetich, and the obi.

I see African and Asiatic towns,
I see Algiers, Tripoli, Derne, Mogadore, Timbuctoo, Mon-
  rovia,
I see the swarms of Pekin, Canton, Benares, Delhi, Calcutta,
  Tokio,
I see the Kruman in his hut, and the Dahoman and Ashantee-
  man in their huts,
I see the Turk smoking opium in Aleppo,
I see the picturesque crowds at the fairs of Khiva and those of
  Herat,
I see Teheran, I see Muscat and Medina and the intervening
  sands, I see the caravans toiling onward,
I see Egypt and the Egyptians, I see the pyramids and obelisks,
I look on chisell'd histories, records of conquering kings,
  dynasties, cut in slabs of sand-stone, or on granite-
  blocks.

I see at Memphis mummy-pits containing mummies embalm'd, swathed in linen-cloth, lying there many centuries,
I look on the fall'n Theban, the large-ball'd eyes, the side-drooping neck, the hands folded across the breast.

I see all the menials of the earth, laboring,
I see all the prisoners in the prisons,
I see the defective human bodies of the earth,
The blind, the deaf and dumb, idiots, hunchbacks, lunatics,
The pirates, thieves, betrayers, murderers, slave-makers of the earth,
The helpless infants, and the helpless old men and women.

I see male and female everywhere,
I see the serene brotherhood of philosophs,
I see the constructiveness of my race,
I see the results of the perseverance and industry of my race,
I see ranks, colors, barbarisms, civilizations, I go among them, I mix indiscriminately,
And I salute all the inhabitants of the earth.

11

You whoever you are!
You daughter or son of England!
You of the mighty Slavic tribes and empires! you Russ in Russia!
You dim-descended, black, divine-soul'd African, large, fine-headed, nobly-form'd, superbly destin'd, on equal terms with me!
You Norwegian! Swede! Dane! Icelander! you Prussian!
You Spaniard of Spain! you Portuguese!
You Frenchwoman and Frenchman of France!
You Belge! you liberty-lover of the Netherlands! (you stock whence I myself have descended ;)
You sturdy Austrian! you Lombard! Hun! Bohemian! farmer of Styria!
You neighbor of the Danube!
You working-man of the Rhine, the Elbe, or the Weser! you working-woman too!

You Sardinian! you Bavarian! Swabian! Saxon! Wallachian!
    Bulgarian!

You Roman! Neapolitan! you Greek!

You lithe matador in the arena at Seville!

You mountaineer living lawlessly on the Taurus or Caucasus!

You Bokh horse-herd watching your mares and stallions
    feeding!

You beautiful-bodied Persian at full speed in the saddle
    shooting arrows to the mark!

You Chinaman and Chinawoman of China! you Tartar of
    Tartary!

You women of the earth subordinated at your tasks!

You Jew journeying in your old age through every risk to
    stand once on Syrian ground!

You other Jews waiting in all lands for your Messiah!

You thoughtful Armenian pondering by some stream of the
    Euphrates! you peering amid the ruins of Nineveh! you
    ascending mount Ararat!

You foot-worn pilgrim welcoming the far-away sparkle of
    the minarets of Mecca!

You sheiks along the stretch from Suez to Bab-el-mandeb
    ruling your families and tribes!

You olive-grower tending your fruit on fields of Nazareth,
    Damascus, or lake Tiberias!

You Thibet trader on the wide inland or bargaining in the
    shops of Lassa!

You Japanese man or woman! you liver in Madagascar,
    Ceylon, Sumatra, Borneo!

All you continentals of Asia, Africa, Europe, Australia, in-
    different of place!

All you on the numberless islands of the archipelagoes of the
    sea!

And you of centuries hence when you listen to me!

And you each and everywhere whom I specify not, but in-
    clude just the same!

Health to you! good will to you all, from me and America sent!

Each of us inevitable,

Each of us limitless—each of us with his or her right upon
    the earth,

Each of us allow'd the eternal purports of the earth,
Each of us here as divinely as any is here.

12

You Hottentot with clicking palate! you woolly-hair'd
hordes!
You own'd persons dropping sweat-drops or blood-drops!
You human forms with the fathomless ever-impressive coun-
tenances of brutes!
You poor koboo whom the meanest of the rest look down
upon for all your glimmering language and spirituality!
You dwarf'd Kamtschatkan, Greenlander, Lapp!
You Austral negro, naked, red, sooty, with protrusive lip,
groveling, seeking your food!
You Caffre, Berber, Soudanese!
You haggard, uncouth, untutor'd Bedowee!
You plague-swarms in Madras, Nankin, Kaubul, Cairo!
You benighted roamer of Amazonia! you Patagonian! you
Feejee-man!
I do not prefer others so very much before you either,
I do not say one word against you, away back there where
you stand,
(You will come forward in due time to my side.)

13

My spirit has pass'd in compassion and determination around
the whole earth,
I have look'd for equals and lovers and found them ready for
me in all lands,
I think some divine rapport has equalized me with them.

You vapors, I think I have risen with you, moved away
to distant continents, and fallen down there, for
reasons,
I think I have blown with you you winds;
You waters I have finger'd every shore with you,
I have run through what any river or strait of the globe has
run through,

I have taken my stand on the bases of peninsulas and on the
    high embedded rocks, to cry thence:

Salut au monde!
What cities the light or warmth penetrates I penetrate those
    cities myself,
All islands to which birds wing their way I wing my way
    myself.

Toward you all, in America's name,
I raise high the perpendicular hand, I make the signal,
To remain after me in sight forever,
For all the haunts and homes of men.
1856   1881

Song of the Open Road

1

AFOOT and light-hearted I take to the open road,
Healthy, free, the world before me,
The long brown path before me leading wherever I choose.

Henceforth I ask not good-fortune, I myself am good-for-
    tune,
Henceforth I whimper no more, postpone no more, need
    nothing,
Done with indoor complaints, libraries, querulous criticisms,
Strong and content I travel the open road.

The earth, that is sufficient,
I do not want the constellations any nearer,
I know they are very well where they are,
I know they suffice for those who belong to them.

(Still here I carry my old delicious burdens,
I carry them, men and women, I carry them with me wher-
    ever I go,

I swear it is impossible for me to get rid of them,
I am fill'd with them; and I will fill them in return.)

2

You road I enter upon and look around, I believe you are
    not all that is here,
I believe that much unseen is also here.

Here the profound lesson of reception, nor preference nor
    denial,
The black with his woolly head, the felon, the diseas'd, the
    illiterate person, are not denied;
The birth, the hasting after the physician, the beggar's tramp,
    the drunkard's stagger, the laughing party of mechanics,
The escaped youth, the rich person's carriage, the fop, the
    eloping couple,
The early market-man, the hearse, the moving of furniture
    into the town, the return back from the town,
They pass, I also pass, any thing passes, none can be inter-
    dicted,
None but are accepted, none but shall be dear to me.

3

You air that serves me with breath to speak!
You objects that call from diffusion my meanings and give
    them shape!
You light that wraps me and all things in delicate equable
    showers!
You paths worn in the irregular hollows by the roadsides!
I believe you are latent with unseen existences, you are so
    dear to me.

You flagg'd walks of the cities! you strong curbs at the edges!
You ferries! you planks and posts of wharves! you timber-
    lined sides! you distant ships!
You rows of houses! you window-pierc'd façades! you roofs!
You porches and entrances! you copings and iron guards!
You windows whose transparent shells might expose so
    much!

You doors and ascending steps! you arches!
You gray stones of interminable pavements! you trodden
crossings!
From all that has touch'd you I believe you have imparted to
yourselves, and now would impart the same secretly to
me,
From the living and the dead you have peopled your im-
passive surfaces, and the spirits thereof would be evident
and amicable with me.

4

The earth expanding right hand and left hand,
The picture alive, every part in its best light,
The music falling in where it is wanted, and stopping where
it is not wanted,
The cheerful voice of the public road, the gay fresh sentiment
of the road.

O highway I travel, do you say to me *Do not leave me?*
Do you say *Venture not—if you leave me you are lost?*
Do you say *I am already prepared, I am well-beaten and un-
denied, adhere to me?*

O public road, I say back I am not afraid to leave you, yet I
love you,
You express me better than I can express myself,
You shall be more to me than my poem.

I think heroic deeds were all conceiv'd in the open air, and all
free poems also,
I think I could stop here myself and do miracles,
I think whatever I shall meet on the road I shall like, and
whoever beholds me shall like me,
I think whoever I see must be happy.

5

From this hour I ordain myself loos'd of limits and imagin-
ary lines,
Going where I list, my own master total and absolute,
Listening to others, considering well what they say,

Pausing, searching, receiving, contemplating,
Gently, but with undeniable will, divesting myself of the
    holds that would hold me.

I inhale great draughts of space,
The east and the west are mine, and the north and the south
    are mine.

I am larger, better than I thought,
I did not know I held so much goodness.

All seems beautiful to me,
I can repeat over to men and women You have done such
    good to me I would do the same to you,
I will recruit for myself and you as I go,
I will scatter myself among men and women as I go,
I will toss a new gladness and roughness among them,
Whoever denies me it shall not trouble me,
Whoever accepts me he or she shall be blessed and shall bless
    me.

6

Now if a thousand perfect men were to appear it would not
    amaze me,
Now if a thousand beautiful forms of women appear'd it
    would not astonish me.

Now I see the secret of the making of the best persons,
It is to grow in the open air and to eat and sleep with the
    earth.

Here a great personal deed has room,
(Such a deed seizes upon the hearts of the whole race of men,
Its effusion of strength and will overwhelms law and mocks
    all authority and all argument against it.)

Here is the test of wisdom,
Wisdom is not finally tested in schools,
Wisdom cannot be pass'd from one having it to another not
    having it,

Wisdom is of the soul, is not susceptible of proof, is its own
  proof,
Applies to all stages and objects and qualities and is content,
Is the certainty of the reality and immortality of things, and
  the excellence of things;
Something there is in the float of the sight of things that pro-
  vokes it out of the soul.

Now I re-examine philosophies and religions,
They may prove well in lecture-rooms, yet not prove at all
  under the spacious clouds and along the landscape and
  flowing currents.

Here is realization,
Here is a man tallied—he realizes here what he has in him,
The past, the future, majesty, love—if they are vacant of you,
  you are vacant of them.

Only the kernel of every object nourishes;
Where is he who tears off the husks for you and me?
Where is he that undoes stratagems and envelopes for you
  and me?

Here is adhesiveness, it is not previously fashion'd, it is
  apropos;
Do you know what it is as you pass to be loved by strangers?
Do you know the talk of those turning eye-balls?

7

Here is the efflux of the soul,
The efflux of the soul comes from within through embower'd
  gates, ever provoking questions,
These yearnings why are they? these thoughts in the darkness
  why are they?
Why are there men and women that while they are nigh me
  the sunlight expands my blood?
Why when they leave me do my pennants of joy sink flat and
  lank?
Why are there trees I never walk under but large and melo-
  dious thoughts descend upon me?

(I think they hang there winter and summer on those trees
    and always drop fruit as I pass;)
What is it I interchange so suddenly with strangers?
What with some driver as I ride on the seat by his side?
What with some fisherman drawing his seine by the shore as
    I walk by and pause?
What gives me to be free to a woman's and man's good-will?
    what gives them to be free to mine?

8

The efflux of the soul is happiness, here is happiness,
I think it pervades the open air, waiting at all times,
Now it flows unto us, we are rightly charged.

Here rises the fluid and attaching character,
The fluid and attaching character is the freshness and sweet-
    ness of man and woman,
(The herbs of the morning sprout no fresher and sweeter
    every day out of the roots of themselves, than it sprouts
    fresh and sweet continually out of itself.)
Toward the fluid and attaching character exudes the sweat of
    the love of young and old,
From it falls distill'd the charm that mocks beauty and
    attainments,
Toward it heaves the shuddering longing ache of con-
    tact.

9

Allons! whoever you are come travel with me!
Traveling with me you find what never tires.

The earth never tires,
The earth is rude, silent, incomprehensible at first, Nature is
    rude and incomprehensible at first,
Be not discouraged, keep on, there are divine things well
    envelop'd,
I swear to you there are divine things more beautiful than
    words can tell.

Allons! we must not stop here,
However sweet these laid-up stores, however convenient this
　　dwelling we cannot remain here,
However shelter'd this port and however calm these waters
　　we must not anchor here,
However welcome the hospitality that surrounds us we are
　　permitted to receive it but a little while.

10

Allons! the inducements shall be greater,
We will sail pathless and wild seas,
We will go where winds blow, waves dash, and the Yankee
　　clipper speeds by under full sail.

Allons! with power, liberty, the earth, the elements,
Health, defiance, gayety, self-esteem, curiosity;
Allons! from all formules!
From your formules, O bat-eyed and materialistic priests.

The stale cadaver blocks up the passage—the burial waits no
　　longer.

Allons! yet take warning!
He traveling with me needs the best blood, thews, endurance,
None may come to the trial till he or she bring courage and
　　health,
Come not here if you have already spent the best of yourself,
Only those may come who come in sweet and determin'd
　　bodies,
No diseas'd person, no rum-drinker or venereal taint is per-
　　mitted here.

(I and mine do not convince by arguments, similes, rhymes,
We convince by our presence.)

11

Listen! I will be honest with you,
I do not offer the old smooth prizes, but offer rough new
　　prizes,
These are the days that must happen to you:

You shall not heap up what is call'd riches,

You shall scatter with lavish hand all that you earn or achieve,

You but arrive at the city to which you were destin'd, you hardly settle yourself to satisfaction before you are call'd by an irresistible call to depart,

You shall be treated to the ironical smiles and mockings of those who remain behind you,

What beckonings of love you receive you shall only answer with passionate kisses of parting,

You shall not allow the hold of those who spread their reach'd hands toward you.

12

Allons! after the great Companions, and to belong to them!

They too are on the road—they are the swift and majestic men—they are the greatest women,

Enjoyers of calms of seas and storms of seas,

Sailors of many a ship, walkers of many a mile of land,

Habituès of many distant countries, habituès of far-distant dwellings,

Trusters of men and women, observers of cities, solitary toilers,

Pausers and contemplators of tufts, blossoms, shells of the shore,

Dancers at wedding-dances, kissers of brides, tender helpers of children, bearers of children,

Soldiers of revolts, standers by gaping graves, lowerers-down of coffins,

Journeyers over consecutive seasons, over the years, the curious years each emerging from that which preceded it,

Journeyers as with companions, namely their own diverse phases,

Forth-steppers from the latent unrealized baby-days,

Journeyers gayly with their own youth, journeyers with their bearded and well-grain'd manhood,

Journeyers with their womanhood, ample, unsurpass'd, content,

Journeyers with their own sublime old age of manhood or womanhood,

Old age, calm, expanded, broad with the haughty breadth of
the universe,
Old age, flowing free with the delicious near-by freedom of
death.

13

Allons! to that which is endless as it was beginningless,
To undergo much, tramps of days, rests of nights,
To merge all in the travel they tend to, and the days and
nights they tend to,
Again to merge them in the start of superior journeys,
To see nothing anywhere but what you may reach it and pass
it,
To conceive no time, however distant, but what you may
reach it and pass it,
To look up or down no road but it stretches and waits for
you, however long but it stretches and waits for you,
To see no being, not God's or any, but you also go thither,
To see no possession but you may possess it, enjoying all
without labor or purchase, abstracting the feast yet not
abstracting one particle of it,
To take the best of the farmer's farm and the rich man's
elegant villa, and the chaste blessings of the well-married
couple, and the fruits of orchards and flowers of gardens,
To take to your use out of the compact cities as you pass
through,
To carry buildings and streets with you afterward wherever
you go,
To gather the minds of men out of their brains as you en-
counter them, to gather the love out of their hearts,
To take your lovers on the road with you, for all that you
leave them behind you,
To know the universe itself as a road, as many roads, as roads
for traveling souls.

All parts away for the progress of souls,
All religion, all solid things, arts, governments—all that was
or is apparent upon this globe or any globe, falls into
niches and corners before the procession of souls along
the grand roads of the universe.

Of the progress of the souls of men and women along the grand roads of the universe, all other progress is the needed emblem and sustenance.

Forever alive, forever forward,
Stately, solemn, sad, withdrawn, baffled, mad, turbulent, feeble, dissatisfied,
Desperate, proud, fond, sick, accepted by men, rejected by men,
They go! they go! I know that they go, but I know not where they go,
But I know that they go toward the best—toward something great.

Whoever you are, come forth! or man or woman come forth!
You must not stay sleeping and dallying there in the house, though you built it, or though it has been built for you.

Out of the dark confinement! out from behind the screen!
It is useless to protest, I know all and expose it.

Behold through you as bad as the rest,
Through the laughter, dancing, dining, supping, of people,
Inside of dresses and ornaments, inside of those wash'd and trimm'd faces,
Behold a secret silent loathing and despair.

No husband, no wife, no friend, trusted to hear the confession,
Another self, a duplicate of every one, skulking and hiding it goes,
Formless and wordless through the streets of the cities, polite and bland in the parlors,
In the cars of railroads, in steamboats, in the public assembly,
Home to the houses of men and women, at the table, in the bedroom, everywhere,
Smartly attired, countenance smiling, form upright, death under the breast-bones, hell under the skull-bones,
Under the broadcloth and gloves, under the ribbons and artificial flowers,

Keeping fair with the customs, speaking not a syllable of
    itself,
Speaking of any thing else but never of itself.

14

Allons! through struggles and wars!
The goal that was named cannot be countermanded.

Have the past struggles succeeded?
What has succeeded? yourself? your nation? Nature?
Now understand me well—it is provided in the essence of
    things that from any fruition of success, no matter what,
    shall come forth something to make a greater struggle
    necessary.

My call is the call of battle, I nourish active rebellion,
He going with me must go well arm'd,
He going with me goes often with spare diet, poverty, angry
    enemies, desertions.

15

Allons! the road is before us!
It is safe—I have tried it—my own feet have tried it well—be
    not detain'd!
Let the paper remain on the desk unwritten, and the book on
    the shelf unopen'd!

Let the tools remain in the workshop! let the money remain
    unearn'd!
Let the school stand! mind not the cry of the teacher!
Let the preacher preach in his pulpit! let the lawyer plead in
    the court, and the judge expound the law.

Camerado, I give you my hand!
I give you my love more precise than money,
I give you myself before preaching or law;
Will you give me yourself? will you come travel with me?
Shall we stick by each other as long as we live?
1856   1881

Crossing Brooklyn Ferry

1

FLOOD-TIDE below me! I see you face to face!
Clouds of the west—sun there half an hour high—I see you
   also face to face.

Crowds of men and women attired in the usual costumes,
   how curious you are to me!
On the ferry-boats the hundreds and hundreds that cross,
   returning home, are more curious to me than you sup-
   pose,
And you that shall cross from shore to shore years hence are
   more to me, and more in my meditations, than you
   might suppose.

2

The impalpable sustenance of me from all things at all hours
   of the day,
The simple, compact, well-join'd scheme, myself disinte-
   grated, every one disintegrated yet part of the scheme,
The similitudes of the past and those of the future,
The glories strung like beads on my smallest sights and
   hearings, on the walk in the street and the passage over
   the river,
The current rushing so swiftly and swimming with me far
   away,
The others that are to follow me, the ties between me and
   them,
The certainty of others, the life, love, sight, hearing of others.

Others will enter the gates of the ferry and cross from shore
   to shore,
Others will watch the run of the flood-tide,
Others will see the shipping of Manhattan north and west,
   and the heights of Brooklyn to the south and east,
Others will see the islands large and small;

Fifty years hence, others will see them as they cross, the sun half an hour high,
A hundred years hence, or ever so many hundred years hence, others will see them,
Will enjoy the sunset, the pouring-in of the flood-tide, the falling-back to the sea of the ebb-tide.

3

It avails not, time nor place—distance avails not,
I am with you, you men and women of a generation, or ever so many generations hence,
Just as you feel when you look on the river and sky, so I felt,
Just as any of you is one of a living crowd, I was one of a crowd,
Just as you are refresh'd by the gladness of the river and the bright flow, I was refresh'd,
Just as you stand and lean on the rail, yet hurry with the swift current, I stood yet was hurried,
Just as you look on the numberless masts of ships and the thick-stemm'd pipes of steamboats, I look'd.

I too many and many a time cross'd the river of old,
Watched the Twelfth-month sea-gulls, saw them high in the air floating with motionless wings, oscillating their bodies,
Saw how the glistening yellow lit up parts of their bodies and left the rest in strong shadow,
Saw the slow-wheeling circles and the gradual edging toward the south,
Saw the reflection of the summer sky in the water,
Had my eyes dazzled by the shimmering track of beams,
Look'd at the fine centrifugal spokes of light round the shape of my head in the sunlit water,
Look'd on the haze on the hills southward and south-westward,
Look'd on the vapor as it flew in fleeces tinged with violet,
Look'd toward the lower bay to notice the vessels arriving,
Saw their approach, saw aboard those that were near me,
Saw the white sails of schooners and sloops, saw the ships at anchor,

The sailors at work in the rigging or out astride the spars,
The round masts, the swinging motion of the hulls, the slender serpentine pennants,
The large and small steamers in motion, the pilots in their pilot-houses,
The white wake left by the passage, the quick tremulous whirl of the wheels,
The flags of all nations, the falling of them at sunset,
The scallop-edged waves in the twilight, the ladled cups, the frolicsome crests and glistening,
The stretch afar growing dimmer and dimmer, the gray walls of the granite storehouses by the docks,
On the river the shadowy group, the big steam-tug closely flank'd on each side by the barges, the hay-boat, the belated lighter,
On the neighboring shore the fires from the foundry chimneys burning high and glaringly into the night,
Casting their flicker of black contrasted with wild red and yellow light over the tops of houses, and down into the clefts of streets.

4

These and all else were to me the same as they are to you,
I loved well those cities, loved well the stately and rapid river,
The men and women I saw were all near to me,
Others the same—others who look back on me because I look'd forward to them,
(The time will come, though I stop here to-day, and to-night.)

5

What is it then between us?
What is the count of the scores or hundreds of years between us?

Whatever it is, it avails not—distance avails not, and place avails not,
I too lived, Brooklyn of ample hills was mine,
I too walk'd the streets of Manhattan island, and bathed in the waters around it,
I too felt the curious abrupt questionings stir within me.

In the day among crowds of people sometimes they came
    upon me,
In my walks home late at night or as I lay in my bed they
    came upon me,
I too had been struck from the float forever held in solution,
I too had receiv'd identity by my body,
That I was I knew was of my body, and what I should be I
    knew I should be of my body.

6

It is not upon you alone the dark patches fall,
The dark threw its patches down upon me also,
The best I had done seem'd to me blank and suspicious,
My great thoughts as I supposed them, were they not in
    reality meagre?
Nor is it you alone who know what it is to be evil,
I am he who knew what it was to be evil,
I too knitted the old knot of contrariety,
Blabb'd, blush'd, resented, lied, stole, grudg'd,
Had guile, anger, lust, hot wishes I dared not speak,
Was wayward, vain, greedy, shallow, sly, cowardly, malig-
    nant,
The wolf, the snake, the hog, not wanting in me,
The cheating look, the frivolous word, the adulterous wish,
    not wanting,
Refusals, hates, postponements, meanness, laziness, none of
    these wanting,
Was one with the rest, the days and haps of the rest,
Was call'd by my nighest name by clear loud voices of young
    men as they saw me approaching or passing,
Felt their arms on my neck as I stood, or the negligent lean-
    ing of their flesh against me as I sat,
Saw many I loved in the street or ferry-boat or public assem-
    bly, yet never told them a word,
Lived the same life with the rest, the same old laughing,
    gnawing, sleeping,
Play'd the part that still looks back on the actor or actress,
The same old role, the role that is what we make it, as great
    as we like,
Or as small as we like, or both great and small.

7

Closer yet I approach you,
What thought you have of me now, I had as much of you—I
    laid in my stores in advance,
I consider'd long and seriously of you before you were born.

Who was to know what should come home to me?
Who knows but I am enjoying this?
Who knows, for all the distance, but I am as good as looking
    at you now, for all you cannot see me?

8

Ah, what can ever be more stately and admirable to me than
    mast-hemm'd Manhattan?
River and sunset and scallop-edg'd waves of flood-tide?
The sea-gulls oscillating their bodies, the hay-boat in the
    twilight, and the belated lighter?

What gods can exceed these that clasp me by the hand, and
    with voices I love call me promptly and loudly by my
    nighest name as I approach?

What is more subtle than this which ties me to the woman or
    man that looks in my face?
Which fuses me into you now, and pours my meaning into
    you?

We understand then do we not?
What I promis'd without mentioning it, have you not ac-
    cepted?
What the study could not teach—what the preaching could
    not accomplish is accomplish'd, is it not?

9

Flow on, river! flow with the flood-tide, and ebb with the
    ebb-tide!
Frolic on, crested and scallop-edg'd waves!
Gorgeous clouds of the sunset! drench with your splendor
    me, or the men and women generations after me!

Cross from shore to shore, countless crowds of passengers!

Stand up, tall masts of Mannahatta! stand up, beautiful hills of Brooklyn!

Throb, baffled and curious brain! throw out questions and answers!

Suspend here and everywhere, eternal float of solution!

Gaze, loving and thirsting eyes, in the house or street or public assembly!

Sound out, voices of young men! loudly and musically call me by my nighest name!

Live, old life! play the part that looks back on the actor or actress!

Play the old role, the role that is great or small according as one makes it!

Consider, you who peruse me, whether I may not in unknown ways be looking upon you;

Be firm, rail over the river, to support those who lean idly, yet haste with the hasting current;

Fly on, sea-birds! fly sideways, or wheel in large circles high in the air;

Receive the summer sky, you water, and faithfully hold it till all downcast eyes have time to take it from you!

Diverge, fine spokes of light, from the shape of my head, or any one's head, in the sunlit water!

Come on, ships from the lower bay! pass up or down, white-sail'd schooners, sloops, lighters!

Flaunt away, flags of all nations! be duly lower'd at sunset!

Burn high your fires, foundry chimneys! cast black shadows at nightfall! cast red and yellow light over the tops of the houses!

Appearances, now or henceforth, indicate what you are,

You necessary film, continue to envelop the soul,

About my body for me, and your body for you, be hung our divinest aromas,

Thrive, cities—bring your freight, bring your shows, ample and sufficient rivers,

Expand, being than which none else is perhaps more spiritual,

Keep your places, objects than which none else is more lasting.

You have waited, you always wait, you dumb, beautiful
    ministers,
We receive you with free sense at last, and are insatiate hence-
    forward,
Not you any more shall be able to foil us, or withhold your-
    selves from us,
We use you, and do not cast you aside—we plant you per-
    manently within us,
We fathom you not—we love you—there is perfection in you
    also,
You furnish your parts toward eternity,
Great or small, you furnish your parts toward the soul.
1856   1881

Song of the Answerer

Now list to my morning's romanza, I tell the signs of the
    Answerer,
To the cities and farms I sing as they spread in the sunshine
    before me.

A young man comes to me bearing a message from his brother,
How shall the young man know the whether and when of his
    brother?
Tell him to send me the signs.

And I stand before the young man face to face, and take his
    right hand in my left hand and his left hand in my right
    hand,
And I answer for his brother and for men, and I answer for
    him that answers for all, and send these signs.

Him all wait for, him all yield up to, his word is decisive and
    final,
Him they accept, in him lave, in him perceive themselves as
    amid light,
Him they immerse and he immerses them.

Beautiful women, the haughtiest nations, laws, the landscape,
    people, animals,
The profound earth and its attributes and the unquiet ocean,
    (so tell I my morning's romanza,)
All enjoyments and properties and money, and whatever
    money will buy,
The best farms, others toiling and planting and he unavoid-
    ably reaps,
The noblest and costliest cities, others grading and building
    and he domiciles there,
Nothing for any one but what is for him, near and far are for
    him, the ships in the offing,
The perpetual shows and marches on land are for him if they
    are for anybody.

He puts things in their attitudes,
He puts to-day out of himself with plasticity and love,
He places his own times, reminiscences, parents, brothers
    and sisters, associations, employment, politics, so that
    the rest never shame them afterward, nor assume to
    command them.

He is the Answerer,
What can be answer'd he answers, and what cannot be
    answer'd he shows how it cannot be answer'd.

A man is a summons and challenge,
(It is vain to skulk—do you hear that mocking and laughter?
    do you hear the ironical echoes?)

Books, friendships, philosophers, priests, action, pleasure,
    pride, beat up and down seeking to give satisfaction,
He indicates the satisfaction, and indicates them that beat up
    and down also.

Whichever the sex, whatever the season or place, he may go
    freshly and gently and safely by day or by night,
He has the pass-key of hearts, to him the response of the
    prying of hands on the knobs.

His welcome is universal, the flow of beauty is not more wel-
come or universal than he is,
The person he favors by day or sleeps with at night is blessed.

Every existence has its idiom, every thing has an idiom and
tongue,
He resolves all tongues into his own and bestows it upon
men, and any man translates, and any man translates
himself also,
One part does not counteract another part, he is the joiner,
he sees how they join.

He says indifferently and alike *How are you friend?* to the
President at his levee,
And he says *Good-day my brother*, to Cudge that hoes in the
sugar-field,
And both understand him and know that his speech is right.

He walks with perfect ease in the capitol,
He walks among the Congress, and one Representative says
to another, *Here is our equal appearing and new.*

Then the mechanics take him for a mechanic,
And the soldiers suppose him to be a soldier, and the sailors
that he has follow'd the sea,
And the authors take him for an author, and the artists for
an artist,
And the laborers perceive he could labor with them and love
them,
No matter what the work is, that he is the one to follow it or
has follow'd it,
No matter what the nation, that he might find his brothers
and sisters there.

The English believe he comes of their English stock,
A Jew to the Jew he seems, a Russ to the Russ, usual and
near, removed from none.

Whoever he looks at in the traveler's coffee-house claims him,
The Italian or Frenchman is sure, the German is sure, the
Spaniard is sure, and the island Cuban is sure,

The engineer, the deck-hand on the great lakes, or on the Mississippi or St. Lawrence or Sacramento, or Hudson or Paumanok sound, claims him.

The gentleman of perfect blood acknowledges his perfect blood,
The insulter, the prostitute, the angry person, the beggar, see themselves in the ways of him, he strangely transmutes them,
They are not vile any more, they hardly know themselves they are so grown.

2

The indications and tally of time,
Perfect sanity shows the master among philosophs,
Time, always without break, indicates itself in parts,
What always indicates the poet is the crowd of the pleasant company of singers, and their words,
The words of the singers are the hours or minutes of the light or dark, but the words of the maker of poems are the general light and dark,
The maker of poems settles justice, reality, immortality,
His insight and power encircle things and the human race,
He is the glory and extract thus far of things and of the human race.

The singers do not beget, only the Poet begets,
The singers are welcom'd, understood, appear often enough, but rare has the day been, likewise the spot, of the birth of the maker of poems, the Answerer,
(Not every century nor every five centuries has contain'd such a day, for all its names.)

The singers of successive hours of centuries may have ostensible names, but the name of each of them is one of the singers,
The name of each is, eye-singer, ear-singer, head-singer, sweet-singer, night-singer, parlor-singer, love-singer, weird-singer, or something else.

All this time and at all times wait the words of true poems,
The words of true poems do not merely please,
The true poets are not followers of beauty but the august
    masters of beauty;
The greatness of sons is the exuding of the greatness of
    mothers and fathers,
The words of true poems are the tuft and final applause of
    science.

Divine instinct, breadth of vision, the law of reason, health,
    rudeness of body, withdrawnness,
Gayety, sun-tan, air-sweetness, such are some of the words of
    poems.

The sailor and traveler underlie the maker of poems, the
    Answerer,
The builder, geometer, chemist, anatomist, phrenologist,
    artist, all these underlie the maker of poems, the
    Answerer.

The words of the true poems give you more than poems,
They give you to form for yourself poems, religions, politics,
    war, peace, behavior, histories, essays, daily life, and
    every thing else,
They balance ranks, colors, races, creeds, and the sexes,
They do not seek beauty, they are sought,
Forever touching them or close upon them follows beauty,
    longing, fain, love-sick.

They prepare for death, yet they are not the finish, but rather
    the outset,
They bring none to his or her terminus or to be content and
    full,
Whom they take they take into space to behold the birth of
    stars, to learn one of the meanings,
To launch off with absolute faith, to sweep through the cease-
    less rings and never be quiet again.

1855   1881

Our Old Feuillage

ALWAYS our old feuillage!

Always Florida's green peninsula—always the priceless delta
of Louisiana—always the cotton-fields of Alabama and
Texas,

Always California's golden hills and hollows, and the silver
mountains of New Mexico—always soft-breath'd Cuba,

Always the vast slope drain'd by the Southern sea, inseparable
with the slopes drain'd by the Eastern and Western seas,

The area the eighty-third year of these States, the three and a
half millions of square miles,

The eighteen thousand miles of sea-coast and bay-coast on
the main, the thirty thousand miles of river navigation,

The seven millions of distinct families and the same number
of dwellings—always these, and more, branching forth
into numberless branches,

Always the free range and diversity—always the continent of
Democracy;

Always the prairies, pastures, forests, vast cities, travelers,
Kanada, the snows;

Always these compact lands tied at the hips with the belt
stringing the huge oval lakes;

Always the West with strong native persons, the increasing
density there, the habitans, friendly, threatening, ironi-
cal, scorning invaders;

All sights, South, North, East—all deeds promiscuously done
at all times,

All characters, movements, growths, a few noticed, myriads
unnoticed,

Through Mannahatta's streets I walking, these things
gathering,

On interior rivers by night in the glare of pine knots, steam-
boats wooding up,

Sunlight by day on the valley of the Susquehanna, and on the
valleys of the Potomac and Rappahannock, and the
valleys of the Roanoke and Delaware,

In their northerly wilds beasts of prey haunting the Adiron-
dacks the hills, or lapping the Saginaw waters to drink,

In a lonesome inlet a sheldrake lost from the flock, sitting on
the water rocking silently,

In farmers' barns oxen in the stable, their harvest labor done,
they rest standing, they are too tired,

Afar on arctic ice the she-walrus lying drowsily while her cubs
play around,

The hawk sailing where men have not yet sail'd, the farthest
polar sea, ripply, crystalline, open, beyond the floes,

White drift spooning ahead where the ship in the tempest
dashes,

On solid land what is done in cities as the bells strike mid-
night together,

In primitive woods the sounds there also sounding, the howl
of the wolf, the scream of the panther, and the hoarse
bellow of the elk,

In winter beneath the hard blue ice of Moosehead lake, in
summer visible through the clear waters, the great trout
swimming,

In lower latitudes in warmer air in the Carolinas the large
black buzzard floating slowly high beyond the tree
tops,

Below, the red cedar festoon'd with tylandria, the pines and
cypresses growing out of the white sand that spreads far
and flat,

Rude boats descending the big Pedee, climbing plants, para-
sites with color'd flowers and berries enveloping huge
trees,

The waving drapery on the live-oak trailing long and low,
noiselessly waved by the wind,

The camp of Georgia wagoners just after dark, the supper-
fires and the cooking and eating by whites and negroes,

Thirty or forty great wagons, the mules, cattle, horses, feed-
ing from troughs,

The shadows, gleams, up under the leaves of the old syca-
more-trees, the flames with the black smoke from the
pitch-pine curling and rising;

Southern fishermen fishing, the sounds and inlets of North
Carolina's coast, the shad-fishery and the herring-

fishery, the large sweep-seines, the windlasses on shore work'd by horses, the clearing, curing, and packing-houses;

Deep in the forest in piney woods turpentine dropping from the incisions in the trees, there are the turpentine works,

There are the negroes at work in good health, the ground in all directions is cover'd with pine straw;

In Tennessee and Kentucky slaves busy in the coalings, at the forge, by the furnace-blaze, or at the corn-shucking,

In Virginia, the planter's son returning after a long absence, joyfully welcom'd and kiss'd by the aged mulatto nurse,

On rivers boatmen safely moor'd at nightfall in their boats under shelter of high banks,

Some of the younger men dance to the sound of the banjo or fiddle, others sit on the gunwale smoking and talking;

Late in the afternoon the mocking-bird, the American mimic, singing in the Great Dismal Swamp,

There are the greenish waters, the resinous odor, the plenteous moss, the cypress-tree, and the juniper-tree;

Northward, young men of Mannahatta, the target company from an excursion returning home at evening, the musket-muzzles all bear bunches of flowers presented by women;

Children at play, or on his father's lap a young boy fallen asleep, (how his lips move! how he smiles in his sleep!)

The scout riding on horseback over the plains west of the Mississippi, he ascends a knoll and sweeps his eyes around;

California life, the miner, bearded, dress'd in his rude costume, the stanch California friendship, the sweet air, the graves one in passing meets solitary just aside the horse-path;

Down in Texas the cotton-field, the negro-cabins, drivers driving mules or oxen before rude carts, cotton bales piled on banks and wharves;

Encircling all, vast-darting up and wide, the American Soul, with equal hemispheres, one Love, one Dilation or Pride;

In arriere the peace-talk with the Iroquois the aborigines, the calumet, the pipe of good-will, arbitration, and indorsement,

The sachem blowing the smoke first toward the sun and then
    toward the earth,

The drama of the scalp-dance enacted with painted faces and
    guttural exclamations,

The setting out of the war-party, the long and stealthy march,

The single file, the swinging hatchets, the surprise and
    slaughter of enemies;

All the acts, scenes, ways, persons, attitudes of these States,
    reminiscences, institutions,

All these States compact, every square mile of these States
    without excepting a particle;

Me pleas'd, rambling in lanes and country fields, Paumanok's
    fields,

Observing the spiral flight of two little yellow butterflies
    shuffling between each other, ascending high in the
    air,

The darting swallow, the destroyer of insects, the fall traveler
    southward but returning northward early in the spring,

The country boy at the close of the day driving the herd of
    cows and shouting to them as they loiter to browse by
    the roadside,

The city wharf, Boston, Philadelphia, Baltimore, Charleston,
    New Orleans, San Francisco,

The departing ships when the sailors heave at the capstan;

Evening—me in my room—the setting sun,

The setting summer sun shining in my open window, showing
    the swarm of flies, suspended, balancing in the air in the
    centre of the room, darting athwart, up and down, cast-
    ing swift shadows in specks on the opposite wall where
    the shine is;

The athletic American matron speaking in public to crowds
    of listeners,

Males, females, immigrants, combinations, the copiousness,
    the individuality of the States, each for itself—the
    money-makers,

Factories, machinery, the mechanical forces, the windlass,
    lever, pulley, all certainties,

The certainty of space, increase, freedom, futurity,

In space the sporades, the scatter'd islands, the stars—on the
    firm earth, the lands, my lands,

O lands! all so dear to me—what you are, (whatever it is,) I
 putting it at random in these songs, become a part of
 that, whatever it is,

Southward there, I screaming, with wings slow flapping, with
 the myriads of gulls wintering along the coasts of
 Florida,

Otherways there atwixt the banks of the Arkansas, the Rio
 Grande, the Nueces, the Brazos, the Tombigbee, the
 Red River, the Saskatchewan or the Osage, I with the
 spring waters laughing and skipping and running,

Northward, on the sands, on some shallow bay of Paumanok,
 I with parties of snowy herons wading in the wet to seek
 worms and aquatic plants,

Retreating, triumphantly twittering, the king-bird, from
 piercing the crow with its bill, for amusement—and I
 triumphantly twittering,

The migrating flock of wild geese alighting in autumn to
 refresh themselves, the body of the flock feed, the sen-
 tinels outside move around with erect heads watching,
 and are from time to time reliev'd by other sentinels—
 and I feeding and taking turns with the rest,

In Kanadian forests the moose, large as an ox, corner'd by
 hunters, rising desperately on his hind-feet, and plung-
 ing with his fore-feet, the hoofs as sharp as knives—and
 I, plunging at the hunters, corner'd and desperate,

In the Mannahatta, streets, piers, shipping, store-houses, and
 the countless workmen working in the shops,

And I too of the Mannahatta, singing thereof—and no less in
 myself than the whole of the Mannahatta in itself,

Singing the song of These, my ever-united lands—my body
 no more inevitably united, part to part, and made out of
 a thousand diverse contributions one identity, any more
 than my lands are inevitably united and made ONE
 IDENTITY;

Nativities, climates, the grass of the great pastoral Plains,

Cities, labors, death, animals, products, war, good and evil—
 these me,

These affording, in all their particulars, the old feuillage to
 me and to America, how can I do less than pass the clew
 of the union of them, to afford the like to you?

Whoever you are! how can I but offer you divine leaves, that
    you also be eligible as I am?
How can I but as here chanting, invite you for yourself to
    collect bouquets of the incomparable feuillage of these
    States?
1860   1881

A Song of Joys

O TO make the most jubilant song!
Full of music—full of manhood, womanhood, infancy!
Full of common employments—full of grain and trees.

O for the voices of animals—O for the swiftness and balance
    of fishes!
O for the dropping of raindrops in a song!
O for the sunshine and motion of waves in a song!

O the joy of my spirit—it is uncaged—it darts like lightning!
It is not enough to have this globe or a certain time,
I will have thousands of globes and all time.

O the engineer's joys! to go with a locomotive!
To hear the hiss of steam, the merry shriek, the steam-whistle,
    the laughing locomotive!
To push with resistless way and speed off in the distance.

O the gleesome saunter over fields and hillsides!
The leaves and flowers of the commonest weeds, the moist
    fresh stillness of the woods,
The exquisite smell of the earth at daybreak, and all through
    the forenoon.

O the horseman's and horsewoman's joys!
The saddle, the gallop, the pressure upon the seat, the cool
    gurgling by the ears and hair.

O the fireman's joys!
I hear the alarm at dead of night,
I hear bells, shouts! I pass the crowd, I run!
The sight of the flames maddens me with pleasure.

O the joy of the strong-brawn'd fighter, towering in the arena
　　in perfect condition, conscious of power, thirsting to
　　meet his opponent.

O the joy of that vast elemental sympathy which only the
　　human soul is capable of generating and emitting in
　　steady and limitless floods.

O the mother's joys!
The watching, the endurance, the precious love, the anguish,
　　the patiently yielded life.

O the joy of increase, growth, recuperation,
The joy of soothing and pacifying, the joy of concord and
　　harmony.

O to go back to the place where I was born,
To hear the birds sing once more,
To ramble about the house and barn and over the fields once
　　more,
And through the orchard and along the old lanes once more.

O to have been brought up on bays, lagoons, creeks, or along
　　the coast,
To continue and be employ'd there all my life,
The briny and damp smell, the shore, the salt weeds exposed
　　at low water,
The work of fishermen, the work of the eel-fisher and clam-
　　fisher;
I come with my clam-rake and spade, I come with my eel-
　　spear,
Is the tide out? I join the group of clam-diggers on the flats,
I laugh and work with them, I joke at my work like a mettle-
　　some young man;
In winter I take my eel-basket and eel-spear and travel out on
　　foot on the ice—I have a small axe to cut holes in the ice,

Behold me well-clothed going gayly or returning in the
  afternoon, my brood of tough boys accompanying
  me,
My brood of grown and part-grown boys, who love to be
  with no one else so well as they love to be with me,
By day to work with me, and by night to sleep with me.

Another time in warm weather out in a boat, to lift the
  lobster-pots where they are sunk with heavy stones, (I
  know the buoys,)
O the sweetness of the Fifth-month morning upon the water
  as I row just before sunrise toward the buoys,
I pull the wicker pots up slantingly, the dark green lobsters
  are desperate with their claws as I take them out, I insert
  wooden pegs in the joints of their pincers,
I go to all the places one after another, and then row back to
  the shore,
There in a huge kettle of boiling water the lobsters shall be
  boil'd till their color becomes scarlet.

Another time mackerel-taking,
Voracious, mad for the hook, near the surface, they seem to
  fill the water for miles;
Another time fishing for rock-fish in Chesapeake Bay, I one
  of the brown-faced crew;
Another time trailing for blue-fish off Paumanok, I stand
  with braced body,
My left foot is on the gunwale, my right arm throws far out
  the coils of slender rope,
In sight around me the quick veering and darting of fifty
  skiffs, my companions.

O boating on the rivers,
The voyage down the St. Lawrence, the superb scenery, the
  steamers,
The ships sailing, the Thousand Islands, the occasional tim-
  ber-raft and the raftsmen with long-reaching sweep-
  oars,
The little huts on the rafts, and the stream of smoke when
  they cook supper at evening.

(O something pernicious and dread!
Something far away from a puny and pious life!
Something unproved! something in a trance!
Something escaped from the anchorage and driving free.)

O to work in mines, or forging iron,
Foundry casting, the foundry itself, the rude high roof, the
    ample and shadow'd space,
The furnace, the hot liquid pour'd out and running.

O to resume the joys of the soldier!
To feel the presence of a brave commanding officer—to feel
    his sympathy!
To behold his calmness—to be warm'd in the rays of his
    smile!
To go to battle—to hear the bugles play and the drums beat!
To hear the crash of artillery—to see the glittering of the
    bayonets and musket-barrels in the sun!
To see men fall and die and not complain!
To taste the savage taste of blood—to be so devilish!
To gloat so over the wounds and deaths of the enemy.

O the whaleman's joys! O I cruise my old cruise again!
I feel the ship's motion under me, I feel the Atlantic breezes
    fanning me,
I hear the cry again sent down from the mast-head, *There—
    she blows!*
Again I spring up the rigging to look with the rest—we de-
    scend, wild with excitement,
I leap in the lower'd boat, we row toward our prey where he
    lies,
We approach stealthy and silent, I see the mountainous mass,
    lethargic, basking,
I see the harpooner standing up, I see the weapon dart from
    his vigorous arm;
O swift again far out in the ocean the wounded whale,
    settling, running to windward, tows me,
Again I see him rise to breathe, we row close again,
I see a lance driven through his side, press'd deep, turn'd in
    the wound,

Again we back off, I see him settle again, the life is leaving
    him fast,
As he rises he spouts blood, I see him swim in circles nar-
    rower and narrower, swiftly cutting the water—I see
    him die,
He gives one convulsive leap in the centre of the circle, and
    then falls flat and still in the bloody foam.

O the old manhood of me, my noblest joy of all!
My children and grand-children, my white hair and beard,
My largeness, calmness, majesty, out of the long stretch of
    my life.

O ripen'd joy of womanhood! O happiness at last!
I am more than eighty years of age, I am the most venerable
    mother,
How clear is my mind—how all people draw nigh to me!
What attractions are these beyond any before? what bloom
    more than the bloom of youth?
What beauty is this that descends upon me and rises out of me?

O the orator's joys!
To inflate the chest, to roll the thunder of the voice out from
    the ribs and throat,
To make the people rage, weep, hate, desire, with yourself,
To lead America—to quell America with a great tongue.

O the joy of my soul leaning pois'd on itself, receiving iden-
    tity through materials and loving them, observing char-
    acters and absorbing them,
My soul vibrated back to me from them, from sight, hearing,
    touch, reason, articulation, comparison, memory, and
    the like,
The real life of my senses and flesh transcending my senses
    and flesh,
My body done with materials, my sight done with my
    material eyes,
Proved to me this day beyond cavil that it is not my material
    eyes which finally see,
Nor my material body which finally loves, walks, laughs,
    shouts, embraces, procreates.

O the farmer's joys!
Ohioan's, Illinoisian's, Wisconsinese', Kanadian's, Iowan's,
   Kansian's, Missourian's, Oregonese' joys!
To rise at peep of day and pass forth nimbly to work,
To plough land in the fall for winter-sown crops,
To plough land in the spring for maize,
To train orchards, to graft the trees, to gather apples in the
   fall.

O to bathe in the swimming-bath, or in a good place along
   shore,
To splash the water! to walk ankle-deep, or race naked along
   the shore.

O to realize space!
The plenteousness of all, that there are no bounds,
To emerge and be of the sky, of the sun and moon and flying
   clouds, as one with them.

O the joy of a manly self-hood!
To be servile to none, to defer to none, not to any tyrant
   known or unknown,
To walk with erect carriage, a step springy and elastic,
To look with calm gaze or with a flashing eye,
To speak with a full and sonorous voice out of a broad chest,
To confront with your personality all the other personalities
   of the earth.

Know'st thou the excellent joys of youth?
Joys of the dear companions and of the merry word and
   laughing face?
Joy of the glad light-beaming day, joy of the wide-breath'd
   games?
Joy of sweet music, joy of the lighted ball-room and the
   dancers?
Joy of the plenteous dinner, strong carouse and drinking?

Yet O my soul supreme!
Know'st thou the joys of pensive thought?
Joys of the free and lonesome heart, the tender, gloomy
   heart?

Joys of the solitary walk, the spirit bow'd yet proud, the
  suffering and the struggle?
The agonistic throes, the ecstasies, joys of the solemn mus-
  ings day or night?
Joys of the thought of Death, the great spheres Time and
  Space?
Prophetic joys of better, loftier love's ideals, the divine wife,
  the sweet, eternal, perfect comrade?
Joys all thine own undying one, joys worthy thee O soul.

O while I live to be the ruler of life, not a slave,
To meet life as a powerful conqueror,
No fumes, no ennui, no more complaints or scornful
  criticisms,
To these proud laws of the air, the water and the ground,
  proving my interior soul impregnable,
And nothing exterior shall ever take command of me.

For not life's joys alone I sing, repeating—the joy of death!
The beautiful touch of Death, soothing and benumbing a
  few moments, for reasons,
Myself discharging my excrementitious body to be burn'd, or
  render'd to powder, or buried,
My real body doubtless left to me for other spheres,
My voided body nothing more to me, returning to the puri-
  fications, further offices, eternal uses of the earth.

O to attract by more than attraction!
How it is I know not—yet behold! the something which
  obeys none of the rest,
It is offensive, never defensive—yet how magnetic it draws.

O to struggle against great odds, to meet enemies undaunted!
To be entirely alone with them, to find how much one can
  stand!
To look strife, torture, prison, popular odium, face to
  face!
To mount the scaffold, to advance to the muzzles of guns
  with perfect nonchalance!
To be indeed a God!

O to sail to sea in a ship!
To leave this steady unendurable land,
To leave the tiresome sameness of the streets, the sidewalks
　　and the houses,
To leave you O you solid motionless land, and entering a
　　ship,
To sail and sail and sail!

O to have life henceforth a poem of new joys!
To dance, clap hands, exult, shout, skip, leap, roll on, float
　　on!
To be a sailor of the world bound for all ports,
A ship itself, (see indeed these sails I spread to the sun and
　　air,)
A swift and swelling ship full of rich words, full of joys.
1860　　　　　　　　　　　　　　　　　　　　　　1881

Song of the Broad-Axe

1

WEAPON shapely, naked, wan,
Head from the mother's bowels drawn,
Wooded flesh and metal bone, limb only one and lip only
　　one,
Gray-blue leaf by red-heat grown, helve produced from a
　　little seed sown,
Resting the grass amid and upon,
To be lean'd and to lean on.

Strong shapes and attributes of strong shapes, masculine
　　trades, sights and sounds,
Long varied train of an emblem, dabs of music,
Fingers of the organist skipping staccato over the keys of the
　　great organ.

2

Welcome are all earth's lands, each for its kind,
Welcome are lands of pine and oak,

Welcome are lands of the lemon and fig,
Welcome are lands of gold,
Welcome are lands of wheat and maize, welcome those of the
grape,
Welcome are lands of sugar and rice,
Welcome the cotton-lands, welcome those of the white
potato and sweet potato,
Welcome are mountains, flats, sands, forests, prairies,
Welcome the rich borders of rivers, table-lands, openings,
Welcome the measureless grazing-lands, welcome the teem-
ing soil of orchards, flax, honey, hemp;
Welcome just as much the other more hard-faced lands,
Lands rich as lands of gold or wheat and fruit lands,
Lands of mines, lands of the manly and rugged ores,
Lands of coal, copper, lead, tin, zinc,
Lands of iron—lands of the make of the axe.

3

The log at the wood-pile, the axe supported by it,
The sylvan hut, the vine over the doorway, the space clear'd
for a garden,
The irregular tapping of rain down on the leaves after the
storm is lull'd,
The wailing and moaning at intervals, the thought of the sea,
The thought of ships struck in the storm and put on their
beam ends, and the cutting away of masts,
The sentiment of the huge timbers of old-fashion'd houses
and barns,
The remember'd print or narrative, the voyage at a venture
of men, families, goods,
The disembarkation, the founding of a new city,
The voyage of those who sought a New England and found
it, the outset anywhere,
The settlements of the Arkansas, Colorado, Ottawa, Willa-
mette,
The slow progress, the scant fare, the axe, rifle, saddle-bags;
The beauty of all adventurous and daring persons,
The beauty of wood-boys and wood-men with their clear
untrimm'd faces,

The beauty of independence, departure, actions that rely on
themselves,

The American contempt for statutes and ceremonies, the
boundless impatience of restraint,

The loose drift of character, the inkling through random
types, the solidification;

The butcher in the slaughter-house, the hands aboard
schooners and sloops, the raftsmen, the pioneer,

Lumbermen in their winter camp, daybreak in the woods,
stripes of snow on the limbs of trees, the occasional
snapping,

The glad clear sound of one's own voice, the merry song, the
natural life of the woods, the strong day's work,

The blazing fire at night, the sweet taste of supper, the talk,
the bed of hemlock-boughs and the bear-skin;

The house-builder at work in cities or anywhere,

The preparatory jointing, squaring, sawing, mortising,

The hoist-up of beams, the push of them in their places,
laying them regular,

Setting the studs by their tenons in the mortises according as
they were prepared,

The blows of mallets and hammers, the attitudes of the men,
their curv'd limbs,

Bending, standing, astride the beams, driving in pins, holding
on by posts and braces,

The hook'd arm over the plate, the other arm wielding the
axe,

The floor-men forcing the planks close to be nail'd,

Their postures bringing their weapons downward on the
bearers,

The echoes resounding through the vacant building;

The huge storehouse carried up in the city well under way,

The six framing-men, two in the middle and two at each end,
carefully bearing on their shoulders a heavy stick for a
cross-beam,

The crowded line of masons with trowels in their right hands
rapidly laying the long side-wall, two hundred feet from
front to rear,

The flexible rise and fall of backs, the continual click of the
trowels striking the bricks,

The bricks one after another each laid so workmanlike in its
place, and set with a knock of the trowel-handle,
The piles of materials, the mortar on the mortar-boards, and
the steady replenishing by the hod-men;
Spar-makers in the spar-yard, the swarming row of well-
grown apprentices,
The swing of their axes on the square-hew'd log shaping it
toward the shape of a mast,
The brisk short crackle of the steel driven slantingly into the
pine,
The butter-color'd chips flying off in great flakes and slivers,
The limber motion of brawny young arms and hips in easy
costumes,
The constructor of wharves, bridges, piers, bulk-heads, floats,
stays against the sea;
The city fireman, the fire that suddenly bursts forth in the
close-pack'd square,
The arriving engines, the hoarse shouts, the nimble stepping
and daring,
The strong command through the fire-trumpets, the falling in
line, the rise and fall of the arms forcing the water,
The slender, spasmic, blue-white jets, the bringing to bear of
the hooks and ladders and their execution,
The crash and cut away of connecting wood-work, or
through floors if the fire smoulders under them,
The crowd with their lit faces watching, the glare and dense
shadows;
The forger at his forge-furnace and the user of iron after him,
The maker of the axe large and small, and the welder and
temperer,
The chooser breathing his breath on the cold steel and trying
the edge with his thumb,
The one who clean-shapes the handle and sets it firmly in the
socket;
The shadowy processions of the portraits of the past users
also,
The primal patient mechanics, the architects and engineers,
The far-off Assyrian edifice and Mizra edifice,
The Roman lictors preceding the consuls,
The antique European warrior with his axe in combat,

The uplifted arm, the clatter of blows on the helmeted head,
The death-howl, the limpsy tumbling body, the rush of
    friend and foe thither,
The siege of revolted lieges determin'd for liberty,
The summons to surrender, the battering at castle gates, the
    truce and parley,
The sack of an old city in its time,
The bursting in of mercenaries and bigots tumultuously and
    disorderly,
Roar, flames, blood, drunkenness, madness,
Goods freely rifled from houses and temples, screams of
    women in the gripe of brigands,
Craft and thievery of camp-followers, men running, old per-
    sons despairing,
The hell of war, the cruelties of creeds,
The list of all executive deeds and words just or unjust,
The power of personality just or unjust.

4

Muscle and pluck forever!
What invigorates life invigorates death,
And the dead advance as much as the living advance,
And the future is no more uncertain than the present,
For the roughness of the earth and of man encloses as much
    as the delicatesse of the earth and of man,
And nothing endures but personal qualities.

What do you think endures?
Do you think a great city endures?
Or a teeming manufacturing state? or a prepared constitu-
    tion? or the best built steamships?
Or hotels of granite and iron? or any chef-d'œuvres of en-
    gineering, forts, armaments?

Away! these are not to be cherish'd for themselves,
They fill their hour, the dancers dance, the musicians play for
    them,
The show passes, all does well enough of course,
All does very well till one flash of defiance.

A great city is that which has the greatest men and women,
If it be a few ragged huts it is still the greatest city in the
    whole world.

5

The place where a great city stands is not the place of
    stretch'd wharves, docks, manufactures, deposits of
    produce merely,
Nor the place of ceaseless salutes of new-comers or the
    anchor-lifters of the departing,
Nor the place of the tallest and costliest buildings or shops
    selling goods from the rest of the earth,
Nor the place of the best libraries and schools, nor the place
    where money is plentiest,
Nor the place of the most numerous population.

Where the city stands with the brawniest breed of orators and
    bards,
Where the city stands that is belov'd by these, and loves them
    in return and understands them,
Where no monuments exist to heroes but in the common
    words and deeds,
Where thrift is in its place, and prudence is in its place,
Where the men and women think lightly of the laws,
Where the slave ceases, and the master of slaves ceases,
Where the populace rise at once against the never-ending
    audacity of elected persons,
Where fierce men and women pour forth as the sea to the
    whistle of death pours its sweeping and unript waves,
Where outside authority enters always after the precedence
    of inside authority,
Where the citizen is always the head and ideal, and Presi-
    dent, Mayor, Governor and what not, are agents for
    pay,
Where children are taught to be laws to themselves, and to
    depend on themselves,
Where equanimity is illustrated in affairs,
Where speculations on the soul are encouraged,
Where women walk in public processions in the streets the
    same as the men,

Where they enter the public assembly and take places the
    same as the men;
Where the city of the faithfulest friends stands,
Where the city of the cleanliness of the sexes stands,
Where the city of the healthiest fathers stands,
Where the city of the best-bodied mothers stands,
There the great city stands.

6

How beggarly appear arguments before a defiant deed!
How the floridness of the materials of cities shrivels before a
    man's or woman's look!

All waits or goes by default till a strong being appears;
A strong being is the proof of the race and of the ability of the
    universe,
When he or she appears materials are overaw'd,
The dispute on the soul stops,
The old customs and phrases are confronted, turn'd back, or
    laid away.

What is your money-making now? what can it do now?
What is your respectability now?
What are your theology, tuition, society, traditions, statute-
    books, now?
Where are your jibes of being now?
Where are your cavils about the soul now?

7

A sterile landscape covers the ore, there is as good as the best
    for all the forbidding appearance,
There is the mine, there are the miners,
The forge-furnace is there, the melt is accomplish'd, the
    hammers-men are at hand with their tongs and hammers,
What always served and always serves is at hand.

Than this nothing has better served, it has served all,
Served the fluent-tongued and subtle-sensed Greek, and long
    ere the Greek,
Served in building the buildings that last longer than any,

Served the Hebrew, the Persian, the most ancient Hindu-
stanee,
Served the mound-raiser on the Mississippi, served those
whose relics remain in Central America,
Served Albic temples in woods or on plains, with unhewn
pillars and the druids,
Served the artificial clefts, vast, high, silent, on the snow-
cover'd hills of Scandinavia,
Served those who time out of mind made on the granite
walls rough sketches of the sun, moon, stars, ships,
ocean waves,
Served the paths of the irruptions of the Goths, served the
pastoral tribes and nomads,
Served the long distant Kelt, served the hardy pirates of the
Baltic,
Served before any of those the venerable and harmless men
of Ethiopia,
Served the making of helms for the galleys of pleasure and
the making of those for war,
Served all great works on land and all great works on the sea,
For the mediæval ages and before the mediæval ages,
Served not the living only then as now, but served the dead.

8

I see the European headsman,
He stands mask'd, clothed in red, with huge legs and strong
naked arms,
And leans on a ponderous axe.

(Whom have you slaughter'd lately European headsman?
Whose is that blood upon you so wet and sticky?)

I see the clear sunsets of the martyrs,
I see from the scaffolds the descending ghosts,
Ghosts of dead lords, uncrown'd ladies, impeach'd ministers,
rejected kings,
Rivals, traitors, poisoners, disgraced chieftains and the rest.

I see those who in any land have died for the good cause,
The seed is spare, nevertheless the crop shall never run out,

(Mind you O foreign kings, O priests, the crop shall never
    run out.)

I see the blood wash'd entirely away from the axe,
Both blade and helve are clean,
They spirt no more the blood of European nobles, they clasp
    no more the necks of queens.

I see the headsman withdraw and become useless,
I see the scaffold untrodden and mouldy, I see no longer any
    axe upon it,
I see the mighty and friendly emblem of the power of my own
    race, the newest, largest race.

9

(America! I do not vaunt my love for you,
I have what I have.)

The axe leaps!
The solid forest gives fluid utterances,
They tumble forth, they rise and form,
Hut, tent, landing, survey,
Flail, plough, pick, crowbar, spade,
Shingle, rail, prop, wainscot, jamb, lath, panel, gable,
Citadel, ceiling, saloon, academy, organ, exhibition-house,
    library,
Cornice, trellis, pilaster, balcony, window, turret, porch,
Hoe, rake, pitchfork, pencil, wagon, staff, saw, jack-plane,
    mallet, wedge, rounce,
Chair, tub, hoop, table, wicket, vane, sash, floor,
Work-box, chest, string'd instrument, boat, frame, and what
    not,
Capitols of States, and capitol of the nation of States,
Long stately rows in avenues, hospitals for orphans or for
    the poor or sick,
Manhattan steamboats and clippers taking the measure of all
    seas.

The shapes arise!
Shapes of the using of axes anyhow, and the users and all that
    neighbors them,

Cutters down of wood and haulers of it to the Penobscot or Kennebec,

Dwellers in cabins among the Californian mountains or by the little lakes, or on the Columbia,

Dwellers south on the banks of the Gila or Rio Grande, friendly gatherings, the characters and fun,

Dwellers along the St. Lawrence, or north in Kanada, or down by the Yellowstone, dwellers on coasts and off coasts,

Seal-fishers, whalers, arctic seamen breaking passages through the ice.

The shapes arise!

Shapes of factories, arsenals, foundries, markets,

Shapes of the two-threaded tracks of railroads,

Shapes of the sleepers of bridges, vast frameworks, girders, arches,

Shapes of the fleets of barges, tows, lake and canal craft, river craft,

Ship-yards and dry-docks along the Eastern and Western seas, and in many a bay and by-place,

The live-oak kelsons, the pine planks, the spars, the hackmatack-roots for knees,

The ships themselves on their ways, the tiers of scaffolds, the workmen busy outside and inside,

The tools lying around, the great auger and little auger, the adze, bolt, line, square, gouge, and bead-plane.

10

The shapes arise!

The shape measur'd, saw'd, jack'd, join'd, stain'd,

The coffin-shape for the dead to lie within in his shroud,

The shape got out in posts, in the bedstead posts, in the posts of the bride's bed,

The shape of the little trough, the shape of the rockers beneath, the shape of the babe's cradle,

The shape of the floor-planks, the floor-planks for dancer's feet,

The shape of the planks of the family home, the home of the friendly parents and children,

The shape of the roof of the home of the happy young man
and woman, the roof over the well-married young man
and woman,
The roof over the supper joyously cook'd by the chaste wife,
and joyously eaten by the chaste husband, content after
his day's work.

The shapes arise!
The shape of the prisoner's place in the court-room, and of
him or her seated in the place.
The shape of the liquor-bar lean'd against by the young rum-
drinker and the old rum-drinker,
The shape of the shamed and angry stairs trod by sneaking
footsteps,
The shape of the sly settee, and the adulterous unwholesome
couple,
The shape of the gambling-board with its devilish winnings
and losings,
The shape of the step-ladder for the convicted and sentenced
murderer, the murderer with haggard face and pinion'd
arms,
The sheriff at hand with his deputies, the silent and white-
lipp'd crowd, the dangling of the rope.

The shapes arise!
Shapes of doors giving many exits and entrances,
The door passing the dissever'd friend flush'd and in haste,
The door that admits good news and bad news,
The door whence the son left home confident and puff'd up,
The door he enter'd again from a long and scandalous ab-
sence, diseas'd, broken down, without innocence, with-
out means.

11

Her shape arises,
She less guarded than ever, yet more guarded than ever,
The gross and soil'd she moves among do not make her gross
and soil'd,
She knows the thoughts as she passes, nothing is conceal'd
from her,

She is none the less considerate or friendly therefor,
She is the best belov'd, it is without exception, she has no
    reason to fear and she does not fear,
Oaths, quarrels, hiccupp'd songs, smutty expressions are idle
    to her as she passes,
She is silent, she is possess'd of herself, they do not offend
    her,
She receives them as the laws of Nature receive them, she is
    strong,
She too is a law of Nature—there is no law stronger than
    she is.

12

The main shapes arise!
Shapes of Democracy total, result of centuries,
Shapes ever projecting other shapes,
Shapes of turbulent manly cities,
Shapes of the friends and home-givers of the whole earth,
Shapes bracing the earth and braced with the whole earth.
1856   1881

Song of the Exposition

1

(AH little recks the laborer,
How near his work is holding him to God,
The loving Laborer through space and time.)

After all not to create only, or found only,
But to bring perhaps from afar what is already founded,
To give it our own identity, average, limitless, free,
To fill the gross the torpid bulk with vital religious fire,
Not to repel or destroy so much as accept, fuse, rehabilitate,
To obey as well as command, to follow more than to lead,
These also are the lessons of our New World;
While how little the New after all, how much the Old, Old
    World!

Long and long has the grass been growing,
Long and long has the rain been falling,
Long has the globe been rolling round.

2

Come Muse migrate from Greece and Ionia,
Cross out please those immensely overpaid accounts,
That matter of Troy and Achilles' wrath, and Æneas', Odys-
    seus' wanderings,
Placard "Removed" and "To Let" on the rocks of your
    snowy Parnassus,
Repeat at Jerusalem, place the notice high on Jaffa's gate and
    on Mount Moriah,
The same on the walls of your German, French and Spanish
    castles, and Italian collections,
For know a better, fresher, busier sphere, a wide, untried
    domain awaits, demands you.

3

Responsive to our summons,
Or rather to her long-nurs'd inclination,
Join'd with an irresistible, natural gravitation,
She comes! I hear the rustling of her gown,
I scent the odor of her breath's delicious fragrance,
I mark her step divine, her curious eyes a-turning, rolling,
Upon this very scene.

The dame of dames! can I believe then,
Those ancient temples, sculptures classic, could none of them
    retain her?
Nor shades of Virgil and Dante, nor myriad memories,
    poems, old associations, magnetize and hold on to her?
But that she's left them all—and here?

Yes, if you will allow me to say so,
I, my friends, if you do not, can plainly see her,
The same undying soul of earth's, activity's, beauty's, hero-
    ism's expression,
Out from her evolutions hither come, ended the strata of her
    former themes,

Hidden and cover'd by to-day's, foundation of to-day's,

Ended, deceas'd through time, her voice by Castaly's fountain,

Silent the broken-lipp'd Sphynx in Egypt, silent all those century-baffling tombs,

Ended for aye the epics of Asia's, Europe's helmeted warriors, ended the primitive call of the muses,

Calliope's call forever closed, Clio, Melpomene, Thalia dead,

Ended the stately rhythmus of Una and Oriana, ended the quest of the Holy Graal,

Jerusalem a handful of ashes blown by the wind, extinct,

The Crusaders' streams of shadowy midnight troops sped with the sunrise,

Amadis, Tancred, utterly gone, Charlemagne, Roland, Oliver gone,

Palmerin, ogre, departed, vanish'd the turrets that Usk from its waters reflected,

Arthur vanish'd with all his knights, Merlin and Lancelot and Galahad, all gone, dissolv'd utterly like an exhalation;

Pass'd! pass'd! for us, forever pass'd, that once so mighty world, now void, inanimate, phantom world,

Embroider'd, dazzling, foreign world, with all its gorgeous legends, myths,

Its kings and castles proud, its priests and warlike lords and courtly dames,

Pass'd to its charnel vault, coffin'd with crown and armor on,

Blazon'd with Shakspere's purple page,

And dirged by Tennyson's sweet sad rhyme.

I say I see, my friends, if you do not, the illustrious emigré, (having it is true in her day, although the same, changed, journey'd considerable,)

Making directly for this rendezvous, vigorously clearing a path for herself, striding through the confusion,

By thud of machinery and shrill steam-whistle undismay'd,

Bluff'd not a bit by drain-pipe, gasometers, artificial fertilizers,

Smiling and pleas'd with palpable intent to stay,

She's here, install'd amid the kitchen ware!

4

But hold—don't I forget my manners?
To introduce the stranger, (what else indeed do I live to
    chant for?) to thee Columbia;
In liberty's name welcome immortal! clasp hands,
And ever henceforth sisters dear be both.

Fear not O Muse! truly new ways and days receive, surround
    you,
I candidly confess a queer, queer race, of novel fashion,
And yet the same old human race, the same within, without,
Faces and hearts the same, feelings the same, yearnings the
    same,
The same old love, beauty and use the same.

5

We do not blame thee elder World, nor really separate our-
    selves from thee,
(Would the son separate himself from the father?)
Looking back on thee, seeing thee to thy duties, grandeurs,
    through past ages bending, building,
We build to ours to-day.

Mightier than Egypt's tombs,
Fairer than Grecia's, Roma's temples,
Prouder then Milan's statued, spired, cathedral,
More picturesque than Rhenish castle-keeps,
We plan even now to raise, beyond them all,
Thy great cathedral sacred industry, no tomb,
A keep for life for practical invention.

As in a waking vision,
E'en while I chant I see it rise, I scan and prophesy outside
    and in,
Its manifold ensemble.

Around a palace, loftier, fairer, ampler than any yet,
Earth's modern wonder, history's seven outstripping,
High rising tier on tier with glass and iron façades,
Gladdening the sun and sky, enhued in cheerfulest hues,

Bronze, lilac, robin's-egg, marine and crimson,
Over whose golden roof shall flaunt, beneath thy banner
    Freedom,
The banners of the States and flags of every land,
A brood of lofty, fair, but lesser palaces shall cluster.

Somewhere within their walls shall all that forwards perfect
    human life be started,
Tried, taught, advanced, visibly exhibited.

Not only all the world of works, trade, products,
But all the workmen of the world here to be represented.

Here shall you trace in flowing operation,
In every state of practical, busy movement, the rills of civili-
    zation,
Materials here under your eye shall change their shape as if
    by magic,
The cotton shall be pick'd almost in the very field,
Shall be dried, clean'd, ginn'd, baled, spun into thread and
    cloth before you,
You shall see hands at work at all the old processes and all
    the new ones,
You shall see the various grains and how flour is made and
    then bread baked by the bakers,
You shall see the crude ores of California and Nevada pass-
    ing on and on till they become bullion,
You shall watch how the printer sets type, and learn what a
    composing-stick is,
You shall mark in amazement the Hoe press whirling its
    cylinders, shedding the printed leaves steady and fast,
The photograph, model, watch, pin, nail, shall be created
    before you.

In large calm halls, a stately museum shall teach you the
    infinite lessons of minerals,
In another, woods, plants, vegetation shall be illustrated—in
    another animals, animal life and development.

One stately house shall be the music house,
Others for other arts—learning, the sciences, shall all be here,

None shall be slighted, none but shall here be honor'd,
    help'd, exampled.

6

(This, this and these, America, shall be *your* pyramids and
    obelisks,
Your Alexandrian Pharos, gardens of Babylon,
Your temple at Olympia.)

The male and female many laboring not,
Shall ever here confront the laboring many,
With precious benefits to both, glory to all,
To thee America, and thee eternal Muse.

And here shall ye inhabit powerful Matrons!
In your vast state vaster than all the old,
Echoed through long, long centuries to come,
To sound of different, prouder songs, with stronger themes,
Practical, peaceful life, the people's life, the People them-
    selves,
Lifted, illumin'd, bathed in peace—elate, secure in peace.

7

Away with themes of war! away with war itself!
Hence from my shuddering sight to never more return that
    show of blacken'd, mutilated corpses!
That hell unpent and raid of blood, fit for wild tigers or for
    lop-tongued wolves, not reasoning men,
And in its stead speed industry's campaigns,
With thy undaunted armies, engineering,
Thy pennants labor, loosen'd to the breeze,
Thy bugles sounding loud and clear.

Away with old romance!
Away with novels, plots and plays of foreign courts,
Away with love-verses, sugar'd in rhyme, the intrigues,
    amours of idlers,
Fitted for only banquets of the night where dancers to late
    music slide,
The unhealthy pleasures, extravagant dissipation of the few,

With perfumes, heat and wine, beneath the dazzling chan-
deliers.

To you ye reverent sane sisters,
I raise a voice for far superber themes for poets and for art,
To exalt the present and the real,
To teach the average man the glory of his daily walk and
trade,
To sing in songs how exercise and chemical life are never to
be baffled,
To manual work for each and all, to plough, hoe, dig,
To plant and tend the tree, the berry, vegetables, flowers,
For every man to see to it that he really do something, for
every woman too;
To use the hammer and the saw, (rip, or cross-cut,)
To cultivate a turn for carpentering, plastering, painting,
To work as tailor, tailoress, nurse, hostler, porter,
To invent a little, something ingenious, to aid the washing,
cooking, cleaning,
And hold it no disgrace to take a hand at them themselves.

I say I bring thee Muse to-day and here,
All occupations, duties broad and close,
Toil, healthy toil and sweat, endless, without cessation,
The old, old practical burdens, interests, joys,
The family, parentage, childhood, husband and wife,
The house-comforts, the house itself and all its belongings,
Food and its preservation, chemistry applied to it,
Whatever forms the average, strong, complete, sweet-blooded
man or woman, the perfect longeve personality,
And helps its present life to health and happiness, and shapes
its soul,
For the eternal real life to come.

With latest connections, works, the inter-transportation of
the world,
Steam-power, the great express lines, gas, petroleum,
These triumphs of our time, the Atlantic's delicate cable,
The Pacific railroad, the Suez canal, the Mont Cenis and
Gothard and Hoosac tunnels, the Brooklyn bridge,

This earth all spann'd with iron rails, with lines of steamships
    threading every sea,
Our own rondure, the current globe I bring.

8

And thou America,
Thy offspring towering e'er so high, yet higher Thee above all
    towering,
With Victory on thy left, and at thy right hand Law;
Thou Union holding all, fusing, absorbing, tolerating all,
Thee, ever thee, I sing.

Thou, also thou, a World,
With all thy wide geographies, manifold, different, distant,
Rounded by thee in one—one common orbic language,
One common indivisible destiny for All.

And by the spells which ye vouchsafe to those your ministers
    in earnest,
I here personify and call my themes, to make them pass
    before ye.

Behold, America! (and thou, ineffable guest and sister!)
For thee come trooping up thy waters and thy lands;
Behold! thy fields and farms, thy far-off woods and moun-
    tains,
As in procession coming.

Behold, the sea itself,
And on its limitless, heaving breast, the ships;
See, where their white sails, bellying in the wind, speckle the
    green and blue,
See, the steamers coming and going, steaming in or out of
    port,
See, dusky and undulating, the long pennants of smoke.

Behold, in Oregon, far in the north and west,
Or in Maine, far in the north and east, thy cheerful axemen,
Wielding all day their axes.

Behold, on the lakes, thy pilots at their wheels, thy oarsmen,
How the ash writhes under those muscular arms!

There by the furnace, and there by the anvil,
Behold thy sturdy blacksmiths swinging their sledges,
Overhand so steady, overhand they turn and fall with joyous
    clank,
Like a tumult of laughter.

Mark the spirit of invention everywhere, thy rapid patents,
Thy continual workshops, foundries, risen or rising,
See, from their chimneys how the tall flame-fires stream.

Mark, thy interminable farms, North, South,
Thy wealthy daughter-states, Eastern and Western,
The varied products of Ohio, Pennsylvania, Missouri,
    Georgia, Texas, and the rest,
Thy limitless crops, grass, wheat, sugar, oil, corn, rice, hemp,
    hops,
Thy barns all fill'd, the endless freight-train and the bulging
    storehouse,
The grapes that ripen on thy vines, the apples in thy orchards,
Thy incalculable lumber, beef, pork, potatoes, thy coal, thy
    gold and silver,
The inexhaustible iron in thy mines.

All thine, O sacred Union!
Ships, farms, shops, barns, factories, mines,
City and State, North, South, item and aggregate,
We dedicate, dread Mother, all to thee!

Protectress absolute, thou! bulwark of all!
For well we know that while thou givest each and all, (gener-
    ous as God,)
Without thee neither all nor each, nor land, home,
Nor ship, nor mine, nor any here this day secure,
Nor aught, nor any day secure.

9

And thou, the Emblem waving over all!
Delicate beauty, a word to thee, (it may be salutary,)

Remember thou hast not always been as here to-day so com-
      fortably ensovereign'd,
In other scenes than these have I observ'd thee flag,
Not quite so trim and whole and freshly blooming in folds of
      stainless silk,
But I have seen thee bunting, to tatters torn upon thy splin-
      ter'd staff,
Or clutch'd to some young color-bearer's breast with des-
      perate hands,
Savagely struggled for, for life or death, fought over long,
'Mid cannons' thunder-crash and many a curse and groan
      and yell, and rifle-volleys cracking sharp,
And moving masses as wild demons surging, and lives as
      nothing risk'd,
For thy mere remnant grimed with dirt and smoke and
      sopp'd in blood,
For sake of that, my beauty, and that thou might'st dally as
      now secure up there,
Many a good man have I seen go under.

Now here and these and hence in peace, all thine, O flag!
And here and hence for thee, O universal Muse! and thou for
      them!
And here and hence O Union, all the work and workmen
      thine!
None separate from thee—henceforth One only, we and thou,
(For the blood of the children, what is it, only the blood
      maternal?
And lives and works, what are they all at last, except the
      roads to faith and death?)

While we rehearse our measureless wealth, it is for thee, dear
      Mother,
We own it all and several to-day indissoluble in thee;
Think not our chant, our show, merely for products gross or
      lucre—it is for thee, the soul in thee, electric, spiritual!
Our farms, inventions, crops, we own in thee! cities and
      States in thee!
Our freedom all in thee! our very lives in thee!
1871   1881

Song of the Redwood-Tree

1

A CALIFORNIA song,
A prophecy and indirection, a thought impalpable to breathe
     as air,
A chorus of dryads, fading, departing, or hamadryads de-
     parting,
A murmuring, fateful, giant voice, out of the earth and
     sky,
Voice of a mighty dying tree in the redwood forest dense.

Farewell my brethren,
Farewell O earth and sky, farewell ye neighboring waters,
My time has ended, my term has come.

Along the northern coast,
Just back from the rock-bound shore and the caves,
In the saline air from the sea in the Mendocino country,
With the surge for base and accompaniment low and hoarse,
With crackling blows of axes sounding musically driven by
     strong arms,
Riven deep by the sharp tongues of the axes, there in the red-
     wood forest dense,
I heard the mighty tree its death-chant chanting.

The choppers heard not, the camp shanties echoed not,
The quick-ear'd teamsters and chain and jack-screw men
     heard not,
As the wood-spirits came from their haunts of a thousand
     years to join the refrain,
But in my soul I plainly heard.

Murmuring out of its myriad leaves,
Down from its lofty top rising two hundred feet high,
Out of its stalwart trunk and limbs, out of its foot-thick
     bark,

That chant of the seasons and time, chant not of the past
  only but the future.

You untold life of me,
And all you venerable and innocent joys,
Perennial hardy life of me with joys 'mid rain and many a
  summer sun,
And the white snows and night and the wild winds;
O the great patient rugged joys, my soul's strong joys unreck'd
  by man,
(For know I bear the soul befitting me, I too have conscious-
  ness, identity,
And all the rocks and mountains have, and all the earth,)
Joys of the life befitting me and brothers mine,
Our time, our term has come.

Nor yield we mournfully majestic brothers,
We who have grandly fill'd our time;
With Nature's calm content, with tacit huge delight,
We welcome what we wrought for through the past,
And leave the field for them.
For them predicted long,
For a superber race, they too to grandly fill their time,
For them we abdicate, in them ourselves ye forest kings!
In them these skies and airs, these mountain peaks, Shasta,
  Nevadas,
These huge precipitous cliffs, this amplitude, these valleys, far
  Yosemite,
To be in them absorb'd, assimilated.

Then to a loftier strain,
Still prouder, more ecstatic rose the chant,
As if the heirs, the deities of the West,
Joining with master-tongue bore part.

Not wan from Asia's fetiches,
Nor red from Europe's old dynastic slaughter-house,
(Area of murder-plots of thrones, with scent left yet of wars and
  scaffolds everywhere,)
But come from Nature's long and harmless throes, peacefully
  builded thence,

These virgin lands, lands of the Western shore,
To the new culminating man, to you, the empire new,
You promis'd long, we pledge, we dedicate.

You occult deep volitions,
You average spiritual manhood, purpose of all, pois'd on your-
*   self, giving not taking law,*
You womanhood divine, mistress and source of all, whence life
*   and love and aught that comes from life and love,*
You unseen moral essence of all the vast materials of America,
*   (age upon age working in death the same as life,)*
You that, sometimes known, oftener unknown, really shape
*   and mould the New World, adjusting it to Time and*
*   Space,*
You hidden national will lying in your abysms, conceal'd but
*   ever alert,*
You past and present purposes tenaciously pursued, may-be
*   unconscious of yourselves,*
Unswerv'd by all the passing errors, perturbations of the sur-
*   face;*
You vital, universal, deathless germs, beneath all creeds, arts,
*   statutes, literatures,*
Here build your homes for good, establish here, these areas
*   entire, lands of the Western shore,*
We pledge, we dedicate to you.

For man of you, your characteristic race,
Here may he hardy, sweet, gigantic grow, here tower propor-
*   tionate to Nature,*
Here climb the vast pure spaces unconfined, uncheck'd by wall
*   or roof,*
Here laugh with storm or sun, here joy, here patiently inure,
Here heed himself, unfold himself, (not others' formulas heed,)
*   here fill his time,*
To duly fall, to aid, unreck'd at last,
To disappear, to serve.

Thus on the northern coast,
In the echo of teamsters' calls and the clinking chains, and
    the music of choppers' axes,

The falling trunk and limbs, the crash, the muffled shriek,
    the groan,
Such words combined from the redwood-tree, as of voices
    ecstatic, ancient and rustling,
The century-lasting, unseen dryads, singing, withdrawing,
All their recesses of forests and mountains leaving,
From the Cascade range to the Wasatch, or Idaho far, or
    Utah,
To the deities of the modern henceforth yielding,
The chorus and indications, the vistas of coming humanity,
    the settlements, features all,
In the Mendocino woods I caught.

2

The flashing and golden pageant of California,
The sudden and gorgeous drama, the sunny and ample lands,
The long and varied stretch from Puget sound to Colorado
    south,
Lands bathed in sweeter, rarer, healthier air, valleys and
    mountain cliffs,
The fields of Nature long prepared and fallow, the silent,
    cyclic chemistry,
The slow and steady ages plodding, the unoccupied surface
    ripening, the rich ores forming beneath;
At last the New arriving, assuming, taking possession,
A swarming and busy race settling and organizing every-
    where,
Ships coming in from the whole round world, and going out
    to the whole world,
To India and China and Australia and the thousand island
    paradises of the Pacific,
Populous cities, the latest inventions, the steamers on the
    rivers, the railroads, with many a thrifty farm, with
    machinery,
And wood and wheat and the grape, and diggings of yellow
    gold.

3

But more in you than these, lands of the Western shore,
(These but the means, the implements, the standing-ground,)

I see in you, certain to come, the promise of thousands of
    years, till now deferr'd,
Promis'd to be fulfill'd, our common kind, the race.

The new society at last, proportionate to Nature,
In man of you, more than your mountain peaks or stalwart
    trees imperial,
In woman more, far more, than all your gold or vines, or
    even vital air.

Fresh come, to a new world indeed, yet long prepared,
I see the genius of the modern, child of the real and
    ideal,
Clearing the ground for broad humanity, the true America,
    heir of the past so grand,
To build a grander future.
1874   1881

A Song for Occupations

1

A SONG for occupations!
In the labor of engines and trades and the labor of fields I
    find the developments,
And find the eternal meanings.

Workmen and Workwomen!
Were all educations practical and ornamental well display'd
    out of me, what would it amount to?
Were I as the head teacher, charitable proprietor, wise states-
    man, what would it amount to?
Were I to you as the boss employing and paying you, would
    that satisfy you?

The learn'd, virtuous, benevolent, and the usual terms,
A man like me and never the usual terms.

Neither a servant nor a master I,

I take no sooner a large price than a small price, I will have my own whoever enjoys me,

I will be even with you and you shall be even with me.

If you stand at work in a shop I stand as nigh as the nighest in the same shop,

If you bestow gifts on your brother or dearest friend I demand as good as your brother or dearest friend,

If your lover, husband, wife, is welcome by day or night, I must be personally as welcome,

If you become degraded, criminal, ill, then I become so for your sake,

If you remember your foolish and outlaw'd deeds, do you think I cannot remember my own foolish and outlaw'd deeds?

If you carouse at the table I carouse at the opposite side of the table,

If you meet some stranger in the streets and love him or her, why I often meet strangers in the street and love them.

Why what have you thought of yourself?

Is it you then that thought yourself less?

Is it you that thought the President greater than you?

Or the rich better off than you? or the educated wiser than you?

(Because you are greasy or pimpled, or were once drunk, or a thief,

Or that you are diseas'd, or rheumatic, or a prostitute,

Or from frivolity or impotence, or that you are no scholar and never saw your name in print,

Do you give in that you are any less immortal?)

2

Souls of men and women! it is not you I call unseen, unheard, untouchable and untouching,

It is not you I go argue pro and con about, and to settle whether you are alive or no,

I own publicly who you are, if nobody else owns.

Grown, half-grown and babe, of this country and every
    country, indoors and out-doors, one just as much as the
    other, I see,
And all else behind or through them.

The wife, and she is not one jot less than the husband,
The daughter, and she is just as good as the son,
The mother, and she is every bit as much as the father.

Offspring of ignorant and poor, boys apprenticed to trades,
Young fellows working on farms and old fellows working on
    farms,
Sailor-men, merchant-men, coasters, immigrants,
All these I see, but nigher and farther the same I see,
None shall escape me and none shall wish to escape me.

I bring what you much need yet always have,
Not money, amours, dress, eating, erudition, but as good,
I send no agent or medium, offer no representative of value,
    but offer the value itself.

There is something that comes to one now and perpetually,
It is not what is printed, preach'd, discussed, it eludes dis-
    cussion and print,
It is not to be put in a book, it is not in this book,
It is for you whoever you are, it is no farther from you than
    your hearing and sight are from you,
It is hinted by nearest, commonest, readiest, it is ever pro-
    voked by them.

You may read in many languages, yet read nothing about it,
You may read the President's message and read nothing
    about it there,
Nothing in the reports from the State department or Trea-
    sury department, or in the daily papers or weekly papers,
Or in the census or revenue returns, prices current, or any
    accounts of stock.

3

The sun and stars that float in the open air,
The apple-shaped earth and we upon it, surely the drift of
    them is something grand,

I do not know what it is except that it is grand, and that it is
  happiness,
And that the enclosing purport of us here is not a speculation
  or bon-mot or reconnoissance,
And that it is not something which by luck may turn out well
  for us, and without luck must be a failure for us,
And not something which may yet be retracted in a certain
  contingency.

The light and shade, the curious sense of body and identity,
  the greed that with perfect complaisance devours all
  things,
The endless pride and outstretching of man, unspeakable
  joys and sorrows,
The wonder every one sees in every one else he sees, and the
  wonders that fill each minute of time forever,
What have you reckon'd them for, camerado?
Have you reckon'd them for your trade or farm-work? or for
  the profits of your store?
Or to achieve yourself a position? or to fill a gentleman's
  leisure, or a lady's leisure?

Have you reckon'd that the landscape took substance and
  form that it might be painted in a picture?
Or men and women that they might be written of, and songs
  sung?
Or the attraction of gravity, and the great laws and harmoni-
  ous combinations and the fluids of the air, as subjects
  for the savans?
Or the brown land and the blue sea for maps and charts?
Or the stars to be put in constellations and named fancy
  names?
Or that the growth of seeds is for agricultural tables, or
  agriculture itself?

Old institutions, these arts, libraries, legends, collections, and
  the practice handed along in manufactures, will we rate
  them so high?
Will we rate our cash and business high? I have no objection,
I rate them as high as the highest—then a child born of a
  woman and man I rate beyond all rate.

We thought our Union grand, and our Constitution grand,
I do not say they are not grand and good, for they are,
I am this day just as much in love with them as you,
Then I am in love with You, and with all my fellows upon the
earth.

We consider bibles and religions divine—I do not say they
are not divine,
I say they have all grown out of you, and may grow out of
you still,
It is not they who give the life, it is you who give the life,
Leaves are not more shed from the trees, or trees from the
earth, than they are shed out of you.

4

The sum of all known reverence I add up in you whoever you
are,
The President is there in the White House for you, it is not
you who are here for him,
The Secretaries act in their bureaus for you, not you here for
them,
The Congress convenes every Twelfth-month for you,
Laws, courts, the forming of States, the charters of cities, the
going and coming of commerce and mails, are all for
you.

List close my scholars dear,
Doctrines, politics and civilization exurge from you,
Sculpture and monuments and any thing inscribed anywhere
are tallied in you,
The gist of histories and statistics as far back as the records
reach is in you this hour, and myths and tales the same,
If you were not breathing and walking here, where would
they all be?
The most renown'd poems would be ashes, orations and
plays would be vacuums.

All architecture is what you do to it when you look upon it,
(Did you think it was in the white or gray stone? or the lines
of the arches and cornices?)

All music is what awakes from you when you are reminded
　　by the instruments,
It is not the violins and the cornets, it is not the oboe nor the
　　beating drums, nor the score of the baritone singer sing-
　　ing his sweet romanza, nor that of the men's chorus, nor
　　that of the women's chorus,
It is nearer and farther than they.

5

Will the whole come back then?
Can each see signs of the best by a look in the looking-glass?
　　is there nothing greater or more?
Does all sit there with you, with the mystic unseen soul?

Strange and hard that paradox true I give,
Objects gross and the unseen soul are one.

House-building, measuring, sawing the boards,
Blacksmithing, glass-blowing, nail-making, coopering, tin-
　　roofing, shingle-dressing,
Ship-joining, dock-building, fish-curing, flagging of side-
　　walks by flaggers,
The pump, the pile-driver, the great derrick, the coal-kiln
　　and brick-kiln,
Coal-mines and all that is down there, the lamps in the dark-
　　ness, echoes, songs, what meditations, what vast native
　　thoughts looking through smutch'd faces,
Iron-works, forge-fires in the mountains or by river-banks,
　　men around feeling the melt with huge crowbars, lumps
　　of ore, the due combining of ore, limestone, coal,
The blast-furnace and the puddling-furnace, the loup-lump
　　at the bottom of the melt at last, the rolling-mill, the
　　stumpy bars of pig-iron, the strong, clean-shaped T-rail
　　for railroads,
Oil-works, silk-works, white-lead-works, the sugar-house,
　　steam-saws, the great mills and factories,
Stone-cutting, shapely trimmings for façades or window or
　　door-lintels, the mallet, the tooth-chisel, the jib to pro-
　　tect the thumb,
The calking-iron, the kettle of boiling vault-cement, and the
　　fire under the kettle,

The cotton-bale, the stevedore's hook, the saw and buck of
    the sawyer, the mould of the moulder, the working-knife
    of the butcher, the ice-saw, and all the work with ice,
The work and tools of the rigger, grappler, sail-maker, block-
    maker,
Goods of gutta-percha, papier-maché, colors, brushes, brush-
    making, glazier's implements,
The veneer and glue-pot, the confectioner's ornaments, the
    decanter and glasses, the shears and flat-iron,
The awl and knee-strap, the pint measure and quart measure,
    the counter and stool, the writing-pen of quill or metal,
    the making of all sorts of edged tools,
The brewery, brewing, the malt, the vats, everything that is
    done by brewers, wine-makers, vinegar-makers,
Leather-dressing, coach-making, boiler-making, rope-twist-
    ing, distilling, sign-painting, lime-burning, cotton-pick-
    ing, electroplating, electrotyping, stereotyping,
Stave-machines, planing-machines, reaping-machines,
    ploughing-machines, thrashing-machines, steam wagons,
The cart of the carman, the omnibus, the ponderous dray,
Pyrotechny, letting off color'd fireworks at night, fancy
    figures and jets;
Beef on the butcher's stall, the slaughter-house of the butcher,
    the butcher in his killing-clothes,
The pens of live pork, the killing-hammer, the hog-hook, the
    scalder's tub, gutting, the cutter's cleaver, the packer's
    maul, and the plenteous winterwork of pork-packing,
Flour-works, grinding of wheat, rye, maize, rice, the barrels
    and the half and quarter barrels, the loaded barges, the
    high piles on wharves and levees,
The men and the work of the men on ferries, railroad,
    coasters, fish-boats, canals;
The hourly routine of your own or any man's life, the shop,
    yard, store, or factory,
These shows all near you by day and night—workman! who-
    ever you are, your daily life!
In that and them the heft of the heaviest—in that and them
    far more than you estimated, (and far less also,)
In them realities for you and me, in them poems for you and
    me,

In them, not yourself—you and your soul enclose all things, regardless of estimation,
In them the development good—in them all themes, hints, possibilities.

I do not affirm that what you see beyond is futile, I do not advise you to stop,
I do not say leadings you thought great are not great,
But I say that none lead to greater than these lead to.

6

Will you seek afar off? you surely come back at last,
In things best known to you finding the best, or as good as the best,
In folks nearest to you finding the sweetest, strongest, lovingest,
Happiness, knowledge, not in another place but this place, not for another hour but this hour,
Man in the first you see or touch, always in friend, brother, nighest neighbor—woman in mother, sister, wife,
The popular tastes and employments taking precedence in poems or anywhere,
You workwomen and workmen of these States having your own divine and strong life,
And all else giving place to men and women like you.

When the psalm sings instead of the singer,
When the script preaches instead of the preacher,
When the pulpit descends and goes instead of the carver that carved the supporting desk,
When I can touch the body of books by night or by day, and when they touch my body back again,
When a university course convinces like a slumbering woman and child convince,
When the minted gold in the vault smiles like the night-watchman's daughter,
When warrantee deeds loafe in chairs opposite and are my friendly companions,
I intend to reach them my hand, and make as much of them as I do of men and women like you.

1855   1881

A Song of the Rolling Earth

1

A SONG of the rolling earth, and of words according,
Were you thinking that those were the words, those upright
lines? those curves, angles, dots?
No, those are not the words, the substantial words are in the
ground and sea,
They are in the air, they are in you.

Were you thinking that those were the words, those delicious
sounds out of your friends' mouths?
No, the real words are more delicious than they.

Human bodies are words, myriads of words,
(In the best poems re-appears the body, man's or woman's,
well-shaped, natural, gay,
Every part able, active, receptive, without shame or the need
of shame.)

Air, soil, water, fire—those are words,
I myself am a word with them—my qualities interpenetrate
with theirs—my name is nothing to them,
Though it were told in the three thousand languages, what
would air, soil, water, fire, know of my name?

A healthy presence, a friendly or commanding gesture, are
words, sayings, meanings,
The charms that go with the mere looks of some men and
women, are sayings and meanings also.

The workmanship of souls is by those inaudible words of the
earth,
The masters know the earth's words and use them more than
audible words.

Amelioration is one of the earth's words,
The earth neither lags nor hastens,

It has all attributes, growths, effects, latent in itself from the
     jump,
It is not half beautiful only, defects and excrescences show
     just as much as perfections show.

The earth does not withhold, it is generous enough,
The truths of the earth continually wait, they are not so con-
     ceal'd either,
They are calm, subtle, untransmissible by print,
They are imbued through all things conveying themselves
     willingly,
Conveying a sentiment and invitation, I utter and utter,
I speak not, yet if you hear me not of what avail am I to you?
To bear, to better, lacking these of what avail am I?

(Accouche! accouchez!
Will you rot your own fruit in yourself there?
Will you squat and stifle there?)

The earth does not argue,
Is not pathetic, has no arrangements,
Does not scream, haste, persuade, threaten, promise,
Makes no discriminations, has no conceivable failures,
Closes nothing, refuses nothing, shuts none out,
Of all the powers, objects, states, it notifies, shuts none out.

The earth does not exhibit itself nor refuse to exhibit itself,
     possesses still underneath,
Underneath the ostensible sounds, the august chorus of
     heroes, the wail of slaves,
Persuasions of lovers, curses, gasps of the dying, laughter of
     young people, accents of bargainers,
Underneath these possessing words that never fail.

To her children the words of the eloquent dumb great mother
     never fail,
The true words do not fail, for motion does not fail and re-
     flection does not fail,
Also the day and night do not fail, and the voyage we pursue
     does not fail.

Of the interminable sisters,
Of the ceaseless cotillions of sisters,
Of the centripetal and centrifugal sisters, the elder and
     younger sisters,
The beautiful sister we know dances on with the rest.

With her ample back towards every beholder,
With the fascinations of youth and the equal fascinations of
     age,
Sits she whom I too love like the rest, sits undisturb'd,
Holding up in her hand what has the character of a mirror,
     while her eyes glance back from it,
Glance as she sits, inviting none, denying none,
Holding a mirror day and night tirelessly before her own face.

Seen at hand or seen at a distance,
Duly the twenty-four appear in public every day,
Duly approach and pass with their companions or a com-
     panion,
Looking from no countenances of their own, but from the
     countenances of those who are with them,
From the countenances of children or women or the manly
     countenance,
From the open countenances of animals or from inanimate
     things,
From the landscape or waters or from the exquisite appari-
     tion of the sky,
From our countenances, mine and yours, faithfully returning
     them,
Every day in public appearing without fail, but never twice
     with the same companions.

Embracing man, embracing all, proceed the three hundred
     and sixty-five resistlessly round the sun;
Embracing all, soothing, supporting, follow close three
     hundred and sixty-five offsets of the first, sure and neces-
     sary as they.

Tumbling on steadily, nothing dreading,
Sunshine, storm, cold, heat, forever withstanding, passing,
     carrying,

The soul's realization and determination still inheriting,
The fluid vacuum around and ahead still entering and dividing,
No balk retarding, no anchor anchoring, on no rock striking,
Swift, glad, content, unbereav'd, nothing losing,
Of all able and ready at any time to give strict account,
The divine ship sails the divine sea.

2

Whoever you are! motion and reflection are especially for you,
The divine ship sails the divine sea for you.

Whoever you are! you are he or she for whom the earth is
    solid and liquid,
You are he or she for whom the sun and moon hang in the sky,
For none more than you are the present and the past,
For none more than you is immortality.

Each man to himself and each woman to herself, is the word
    of the past and present, and the true word of immortality;
No one can acquire for another—not one,
Not one can grow for another—not one.

The song is to the singer, and comes back most to him,
The teaching is to the teacher, and comes back most to him,
The murder is to the murderer, and comes back most to him,
The theft is to the thief, and comes back most to him,
The love is to the lover, and comes back most to him,
The gift is to the giver, and comes back most to him—it
    cannot fail,
The oration is to the orator, the acting is to the actor and
    actress not to the audience,
And no man understands any greatness or goodness but his
    own, or the indication of his own.

3

I swear the earth shall surely be complete to him or her who
    shall be complete,
The earth remains jagged and broken only to him or her who
    remains jagged and broken.

I swear there is no greatness or power that does not emulate
those of the earth,
There can be no theory of any account unless it corroborate
the theory of the earth,
No politics, song, religion, behavior, or what not, is of
account, unless it compare with the amplitude of the
earth,
Unless it face the exactness, vitality, impartiality, rectitude of
the earth.

I swear I begin to see love with sweeter spasms than that
which responds love,
It is that which contains itself, which never invites and never
refuses.

I swear I begin to see little or nothing in audible words,
All merges toward the presentation of the unspoken mean-
ings of the earth,
Toward him who sings the songs of the body and of the
truths of the earth,
Toward him who makes the dictionaries of words that print
cannot touch.

I swear I see what is better than to tell the best,
It is always to leave the best untold.

When I undertake to tell the best I find I cannot,
My tongue is ineffectual on its pivots,
My breath will not be obedient to its organs,
I become a dumb man.

The best of the earth cannot be told anyhow, all or any is
best,
It is not what you anticipated, it is cheaper, easier, nearer,
Things are not dismiss'd from the places they held before,
The earth is just as positive and direct as it was before,
Facts, religions, improvements, politics, trades, are as real as
before,
But the soul is also real, it too is positive and direct,
No reasoning, no proof has establish'd it,
Undeniable growth has establish'd it.

4

These to echo the tones of souls and the phrases of souls,
(If they did not echo the phrases of souls what were they
    then?
If they had not reference to you in especial what were they
    then?)

I swear I will never henceforth have to do with the faith that
    tells the best,
I will have to do only with that faith that leaves the best
    untold.

Say on, sayers! sing on, singers!
Delve! mould! pile the words of the earth!
Work on, age after age, nothing is to be lost,
It may have to wait long, but it will certainly come in use,
When the materials are all prepared and ready, the architects
    shall appear.

I swear to you the architects shall appear without fail,
I swear to you they will understand you and justify you,
The greatest among them shall be he who best knows you,
    and encloses all and is faithful to all,
He and the rest shall not forget you, they shall perceive that
    you are not an iota less than they,
You shall be fully glorified in them.
1856   1881

YOUTH, DAY, OLD AGE AND NIGHT

YOUTH, large, lusty, loving—youth full of grace, force,
    fascination,
Do you know that Old Age may come after you with equal
    grace, force, fascination?

Day full-blown and splendid—day of the immense sun,
    action, ambition, laughter,
The Night follows close with millions of suns, and sleep and
    restoring darkness.
1881   1881

Birds of Passage

SONG OF THE UNIVERSAL

1

COME said the Muse,
Sing me a song no poet yet has chanted,
Sing me the universal.

In this broad earth of ours,
Amid the measureless grossness and the slag,
Enclosed and safe within its central heart,
Nestles the seed perfection.

By every life a share or more or less,
None born but it is born, conceal'd or unconceal'd the seed
    is waiting.

2

Lo! keen-eyed towering science,
As from tall peaks the modern overlooking,
Successive absolute fiats issuing.

Yet again, lo! the soul, above all science,
For it has history gather'd like husks around the globe,
For it the entire star-myriads roll through the sky.

In spiral routes by long detours,
(As a much-tacking ship upon the sea,)
For it the partial to the permanent flowing,
For it the real to the ideal tends.

For it the mystic evolution,
Not the right only justified, what we call evil also justified.

Forth from their masks, no matter what,
From the huge festering trunk, from craft and guile and tears,
Health to emerge and joy, joy universal.

Out of the bulk, the morbid and the shallow,
Out of the bad majority, the varied countless frauds of men
    and states,
Electric, antiseptic yet, cleaving, suffusing all,
Only the good is universal.

3

Over the mountain-growths disease and sorrow,
An uncaught bird is ever hovering, hovering,
High in the purer, happier air.

From imperfection's murkiest cloud,
Darts always forth one ray of perfect light,
One flash of heaven's glory.

To fashion's, custom's discord,
To the mad Babel-din, the deafening orgies,
Soothing each lull a strain is heard, just heard,
From some far shore the final chorus sounding.

O the blest eyes, the happy hearts,
That see, that know the guiding thread so fine,
Along the mighty labyrinth.

4

And thou America,
For the scheme's culmination, its thought and its reality,
For these (not for thyself) thou hast arrived.

Thou too surroundest all,
Embracing carrying welcoming all, thou too by pathways
    broad and new,
To the ideal tendest.

The measur'd faiths of other lands, the grandeurs of the past,
Are not for thee, but grandeurs of thine own,
Deific faiths and amplitudes, absorbing, comprehending all,
All eligible to all.

All, all for immortality,
Love like the light silently wrapping all,
Nature's amelioration blessing all,
The blossoms, fruits of ages, orchards divine and certain,
Forms, objects, growths, humanities, to spiritual images
    ripening.

Give me O God to sing that thought,
Give me, give him or her I love this quenchless faith
In Thy ensemble, whatever else withheld withhold not from us,
Belief in plan of Thee enclosed in Time and Space,
Health, peace, salvation universal.

Is it a dream?
Nay but the lack of it the dream,
And failing it life's lore and wealth a dream,
And all the world a dream.
1874   1881

PIONEERS! O PIONEERS!

COME my tan-faced children,
Follow well in order, get your weapons ready,
Have you your pistols? have you your sharp-edged axes?
    Pioneers! O pioneers!

For we cannot tarry here,
We must march my darlings, we must bear the brunt of
    danger,
We the youthful sinewy races, all the rest on us depend,
    Pioneers! O pioneers!

O you youths, Western youths,
So impatient, full of action, full of manly pride and friendship,
Plain I see you Western youths, see you tramping with the
    foremost,
    Pioneers! O pioneers!

Have the elder races halted?
Do they droop and end their lesson, wearied over there be-
    yond the seas?

We take up the task eternal, and the burden and the lesson,
   Pioneers! O pioneers!

All the past we leave behind,
We debouch upon a newer mightier world, varied world,
Fresh and strong the world we seize, world of labor and the
  march,
   Pioneers! O pioneers!

We detachments steady throwing,
Down the edges, through the passes, up the mountains steep,
Conquering, holding, daring, venturing as we go the un-
  known ways,
   Pioneers! O pioneers!

We primeval forests felling,
We the rivers stemming, vexing we and piercing deep the
  mines within,
We the surface broad surveying, we the virgin soil upheaving,
   Pioneers! O pioneers!

Colorado men are we,
From the peaks gigantic, from the great sierras and the high
  plateaus,
From the mine and from the gully, from the hunting trail we
  come,
   Pioneers! O pioneers!

From Nebraska, from Arkansas,
Central inland race are we, from Missouri, with the conti-
  nental blood intervein'd,
All the hands of comrades clasping, all the Southern, all the
  Northern,
   Pioneers! O pioneers!

O resistless restless race!
O beloved race in all! O my breast aches with tender love for
  all!
O I mourn and yet exult, I am rapt with love for all,
   Pioneers! O pioneers!

Raise the mighty mother mistress,
Waving high the delicate mistress, over all the starry mistress,
(bend your heads all,)
Raise the fang'd and warlike mistress, stern, impassive,
weapon'd mistress,
Pioneers! O pioneers!

See my children, resolute children,
By those swarms upon our rear we must never yield or falter,
Ages back in ghostly millions frowning there behind us
urging,
Pioneers! O pioneers!

On and on the compact ranks,
With accessions ever waiting, with the places of the dead
quickly fill'd,
Through the battle, through defeat, moving yet and never
stopping,
Pioneers! O pioneers!

O to die advancing on!
Are there some of us to droop and die? has the hour come?
Then upon the march we fittest die, soon and sure the gap is
fill'd,
Pioneers! O pioneers!

All the pulses of the world,
Falling in they beat for us, with the Western movement beat,
Holding single or together, steady moving to the front, all
for us,
Pioneers! O pioneers!

Life's involv'd and varied pageants,
All the forms and shows, all the workmen at their work,
All the seamen and the landsmen, all the masters with their
slaves,
Pioneers! O pioneers!

All the hapless silent lovers,
All the prisoners in the prisons, all the righteous and the
wicked,

All the joyous, all the sorrowing, all the living, all the dying,
           Pioneers! O pioneers!

          I too with my soul and body,
We, a curious trio, picking, wandering on our way,
Through these shores amid the shadows, with the apparitions
    pressing,
           Pioneers! O pioneers!

          Lo, the darting bowling orb!
Lo, the brother orbs around, all the clustering suns and
    planets,
All the dazzling days, all the mystic nights with dreams,
           Pioneers! O pioneers!

          These are of us, they are with us,
All for primal needed work, while the followers there in em-
    bryo wait behind,
We to-day's procession heading, we the route for travel
    clearing,
           Pioneers! O pioneers!

          O you daughters of the West!
O you young and elder daughters! O you mothers and you
    wives!
Never must you be divided, in our ranks you move united,
           Pioneers! O pioneers!

          Minstrels latent on the prairies!
(Shrouded bards of other lands, you may rest, you have done
    your work,)
Soon I hear you coming warbling, soon you rise and tramp
    amid us,
           Pioneers! O pioneers!

          Not for delectations sweet,
Not the cushion and the slipper, not the peaceful and the
    studious,
Not the riches safe and palling, not for us the tame enjoy-
    ment,
           Pioneers! O pioneers!

Do the feasters gluttonous feast?
Do the corpulent sleepers sleep? have they lock'd and bolted
doors?
Still be ours the diet hard, and the blanket on the ground,
Pioneers! O pioneers!

Has the night descended?
Was the road of late so toilsome? did we stop discouraged
nodding on our way?
Yet a passing hour I yield you in your tracks to pause obli-
vious,
Pioneers! O pioneers!

Till with sound of trumpet,
Far, far off the daybreak call—hark! how loud and clear I
hear it wind,
Swift! to the head of the army!—swift! spring to your places,
Pioneers! O pioneers!

1865   1881

TO YOU

WHOEVER you are, I fear you are walking the walks of dreams,
I fear these supposed realities are to melt from under your
feet and hands,
Even now your features, joys, speech, house, trade, manners,
troubles, follies, costume, crimes, dissipate away from
you,
Your true soul and body appear before me,
They stand forth out of affairs, out of commerce, shops,
work, farms, clothes, the house, buying, selling, eating,
drinking, suffering, dying.

Whoever you are, now I place my hand upon you, that you
be my poem,
I whisper with my lips close to your ear,
I have loved many women and men, but I love none better
than you.

O I have been dilatory and dumb,
I should have made my way straight to you long ago,

I should have blabb'd nothing but you, I should have chanted
    nothing but you.

I will leave all and come and make the hymns of you,
None has understood you, but I understand you,
None has done justice to you, you have not done justice to
    yourself,
None but has found you imperfect, I only find no imperfec-
    tion in you,
None but would subordinate you, I only am he who will
    never consent to subordinate you,
I only am he who places over you no master, owner, better,
    God, beyond what waits intrinsically in yourself.

Painters have painted their swarming groups and the centre-
    figure of all,
From the head of the centre-figure spreading a nimbus of
    gold-color'd light,
But I paint myriads of heads, but paint no head without its
    nimbus of gold-color'd light,
From my hand from the brain of every man and woman it
    streams, effulgently flowing forever.

O I could sing such grandeurs and glories about you!
You have not known what you are, you have slumber'd upon
    yourself all your life,
Your eyelids have been the same as closed most of the time,
What you have done returns already in mockeries,
(Your thrift, knowledge, prayers, if they do not return in
    mockeries, what is their return?)

The mockeries are not you,
Underneath them and within them I see you lurk,
I pursue you where none else has pursued you,
Silence, the desk, the flippant expression, the night, the
    accustom'd routine, if these conceal you from others or
    from yourself, they do not conceal you from me,
The shaved face, the unsteady eye, the impure complexion, if
    these balk others they do not balk me,
The pert apparel, the deform'd attitude, drunkenness, greed,
    premature death, all these I part aside.

There is no endowment in man or woman that is not tallied
    in you,
There is no virtue, no beauty in man or woman, but as good
    is in you,
No pluck, no endurance in others, but as good is in you,
No pleasure waiting for others, but an equal pleasure waits
    for you.

As for me, I give nothing to any one except I give the like
    carefully to you,
I sing the songs of the glory of none, not God, sooner than I
    sing the songs of the glory of you.

Whoever you are! claim your own at any hazard!
These shows of the East and West are tame compared to you,
These immense meadows, these interminable rivers, you are
    immense and interminable as they,
These furies, elements, storms, motions of Nature, throes of
    apparent dissolution, you are he or she who is master or
    mistress over them,
Master or mistress in your own right over Nature, elements,
    pain, passion, dissolution.

The hopples fall from your ankles, you find an unfailing
    sufficiency,
Old or young, male or female, rude, low, rejected by the rest,
    whatever you are promulges itself,
Through birth, life, death, burial, the means are provided,
    nothing is scanted,
Through angers, losses, ambition, ignorance, ennui, what you
    are picks its way.

1856   1881

FRANCE

The 18th Year of these States

A GREAT year and place,
A harsh discordant natal scream out-sounding, to touch the
    mother's heart closer than any yet.

I walk'd the shores of my Eastern sea,
Heard over the waves the little voice,
Saw the divine infant where she woke mournfully wailing,
    amid the roar of cannon, curses, shouts, crush of falling
    buildings,
Was not so sick from the blood in the gutters running, nor
    from the single corpses, nor those in heaps, nor those
    borne away in the tumbrils,
Was not so desperate at the battues of death—was not so
    shock'd at the repeated fusillades of the guns.

Pale, silent, stern, what could I say to that long-accrued re-
    tribution?
Could I wish humanity different?
Could I wish the people made of wood and stone?
Or that there be no justice in destiny or time?

O liberty! O mate for me!
Here too the blaze, the grape-shot and the axe, in reserve, to
    fetch them out in case of need,
Here too, though long represt, can never be destroy'd,
Here too could rise at last murdering and ecstatic,
Here too demanding full arrears of vengeance.

Hence I sign this salute over the sea,
And I do not deny that terrible red birth and baptism,
But remember the little voice that I heard wailing, and wait
    with perfect trust, no matter how long,
And from to-day sad and cogent I maintain the bequeath'd
    cause, as for all lands,
And I send these words to Paris with my love,
And I guess some chansonniers there will understand them,
For I guess there is latent music yet in France, floods of it,
O I hear already the bustle of instruments, they will soon be
    drowning all that would interrupt them,
O I think the east wind brings a triumphal and free march,
It reaches hither, it swells me to joyful madness,
I will run transpose it in words, to justify it,
I will yet sing a song for you ma femme.
1860   1871

MYSELF AND MINE

MYSELF and mine gymnastic ever,
To stand the cold or heat, to make good aim with a gun, to
    sail a boat, to manage horses, to beget superb chil-
    dren,
To speak readily and clearly, to feel at home among common
    people,
And to hold our own in terrible positions on land and sea.

Not for an embroiderer,
(There will always be plenty of embroiderers, I welcome
    them also,)
But for the fibre of things and for inherent men and women.

Not to chisel ornaments,
But to chisel with free stroke the heads and limbs of plen-
    teous supreme Gods, that the States may realize them
    walking and talking.

Let me have my own way,
Let others promulge the laws, I will make no account of the
    laws,
Let others praise eminent men and hold up peace, I hold up
    agitation and conflict,
I praise no eminent man, I rebuke to his face the one that was
    thought most worthy.

(Who are you? and what are you secretly guilty of all your
    life?
Will you turn aside all your life? will you grub and chatter all
    your life?
And who are you, blabbing by rote, years, pages, languages,
    reminiscences,
Unwitting to-day that you do not know how to speak pro-
    perly a single word?)

Let others finish specimens, I never finish specimens,
I start them by exhaustless laws as Nature does, fresh and
    modern continually.

I give nothing as duties,
What others give as duties I give as living impulses,
(Shall I give the heart's action as a duty?)

Let others dispose of questions, I dispose of nothing, I
    arouse unanswerable questions,
Who are they I see and touch, and what about them?
What about these likes of myself that draw me so close by
    tender directions and indirections?

I call to the world to distrust the accounts of my friends, but
    listen to my enemies, as I myself do,
I charge you forever reject those who would expound me, for
    I cannot expound myself,
I charge that there be no theory or school founded out of
    me,
I charge you to leave all free, as I have left all free.

After me, vista!
O I see life is not short, but immeasurably long,
I henceforth tread the world chaste, temperate, an early
    riser, a steady grower,
Every hour the semen of centuries, and still of centuries.

I must follow up these continual lessons of the air, water,
    earth,
I perceive I have no time to lose.
1860   1881

YEAR OF METEORS

(1859–60)

YEAR of meteors! brooding year!
I would bind in words retrospective some of your deeds and
    signs,
I would sing your contest for the 19th Presidentiad,
I would sing how an old man, tall, with white hair, mounted
    the scaffold in Virginia,
(I was at hand, silent I stood with teeth shut close, I
    watch'd,

I stood very near you old man when cool and indifferent, but
    trembling with age and your unheal'd wounds, you
    mounted the scaffold;)
I would sing in my copious song your census returns of the
    States,
The tables of population and products, I would sing of your
    ships and their cargoes,
The proud black ships of Manhattan arriving, some fill'd with
    immigrants, some from the isthmus with cargoes of gold,
Songs thereof would I sing, to all that hitherward comes
    would I welcome give,
And you would I sing, fair stripling! welcome to you from
    me, young prince of England!
(Remember you surging Manhattan's crowds as you pass'd
    with your cortege of nobles?
There in the crowds stood I, and singled you out with
    attachment;)
Nor forget I to sing of the wonder, the ship as she swam up
    my bay,
Well-shaped and stately the Great Eastern swam up my bay,
    she was 600 feet long,
Her moving swiftly surrounded by myriads of small craft I
    forget not to sing;
Nor the comet that came unannounced out of the north
    flaring in heaven,
Nor the strange huge meteor-procession dazzling and clear
    shooting over our heads,
(A moment, a moment long it sail'd its balls of unearthly
    light over our heads,
Then departed, dropt in the night, and was gone;)
Of such, and fitful as they, I sing—with gleams from them
    would I gleam and patch these chants,
Your chants, O year all mottled with evil and good—year of
    forebodings!
Year of comets and meteors transient and strange—lo! even
    here one equally transient and strange!
As I flit through you hastily, soon to fall and be gone, what
    is this chant,
What am I myself but one of your meteors?

(1860?)   1881

WITH ANTECEDENTS

1

WITH antecedents,

With my fathers and mothers and the accumulations of past ages,

With all which, had it not been, I would not now be here, as I am,

With Egypt, India, Phenicia, Greece and Rome,

With the Kelt, the Scandinavian, the Alb and the Saxon,

With antique maritime ventures, laws, artisanship, wars and journeys,

With the poet, the skald, the saga, the myth, and the oracle,

With the sale of slaves, with enthusiasts, with the troubadour, the crusader, and the monk,

With those old continents whence we have come to this new continent,

With the fading kingdoms and kings over there,

With the fading religions and priests,

With the small shores we look back to from our own large and present shores,

With countless years drawing themselves onward and arrived at these years,

You and me arrived—America arrived and making this year,

This year! sending itself ahead countless years to come.

2

O but it is not the years—it is I, it is You,

We touch all laws and tally all antecedents,

We are the skald, the oracle, the monk and the knight, we easily include them and more,

We stand amid time beginningless and endless, we stand amid evil and good,

All swings around us, there is as much darkness as light,

The very sun swings itself and its system of planets around us,

Its sun, and its again, all swing around us.

As for me, (torn, stormy, amid these vehement days,)

I have the idea of all, and am all and believe in all,

I believe materialism is true and spiritualism is true, I reject
no part.

(Have I forgotten any part? any thing in the past?
Come to me whoever and whatever, till I give you recogni-
tion.)

I respect Assyria, China, Teutonia, and the Hebrews,
I adopt each theory, myth, god, and demi-god,
I see that the old accounts, bibles, genealogies, are true,
without exception,
I assert that all past days were what they must have been,
And that they could no-how have been better than they were,
And that to-day is what it must be, and that America is,
And that to-day and America could no-how be better than
they are.

3

In the name of these States and in your and my name, the
Past,
And in the name of these States and in your and my name,
the Present time.

I know that the past was great and the future will be great,
And I know that both curiously conjoint in the present time,
(For the sake of him I typify, for the common average man's
sake, your sake if you are he,)
And that where I am or you are this present day, there is the
centre of all days, all races,
And there is the meaning to us of all that has ever come of
races and days, or ever will come.

1860   1881

A Broadway Pageant

1

OVER the Western sea hither from Niphon come,
Courteous, the swart-cheek'd two-sworded envoys,
Leaning back in their open barouches, bare-headed, impassive,
Ride to-day through Manhattan.

Libertad! I do not know whether others behold what I behold,
In the procession along with the nobles of Niphon, the errand-bearers,
Bringing up the rear, hovering above, around, or in the ranks marching,
But I will sing you a song of what I behold Libertad.

When million-footed Manhattan unpent descends to her pavements,
When the thunder-cracking guns arouse me with the proud roar I love,
When the round-mouth'd guns out of the smoke and smell I love spit their salutes,
When the fire-flashing guns have fully alerted me, and heaven clouds canopy my city with a delicate thin haze,
When gorgeous the countless straight stems, the forests at the wharves, thicken with colors,
When every ship richly drest carries her flag at the peak,
When pennants trail and street-festoons hang from the windows,
When Broadway is entirely given up to foot-passengers and foot-standers, when the mass is densest,
When the façades of the houses are alive with people, when eyes gaze riveted tens of thousands at a time,

224

When the guests from the islands advance, when the pageant
    moves forward visible,
When the summons is made, when the answer that waited
    thousands of years answers,
I too arising, answering, descend to the pavements, merge
    with the crowd, and gaze with them.

2

Superb-faced Manhattan!
Comrade Americanos! to us, then at last the Orient comes.

To us, my city,
Where our tall-topt marble and iron beauties range on
    opposite sides, to walk in the space between,
To-day our Antipodes comes.

The Originatress comes,
The nest of languages, the bequeather of poems, the race of
    eld,
Florid with blood, pensive, rapt with musings, hot with
    passion,
Sultry with perfume, with ample and flowing garments,
With sunburnt visage, with intense soul and glittering eyes,
The race of Brahma comes.

See my cantabile! these and more are flashing to us from the
    procession,
As it moves changing, a kaleidoscope divine it moves chang-
    ing before us.

For not the envoys nor the tann'd Japanee from his island
    only,
Lithe and silent the Hindoo appears, the Asiatic continent
    itself appears, the past, the dead,
The murky night-morning of wonder and fable inscrutable,
The envelop'd mysteries, the old and unknown hive-bees,
The north, the sweltering south, eastern Assyria, the He-
    brews, the ancient of ancients,
Vast desolated cities, the gliding present, all of these and
    more are in the pageant-procession.

Geography, the world, is in it,

The Great Sea, the brood of islands, Polynesia, the coast beyond,

The coast you henceforth are facing—you, Libertad! from your Western golden shores,

The countries there with their populations, the millions en-masse are curiously here,

The swarming market-places, the temples with idols ranged along the sides or at the end, bonze, brahmin, and llama,

Mandarin, farmer, merchant, mechanic, and fisherman,

The singing-girl and the dancing-girl, the ecstatic persons, the secluded emperors,

Confucius himself, the great poets and heroes, the warriors, the castes, all,

Trooping up, crowding from all directions, from the Altay mountains,

From Thibet, from the four winding and far-flowing rivers of China,

From the southern peninsulas and the demi-continental islands, from Malaysia,

These and whatever belongs to them palpable show forth to me, and are seiz'd by me,

And I am seiz'd by them, and friendlily held by them,

Till as here them all I chant, Libertad! for themselves and for you.

For I too raising my voice join the ranks of this pageant,

I am the chanter, I chant aloud over the pageant,

I chant the world on my Western sea,

I chant copious the islands beyond, thick as stars in the sky,

I chant the new empire grander than any before, as in a vision it comes to me,

I chant America the mistress, I chant a greater supremacy,

I chant projected a thousand blooming cities yet in time on those groups of sea-islands,

My sail-ships and steam-ships threading the archipelagoes,

My stars and stripes fluttering in the wind,

Commerce opening, the sleep of ages having done its work, races reborn, refresh'd,

Lives, works resumed—the object I know not—but the old, the Asiatic renew'd as it must be,
Commencing from this day surrounded by the world.

3

And you Libertad of the world!
You shall sit in the middle well-pois'd thousands and thousands of years,
As to-day from one side the nobles of Asia come to you,
As to-morrow from the other side the queen of England sends her eldest son to you.

The sign is reversing, the orb is enclosed,
The ring is circled, the journey is done,
The box-lid is but perceptibly open'd, nevertheless the perfume pours copiously out of the whole box.

Young Libertad! with the venerable Asia, the all-mother,
Be considerate with her now and ever hot Libertad, for you are all,
Bend your proud neck to the long-off mother now sending messages over the archipelagoes to you,
Bend your proud neck low for once, young Libertad.

Were the children straying westward so long? so wide the tramping?
Were the precedent dim ages debouching westward from Paradise so long?
Were the centuries steadily footing it that way, all the while unknown, for you, for reasons?

They are justified, they are accomplish'd, they shall now be turn'd the other way also, to travel toward you thence,
They shall now also march obediently eastward for your sake Libertad.

(1860?)   1881

Sea-Drift

OUT OF THE CRADLE ENDLESSLY ROCKING

OUT of the cradle endlessly rocking,
Out of the mocking-bird's throat, the musical shuttle,
Out of the Ninth-month midnight,
Over the sterile sands and the fields beyond, where the child
    leaving his bed wander'd alone, bareheaded, barefoot,
Down from the shower'd halo,
Up from the mystic play of shadows twining and twisting as
    if they were alive,
Out from the patches of briers and blackberries,
From the memories of the bird that chanted to me,
From your memories sad brother, from the fitful risings and
    fallings I heard,
From under that yellow half-moon late-risen and swollen as
    if with tears,
From those beginning notes of yearning and love there in the
    mist,
From the thousand responses of my heart never to cease,
From the myriad thence-arous'd words,
From the word stronger and more delicious than any,
From such as now they start the scene revisiting,
As a flock, twittering, rising, or overhead passing,
Borne hither, ere all eludes me, hurriedly,
A man, yet by these tears a little boy again,
Throwing myself on the sand, confronting the waves,
I, chanter of pains and joys, uniter of here and hereafter,
Taking all hints to use them, but swiftly leaping beyond them,
A reminiscence sing.

Once Paumanok,
When the lilac-scent was in the air and Fifth-month grass
    was growing,

Up this seashore in some briers,
Two feather'd guests from Alabama, two together,
And their nest, and four light-green eggs spotted with brown,
And every day the he-bird to and fro near at hand,
And every day the she-bird crouch'd on her nest, silent, with
    bright eyes,
And every day I, a curious boy, never too close, never dis-
    turbing them,
Cautiously peering, absorbing, translating.

Shine ! shine ! shine !
Pour down your warmth, great sun !
While we bask, we two together.

Two together !
Winds blow south, or winds blow north,
Day come white, or night come black,
Home, or rivers and mountains from home,
Singing all time, minding no time,
While we two keep together.

Till of a sudden,
May-be kill'd, unknown to her mate,
One forenoon the she-bird crouch'd not on the nest,
Nor return'd that afternoon, nor the next,
Nor ever appear'd again.

And thenceforward all summer in the sound of the sea,
And at night under the full of the moon in calmer weather,
Over the hoarse surging of the sea,
Or flitting from brier to brier by day,
I saw, I heard at intervals the remaining one, the he-bird,
The solitary guest from Alabama.

Blow ! blow ! blow !
Blow up sea-winds along Paumanok's shore;
I wait and I wait till you blow my mate to me.

Yes, when the stars glisten'd,
All night long on the prong of a moss-scallop'd stake,

Down almost amid the slapping waves,
Sat the lone singer wonderful causing tears.

He call'd on his mate,
He pour'd forth the meanings which I of all men know.

Yes my brother I know,
The rest might not, but I have treasur'd every note,
For more than once dimly down to the beach gliding,
Silent, avoiding the moonbeams, blending myself with the
    shadows,
Recalling now the obscure shapes, the echoes, the sounds
    and sights after their sorts,
The white arms out in the breakers tirelessly tossing,
I, with bare feet, a child, the wind wafting my hair,
Listen'd long and long.

Listen'd to keep, to sing, now translating the notes,
Following you my brother.

Soothe! soothe! soothe!
Close on its wave soothes the wave behind,
And again another behind embracing and lapping, every one
    close,
But my love soothes not me, not me.

Low hangs the moon, it rose late,
It is lagging—O I think it is heavy with love, with love.

O madly the sea pushes upon the land,
With love, with love.

O night! do I not see my love fluttering out among the
    breakers?
What is that little black thing I see there in the white?

Loud! loud! loud!
Loud I call to you, my love!
High and clear I shoot my voice over the waves,
Surely you must know who is here, is here,
You must know who I am, my love.

Low-hanging moon !
What is that dusky spot in your brown yellow?
O it is the shape, the shape of my mate !
O moon do not keep her from me any longer.

Land ! land ! O land !
Whichever way I turn, O I think you could give me my mate
  back again if you only would,
For I am almost sure I see her dimly whichever way I look.

O rising stars !
Perhaps the one I want so much will rise, will rise with some of
  you.

O throat ! O trembling throat !
Sound clearer through the atmosphere !
Pierce the woods, the earth,
Somewhere listening to catch you must be the one I want.

Shake out carols !
Solitary here, the night's carols !
Carols of lonesome love ! death's carols !
Carols under that lagging, yellow, waning moon !
O under that moon where she droops almost down into the sea !
O reckless despairing carols.

But soft ! sink low !
Soft ! let me just murmur,
And do you wait a moment you husky-nois'd sea,
For somewhere I believe I heard my mate responding to me,
So faint, I must be still, be still to listen,
But not altogether still, for then she might not come immediately
  to me.

Hither my love !
Here I am ! here !
With this just-sustain'd note I announce myself to you,
This gentle call is for you my love, for you.

Do not be decoy'd elsewhere,
That is the whistle of the wind, it is not my voice,

That is the fluttering, the fluttering of the spray,
Those are the shadows of leaves.

O darkness! O in vain!
O I am very sick and sorrowful.

O brown halo in the sky near the moon, drooping upon the sea!
O troubled reflection in the sea!
O throat! O throbbing heart!
And I singing uselessly, uselessly all the night.

O past! O happy life! O songs of joy!
In the air, in the woods, over fields,
Loved! loved! loved! loved! loved!
But my mate no more, no more with me!
We two together no more.

The aria sinking,
All else continuing, the stars shining,
The winds blowing, the notes of the bird continuous echoing,
With angry moans the fierce old mother incessantly moaning,
On the sands of Paumanok's shore gray and rustling,
The yellow half-moon enlarged, sagging down, drooping, the
      face of the sea almost touching,
The boy ecstatic, with his bare feet the waves, with his hair
      the atmosphere dallying,
The love in the heart long pent, now loose, now at last
      tumultuously bursting,
The aria's meaning, the ears, the soul, swiftly depositing,
The strange tears down the cheeks coursing,
The colloquy there, the trio, each uttering,
The undertone, the savage old mother incessantly crying,
To the boy's soul's questions sullenly timing, some drown'd
      secret hissing,
To the outsetting bard.

Demon or bird! (said the boy's soul,)
Is it indeed toward your mate you sing? or is it really to me?
For I, that was a child, my tongue's use sleeping, now I have
      heard you,
Now in a moment I know what I am for, I awake,

And already a thousand singers, a thousand songs, clearer,
  louder and more sorrowful than yours,
A thousand warbling echoes have started to life within me,
  never to die.

O you singer solitary, singing by yourself, projecting me,
O solitary me listening, never more shall I cease perpetuating
  you,
Never more shall I escape, never more the reverberations,
Never more the cries of unsatisfied love be absent from me,
Never again leave me to be the peaceful child I was before
  what there in the night,
By the sea under the yellow and sagging moon,
The messenger there arous'd, the fire, the sweet hell within,
The unknown want, the destiny of me.

O give me the clew! (it lurks in the night here somewhere,)
O if I am to have so much, let me have more!

A word then, (for I will conquer it,)
The word final, superior to all,
Subtle, sent up—what is it?—I listen;
Are you whispering it, and have been all the time, you sea
  waves?
Is that it from your liquid rims and wet sands?

Whereto answering, the sea,
Delaying not, hurrying not,
Whisper'd me through the night, and very plainly before
  daybreak,
Lisp'd to me the low and delicious word death,
And again death, death, death, death,
Hissing melodious, neither like the bird nor like my arous'd
  child's heart,
But edging near as privately for me rustling at my feet,
Creeping thence steadily up to my ears and laving me softly
  all over,
Death, death, death, death, death.

Which I do not forget,
But fuse the song of my dusky demon and brother,

That he sang to me in the moonlight on Paumanok's gray
      beach,
With the thousand responsive songs at random,
My own songs awaked from that hour,
And with them the key, the word up from the waves,
The word of the sweetest song and all songs,
That strong and delicious word which, creeping to my feet,
(Or like some old crone rocking the cradle, swathed in sweet
      garments, bending aside,)
The sea whisper'd me.
1859   1881

AS I EBB'D WITH THE OCEAN OF LIFE

1

As I ebb'd with the ocean of life,
As I wended the shores I know,
As I walk'd where the ripples continually wash you Paumanok,
Where they rustle up hoarse and sibilant,
Where the fierce old mother endlessly cries for her castaways,
I musing late in the autumn day, gazing off southward,
Held by this electric self out of the pride of which I utter
      poems,
Was seiz'd by the spirit that trails in the lines underfoot,
The rim, the sediment that stands for all the water and all the
      land of the globe.

Fascinated, my eyes reverting from the south, dropt, to
      follow those slender windrows,
Chaff, straw, splinters of wood, weeds, and the sea-gluten,
Scum, scales from shining rocks, leaves of salt-lettuce, left by
      the tide,
Miles walking, the sound of breaking waves the other side of
      me,
Paumanok there and then as I thought the old thought of
      likenesses,
These you presented to me you fish-shaped island,
As I wended the shores I know,
As I walk'd with that electric self seeking types.

2

As I wend to the shores I know not,
As I list to the dirge, the voices of men and women wreck'd,
As I inhale the impalpable breezes that set in upon me,
As the ocean so mysterious rolls toward me closer and closer,
I too but signify at the utmost a little wash'd-up drift,
A few sands and dead leaves to gather,
Gather, and merge myself as part of the sands and drift.

O baffled, balk'd, bent to the very earth,
Oppress'd with myself that I have dared to open my mouth,
Aware now that amid all that blab whose echoes recoil upon
    me I have not once had the least idea who or what I am,
But that before all my arrogant poems the real Me stands yet
    untouch'd, untold, altogether unreach'd,
Withdrawn far, mocking me with mock-congratulatory signs
    and bows,
With peals of distant ironical laughter at every word I have
    written,
Pointing in silence to these songs, and then to the sand be-
    neath.
I perceive I have not really understood any thing, not a
    single object, and that no man ever can,
Nature here in sight of the sea taking advantage of me to dart
    upon me and sting me,
Because I have dared to open my mouth to sing at all.

3

You oceans both, I close with you,
We murmur alike reproachfully rolling sands and drift,
    knowing not why,
These little shreds indeed standing for you and me and all.

You friable shore with trails of debris,
You fish-shaped island, I take what is underfoot,
What is yours is mine my father.

I too Paumanok,
I too have bubbled up, floated the measureless float, and
    been wash'd on your shores,

I too am but a trail of drift and debris,
I too leave little wrecks upon you, you fish-shaped island.

I throw myself upon your breast my father,
I cling to you so that you cannot unloose me,
I hold you so firm till you answer me something.

Kiss me my father,
Touch me with your lips as I touch those I love,
Breathe to me while I hold you close the secret of the murmuring I envy.

4

Ebb, ocean of life, (the flow will return,)
Cease not your moaning you fierce old mother,
Endlessly cry for your castaways, but fear not, deny not me,
Rustle not up so hoarse and angry against my feet as I touch you or gather from you.

I mean tenderly by you and all,
I gather for myself and for this phantom looking down where we lead, and following me and mine.

Me and mine, loose windrows, little corpses,
Froth, snowy white, and bubbles,
(See, from my dead lips the ooze exuding at last,
See, the prismatic colors glistening and rolling,)
Tufts of straw, sands, fragments,
Buoy'd hither from many moods, one contradicting another,
From the storm, the long calm, the darkness, the swell,
Musing, pondering, a breath, a briny tear, a dab of liquid or soil,
Up just as much out of fathomless workings fermented and thrown,
A limp blossom or two, torn, just as much over waves floating, drifted at random,
Just as much for us that sobbing dirge of Nature,
Just as much whence we come that blare of the cloud-trumpets,
We, capricious, brought hither we know not whence, spread out before you,

You up there walking or sitting,
Whoever you are, we too lie in drifts at your feet.
1860   1881

TEARS

TEARS! tears! tears!
In the night, in solitude, tears,
On the white shore dripping, dripping, suck'd in by the sand,
Tears, not a star shining, all dark and desolate,
Moist tears from the eyes of a muffled head;
O who is that ghost? that form in the dark, with tears?
What shapeless lump is that, bent, crouch'd there on the
     sand?
Streaming tears, sobbing tears, throes, choked with wild
     cries;
O storm, embodied, rising, careering with swift steps along
     the beach!
O wild and dismal night storm, with wind—O belching and
     desperate!
O shade so sedate and decorous by day, with calm counten-
     ance and regulated pace,
But away at night as you fly, none looking—O then the un-
     loosen'd ocean,
Of tears! tears! tears!
1867   1871

TO THE MAN-OF-WAR-BIRD

THOU who hast slept all night upon the storm,
Waking renew'd on thy prodigious pinions,
(Burst the wild storm? above it thou ascended'st,
And rested on the sky, thy slave that cradled thee,)
Now a blue point, far, far in heaven floating,
As to the light emerging here on deck I watch thee,
(Myself a speck, a point on the world's floating vast.)
Far, far at sea,
After the night's fierce drifts have strewn the shore with
     wrecks,

With re-appearing day as now so happy and serene,
The rosy and elastic dawn, the flashing sun,
The limpid spread of air cerulean,
Thou also re-appearest.

Thou born to match the gale, (thou art all wings,)
To cope with heaven and earth and sea and hurricane,
Thou ship of air that never furl'st thy sails,
Days, even weeks untired and onward, through spaces,
    realms gyrating,
At dusk that look'st on Senegal, at morn America,
That sport'st amid the lightning-flash and thunder-cloud,
In them, in thy experiences, had'st thou my soul,
What joys! what joys were thine!
1876   1881

ABOARD AT A SHIP'S HELM

ABOARD at a ship's helm,
A young steersman steering with care.

Through fog on a sea-coast dolefully ringing,
An ocean-bell—O a warning bell, rock'd by the waves.

O you give good notice indeed, you bell by the sea-reefs
    ringing,
Ringing, ringing, to warn the ship from its wreck-place.

For as on the alert O steersman, you mind the loud admoni-
    tion,
The bows turn, the freighted ship tacking speeds away under
    her gray sails,
The beautiful and noble ship with all her precious wealth
    speeds away gayly and safe.

But O the ship, the immortal ship! O ship aboard the ship!
Ship of the body, ship of the soul, voyaging, voyaging,
    voyaging.
1867   1871

ON THE BEACH AT NIGHT

On the beach at night,
Stands a child with her father,
Watching the east, the autumn sky.

Up through the darkness,
While ravening clouds, the burial clouds, in black masses
    spreading,
Lower sullen and fast athwart and down the sky,
Amid a transparent clear belt of ether yet left in the east,
Ascends large and calm the lord-star Jupiter,
And nigh at hand, only a very little above,
Swim the delicate sisters the Pleiades.

From the beach the child holding the hand of her father,
Those burial clouds that lower victorious soon to devour all,
Watching, silently weeps.

Weep not, child,
Weep not, my darling,
With these kisses let me remove your tears,
The ravening clouds shall not long be victorious,
They shall not long possess the sky, they devour the stars
    only in apparition,
Jupiter shall emerge, be patient, watch again another night,
    the Pleiades shall emerge,
They are immortal, all those stars both silvery and golden
    shall shine out again,
The great stars and the little ones shall shine out again, they
    endure,
The vast immortal suns and the long-enduring pensive moons
    shall again shine.

Then dearest child mournest thou only for Jupiter?
Considerest thou alone the burial of the stars?
Something there is,
(With my lips soothing thee, adding I whisper,
I give thee the first suggestion, the problem and indirection,)
Something there is more immortal even than the stars,

(Many the burials, many the days and nights, passing away,)
Something that shall endure longer even than lustrous
    Jupiter,
Longer than sun or any revolving satellite,
Or the radiant sisters the Pleiades.
1871   1871

THE WORLD BELOW THE BRINE

THE world below the brine,
Forests at the bottom of the sea, the branches and leaves,
Sea-lettuce, vast lichens, strange flowers and seeds, the thick
    tangle, openings, and pink turf,
Different colors, pale gray and green, purple, white, and gold,
    the play of light through the water,
Dumb swimmers there among the rocks, coral, gluten, grass,
    rushes, and the aliment of the swimmers,
Sluggish existences grazing there suspended, or slowly crawl-
    ing close to the bottom,
The sperm-whale at the surface blowing air and spray, or
    disporting with his flukes,
The leaden-eyed shark, the walrus, the turtle, the hairy sea-
    leopard, and the sting-ray,
Passions there, wars, pursuits, tribes, sight in those ocean-
    depths, breathing that thick-breathing air, as so many
    do,
The change thence to the sight here, and to the subtle air
    breathed by beings like us who walk this sphere,
The change onward from ours to that of beings who walk
    other spheres.
1860   1871

ON THE BEACH AT NIGHT ALONE

ON the beach at night alone,
As the old mother sways her to and fro singing her husky
    song,
As I watch the bright stars shining, I think a thought of the
    clef of the universes and of the future.

A vast similitude interlocks all,

All spheres, grown, ungrown, small, large, suns, moons, planets,

All distances of place however wide,

All distances of time, all inanimate forms,

All souls, all living bodies though they be ever so different, or in different worlds,

All gaseous, watery, vegetable, mineral processes, the fishes, the brutes,

All nations, colors, barbarisms, civilizations, languages,

All identities that have existed or may exist on this globe, or any globe,

All lives and deaths, all of the past, present, future,

This vast similitude spans them, and always has spann'd,

And shall forever span them and compactly hold and enclose them.

·856   1881

SONG FOR ALL SEAS, ALL SHIPS

1

TO-DAY a rude brief recitative,

Of ships sailing the seas, each with its special flag or ship-signal,

Of unnamed heroes in the ships—of waves spreading and spreading far as the eye can reach,

Of dashing spray, and the winds piping and blowing,

And out of these a chant for the sailors of all nations,

Fitful, like a surge.

Of sea-captains young or old, and the mates, and of all intrepid sailors,

Of the few, very choice, taciturn, whom fate can never surprise nor death dismay,

Pick'd sparingly without noise by thee old ocean, chosen by thee,

Thou sea that pickest and cullest the race in time, and unitest nations,

Suckled by thee, old husky nurse, embodying thee,

Indomitable, untamed as thee.

(Ever the heroes on water or on land, by ones or twos
    appearing,
Ever the stock preserv'd and never lost, though rare, enough
    for seed preserv'd.)

2

Flaunt out O sea your separate flags of nations!
Flaunt out visible as ever the various ship-signals!
But do you reserve especially for yourself and for the soul of
    man one flag above all the rest,
A spiritual woven signal for all nations, emblem of man elate
    above death,
Token of all brave captains and all intrepid sailors and mates,
And all that went down doing their duty,
Reminiscent of them, twined from all intrepid captains
    young or old,
A pennant universal, subtly waving all time, o'er all brave
    sailors,
All seas, all ships.
1873   1881

PATROLING BARNEGAT

WILD, wild the storm, and the sea high running,
Steady the roar of the gale, with incessant undertone mutter-
    ing,
Shouts of demoniac laughter fitfully piercing and pealing,
Waves, air, midnight, their savagest trinity lashing,
Out in the shadows there milk-white combs careering,
On beachy slush and sand spirts of snow fierce slanting,
Where through the murk the easterly death-wind breasting,
Through cutting swirl and spray watchful and firm advanc-
    ing,
(That in the distance! is that a wreck? is the red signal
    flaring?)
Slush and sand of the beach tireless till daylight wending,
Steadily, slowly, through hoarse roar never remitting,
Along the midnight edge by those milk-white combs career-
    ing,

A group of dim, weird forms, struggling, the night confronting,
That savage trinity warily watching.
1880   1881

AFTER THE SEA-SHIP

AFTER the sea-ship, after the whistling winds,
After the white-gray sails taut to their spars and ropes,
Below, a myriad myriad waves hastening, lifting up their
    necks,
Tending in ceaseless flow toward the track of the ship,
Waves of the ocean bubbling and gurgling, blithely prying,
Waves, undulating waves, liquid, uneven, emulous waves,
Toward that whirling current, laughing and buoyant, with
    curves,
Where the great vessel sailing and tacking displaced the
    surface,
Larger and smaller waves in the spread of the ocean yearn-
    fully flowing,
The wake of the sea-ship after she passes, flashing and frolic-
    some under the sun,
A motley procession with many a fleck of foam and many
    fragments,
Following the stately and rapid ship, in the wake following.
1874   1881

By the Roadside

A BOSTON BALLAD

(1854)

To get betimes in Boston town I rose this morning early,
Here's a good place at the corner, I must stand and see the
show.

Clear the way there Jonathan!
Way for the President's marshal—way for the government
cannon!
Way for the Federal foot and dragoons, (and the apparitions
copiously tumbling.)

I love to look on the Stars and Stripes, I hope the fifes will
play Yankee Doodle.

How bright shine the cutlasses of the foremost troops!
Every man holds his revolver, marching stiff through Boston
town.

A fog follows, antiques of the same come limping,
Some appear wooden-legged, and some appear bandaged
and bloodless.

Why this is indeed a show—it has called the dead out of the
earth!
The old graveyards of the hills have hurried to see!
Phantoms! phantoms countless by flank and rear!
Cock'd hats of mothy mould—crutches made of mist!
Arms in slings—old men leaning on young men's shoulders.

What troubles you Yankee phantoms? what is all this chat-
tering of bare gums?

244

Does the ague convulse your limbs? do you mistake your
    crutches for firelocks and level them?

If you blind your eyes with tears you will not see the Presi-
    dent's marshal,
If you groan such groans you might balk the government
    cannon.

For shame old maniacs—bring down those toss'd arms, and
    let your white hair be,
Here gape your great-grandsons, their wives gaze at them
    from the windows,
See how well dress'd, see how orderly they conduct them-
    selves.

Worse and worse—can't you stand it? are you retreating?
Is this hour with the living too dead for you?

Retreat then—pell-mell!
To your graves—back—back to the hills old limpers!
I do not think you belong here anyhow.

But there is one thing that belongs here—shall I tell you what
    it is, gentlemen of Boston?

I will whisper it to the Mayor, he shall send a committee to
    England,
They shall get a grant from the Parliament, go with a cart to
    the royal vault,
Dig out King George's coffin, unwrap him quick from the
    grave-clothes, box up his bones for a journey,
Find a swift Yankee clipper—here is freight for you, black-
    bellied clipper,
Up with your anchor—shake out your sails—steer straight
    toward Boston bay.

Now call for the President's marshal again, bring out the
    government cannon,
Fetch home the roarers from Congress, make another pro-
    cession, guard it with foot and dragoons.

This centre-piece for them;
Look, all orderly citizens—look from the windows, women!

The committee open the box, set up the regal ribs, glue those
    that will not stay,
Clap the skull on top of the ribs, and clap a crown on top of
    the skull.

You have got your revenge, old buster—the crown is come to
    its own, and more than its own.

Stick your hands in your pockets, Jonathan—you are a made
    man from this day,
You are mighty cute—and here is one of your bargains.
(1854?)   1871

EUROPE

The 72d and 73d Years of These States

SUDDENLY out of its stale and drowsy lair, the lair of
    slaves,
Like lightning it le'pt forth half startled at itself,
Its feet upon the ashes and the rags, its hand tight to the
    throats of kings.

O hope and faith!
O aching close of exiled patriots' lives!
O many a sicken'd heart!
Turn back unto this day and make yourselves afresh.

And you, paid to defile the People—you liars, mark!
Not for numberless agonies, murders, lusts,
For court thieving in its manifold mean forms, worming
    from his simplicity the poor man's wages,
For many a promise sworn by royal lips and broken and
    laugh'd at in the breaking,
Then in their power not for all these did the blows strike
    revenge, or the heads of the nobles fall;
The People scorn'd the ferocity of kings.

But the sweetness of mercy brew'd bitter destruction, and the
    frighten'd monarchs come back,
Each comes in state with his train, hangman, priest, tax-
    gatherer,
Soldier, lawyer, lord, jailer, and sycophant.

Yet behind all lowering stealing, lo, a shape,
Vague as the night, draped interminably, head, front and
    form, in scarlet folds,
Whose face and eyes none may see,
Out of its robes only this, the red robes lifted by the arm,
One finger crook'd pointed high over the top, like the head of
    a snake appears.

Meanwhile corpses lie in new-made graves, bloody corpses of
    young men,
The rope of the gibbet hangs heavily, the bullets of princes
    are flying, the creatures of power laugh aloud,
And all these things bear fruits, and they are good.

Those corpses of young men,
Those martyrs that hang from the gibbets, those hearts
    pierc'd by the gray lead,
Cold and motionless as they seem live elsewhere with un-
    slaughter'd vitality.

They live in other young men O kings!
They live in brothers again ready to defy you,
They were purified by death, they were taught and exalted.

Not a grave of the murder'd for freedom but grows seed for
    freedom, in its turn to bear seed,
Which the winds carry afar and re-sow, and the rains and the
    snows nourish.

Not a disembodied spirit can the weapons of tyrants let loose,
But it stalks invisibly over the earth, whispering, counseling,
    cautioning.

Liberty, let others despair of you—I never despair of you.

Is the house shut? is the master away?
Nevertheless, be ready, be not weary of watching,
He will soon return, his messengers come anon.
1850   1860

A HAND-MIRROR

HOLD it up sternly—see this it sends back, (who is it? is it
    you?)
Outside fair costume, within ashes and filth,
No more a flashing eye, no more a sonorous voice or springy
    step,
Now some slave's eye, voice, hands, step,
A drunkard's breath, unwholesome eater's face, venerealee's
    flesh,
Lungs rotting away piecemeal, stomach sour and cankerous,
Joints rheumatic, bowels clogged with abomination,
Blood circulating dark and poisonous streams,
Words babble, hearing and touch callous,
No brain, no heart left, no magnetism of sex;
Such from one look in this looking-glass ere you go hence,
Such a result so soon—and from such a beginning!
1860   1860

GODS

LOVER divine and perfect Comrade,
Waiting content, invisible yet, but certain,
Be thou my God.

Thou, thou, the Ideal Man,
Fair, able, beautiful, content, and loving,
Complete in body and dilate in spirit,
Be thou my God.

O Death, (for Life has served its turn,)
Opener and usher to the heavenly mansion,
Be thou my God.

Aught, aught of mightiest, best I see, conceive, or know,
(To break the stagnant tie—thee, thee to free, O soul,)
Be thou my God.

All great ideas, the races' aspirations,
All heroisms, deeds of rapt enthusiasts,
Be ye my Gods.

Or Time and Space,
Or shape of Earth divine and wondrous,
Or some fair shape I viewing, worship,
Or lustrous orb of sun or star by night,
Be ye my Gods.

1870   1881

GERMS

Forms, qualities, lives, humanity, language, thoughts,
The ones known, and the ones unknown, the ones on the stars,
The stars themselves, some shaped, others unshaped,
Wonders as of those countries, the soil, trees, cities, inhabi-
    tants, whatever they may be,
Splendid suns, the moons and rings, the countless combina-
    tions and effects,
Such-like, and as good as such-like, visible here or anywhere,
    stand provided for in a handful of space, which I extend
    my arm and half enclose with my hand,
That containing the start of each and all, the virtue, the
    germs of all.

1860   1871

THOUGHTS

Of ownership—as if one fit to own things could not at
    pleasure enter upon all, and incorporate them into him-
    self or herself;
Of vista—suppose some sight in arriere through the forma-
    tive chaos, presuming the growth, fulness, life, now
    attain'd on the journey,
(But I see the road continued, and the journey ever con-
    tinued;)
Of what was once lacking on earth, and in due time has be-
    come supplied—and of what will yet be supplied,
Because all I see and know I believe to have its main purport
    in what will yet be supplied.

1860   1881

WHEN I HEARD THE LEARN'D ASTRONOMER

WHEN I heard the learn'd astronomer,
When the proofs, the figures, were ranged in columns before
    me,
When I was shown the charts and diagrams, to add, divide,
    and measure them,
When I sitting heard the astronomer where he lectured with
    much applause in the lecture-room,
How soon unaccountable I became tired and sick,
Till rising and gliding out I wander'd off by myself,
In the mystical moist night-air, and from time to time,
Look'd up in perfect silence at the stars.
1865   1867

PERFECTIONS

ONLY themselves understand themselves and the like of
    themselves,
As souls only understand souls.
1860   1860

O ME! O LIFE!

O ME! O life! of the questions of these recurring,
Of the endless trains of the faithless, of cities fill'd with the
    foolish,
Of myself forever reproaching myself, (for who more foolish
    than I, and who more faithless?)
Of eyes that vainly crave the light, of the objects mean, of the
    struggle ever renew'd,
Of the poor results of all, of the plodding and sordid crowds
    I see around me,
Of the empty and useless years of the rest, with the rest me
    intertwined,
The question, O me! so sad, recurring—What good amid
    these, O me, O life?

Answer

That you are here—that life exists and identity,
That the powerful play goes on, and you may contribute a
    verse.
1865-6   1867

TO A PRESIDENT

ALL you are doing and saying is to America dangled mirages,
You have not learn'd of Nature—of the politics of Nature
    you have not learn'd the great amplitude, rectitude,
    impartiality,
You have not seen that only such as they are for these States,
And that what is less than they must sooner or later lift off
    from these States.
1860   1860

I SIT AND LOOK OUT

I SIT and look out upon all the sorrows of the world, and
    upon all oppression and shame,
I hear secret convulsive sobs from young men at anguish
    with themselves, remorseful after deeds done,
I see in low life the mother misused by her children, dying,
    neglected, gaunt, desperate,
I see the wife misused by her husband, I see the treacherous
    seducer of young women,
I mark the ranklings of jealousy and unrequited love at-
    tempted to be hid, I see these sights on the earth,
I see the workings of battle, pestilence, tyranny, I see martyrs
    and prisoners,
I observe a famine at sea, I observe the sailors casting lots
    who shall be kill'd to preserve the lives of the rest,
I observe the slights and degradations cast by arrogant per-
    sons upon laborers, the poor, and upon negroes, and the
    like;
All these—all the meanness and agony without end I sitting
    look out upon,
See, hear, and am silent.
1860   1860

TO RICH GIVERS

WHAT you give me I cheerfully accept,
A little sustenance, a hut and garden, a little money, as I
    rendezvous with my poems,

A traveler's lodging and breakfast as I journey through the
　　States,—why should I be ashamed to own such gifts?
　　why to advertise for them?
For I myself am not one who bestows nothing upon man and
　　woman,
For I bestow upon any man or woman the entrance to all the
　　gifts of the universe.
1860　　　　　　　　　　　　　　　　　　　　　　　1867

THE DALLIANCE OF THE EAGLES

SKIRTING the river road, (my forenoon walk, my rest,)
Skyward in air a sudden muffled sound, the dalliance of the
　　eagles,
The rushing amorous contact high in space together,
The clinching interlocking claws, a living, fierce, gyrating
　　wheel,
Four beating wings, two beaks, a swirling mass tight grappling,
In tumbling turning clustering loops, straight downward
　　falling,
Till o'er the river pois'd, the twain yet one, a moment's lull,
A motionless still balance in the air, then parting, talons
　　loosing,
Upward again on slow-firm pinions slanting, their separate
　　diverse flight,
She hers, he his, pursuing.
1880　　　　　　　　　　　　　　　　　　　　　　　1881

ROAMING IN THOUGHT

(*After reading* HEGEL)

ROAMING in thought over the Universe, I saw the little that is
　　Good steadily hastening towards immortality,
And the vast all that is call'd Evil I saw hastening to merge
　　itself and become lost and dead.
1881　　　　　　　　　　　　　　　　　　　　　　　1881

A FARM PICTURE

THROUGH the ample open door of the peaceful country barn,
A sunlit pasture field with cattle and horses feeding,
And haze and vista, and the far horizon fading away.
1865　　　　　　　　　　　　　　　　　　　　　　　1871

A CHILD'S AMAZE

SILENT and amazed even when a little boy,
I remember I heard the preacher every Sunday put God in
    his statements,
As contending against some being or influence.
1865   1867

THE RUNNER

ON a flat road runs the well-train'd runner,
He is lean and sinewy with muscular legs,
He is thinly clothed, he leans forward as he runs,
With lightly closed fists and arms partially rais'd.
1867   1867

BEAUTIFUL WOMEN

WOMEN sit or move to and fro, some old, some young,
The young are beautiful—but the old are more beautiful than
    the young.
1860   1860

MOTHER AND BABE

I SEE the sleeping babe nestling the breast of its mother,
The sleeping mother and babe—hush'd, I study them long
    and long.
1865   1867

THOUGHT

OF obedience, faith, adhesiveness;
As I stand aloof and look there is to me something profoundly
    affecting in large masses of men following the lead of
    those who do not believe in men.
1860   1860

VISOR'D

A MASK, a perpetual natural disguiser of herself,
Concealing her face, concealing her form,
Changes and transformations every hour, every moment,
Falling upon her even when she sleeps.
1860   1867

THOUGHT

OF Justice—as if Justice could be any thing but the same
　　ample law, expounded by natural judges and saviors,
As if it might be this thing or that thing, according to decisions.
1860　　　　　　　　　　　　　　　　　　　　　　　　　1860

GLIDING O'ER ALL

GLIDING o'er all, through all,
Through Nature, Time, and Space,
As a ship on the waters advancing,
The voyage of the soul—not life alone,
Death, many deaths I'll sing.

1871　　　　　　　　　　　　　　　　　　　　　　　　　1871

HAST NEVER COME TO THEE AN HOUR

HAST never come to thee an hour,
A sudden gleam divine, precipitating, bursting all these
　　bubbles, fashions, wealth?
These eager business aims—books, politics, art, amours,
To utter nothingness?
1881　　　　　　　　　　　　　　　　　　　　　　　　　1881

THOUGHT

OF Equality—as if it harm'd me, giving others the same
　　chances and rights as myself—as if it were not indis-
　　pensable to my own rights that others possess the same.
1860　　　　　　　　　　　　　　　　　　　　　　　　　1860

TO OLD AGE

I SEE in you the estuary that enlarges and spreads itself
　　grandly as it pours in the great sea.
1860　　　　　　　　　　　　　　　　　　　　　　　　　1860

LOCATIONS AND TIMES

LOCATIONS and times—what is it in me that meets them all,
　　whenever and wherever, and makes me at home?
Forms, colors, densities, odors—what is it in me that cor-
　　responds with them?
1860　　　　　　　　　　　　　　　　　　　　　　　　　1871

OFFERINGS

A THOUSAND perfect men and women appear,
Around each gathers a cluster of friends, and gay children
    and youths, with offerings.
1860   1871

TO THE STATES

To Identify the 16th, 17th, or 18th Presidentiad

WHY reclining, interrogating? why myself and all drowsing?
What deepening twilight—scum floating atop of the waters,
Who are they as bats and night-dogs askant in the capitol?
What a filthy Presidentiad! (O South, your torrid suns! O
    North, your arctic freezings!)
Are those really Congressmen? are those the great Judges? is
    that the President?
Then I will sleep awhile yet, for I see that these States sleep,
    for reasons;
(With gathering murk, with muttering thunder and lambent
    shoots we all duly awake,
South, North, East, West, inland and seaboard, we will surely
    awake.)
1860   1860

Drum-Taps

FIRST O SONGS FOR A PRELUDE

FIRST O songs for a prelude,
Lightly strike on the stretch'd tympanum pride and joy in
   my city,
How she led the rest to arms, how she gave the cue,
How at once with lithe limbs unwaiting a moment she sprang,
(O superb! O Manhattan, my own, my peerless!
O strongest you in the hour of danger, in crisis! O truer than
   steel!)
How you sprang—how you threw off the costumes of peace
   with indifferent hand,
How your soft opera-music changed, and the drum and fife
   were heard in their stead,
How you led to the war, (that shall serve for our prelude,
   songs of soldiers,)
How Manhattan drum-taps led.

Forty years had I in my city seen soldiers parading,
Forty years as a pageant, till unawares the lady of this teem-
   ing and turbulent city,
Sleepless amid her ships, her houses, her incalculable wealth,
With her million children around her, suddenly,
At dead of night, at news from the south,
Incens'd struck with clinch'd hand the pavement.

A shock electric, the night sustain'd it,
Till with ominous hum our hive at daybreak pour'd out its
   myriads.

From the houses then and the workshops, and through all
   the doorways,
Leapt they tumultuous, and lo! Manhattan arming.

To the drum-taps prompt,
The young men falling in and arming,
The mechanics arming, (the trowel, the jack-plane, the black-
smith's hammer, tost aside with precipitation,)
The lawyer leaving his office and arming, the judge leaving
the court,
The driver deserting his wagon in the street, jumping down,
throwing the reins abruptly down on the horses' backs,
The salesman leaving the store, the boss, book-keeper, por-
ter, all leaving;
Squads gather everywhere by common consent and arm,
The new recruits, even boys, the old men show them how to
wear their accoutrements, they buckle the straps care-
fully,
Outdoors, arming, indoors arming, the flash of the musket-
barrels,
The white tents cluster in camps, the arm'd sentries around,
the sunrise cannon and again at sunset,
Arm'd regiments arrive every day, pass through the city, and
embark from the wharves,
(How good they look as they tramp down to the river, sweaty,
with their guns on their shoulders!
How I love them! how I could hug them, with their brown
faces and their clothes and knapsacks cover'd with
dust!)
The blood of the city up—arm'd! arm'd! the cry everywhere,
The flags flung out from the steeples of churches and from all
the public buildings and stores,
The tearful parting, the mother kisses her son, the son kisses
his mother,
(Loth is the mother to part, yet not a word does she speak to
detain him,)
The tumultuous escort, the ranks of policemen preceding,
clearing the way,
The unpent enthusiasm, the wild cheers of the crowd for
their favorites,
The artillery, the silent cannons bright as gold, drawn along,
rumble lightly over the stones,
(Silent cannons, soon to cease your silence,
Soon unlimber'd to begin the red business;)

All the mutter of preparation, all the determin'd arming,
The hospital service, the lint, bandages and medicines,
The women volunteering for nurses, the work begun for in
    earnest, no mere parade now;
War! an arm'd race is advancing! the welcome for battle, no
    turning away;
War! be it weeks, months, or years, an arm'd race is advanc-
    ing to welcome it.

Mannahatta a-march—and it's O to sing it well!
It's O for a manly life in the camp.

And the sturdy artillery,
The guns bright as gold, the work for giants, to serve well the
    guns,
Unlimber them! (no more as the past forty years for salute or
    courtesies merely,
Put in something now besides powder and wadding.)

And you lady of ships, you Mannahatta,
Old matron of this proud, friendly, turbulent city,
Often in peace and wealth you were pensive or covertly
    frown'd amid all your children,
But now you smile with joy exulting old Mannahatta.
1865   1867

EIGHTEEN SIXTY-ONE

ARM'D year—year of the struggle,
No dainty rhymes or sentimental love verses for you terrible
    year,
Not you as some pale poetling seated at a desk lisping
    cadenzas piano,
But as a strong man erect, clothed in blue clothes, advancing,
    carrying a rifle on your shoulder,
With well-gristled body and sunburnt face and hands, with a
    knife in the belt at your side,
As I heard you shouting loud, your sonorous voice ringing
    across the continent,
Your masculine voice O year, as rising amid the great cities,

Amid the men of Manhattan I saw you as one of the work-
    men, the dwellers in Manhattan,
Or with large steps crossing the prairies out of Illinois and
    Indiana,
Rapidly crossing the West with springy gait and descending
    the Alleghanies,
Or down from the great lakes or in Pennsylvania, or on deck
    along the Ohio river,
Or southward along the Tennessee or Cumberland rivers, or
    at Chattanooga on the mountain top,
Saw I your gait and saw I your sinewy limbs clothed in blue,
    bearing weapons, robust year,
Heard your determin'd voice launch'd forth again and again,
Year that suddenly sang by the mouths of the round-lipp'd
    cannon,
I repeat you, hurrying, crashing, sad, distracted year.
(1861?)   1867

BEAT! BEAT! DRUMS!

BEAT! beat! drums!—blow! bugles! blow!
Through the windows—through doors—burst like a ruthless
    force,
Into the solemn church, and scatter the congregation,
Into the school where the scholar is studying;
Leave not the bridegroom quiet—no happiness must he have
    now with his bride,
Nor the peaceful farmer any peace, ploughing his field or
    gathering his grain,
So fierce you whirr and pound you drums—so shrill you
    bugles blow.

Beat! beat! drums!—blow! bugles! blow!
Over the traffic of cities—over the rumble of wheels in the
    streets;
Are beds prepared for sleepers at night in the houses? no
    sleepers must sleep in those beds,
No bargainers' bargains by day—no brokers or speculators
    —would they continue?
Would the talkers be talking? would the singer attempt to
    sing?

Would the lawyer rise in the court to state his case before the
    judge?
Then rattle quicker, heavier drums—you bugles wilder blow.

Beat! beat! drums!—blow! bugles! blow!
Make no parley—stop for no expostulation,
Mind not the timid—mind not the weeper or prayer,
Mind not the old man beseeching the young man,
Let not the child's voice be heard, nor the mother's entreaties,
Make even the trestles to shake the dead where they lie
    awaiting the hearses,
So strong you thump O terrible drums—so loud you bugles
    blow.
1861   1867

FROM PAUMANOK STARTING I FLY LIKE A BIRD

FROM Paumanok starting I fly like a bird,
Around and around to soar to sing the idea of all,
To the north betaking myself to sing there arctic songs,
To Kanada till I absorb Kanada in myself, to Michigan then,
To Wisconsin, Iowa, Minnesota, to sing their songs, (they
    are inimitable;)
Then to Ohio and Indiana to sing theirs, to Missouri and
    Kansas and Arkansas to sing theirs,
To Tennessee and Kentucky, to the Carolinas and Georgia
    to sing theirs,
To Texas and so along up toward California, to roam
    accepted everywhere;
To sing first, (to the tap of the war-drum if need be,)
The idea of all, of the Western world one and inseparable,
And then the song of each member of these States.
1865   1867

SONG OF THE BANNER AT DAYBREAK

Poet

O A new song, a free song,
Flapping, flapping, flapping, flapping, by sounds, by voices
    clearer,

By the wind's voice and that of the drum,
By the banner's voice and child's voice and sea's voice and
    father's voice,
Low on the ground and high in the air,
On the ground where father and child stand,
In the upward air where their eyes turn,
Where the banner at daybreak is flapping.

Words! book-words! what are you?
Words no more, for hearken and see,
My song is there in the open air, and I must sing,
With the banner and pennant a-flapping.

I'll weave the chord and twine in,
Man's desire and babe's desire, I'll twine them in, I'll put in
    life,
I'll put the bayonet's flashing point, I'll let bullets and slugs
    whizz,
(As one carrying a symbol and menace far into the
    future,
Crying with trumpet voice, *Arouse and beware! Beware and
    arouse!*)
I'll pour the verse with streams of blood, full of volition, full
    of joy,
Then loosen, launch forth, to go and compete,
With the banner and pennant a-flapping.

Pennant

Come up here, bard, bard,
Come up here, soul, soul,
Come up here, dear little child,
To fly in the clouds and winds with me, and play with the
    measureless light.

Child

Father what is that in the sky beckoning to me with long
    finger?
And what does it say to me all the while?

Father

Nothing my babe you see in the sky,
And nothing at all to you it says—but look you my babe,
Look at these dazzling things in the houses, and see you the
    money-shops opening,
And see you the vehicles preparing to crawl along the streets
    with goods;
These, ah these, how valued and toil'd for these!
How envied by all the earth!

Poet

Fresh and rosy red the sun is mounting high,
On floats the sea in distant blue careering through its
    channels,
On floats the wind over the breast of the sea setting in toward
    land,
The great steady wind from west or west-by-south,
Floating so buoyant with milk-white foam on the waters.

But I am not the sea nor the red sun,
I am not the wind with girlish laughter,
Not the immense wind which strengthens, not the wind
    which lashes,
Not the spirit that ever lashes its own body to terror and
    death,
But I am that which unseen comes and sings, sings, sings,
Which babbles in brooks and scoots in showers on the land,
Which the birds know in the woods mornings and evenings,
And the shore-sands know and the hissing wave, and that
    banner and pennant,
Aloft there flapping and flapping.

Child

O father it is alive—it is full of people—it has children,
O now it seems to me it is talking to its children,
I hear it—it talks to me—O it is wonderful!
O it stretches—it spreads and runs so fast—O my father,
It is so broad it covers the whole sky.

Father

Cease, cease, my foolish babe,
What you are saying is sorrowful to me, much it displeases
    me;
Behold with the rest again I say, behold not banners and
    pennants aloft,
But the well-prepared pavements behold, and mark the solid-
    wall'd houses.

Banner and Pennant

Speak to the child O bard out of Manhattan,
To our children all, or north or south of Manhattan,
Point this day, leaving all the rest, to us over all—and yet we
    know not why,
For what are we, mere strips of cloth profiting nothing,
Only flapping in the wind?

Poet

I hear and see not strips of cloth alone,
I hear the tramp of armies, I hear the challenging sentry,
I hear the jubilant shouts of millions of men, I hear Liberty!
I hear the drums beat and the trumpets blowing,
I myself move abroad swift-rising flying then,
I use the wings of the land-bird and use the wings of the sea-
    bird, and look down as from a height,
I do not deny the precious results of peace, I see populous
    cities with wealth incalculable,
I see numberless farms, I see the farmers working in their
    fields or barns,
I see mechanics working, I see buildings everywhere founded,
    going up, or finish'd,
I see trains of cars swiftly speeding along railroad tracks
    drawn by the locomotives,
I see the stores, depots, of Boston, Baltimore, Charleston,
    New Orleans,
I see far in the West the immense area of grain, I dwell awhile
    hovering,

I pass to the lumber forests of the North, and again to the
  Southern plantation, and again to California;
Sweeping the whole I see the countless profit, the busy
  gatherings, earn'd wages,
See the Identity formed out of thirty-eight spacious and
  haughty States, (and many more to come,)
See forts on the shores of harbors, see ships sailing in and
  out;
Then over all, (aye! aye!) my little and lengthen'd pennant
  shaped like a sword,
Runs swiftly up indicating war and defiance—and now the
  halyards have rais'd it,
Side of my banner broad and blue, side of my starry ban-
  ner,
Discarding peace over all the sea and land.

Banner and Pennant

Yet louder, higher, stronger, bard! yet farther, wider cleave!
No longer let our children deem us riches and peace alone,
We may be terror and carnage, and are so now,
Not now are we any one of these spacious and haughty
  States, (nor any five, nor ten,)
Nor market nor depot we, nor money-bank in the city,
But these and all, and the brown and spreading land, and the
  mines below, are ours,
And the shores of the sea are ours, and the rivers great and
  small,
And the fields they moisten, and the crops and the fruits are
  ours,
Bays and channels and ships sailing in and out are ours—
  while we over all,
Over the area spread below, the three or four millions of
  square miles, the capitals,
The forty millions of people,—O bard! in life and death
  supreme,
We, even we, henceforth flaunt out masterful, high up above,
Not for the present alone, for a thousand years chanting
  through you,
This song to the soul of one poor little child.

Child

O my father I like not the houses,
They will never to me be anything, nor do I like money,
But to mount up there I would like, O father dear, that
banner I like,
That pennant I would be and must be.

Father

Child of mine you fill me with anguish,
To be that pennant would be too fearful,
Little you know what it is this day, and after this day, forever,
It is to gain nothing, but risk and defy everything,
Forward to stand in front of wars—and O, such wars!—
what have you to do with them?
With passions of demons, slaughter, premature death?

Banner

Demons and death then I sing,
Put in all, aye all will I, sword-shaped pennant for war,
And a pleasure new and ecstatic, and the prattled yearning of
children,
Blent with the sounds of the peaceful land and the liquid
wash of the sea,
And the black ships fighting on the sea envelop'd in smoke,
And the icy cool of the far, far north, with rustling cedars
and pines,
And the whirr of drums and the sound of soldiers marching,
and the hot sun shining south,
And the beach-waves combing over the beach on my Eastern
shore, and my Western shore the same,
And all between those shores, and my ever running Missis-
sippi with bends and chutes,
And my Illinois fields, and my Kansas fields, and my fields of
Missouri,
The Continent, devoting the whole identity without reserving
an atom,
Pour in! whelm that which asks, which sings, with all and the
yield of all,

Fusing and holding, claiming, devouring the whole,
No more with tender lip, nor musical labial sound,
But out of the night emerging for good, our voice persuasive
    no more,
Croaking like crows here in the wind.

Poet

My limbs, my veins dilate, my theme is clear at last,
Banner so broad advancing out of the night, I sing you
    haughty and resolute,
I burst through where I waited long, too long, deafen'd and
    blinded,
My hearing and tongue are come to me, (a little child taught
    me,)
I hear from above O pennant of war your ironical call and
    demand,
Insensate! insensate (yet I at any rate chant you,) O banner!
Not houses of peace indeed are you, nor any nor all their
    prosperity, (if need be, you shall again have every one of
    those houses to destroy them,
You thought not to destroy those valuable houses, standing
    fast, full of comfort, built with money,
May they stand fast, then? not an hour except you above
    them and all stand fast;)
O banner, not money so precious are you, not farm produce
    you, nor the material good nutriment,
Nor excellent stores, nor landed on wharves from the
    ships,
Not the superb ships with sail-power or steam-power, fetch-
    ing and carrying cargoes,
Nor machinery, vehicles, trade, nor revenues—but you as
    henceforth I see you,
Running up out of the night, bringing your cluster of stars,
    (ever-enlarging stars,)
Divider of daybreak you, cutting the air, touch'd by the sun,
    measuring the sky,
(Passionately seen and yearn'd for by one poor little child,
While others remain busy or smartly talking, forever teach-
    ing thrift, thrift;)

O you up there! O pennant! where you undulate like a snake
  hissing so curious,

Out of reach, an idea only, yet furiously fought for, risking
  bloody death, loved by me,

So loved—O you banner leading the day with stars brought
  from the night!

Valueless, object of eyes, over all and demanding all—(ab-
  solute owner of all)—O banner and pennant!

I too leave the rest—great as it is, it is nothing—houses,
  machines are nothing—I see them not,

I see but you, O warlike pennant! O banner so broad, with
  stripes, I sing you only,

Flapping up there in the wind.

(1861-2?)   1881

RISE O DAYS FROM YOUR FATHOMLESS DEEPS

1

RISE O days from your fathomless deeps, till you loftier,
  fiercer sweep,

Long for my soul hungering gymnastic I devour'd what the
  earth gave me,

Long I roam'd the woods of the north, long I watch'd Nia-
  gara pouring,

I travel'd the prairies over and slept on their breast, I cross'd
  the Nevadas, I cross'd the plateaus,

I ascended the towering rocks along the Pacific, I sail'd out
  to sea,

I sail'd through the storm, I was refresh'd by the storm,

I watch'd with joy the threatening maws of the waves,

I mark'd the white combs where they career'd so high, curling
  over,

I heard the wind piping, I saw the black clouds,

Saw from below what arose and mounted, (O superb! O
  wild as my heart, and powerful!)

Heard the continuous thunder as it bellow'd after the light-
  ning,

Noted the slender and jagged threads of lightning as sudden
  and fast amid the din they chased each other across the
  sky;

These, and such as these, I, elate, saw—saw with wonder, yet
    pensive and masterful,
All the menacing might of the globe uprisen around me,
Yet there with my soul I fed, I fed content, supercilious.

2

'Twas well, O soul—'twas a good preparation you gave me,
Now we advance our latent and ampler hunger to fill,
Now we go forth to receive what the earth and the sea never
    gave us,
Not through the mighty woods we go, but through the
    mightier cities,
Something for us is pouring now more than Niagara pouring,
Torrents of men, (sources and rills of the Northwest are you
    indeed inexhaustible?)
What, to pavements and homesteads here, what were those
    storms of the mountains and sea?
What, to passions I witness around me to-day? was the sea
    risen?
Was the wind piping the pipe of death under the black clouds?
Lo! from deeps more unfathomable, something more deadly
    and savage,
Manhattan rising, advancing with menacing front—Cincin-
    nati, Chicago, unchain'd;
What was that swell I saw on the ocean? behold what comes
    here,
How it climbs with daring feet and hands—how it dashes!
How the true thunder bellows after the lightning—how
    bright the flashes of lightning!
How Democracy with desperate vengeful port strides on,
    shown through the dark by those flashes of lightning!
(Yet a mournful wail and low sob I fancied I heard through
    the dark,
In a lull of the deafening confusion.)

3

Thunder on! stride on, Democracy! strike with vengeful
    stroke!
And do you rise higher than ever yet O days, O cities!

Crash heavier, heavier yet O storms! you have done me
    good,
My soul prepared in the mountains absorbs your immortal
    strong nutriment,
Long had I walk'd my cities, my country roads through
    farms, only half satisfied,
One doubt nauseous undulating like a snake, crawl'd on the
    ground before me,
Continually preceding my steps, turning upon me oft, ironi-
    cally hissing low;
The cities I love so well I abandon'd and left, I sped to the
    certainties suitable to me,
Hungering, hungering, hungering, for primal energies and
    Nature's dauntlessness,
I refresh'd myself with it only, I could relish it only,
I waited the bursting forth of the pent fire—on the water and
    air I waited long;
But now I no longer wait, I am fully satisfied, I am glutted,
I have witness'd the true lightning, I have witness'd my cities
    electric,
I have lived to behold man burst forth and warlike America
    rise,
Hence I will seek no more the food of the northern solitary
    wilds,
No more the mountains roam or sail the stormy sea.
1865   1867

VIRGINIA—THE WEST

THE noble sire fallen on evil days,
I saw with hand uplifted, menacing, brandishing,
(Memories of old in abeyance, love and faith in abeyance,)
The insane knife toward the Mother of All.

The noble son on sinewy feet advancing,
I saw, out of the land of prairies, land of Ohio's waters and of
    Indiana,
To the rescue the stalwart giant hurry his plenteous off-
    spring,
Drest in blue, bearing their trusty rifles on their shoulders.

Then the Mother of All with calm voice speaking,
As to you Rebellious, (I seemed to hear her say,) why strive
     against me, and why seek my life?
When you yourself forever provide to defend me?
For you provided me Washington—and now these also.
1872   1881

CITY OF SHIPS

City of Ships!
(O the black ships! O the fierce ships!
O the beautiful sharp-bow'd steam-ships and sail-ships!)
City of the world! (for all races are here,
All the lands of the earth make contributions here;)
City of the sea! city of hurried and glittering tides!
City whose gleeful tides continually rush or recede, whirling
     in and out with eddies and foam!
City of wharves and stores—city of tall façades of marble and
     iron!
Proud and passionate city—mettlesome, mad, extravagant
     city!
Spring up O city—not for peace alone, but be indeed your-
     self, warlike!
Fear not—submit to no models but your own O city!
Behold me—incarnate me as I have incarnated you!
I have rejected nothing you offer'd me—whom you adopted
     I have adopted,
Good or bad I never question you—I love all—I do not con-
     demn anything,
I chant and celebrate all that is yours—yet peace no more,
In peace I chanted peace, but now the drum of war is mine,
War, red war is my song through your streets, O city!
1865   1867

THE CENTENARIAN'S STORY

*Volunteer of 1861-2, (at Washington Park, Brooklyn, assisting
the Centenarian)*

Give me your hand old Revolutionary,
The hill-top is nigh, but a few steps, (make room gentle-
     men,)

Up the path you have follow'd me well, spite of your hundred
 and extra years,
You can walk old man, though your eyes are almost done,
Your faculties serve you, and presently I must have them
 serve me.

Rest, while I tell what the crowd around us means,
On the plain below recruits are drilling and exercising,
There is the camp, one regiment departs to-morrow,
Do you hear the officers giving their orders?
Do you hear the clank of the muskets?

Why what comes over you now old man?
Why do you tremble and clutch my hand so convulsively?
The troops are but drilling, they are yet surrounded with
 smiles,
Around them at hand the well-drest friends and the women,
While splendid and warm the afternoon sun shines down,
Green the midsummer verdure and fresh blows the dallying
 breeze,
O'er proud and peaceful cities and arm of the sea between.

But drill and parade are over, they march back to quarters,
Only hear that approval of hands! hear what a clapping!

As wending the crowds now part and disperse—but we old
 man,
Not for nothing have I brought you hither—we must remain,
You to speak in your turn, and I to listen and tell.

The Centenarian

When I clutch'd your hand it was not with terror,
But suddenly pouring about me here on every side,
And below there where the boys were drilling, and up the
 slopes they ran,
And where tents are pitch'd, and wherever you see south and
 south-east and south-west,
Over hills, across lowlands and in the skirts of woods,
And along the shores in mire (now fill'd over) came again
 and suddenly raged,

As eighty-five years a-gone no mere parade receiv'd with
    applause of friends,
But a battle which I took part in myself—aye, long ago as it
    is, I took part in it,
Walking then this hilltop, this same ground.

Aye, this is the ground,
My blind eyes even as I speak behold it re-peopled from
    graves,
The years recede, pavements and stately houses disappear,
Rude forts appear again, the old hoop'd guns are mounted,
I see the lines of rais'd earth stretching from river to bay,
I mark the vista of waters, I mark the uplands and slopes;
Here we lay encamp'd, it was this time in summer also.

As I talk I remember all, I remember the Declaration,
It was read here, the whole army paraded, it was read to us
    here,
By his staff surrounded the General stood in the middle, he
    held up his unsheath'd sword,
It glitter'd in the sun in full sight of the army.

'Twas a bold act then—the English war-ships had just arrived,
We could watch down the lower bay where they lay at
    anchor,
And the transports swarming with soldiers.

A few days more and they landed and then the battle.

Twenty thousand were brought against us,
A veteran force furnish'd with good artillery.

I tell not now the whole of the battle,
But one brigade early in the forenoon order'd forward to
    engage the red-coats,
Of that brigade I tell, and how steadily it march'd,
And how long and well it stood confronting death.

Who do you think that was marching steadily sternly con-
    fronting death?

It was the brigade of the youngest men, two thousand strong,
Rais'd in Virginia and Maryland, and most of them known
    personally to the General.

Jauntily forward they went with quick step toward Gowanus'
    waters,
Till of a sudden unlook'd for by defiles through the woods,
    gain'd at night,
The British advancing, rounding in from the east, fiercely
    playing their guns,
That brigade of the youngest was cut off and at the enemy's
    mercy.

The General watch'd them from this hill,
They made repeated desperate attempts to burst their en-
    vironment,
Then drew close together, very compact, their flag flying in
    the middle,
But O from the hills how the cannon were thinning and thin-
    ning them!

It sickens me yet, that slaughter!
I saw the moisture gather in drops on the face of the
    General.
I saw how he wrung his hands in anguish.

Meanwhile the British manœuvr'd to draw us out for a
    pitch'd battle,
But we dared not trust the chances of a pitch'd battle.

We fought the fight in detachments,
Sallying forth we fought at several points, but in each the
    luck was against us,
Our foe advancing, steadily getting the best of it, push'd us
    back to the works on this hill,
Till we turn'd menacing here, and then he left us.

That was the going out of the brigade of the youngest men,
    two thousand strong,
Few return'd, nearly all remain in Brooklyn.

That and here my General's first battle,
No women looking on nor sunshine to bask in, it did not
    conclude with applause,
Nobody clapp'd hands here then.

But in darkness in mist on the ground under a chill rain,
Wearied that night we lay foil'd and sullen,
While scornfully laugh'd many an arrogant lord off against
    us encamp'd,
Quite within hearing, feasting, clinking wineglasses together
    over their victory.

So dull and damp and another day,
But the night of that, mist lifting, rain ceasing,
Silent as a ghost while they thought they were sure of him,
    my General retreated.

I saw him at the river-side,
Down by the ferry lit by torches, hastening the embarcation;
My General waited till the soldiers and wounded were all
    pass'd over,
And then, (it was just ere sunrise,) these eyes rested on him
    for the last time.

Every one else seem'd fill'd with gloom,
Many no doubt thought of capitulation.

But when my General pass'd me,
As he stood in his boat and look'd toward the coming sun,
I saw something different from capitulation.

Terminus

Enough, the Centenarian's story ends,
The two, the past and present, have interchanged,
I myself as connecter, a chansonnier of a great future, am
    now speaking.

And is this the ground Washington trod?
And these waters I listlessly daily cross, are these the waters
    he cross'd,

As resolute in defeat as other generals in their proudest
    triumphs?

I must copy the story, and send it eastward and westward,
I must preserve that look as it beam'd on you rivers of
    Brooklyn.

See—as the annual round returns the phantoms return,
It is the 27th of August and the British have landed,
The battle begins and goes against us, behold through the
    smoke Washington's face,
The brigade of Virginia and Maryland have march'd forth to
    intercept the enemy,
They are cut off, murderous artillery from the hills plays
    upon them,
Rank after rank falls, while over them silently droops the
    flag,
Baptized that day in many a young man's bloody wounds,
In death, defeat, and sisters', mothers' tears.

Ah, hills and slopes of Brooklyn! I perceive you are more
    valuable than your owners supposed;
In the midst of you stands an encampment very old,
Stands forever the camp of that dead brigade.
(1861–2?)   1881

CAVALRY CROSSING A FORD

A LINE in long array where they wind betwixt green islands,
They take a serpentine course, their arms flash in the sun—
    hark to the musical clank,
Behold the silvery river, in it the splashing horses loitering
    stop to drink,
Behold the brown-faced men, each group, each person a
    picture, the negligent rest on the saddles,
Some emerge on the opposite bank, others are just entering
    the ford—while,
Scarlet and blue and snowy white,
The guidon flags flutter gayly in the wind.
1865   1871

BIVOUAC ON A MOUNTAIN SIDE

I SEE before me now a traveling army halting,
Below a fertile valley spread, with barns and the orchards of
    summer,
Behind, the terraced sides of a mountain, abrupt, in places
    rising high,
Broken, with rocks, with clinging cedars, with tall shapes
    dingily seen,
The numerous camp-fires scatter'd near and far, some away
    up on the mountain,
The shadowy forms of men and horses, looming, large-sized,
    flickering,
And over all the sky—the sky! far, far out of reach, studded,
    breaking out, the eternal stars.
1865   1871

AN ARMY CORPS ON THE MARCH

WITH its cloud of skirmishers in advance,
With now the sound of a single shot snapping like a whip,
    and now an irregular volley,
The swarming ranks press on and on, the dense brigades
    press on,
Glittering dimly, toiling under the sun—the dust-cover'd
    men,
In columns rise and fall to the undulations of the ground,
With artillery interspers'd—the wheels rumble, the horses
    sweat,
As the army corps advances.
1865–6   1871

BY THE BIVOUAC'S FITFUL FLAME

BY the bivouac's fitful flame,
A procession winding around me, solemn and sweet and slow
    —but first I note,
The tents of the sleeping army, the fields' and woods' dim
    outline,
The darkness lit by spots of kindled fire, the silence,
Like a phantom far or near an occasional figure moving,

The shrubs and trees, (as I lift my eyes they seem to be
    stealthily watching me,)
While wind in procession thoughts, O tender and wondrous
    thoughts,
Of life and death, of home and the past and loved, and of
    those that are far away;
A solemn and slow procession there as I sit on the ground,
By the bivouac's fitful flame.
1865   1867

COME UP FROM THE FIELDS FATHER

COME up from the fields father, here's a letter from our Pete,
And come to the front door mother, here's a letter from thy
    dear son.

Lo, 'tis autumn,
Lo, where the trees, deeper green, yellower and redder,
Cool and sweeten Ohio's villages with leaves fluttering in the
    moderate wind,
Where apples ripe in the orchards hang and grapes on the
    trellis'd vines,
(Smell you the smell of the grapes on the vines?
Smell you the buckwheat where the bees were lately buzzing?)

Above all, lo, the sky so calm, so transparent after the rain,
    and with wondrous clouds,
Below too, all calm, all vital and beautiful, and the farm
    prospers well.

Down in the fields all prospers well,
But now from the fields come father, come at the daughter's
    call,
And come to the entry mother, to the front door come right
    away.

Fast as she can she hurries, something ominous, her steps
    trembling,
She does not tarry to smooth her hair nor adjust her cap.

Open the envelope quickly,
O this is not our son's writing, yet his name is sign'd,

O a strange hand writes for our dear son, O stricken mother's
　　　soul!
All swims before her eyes, flashes with black, she catches the
　　　main words only,
Sentences broken, *gunshot wound in the breast, cavalry skir-*
　　　mish, taken to hospital,
At present low, but will soon be better.

Ah now the single figure to me,
Amid all teeming and wealthy Ohio with all its cities and
　　　farms,
Sickly white in the face and dull in the head, very faint,
By the jamb of a door leans.

Grieve not so, dear mother, (the just-grown daughter speaks
　　　through her sobs,
The little sisters huddle around speechless and dismay'd,)
See, dearest mother, the letter says Pete will soon be better.

Alas poor boy, he will never be better, (nor may-be needs to
　　　be better, that brave and simple soul,)
While they stand at home at the door he is dead already,
The only son is dead.

But the mother needs to be better,
She with thin form presently drest in black,
By day her meals untouch'd, then at night fitfully sleeping,
　　　often waking,
In the midnight waking, weeping, longing with one deep
　　　longing,
O that she might withdraw unnoticed, silent from life escape
　　　and withdraw,
To follow, to seek, to be with her dear dead son.
1865　　　　　　　　　　　　　　　　　　　　1867

VIGIL STRANGE I KEPT ON THE FIELD ONE NIGHT

VIGIL strange I kept on the field one night;
When you my son and my comrade dropt at my side that
　　　day,

One look I but gave which your dear eyes return'd with a
   look I shall never forget,

One touch of your hand to mine O boy, reach'd up as you
   lay on the ground,

Then onward I sped in the battle, the even-contested battle,

Till late in the night reliev'd to the place at last again I made
   my way,

Found you in death so cold dear comrade, found your body
   son of responding kisses, (never again on earth re-
   sponding,)

Bared your face in the starlight, curious the scene, cool blew
   the moderate night-wind,

Long there and then in vigil I stood, dimly around me the
   battlefield spreading,

Vigil wondrous and vigil sweet there in the fragrant silent
   night,

But not a tear fell, not even a long-drawn sigh, long, long I
   gazed,

Then on the earth partially reclining sat by your side leaning
   my chin in my hands,

Passing sweet hours, immortal and mystic hours with you
   dearest comrade—not a tear, not a word,

Vigil of silence, love and death, vigil for you my son and my
   soldier,

As onward silently stars aloft, eastward new ones upward
   stole,

Vigil final for you brave boy, (I could not save you, swift was
   your death,

I faithfully loved you and cared for you living, I think we
   shall surely meet again,)

Till at latest lingering of the night, indeed just as the dawn
   appear'd,

My comrade I wrapt in his blanket, envelop'd well his
   form,

Folded the blanket well, tucking it carefully over head and
   carefully under feet,

And there and then and bathed by the rising sun, my son in
   his grave, in his rude-dug grave I deposited,

Ending my vigil strange with that, vigil of night and battle-
   field dim,

Vigil for boy of responding kisses, (never again on earth
  responding,)
Vigil for comrade swiftly slain, vigil I never forget, how as
  day brighten'd,
I rose from the chill ground and folded my soldier well in his
  blanket,
And buried him where he fell.
1865   1867

A MARCH IN THE RANKS HARD-PREST, AND
THE ROAD UNKNOWN

A march in the ranks hard-prest, and the road unknown,
A route through a heavy wood with muffled steps in the
  darkness,
Our army foil'd with loss severe, and the sullen remnant
  retreating,
Till after midnight glimmer upon us the lights of a dim-
  lighted building,
We come to an open space in the woods, and halt by the
  dim-lighted building,
'Tis a large old church at the crossing roads, now an im-
  promptu hospital,
Entering but for a minute I see a sight beyond all the pictures
  and poems ever made,
Shadows of deepest, deepest black, just lit by moving candles
  and lamps,
And by one great pitchy torch stationary with wild red flame
  and clouds of smoke,
By these, crowds, groups of forms vaguely I see on the floor,
  some in the pews laid down,
At my feet more distinctly a soldier, a mere lad, in danger of
  bleeding to death, (he is shot in the abdomen,)
I stanch the blood temporarily, (the youngster's face is white
  as a lily,)
Then before I depart I sweep my eyes o'er the scene fain to
  absorb it all,
Faces, varieties, postures beyond description, most in ob-
  scurity, some of them dead,

Surgeons operating, attendants holding lights, the smell of
  ether, the odor of blood,
The crowd, O the crowd of the bloody forms, the yard out-
  side also fill'd,
Some on the bare ground, some on planks or stretchers,
  some in the death-spasm sweating,
An occasional scream or cry, the doctor's shouted orders or
  calls,
The glisten of the little steel instruments catching the glint of
  the torches,
These I resume as I chant, I see again the forms, I smell the
  odor,
Then hear outside the orders given, *Fall in, my men, fall in;*
But first I bend to the dying lad, his eyes open, a half-smile
  gives he me,
Then the eyes close, calmly close, and I speed forth to the
  darkness,
Resuming, marching, ever in darkness marching, on in the
  ranks,
The unknown road still marching.

1865   1867

A SIGHT IN CAMP IN THE DAYBREAK GRAY
AND DIM

A sight in camp in the daybreak gray and dim,
As from my tent I emerge so early sleepless,
As slow I walk in the cool fresh air the path near by the
  hospital tent,
Three forms I see on stretchers lying, brought out there un-
  tended lying,
Over each the blanket spread, ample brownish woolen blanket,
Gray and heavy blanket, folding, covering all.

Curious I halt and silent stand,
Then with light fingers I from the face of the nearest the first
  just lift the blanket;
Who are you elderly man so gaunt and grim, with well-
  gray'd hair, and flesh all sunken about the eyes?
Who are you my dear comrade?

Then to the second I step—and who are you my child and
    darling?
Who are you sweet boy with cheeks yet blooming?

Then to the third—a face nor child nor old, very calm, as of
    beautiful yellow-white ivory;
Young man I think I know you—I think this face is the face
    of the Christ himself,
Dead and divine and brother of all, and here again he lies.
1865   1867

AS TOILSOME I WANDER'D VIRGINIA'S WOODS

As toilsome I wander'd Virginia's woods,
To the music of rustling leaves kick'd by my feet, (for 'twas
    autumn,)
I mark'd at the foot of a tree the grave of a soldier;
Mortally wounded he and buried on the retreat, (easily all
    could I understand,)
The halt of a mid-day hour, when up! no time to lose—yet
    this sign left,
On a tablet scrawl'd and nail'd on the tree by the grave,
Bold, cautious, true, and my loving comrade.

Long, long I muse, then on my way go wandering,
Many a changeful season to follow, and many a scene of life,
Yet at times through changeful season and scene, abrupt,
    alone, or in the crowded street,
Comes before me the unknown soldier's grave, comes the
    inscription rude in Virginia's woods,
Bold, cautious, true, and my loving comrade.
1865   1867

NOT THE PILOT

NOT the pilot has charged himself to bring his ship into port,
    though beaten back and many times baffled;
Not the pathfinder penetrating inland weary and long,
By deserts parch'd, snows chill'd, rivers wet, perseveres till he
    reaches his destination,

More than I have charged myself, heeded or unheeded, to
    compose a march for these States,
For a battle-call, rousing to arms if need be, years, centuries
    hence.
1860   1881

YEAR THAT TREMBLED AND REEL'D BENEATH ME

YEAR that trembled and reel'd beneath me!
Your summer wind was warm enough, yet the air I breathed
    froze me,
A thick gloom fell through the sunshine and darken'd me,
Must I change my triumphant songs? said I to myself,
Must I indeed learn to chant the cold dirges of the baffled?
And sullen hymns of defeat?
1865   1867

THE WOUND-DRESSER

1

AN old man bending I come among new faces,
Years looking backward resuming in answer to children,
Come tell us old man, as from young men and maidens that
    love me,
(Arous'd and angry, I'd thought to beat the alarum, and urge
    relentless war,
But soon my fingers fail'd me, my face droop'd and I re-
    sign'd myself,
To sit by the wounded and soothe them, or silently watch the
    dead;)
Years hence of these scenes, of these furious passions, these
    chances,
Of unsurpass'd heroes, (was one side so brave? the other was
    equally brave;)
Now be witness again, paint the mightiest armies of earth,
Of those armies so rapid so wondrous what saw you to tell us?
What stays with you latest and deepest? of curious panics,
Of hard-fought engagements or sieges tremendous what
    deepest remains?

2

O maidens and young men I love and that love me,
What you ask of my days those the strangest and sudden
    your talking recalls,
Soldier alert I arrive after a long march cover'd with sweat
    and dust,
In the nick of time I come, plunge in the fight, loudly shout
    in the rush of successful charge,
Enter the captur'd works—yet lo, like a swift running river
    they fade,
Pass and are gone they fade—I dwell not on soldiers' perils
    or soldiers' joys,
(Both I remember well—many of the hardships, few the joys,
    yet I was content.)

But in silence, in dreams' projections,
While the world of gain and appearance and mirth goes on,
So soon what is over forgotten, and waves wash the imprints
    off the sand,
With hinged knees returning I enter the doors, (while for you
    up there,
Whoever you are, follow without noise and be of strong
    heart.)

Bearing the bandages, water and sponge,
Straight and swift to my wounded I go,
Where they lie on the ground after the battle brought in,
Where their priceless blood reddens the grass the ground,
Or to the rows of the hospital tent, or under the roof'd
    hospital,
To the long rows of cots up and down each side I return,
To each and all one after another I draw near, not one do I
    miss,
An attendant follows holding a tray, he carries a refuse pail,
Soon to be fill'd with clotted rags and blood, emptied, and
    fill'd again.

I onward go, I stop,
With hinged knees and steady hand to dress wounds,
I am firm with each, the pangs are sharp yet unavoidable,

One turns to me his appealing eyes—poor boy! I never knew
you,
Yet I think I could not refuse this moment to die for you, if
that would save you.

3

On, on I go, (open doors of time! open hospital doors!)
The crush'd head I dress, (poor crazed hand tear not the
bandage away,)
The neck of the cavalry-man with the bullet through and
through I examine,
Hard the breathing rattles, quite glazed already the eye, yet
life struggles hard,
(Come sweet death! be persuaded O beautiful death!
In mercy come quickly.)

From the stump of the arm, the amputated hand,
I undo the clotted lint, remove the slough, wash off the mat-
ter and blood,
Back on his pillow the soldier bends with curv'd neck and
side falling head,
His eyes are closed, his face is pale, he dares not look on the
bloody stump,
And has not yet look'd on it.

I dress a wound in the side, deep, deep,
But a day or two more, for see the frame all wasted and
sinking,
And the yellow-blue countenance see.

I dress the perforated shoulder, the foot with the bullet-
wound,
Cleanse the one with a gnawing and putrid gangrene, so
sickening, so offensive,
While the attendant stands behind aside me holding the tray
and pail.

I am faithful, I do not give out,
The fractur'd thigh, the knee, the wound in the abdomen,
These and more I dress with impassive hand, (yet deep in my
breast a fire, a burning flame.)

4

Thus in silence in dreams' projections,
Returning, resuming, I thread my way through the hospitals,
The hurt and wounded I pacify with soothing hand,
I sit by the restless all the dark night, some are so young,
Some suffer so much, I recall the experience sweet and sad,
(Many a soldier's loving arms about this neck have cross'd
  and rested,
Many a soldier's kiss dwells on these bearded lips.)
1865   1881

LONG, TOO LONG AMERICA

LONG, too long America,
Traveling roads all even and peaceful you learn'd from joys
  and prosperity only,
But now, ah now, to learn from crises of anguish, advancing,
  grappling with direst fate and recoiling not,
And now to conceive and show to the world what your chil-
  dren en-masse really are,
(For who except myself has yet conceiv'd what your children
  en-masse really are?)
1865   1881

GIVE ME THE SPLENDID SILENT SUN

1

GIVE me the splendid silent sun with all his beams full-
  dazzling,
Give me juicy autumnal fruit ripe and red from the orchard,
Give me a field where the unmow'd grass grows,
Give me an arbor, give me the trellis'd grape,
Give me fresh corn and wheat, give me serene-moving
  animals teaching content,
Give me nights perfectly quiet as on high plateaus west of the
  Mississippi, and I looking up at the stars,
Give me odorous at sunrise a garden of beautiful flowers
  where I can walk undisturb'd,
Give me for marriage a sweet-breath'd woman of whom I
  should never tire,

Give me a perfect child, give me away aside from the noise of
the world a rural domestic life,
Give me to warble spontaneous songs recluse by myself, for
my own ears only,
Give me solitude, give me Nature, give me again O Nature
your primal sanities!

These demanding to have them, (tired with ceaseless excite-
ment, and rack'd by the war-strife,)
These to procure incessantly asking, rising in cries from my
heart,
While yet incessantly asking still I adhere to my city,
Day upon day and year upon year O city, walking your
streets,
Where you hold me enchain'd a certain time refusing to give
me up,
Yet giving to make me glutted, enrich'd of soul, you give me
forever faces;
(O I see what I sought to escape, confronting, reversing my
cries,
I see my own soul trampling down what it ask'd for.)

2

Keep your splendid silent sun,
Keep your woods O Nature, and the quiet places by the
woods,
Keep your fields of clover and timothy, and your corn-fields
and orchards,
Keep the blossoming buckwheat fields where the Ninth-
month bees hum;
Give me faces and streets—give me these phantoms incessant
and endless along the trottoirs!
Give me interminable eyes—give me women—give me com-
rades and lovers by the thousand!
Let me see new ones every day—let me hold new ones by the
hand every day!
Give me such shows—give me the streets of Manhattan!
Give me Broadway, with the soldiers marching—give me the
sound of the trumpets and drums!

(The soldiers in companies or regiments—some starting
    away, flush'd and reckless,
Some, their time up, returning with thinn'd ranks, young,
    yet very old, worn, marching, noticing nothing;)
Give me the shores and wharves heavy-fringed with black
    ships!
O such for me! O an intense life, full to repletion and varied!
The life of the theatre, bar-room, huge hotel, for me!
The saloon of the steamer! the crowded excursion for me!
    the torchlight procession!
The dense brigade bound for the war, with high piled military
    wagons following;
People, endless, streaming, with strong voices, passions,
    pageants,
Manhattan streets with their powerful throbs, with beating
    drums as now,
The endless and noisy chorus, the rustle and clank of mus-
    kets, (even the sight of the wounded,)
Manhattan crowds, with their turbulent musical chorus!
Manhattan faces and eyes forever for me.
1865   1867

DIRGE FOR TWO VETERANS

THE last sunbeam
Lightly falls from the finish'd Sabbath,
On the pavement here, and there beyond it is looking,
    Down a new-made double grave.

Lo, the moon ascending,
Up from the east the silvery round moon,
Beautiful over the house-tops, ghastly, phantom moon,
    Immense and silent moon.

I see a sad procession,
And I hear the sound of coming full-key'd bugles,
All the channels of the city streets they're flooding,
    As with voices and with tears.

I hear the great drums pounding,
And the small drums steady whirring,

And every blow of the great convulsive drums,
    Strikes me through and through.

For the son is brought with the father,
(In the foremost ranks of the fierce assault they fell,
Two veterans son and father dropt together,
    And the double grave awaits them.)

Now nearer blow the bugles,
And the drums strike more convulsive,
And the daylight o'er the pavement quite has faded,
    And the strong dead-march enwraps me.

In the eastern sky up-buoying,
The sorrowful vast phantom moves illumin'd,
('Tis some mother's large transparent face,
    In heaven brighter growing.)

O strong dead-march you please me!
O moon immense with your silvery face you soothe me!
O my soldiers twain! O my veterans passing to burial!
    What I have I also give you.

The moon gives you light,
And the bugles and the drums give you music,
And my heart, O my soldiers, my veterans,
    My heart gives you love.

1865–6   1881

OVER THE CARNAGE ROSE PROPHETIC A VOICE

OVER the carnage rose prophetic a voice,
Be not dishearten'd, affection shall solve the problems of
    freedom yet,
Those who love each other shall become invincible,
They shall yet make Columbia victorious.

Sons of the Mother of All, you shall yet be victorious,
You shall yet laugh to scorn the attacks of all the remainder
    of the earth.

No danger shall balk Columbia's lovers,
If need be a thousand shall sternly immolate themselves for
    one.

One from Massachusetts shall be a Missourian's comrade,
From Maine and from hot Carolina, and another an Ore-
    gonese, shall be friends triune,
More precious to each other than all the riches of the earth.

To Michigan, Florida perfumes shall tenderly come,
Not the perfumes of flowers, but sweeter, and wafted beyond
    death.

It shall be customary in the houses and streets to see manly
    affection,
The most dauntless and rude shall touch face to face lightly,
The dependence of Liberty shall be lovers,
The continuance of Equality shall be comrades.

These shall tie you and band you stronger than hoops of iron,
I, ecstatic, O partners! O lands, with the love of lovers tie
    you.

(Were you looking to be held together by lawyers?
Or by an agreement on a paper? or by arms?
Nay, nor the world, nor any living thing, will so cohere.)
1860   1867

I SAW OLD GENERAL AT BAY

I saw old General at bay,
(Old as he was, his gray eyes yet shone out in battle like stars,)
His small force was now completely hemm'd in, in his works,
He call'd for volunteers to run the enemy's lines, a desperate
    emergency,
I saw a hundred and more step forth from the ranks, but two
    or three were selected,
I saw them receive their orders aside, they listen'd with care,
    the adjutant was very grave,
I saw them depart with cheerfulness, freely risking their lives.
1865   1867

THE ARTILLERYMAN'S VISION

WHILE my wife at my side lies slumbering, and the wars are
over long,

And my head on the pillow rests at home, and the vacant
midnight passes,

And through the stillness, through the dark, I hear, just hear,
the breath of my infant,

There in the room as I wake from sleep this vision presses
upon me;

The engagement opens there and then in fantasy unreal,

The skirmishers begin, they crawl cautiously ahead, I hear
the irregular snap! snap!

I hear the sounds of the different missiles, the short *t-h-t!
t-h-t!* of the rifle-balls,

I see the shells exploding leaving small white clouds, I hear
the great shells shrieking as they pass,

The grape like the hum and whirr of wind through the trees,
(tumultuous now the contest rages,)

All the scenes at the batteries rise in detail before me
again,

The crashing and smoking, the pride of the men in their
pieces,

The chief-gunner ranges and sights his piece and selects a fuse
of the right time,

After firing I see him lean aside and look eagerly off to note
the effect;

Elsewhere I hear the cry of a regiment charging, (the young
colonel leads himself this time with brandish'd sword,)

I see the gaps cut by the enemy's volleys, (quickly fill'd up, no
delay,)

I breathe the suffocating smoke, then the flat clouds hover
low concealing all;

Now a strange lull for a few seconds, not a shot fired on
either side,

Then resumed the chaos louder than ever, with eager calls
and orders of officers,

While from some distant part of the field the wind wafts
to my ears a shout of applause, (some special suc-
cess,)

And ever the sound of the cannon far or near, (rousing even
    in dreams a devilish exultation and all the old mad joy in
    the depths of my soul,)
And ever the hastening of infantry shifting positions, bat-
    teries, cavalry, moving hither and thither,
(The falling, dying, I heed not, the wounded dripping and
    red I heed not, some to the rear are hobbling,)
Grime, heat, rush, aides-de-camp galloping by or on a full
    run,
With the patter of small arms, the warning *s-s-t* of the rifles,
    (these in my vision I hear or see,)
And bombs bursting in air, and at night the vari-color'd
    rockets.

1865   1881

ETHIOPIA SALUTING THE COLORS

Who are you dusky woman, so ancient hardly human,
With your woolly-white and turban'd head, and bare bony
    feet?
Why rising by the roadside here, do you the colors greet?

('Tis while our army lines Carolina's sands and pines,
Forth from thy hovel door thou Ethiopia com'st to me,
As under doughty Sherman I march toward the sea.)

Me master years a hundred since from my parents sunder'd,
A little child, they caught me as the savage beast is caught,
Then hither me across the sea the cruel slaver brought.

No further does she say, but lingering all the day,
Her high-borne turban'd head she wags, and rolls her dark-
    ling eye,
And courtesies to the regiments, the guidons moving by.

What is it fateful woman, so blear, hardly human?
Why wag your head with turban bound, yellow, red and
    green?
Are the things so strange and marvelous you see or have
    seen?

1871   1871

NOT YOUTH PERTAINS TO ME

NOT youth pertains to me,
Nor delicatesse, I cannot beguile the time with talk,
Awkward in the parlor, neither a dancer nor elegant,
In the learn'd coterie sitting constrain'd and still, for learning
    inures not to me,
Beauty, knowledge, inure not to me—yet there are two or
    three things inure to me,
I have nourish'd the wounded and sooth'd many a dying
    soldier,
And at intervals waiting or in the midst of camp,
Composed these songs.
1865   1871

RACE OF VETERANS

RACE of veterans—race of victors!
Race of the soil, ready for conflict—race of the conquering
    march!
(No more credulity's race, abiding-temper'd race,)
Race henceforth owning no law but the law of itself,
Race of passion and the storm.
1865–6   1871

WORLD TAKE GOOD NOTICE

    WORLD take good notice, silver stars fading,
    Milky hue ript, weft of white detaching,
    Coals thirty-eight, baleful and burning,
    Scarlet, significant, hands off warning,
    Now and henceforth flaunt from these shores.
1865   1867

O TAN-FACED PRAIRIE-BOY

O TAN-FACED prairie-boy.
Before you came to camp came many a welcome gift,
Praises and presents came and nourishing food, till at last
    among the recruits,

You came, taciturn, with nothing to give—we but look'd on
    each other,
When lo! more than all the gifts of the world you gave me.
1865   1867

LOOK DOWN FAIR MOON

LOOK down fair moon and bathe this scene,
Pour softly down night's nimbus floods on faces ghastly,
    swollen, purple,
On the dead on their backs with arms toss'd wide,
Pour down your unstinted nimbus sacred moon.
1865   1867

RECONCILIATION

WORD over all, beautiful as the sky,
Beautiful that war and all its deeds of carnage must in time
    be utterly lost,
That the hands of the sisters Death and Night incessantly
    softly wash again, and ever again, this soil'd world;
For my enemy is dead, a man divine as myself is dead,
I look where he lies white-faced and still in the coffin—I
    draw near,
Bend down and touch lightly with my lips the white face in
    the coffin.
1865-6   1881

HOW SOLEMN AS ONE BY ONE

(*Washington City, 1865*)

How solemn as one by one,
As the ranks returning worn and sweaty, as the men file by
    where I stand,
As the faces the masks appear, as I glance at the faces study-
    ing the masks,
(As I glance upward out of this page studying you, dear
    friend, whoever you are,)
How solemn the thought of my whispering soul to each in
    the ranks, and to you!

I see behind each mask that wonder a kindred soul,
O the bullet could never kill what you really are, dear friend,
Nor the bayonet stab what you really are;
The soul! yourself I see, great as any, good as the best,
Waiting secure and content, which the bullet could never
    kill,
Nor the bayonet stab O friend.
(1865?)   1871

AS I LAY WITH MY HEAD IN YOUR LAP
CAMERADO

As I lay with my head in your lap camerado,
The confession I made I resume, what I said to you and the
    open air I resume,
I know I am restless and make others so,
I know my words are weapons full of danger, full of death,
For I confront peace, security, and all the settled laws, to
    unsettle them,
I am more resolute because all have denied me than I could
    ever have been had all accepted me,
I heed not and have never heeded either experience, cautions,
    majorities, nor ridicule,
And the threat of what is call'd hell is little or nothing to me,
And the lure of what is call'd heaven is little or nothing to me;
Dear camerado! I confess I have urged you onward with me,
    and still urge you, without the least idea what is our
    destination,
Or whether we shall be victorious, or utterly quell'd and
    defeated.
1865-6   1881

DELICATE CLUSTER

DELICATE cluster! flag of teeming life!
Covering all my lands—all my seashores lining!
Flag of death! (how I watch'd you through the smoke of
    battle pressing!
How I heard you flap and rustle, cloth defiant!)
Flag cerulean—sunny flag, with the orbs of night dappled!

Ah my silvery beauty—ah my woolly white and crimson!
Ah to sing the song of you, my matron mighty!
My sacred one, my mother!
1871   1871

TO A CERTAIN CIVILIAN

DID you ask dulcet rhymes from me?
Did you seek the civilian's peaceful and languishing rhymes?
Did you find what I sang erewhile so hard to follow?
Why I was not singing erewhile for you to follow, to under-
      stand—nor am I now;
(I have been born of the same as the war was born,
The drum-corps' rattle is ever to me sweet music, I love well
      the martial dirge,
With slow wail and convulsive throb leading the officer's
      funeral;)
What to such as you anyhow such a poet as I? therefore leave
      my works,
And go lull yourself with what you can understand, and with
      piano-tunes,
For I lull nobody, and you will never understand me.
1865   1871

LO, VICTRESS ON THE PEAKS

Lo, Victress on the peaks,
Where thou with mighty brow regarding the world,
(The world O Libertad, that vainly conspired against thee,)
Out of its countless beleaguering toils, after thwarting them
      all,
Dominant, with the dazzling sun around thee,
Flauntest now unharm'd in immortal soundness and bloom
      —lo, in these hours supreme,
No poem proud, I chanting bring to thee, nor mastery's rap-
      turous verse,
But a cluster containing night's darkness and blood-dripping
      wounds,
And psalms of the dead.
1865–6   1881

SPIRIT WHOSE WORK IS DONE

(*Washington City*, 1865)

SPIRIT whose work is done—spirit of dreadful hours!
Ere departing fade from my eyes your forests of bayonets;
Spirit of gloomiest fears and doubts, (yet onward ever un-
    faltering pressing,)
Spirit of many a solemn day and many a savage scene—
    electric spirit,
That with muttering voice through the war now closed, like a
    tireless phantom flitted,
Rousing the land with breath of flame, while you beat and
    beat the drum,
Now as the sound of the drum, hollow and harsh to the last,
    reverberates round me,
As your ranks, your immortal ranks, return, return from the
    battles,
As the muskets of the young men yet lean over their shoulders,
As I look on the bayonets bristling over their shoulders,
As those slanted bayonets, whole forests of them appearing
    in the distance, approach and pass on, returning home-
    ward,
Moving with steady motion, swaying to and fro to the right
    and left,
Evenly, lightly rising and falling while the steps keep time;
Spirit of hours I knew, all hectic red one day, but pale as
    death next day,
Touch my mouth ere you depart, press my lips close,
Leave me your pulses of rage—bequeath them to me—fill me
    with currents convulsive,
Let them scorch and blister out of my chants when you are
    gone,
Let them identify you to the future in these songs.
1865–6   1881

ADIEU TO A SOLDIER

ADIEU O soldier,
You of the rude campaigning, (which we shared,)
The rapid march, the life of the camp,

The hot contention of opposing fronts, the long manœuvre,
Red battles with their slaughter, the stimulus, the strong
    terrific game,
Spell of all brave and manly hearts, the trains of time through
    you and like of you all fill'd,
With war and war's expression.

Adieu dear comrade,
Your mission is fulfill'd—but I, more warlike,
Myself and this contentious soul of mine,
Still on our own campaigning bound,
Through untried roads with ambushes opponents lined,
Through many a sharp defeat and many a crisis, often
    baffled,
Here marching, ever marching on, a war fight out—aye
    here,
To fiercer, weightier battles give expression.
1871   1871

TURN O LIBERTAD

TURN O Libertad, for the war is over,
From it and all henceforth expanding, doubting no more,
    resolute, sweeping the world,
Turn from lands retrospective recording proofs of the past,
From the singers that sing the trailing glories of the past,
From the chants of the feudal world, the triumphs of kings,
    slavery, caste,
Turn to the world, the triumphs reserv'd and to come—give
    up that backward world,
Leave to the singers of hitherto, give them the trailing past,
But what remains remains for singers for you—wars to come
    are for you,
(Lo, how the wars of the past have duly inured to you, and
    the wars of the present also inure ;)
Then turn, and be not alarm'd O Libertad—turn your un-
    dying face,
To where the future, greater than all the past,
Is swiftly, surely preparing for you.
1865   1871

TO THE LEAVEN'D SOIL THEY TROD

To the leaven'd soil they trod calling I sing for the last,
(Forth from my tent emerging for good, loosing, untying the
    tent-ropes,)
In the freshness the forenoon air, in the far-stretching circuits
    and vistas again to peace restored,
To the fiery fields emanative and the endless vistas beyond,
    to the South and the North,
To the leaven'd soil of the general Western world to attest
    my songs,
To the Alleghanian hills and the tireless Mississippi,
To the rocks I calling sing, and all the trees in the woods,
To the plains of the poems of heroes, to the prairies spread-
    ing wide,
To the far-off sea and the unseen winds, and the sane im-
    palpable air;
And responding they answer all, (but not in words,)
The average earth, the witness of war and peace, acknow-
    ledges mutely,
The prairie draws me close, as the father to bosom broad the
    son,
The Northern ice and rain that began me nourish me to the
    end,
But the hot sun of the South is to fully ripen my songs.
1865–6   1881

Memories of President Lincoln

WHEN LILACS LAST IN THE DOORYARD BLOOM'D

1

WHEN lilacs last in the dooryard bloom'd,
And the great star early droop'd in the western sky in the
    night,
I mourn'd, and yet shall mourn with ever-returning spring.

Ever-returning spring, trinity sure to me you bring,
Lilac blooming perennial and drooping star in the west,
And thought of him I love.

2

O powerful western fallen star!
O shades of night—O moody, tearful night!
O great star disappear'd—O the black murk that hides the star!
O cruel hands that hold me powerless—O helpless soul of me!
O harsh surrounding cloud that will not free my soul.

3

In the dooryard fronting an old farm-house near the white-
    wash'd palings,
Stands the lilac-bush tall-growing with heart-shaped leaves
    of rich green,
With many a pointed blossom rising delicate, with the per-
    fume strong I love,
With every leaf a miracle—and from this bush in the door-
    yard,
With delicate-color'd blossoms and heart-shaped leaves cf
    rich green,
A sprig with its flower I break.

4

In the swamp in secluded recesses,
A shy and hidden bird is warbling a song.

Solitary the thrush,
The hermit withdrawn to himself, avoiding the settlements,
Sings by himself a song.

Song of the bleeding throat,
Death's outlet song of life, (for well dear brother I know,
If thou wast not granted to sing thou would'st surely die.)

5

Over the breast of the spring, the land, amid cities,
Amid lanes and through old woods, where lately the violets
    peep'd from the ground, spotting the gray debris,
Amid the grass in the fields each side of the lanes, passing the
    endless grass,
Passing the yellow-spear'd wheat, every grain from its shroud
    in the dark-brown fields uprisen,
Passing the apple-tree blows of white and pink in the or-
    chards,
Carrying a corpse to where it shall rest in the grave,
Night and day journeys a coffin.

6

Coffin that passes through lanes and streets,
Through day and night with the great cloud darkening the
    land,
With the pomp of the inloop'd flags with the cities draped in
    black,
With the show of the States themselves as of crape-veil'd
    women standing,
With processions long and winding and the flambeaus of the
    night,
With the countless torches lit, with the silent sea of faces and
    the unbared heads,
With the waiting depot, the arriving coffin, and the sombre
    faces,

With dirges through the night, with the thousand voices
    rising strong and solemn,
With all the mournful voices of the dirges pour'd around the
    coffin,
The dim-lit churches and the shuddering organs—where
    amid these you journey,
With the tolling tolling bells' perpetual clang,
Here, coffin that slowly passes,
I give you my sprig of lilac.

7

(Nor for you, for one alone,
Blossoms and branches green to coffins all I bring,
For fresh as the morning, thus would I chant a song for you
    O sane and sacred death.

All over bouquets of roses,
O death, I cover you over with roses and early lilies,
But mostly and now the lilac that blooms the first,
Copious I break, I break the sprigs from the bushes,
With loaded arms I come, pouring for you,
For you and the coffins all of you O death.)

8

O western orb sailing the heaven,
Now I know what you must have meant as a month since I
    walk'd,
As I walk'd in silence the transparent shadowy night,
As I saw you had something to tell as you bent to me night
    after night,
As you droop'd from the sky low down as if to my side,
    (while the other stars all look'd on,)
As we wander'd together the solemn night, (for something I
    know not what kept me from sleep,)
As the night advanced, and I saw on the rim of the west how
    full you were of woe,
As I stood on the rising ground in the breeze in the cool
    transparent night,
As I watch'd where you pass'd and was lost in the nether-
    ward black of the night,

As my soul in its trouble dissatisfied sank, as where you sad
    orb,
Concluded, dropt in the night, and was gone.

9

Sing on there in the swamp,
O singer bashful and tender, I hear your notes, I hear your
    call,
I hear, I come presently, I understand you,
But a moment I linger, for the lustrous star has detain'd me,
The star my departing comrade holds and detains me.

10

O how shall I warble myself for the dead one there I loved?
And how shall I deck my song for the large sweet soul that
    has gone?
And what shall my perfume be for the grave of him I love?

Sea-winds blown from east and west,
Blown from the Eastern sea and blown from the Western
    sea, till there on the prairies meeting,
These and with these and the breath of my chant,
I'll perfume the grave of him I love.

11

O what shall I hang on the chamber walls?
And what shall the pictures be that I hang on the walls,
To adorn the burial-house of him I love?

Pictures of growing spring and farms and homes,
With the Fourth-month eve at sundown, and the gray smoke
    lucid and bright,
With floods of the yellow gold of the gorgeous, indolent,
    sinking sun, burning, expanding the air,
With the fresh sweet herbage under foot, and the pale green
    leaves of the trees prolific,
In the distance the flowing glaze, the breast of the river, with
    a wind-dapple here and there,
With ranging hills on the banks, with many a line against the
    sky, and shadows,

And the city at hand with dwellings so dense, and stacks of
    chimneys,
And all the scenes of life and the workshops, and the work-
    men homeward returning.

12

Lo, body and soul—this land,
My own Manhattan with spires, and the sparkling and
    hurrying tides, and the ships,
The varied and ample land, the South and the North in the
    light, Ohio's shores and flashing Missouri,
And ever the far-spreading prairies cover'd with grass and
    corn.

Lo, the most excellent sun so calm and haughty,
The violet and purple morn with just-felt breezes,
The gentle soft-born measureless light,
The miracle spreading bathing all, the fulfill'd noon,
The coming eve delicious, the welcome night and the stars,
Over my cities shining all, enveloping man and land.

13

Sing on, sing on you gray-brown bird,
Sing from the swamps, the recesses, pour your chant from
    the bushes,
Limitless out of the dusk, out of the cedars and pines.

Sing on dearest brother, warble your reedy song,
Loud human song, with voice of uttermost woe.

O liquid and free and tender!
O wild and loose to my soul—O wondrous singer!
You only I hear—yet the star holds me, (but will soon
    depart,)
Yet the lilac with mastering odor holds me.

14

Now while I sat in the day and look'd forth,
In the close of the day with its light and the fields of spring,
    and the farmers preparing their crops,
In the large unconscious scenery of my land with its lakes
    and forests,

In the heavenly aerial beauty, (after the perturb'd winds and
    the storms,)
Under the arching heavens of the afternoon swift passing,
    and the voices of children and women,
The many-moving sea-tides, and I saw the ships how they sail'd,
And the summer approaching with richness, and the fields all
    busy with labor,
And the infinite separate houses, how they all went on, each
    with its meals and minutia of daily usages,
And the streets how their throbbings throbb'd, and the cities
    pent—lo, then and there,
Falling upon them all and among them all, enveloping me
    with the rest,
Appear'd the cloud, appear'd the long black trail,
And I knew death, its thought, and the sacred knowledge of
    death.

Then with the knowledge of death as walking one side of me,
And the thought of death close-walking the other side of me,
And I in the middle as with companions, and as holding the
    hands of companions,
I fled forth to the hiding receiving night that talks not,
Down to the shores of the water, the path by the swamp in
    the dimness,
To the solemn shadowy cedars and ghostly pines so still.

And the singer so shy to the rest receiv'd me,
The gray-brown bird I know receiv'd us comrades three,
And he sang the carol of death, and a verse for him I love.

From deep secluded recesses,
From the fragrant cedars and the ghostly pines so still,
Came the carol of the bird.

And the charm of the carol rapt me,
As I held as if by their hands my comrades in the night,
And the voice of my spirit tallied the song of the bird.

Come lovely and soothing death,
Undulate round the world, serenely arriving, arriving,
In the day, in the night, to all, to each,
Sooner or later delicate death

Prais'd be the fathomless universe,
For life and joy, and for objects and knowledge curious,
And for love, sweet love—but praise ! praise ! praise !
For the sure-enwinding arms of cool-enfolding death.

Dark mother always gliding near with soft feet,
Have none chanted for thee a chant of fullest welcome?
Then I chant it for thee, I glorify thee above all,
I bring thee a song that when thou must indeed come, come un-
    falteringly.

Approach strong deliveress,
When it is so, when thou hast taken them I joyously sing the
    dead,
Lost in the loving floating ocean of thee,
Laved in the flood of thy bliss O death.

From me to thee glad serenades,
Dances for thee I propose saluting thee, adornments and feast-
    ings for thee,
And the sights of the open landscape and the high-spread sky
    are fitting,
And life and the fields, and the huge and thoughtful night.

The night in silence under many a star,
The ocean shore and the husky whispering wave whose voice I
    know,
And the soul turning to thee O vast and well-veil'd death,
And the body gratefully nestling close to thee.

Over the tree-tops I float thee a song,
Over the rising and sinking waves, over the myriad fields and
    the prairies wide,
Over the dense-pack'd cities all and the teeming wharves and
    ways,
I float this carol with joy, with joy to thee O death.

15

To the tally of my soul,
Loud and strong kept up the gray-brown bird,
With pure deliberate notes spreading filling the night.

Loud in the pines and cedars dim,
Clear in the freshness moist and the swamp-perfume,
And I with my comrades there in the night.

While my sight that was bound in my eyes unclosed,
As to long panoramas of visions.

And I saw askant the armies,
I saw as in noiseless dreams hundreds of battle-flags,
Borne through the smoke of the battles and pierc'd with missiles I saw them,
And carried hither and yon through the smoke, and torn and bloody,
And at last but a few shreds left on the staffs, (and all in silence,)
And the staffs all splinter'd and broken.

I saw battle-corpses, myriads of them,
And the white skeletons of young men, I saw them,
I saw the debris and debris of all the slain soldiers of the war,
But I saw they were not as was thought,
They themselves were fully at rest, they suffer'd not,
The living remain'd and suffer'd, the mother suffer'd,
And the wife and the child and the musing comrade suffer'd,
And the armies that remain'd suffer'd.

16

Passing the visions, passing the night,
Passing, unloosing the hold of my comrades' hands,
Passing the song of the hermit bird and the tallying song of my soul,
Victorious song, death's outlet song, yet varying ever-altering song,
As low and wailing, yet clear the notes, rising and falling, flooding the night,
Sadly sinking and fainting, as warning and warning, and yet again bursting with joy,
Covering the earth and filling the spread of the heaven,
As that powerful psalm in the night I heard from recesses,

Passing, I leave thee lilac with heart-shaped leaves,
I leave thee there in the door-yard, blooming, returning with
    spring.

I cease from my song for thee,
From my gaze on thee in the west, fronting the west, com-
    muning with thee,
O comrade lustrous with silver face in the night.

Yet each to keep and all, retrievements out of the night,
The song, the wondrous chant of the gray-brown bird,
And the tallying chant, the echo arous'd in my soul,
With the lustrous and drooping star with the countenance
    full of woe,
With the holders holding my hand nearing the call of the bird,
Comrades mine and I in the midst, and their memory ever to
    keep, for the dead I loved so well,
For the sweetest, wisest soul of all my days and lands—and
    this for his dear sake,
Lilac and star and bird twined with the chant of my soul,
There in the fragrant pines and the cedars dusk and dim.
1865–6   1881

O CAPTAIN! MY CAPTAIN!

O CAPTAIN! my Captain! our fearful trip is done,
The ship has weather'd every rack, the prize we sought is won,
The port is near, the bells I hear, the people all exulting,
While follow eyes the steady keel, the vessel grim and daring;
        But O heart! heart! heart!
          O the bleeding drops of red,
             Where on the deck my Captain lies,
             Fallen cold and dead.

O Captain! my Captain! rise up and hear the bells;
Rise up—for you the flag is flung—for you the bugle trills,
For you bouquets and ribbon'd wreaths—for you the shores
    a-crowding,
For you they call, the swaying mass, their eager faces
    turning;
          Here Captain! dear father!
           The arm beneath your head!

It is some dream that on the deck,
    You've fallen cold and dead.

My Captain does not answer, his lips are pale and still,
My father does not feel my arm, he has no pulse nor will,
The ship is anchor'd safe and sound, its voyage closed and
    done,
From fearful trip the victor ship comes in with object won:
    Exult O shores, and ring O bells!
      But I with mournful tread,
        Walk the deck my Captain lies,
          Fallen cold and dead.

1865   1871

HUSH'D BE THE CAMPS TO-DAY

(*May* 4, 1865)

HUSH'D be the camps to-day,
And soldiers let us drape our war-worn weapons,
And each with musing soul retire to celebrate,
Our dear commander's death.

No more for him life's stormy conflicts,
Nor victory, nor defeat—no more time's dark events,
Charging like ceaseless clouds across the sky.

But sing poet in our name,
Sing of the love we bore him—because you—dweller in
    camps, know it truly.

As they invault the coffin there,
Sing—as they close the doors of earth upon him—one verse,
For the heavy hearts of soldiers.

1865   1871

THIS DUST WAS ONCE THE MAN

THIS dust was once the man,
Gentle, plain, just and resolute, under whose cautious hand,
Against the foulest crime in history known in any land or age,
Was saved the Union of these States.

1871   1871

By Blue Ontario's Shore

1

By blue Ontario's shore,
As I mused of these warlike days and of peace return'd, and
the dead that return no more,
A Phantom gigantic superb, with stern visage accosted me,
Chant me the poem, it said, *that comes from the soul of
America, chant me the carol of victory,*
*And strike up the marches of Libertad, marches more powerful
yet,*
*And sing me before you go the song of the throes of Demo-
cracy.*

(Democracy, the destin'd conqueror, yet treacherous lip-
smiles everywhere,
And death and infidelity at every step.)

2

A Nation announcing itself,
I myself make the only growth by which I can be appreciated,
I reject none, accept all, then reproduce all in my own forms.

A breed whose proof is in time and deeds,
What we are we are, nativity is answer enough to objections,
We wield ourselves as a weapon is wielded,
We are powerful and tremendous in ourselves,
We are executive in ourselves, we are sufficient in the variety
of ourselves,
We are the most beautiful to ourselves and in ourselves,
We stand self-pois'd in the middle, branching thence over the
world,
From Missouri, Nebraska, or Kansas, laughing attacks to
scorn.

Nothing is sinful to us outside of ourselves,
Whatever appears, whatever does not appear, we are beautiful or sinful in ourselves only.

(O Mother—O Sisters dear!
If we are lost, no victor else has destroy'd us,
It is by ourselves we go down to eternal night.)

3

Have you thought there could be but a single supreme?
There can be any number of supremes—one does not countervail another any more than one eyesight countervails another, or one life countervails another.

All is eligible to all,
All is for individuals, all is for you,
No condition is prohibited, not God's or any.

All comes by the body, only health puts you rapport with the universe.

Produce great Persons, the rest follows.

4

Piety and conformity to them that like,
Peace, obesity, allegiance, to them that like,
I am he who tauntingly compels men, women, nations,
Crying, Leap from your seats and contend for your lives!

I am he who walks the States with a barb'd tongue, questioning every one I meet,
Who are you that wanted only to be told what you knew before?
Who are you that wanted only a book to join you in your nonsense?

(With pangs and cries as thine own O bearer of many children,
These clamors wild to a race of pride I give.)

O lands, would you be freer than all that has ever been
    before?
If you would be freer than all that has been before, come
    listen to me.

Fear grace, elegance, civilization, delicatesse,
Fear the mellow sweet, the sucking of honey-juice,
Beware the advancing mortal ripening of Nature,
Beware what precedes the decay of the ruggedness of states
    and men.

5

Ages, precedents, have long been accumulating undirected
    materials,
America brings builders, and brings its own styles.

The immortal poets of Asia and Europe have done their
    work and pass'd to other spheres,
A work remains, the work of surpassing all they have done.

America, curious toward foreign characters, stands by its
    own at all hazards,
Stands removed, spacious, composite, sound, initiates the
    true use of precedents,
Does not repel them or the past or what they have produced
    under their forms,
Takes the lesson with calmness, perceives the corpse slowly
    borne from the house,
Perceives that it waits a little while in the door, that it was
    fittest for its days,
That its life has descended to the stalwart and well-shaped
    heir who approaches,
And that he shall be fittest for his days.

Any period one nation must lead,
One land must be the promise and reliance of the future.

These States are the amplest poem,
Here is not merely a nation but a teeming Nation of nations,
Here the doings of men correspond with the broadcast do-
    ings of the day and night,

Here is what moves in magnificent masses careless of par-
ticulars,
Here are the roughs, beards, friendliness, combativeness, the
soul loves,
Here the flowing trains, here the crowds, equality, diversity,
the soul loves.

6

Land of lands and bards to corroborate!
Of them standing among them, one lifts to the light a west-
bred face,
To him the hereditary countenance bequeath'd both mother's
and father's,
His first parts substances, earth, water, animals, trees,
Built of the common stock, having room for far and near,
Used to dispense with other lands, incarnating this land,
Attracting it body and soul to himself, hanging on its neck
with incomparable love,
Plunging his seminal muscle into its merits and demerits,
Making its cities, beginnings, events, diversities, wars, vocal
in him,
Making its rivers, lakes, bays, embouchure in him,
Mississippi with yearly freshets and changing chutes, Colum-
bia, Niagara, Hudson, spending themselves lovingly in
him,
If the Atlantic coast stretch or the Pacific coast stretch, he
stretching with them North or South,
Spanning between them East and West, and touching what-
ever is between them,
Growths growing from him to offset the growths of pine,
cedar, hemlock, live-oak, locust, chestnut, hickory,
cottonwood, orange, magnolia,
Tangles as tangled in him as any cranebake or swamp,
He likening sides and peaks of mountains, forests coated
with northern transparent ice,
Off him pasturage sweet and natural as savanna, upland,
prairie,
Through him flights, whirls, screams, answering those of the
fish-hawk, mocking-bird, night-heron, and eagle,

His spirit surrounding his country's spirit, unclosed to good
and evil,

Surrounding the essences of real things, old times and pre-
sent times,

Surrounding just found shores, islands, tribes of red abori-
gines,

Weather-beaten vessels, landings, settlements, embryo
stature and muscle,

The haughty defiance of the Year One, war, peace, the for-
mation of the Constitution,

The separate States, the simple elastic scheme, the immi-
grants,

The Union always swarming with blatherers and always sure
and impregnable,

The unsurvey'd interior, log-houses, clearings, wild animals,
hunters, trappers,

Surrounding the multiform agriculture, mines, temperature,
the gestation of new States,

Congress convening every Twelfth-month, the members duly
coming up from the uttermost parts,

Surrounding the noble character of mechanics and farmers,
especially the young men,

Responding their manners, speech, dress, friendships, the
gait they have of persons who never knew how it felt to
stand in the presence of superiors,

The freshness and candor of their physiognomy, the copious-
ness and decision of their phrenology,

The picturesque looseness of their carriage, their fierceness
when wrong'd,

The fluency of their speech, their delight in music, their
curiosity, good temper and open-handedness, the whole
composite make,

The prevailing ardor and enterprise, the large amative-
ness,

The perfect equality of the female with the male, the fluid
movement of the population,

The superior marine, free commerce, fisheries, whaling, gold-
digging,

Wharf-hemm'd cities, railroad and steamboat lines inter-
secting all points,

Factories, mercantile life, labor-saving machinery, the North-
east, Northwest, Southwest,
Manhattan firemen, the Yankee swap, southern plantation
life,
Slavery—the murderous, treacherous conspiracy to raise it
upon the ruins of all the rest,
On and on to the grapple with it—Assassin! then your life or
ours be the stake, and respite no more.

7

(Lo, high toward heaven, this day,
Libertad, from the conqueress' field return'd,
I mark the new aureola around your head,
No more of soft astral, but dazzling and fierce,
With war's flames and the lambent lightnings playing,
And your port immovable where you stand,
With still the inextinguishable glance and the clinch'd and
lifted fist,
And your foot on the neck of the menacing one, the scorner
utterly crush'd beneath you,
The menacing arrogant one that strode and advanced with
his senseless scorn, bearing the murderous knife,
The wide-swelling one, the braggart that would yesterday do
so much,
To-day a carrion dead and damn'd, the despised of all the
earth,
An offal rank, to the dunghill maggots spurn'd.)

8

Others take finish, but the Republic is ever constructive and
ever keeps vista,
Others adorn the past, but you O days of the present, I adorn
you,
O days of the future I believe in you—I isolate myself for
your sake,
O America because you build for mankind I build for you,
O well-beloved stone-cutters, I lead them who plan with de-
cision and science,
Lead the present with friendly hand toward the future.

(Bravas to all impulses sending sane children to the next
    age!
But damn that which spends itself with no thought of the
    stain, pains, dismay, feebleness, it is bequeathing.)

9

I listened to the Phantom by Ontario's shore,
I heard the voice arising demanding bards,
By them all native and grand, by them alone can these States
    be fused into the compact organism of a Nation.

To hold men together by paper and seal or by compulsion is
    no account,
That only holds men together which aggregates all in a living
    principle, as the hold of the limbs of the body or the
    fibres of plants.

Of all races and eras these States with veins full of poetica
    stuff most need poets, and are to have the greatest, and
    use them the greatest,
Their Presidents shall not be their common referee so much
    as their poets shall.

(Soul of love and tongue of fire!
Eye to pierce the deepest deeps and sweep the world!
Ah Mother, prolific and full in all besides, yet how long
    barren, barren?)

10

Of these States the poet is the equable man,
Not in him but off from him things are grotesque, eccentric,
    fail of their full returns,
Nothing out of its place is good, nothing in its place is bad,
He bestows on every object or quality its fit proportion,
    neither more nor less,
He is the arbiter of the diverse, he is the key,
He is the equalizer of his age and land,
He supplies what wants supplying, he checks what wants
    checking,

In peace out of him speaks the spirit of peace, large, rich,
thrifty, building populous towns, encouraging agricul-
ture, arts, commerce, lighting the study of man, the soul,
health, immortality, government,
In war he is the best backer of the war, he fetches artillery as
good as the engineer's, he can make every word he
speaks draw blood,
The years straying toward infidelity he withholds by his
steady faith,
He is no arguer, he is judgment, (Nature accepts him abso-
lutely,)
He judges not as the judge judges but as the sun falling round
a helpless thing,
As he sees the farthest he has the most faith,
His thoughts are the hymns of the praise of things,
In the dispute on God and eternity he is silent,
He sees eternity less like a play with a prologue and denoue-
ment,
He sees eternity in men and women, he does not see men and
women as dreams or dots.

For the great Idea, the idea of perfect and free individuals,
For that, the bard walks in advance, leader of leaders,
The attitude of him cheers up slaves and horrifies foreign
despots.

Without extinction is Liberty, without retrograde is Equality,
They live in the feelings of young men and the best women,
(Not for nothing have the indomitable heads of the earth
been always ready to fall for Liberty.)

11

For the great Idea,
That, O my brethren, that is the mission of poets.

Songs of stern defiance ever ready,
Songs of the rapid arming and the march,
The flag of peace quick-folded, and instead the flag we know,
Warlike flag of the great Idea.

(Angry cloth I saw there leaping!
I stand again in leaden rain your flapping folds saluting,
I sing you over all, flying beckoning through the fight—O the
　　hard-contested fight!
The cannons ope their rosy-flashing muzzles—the hurtled
　　balls scream,
The battle-front forms amid the smoke—the volleys pour
　　incessant from the line,
Hark, the ringing word *Charge!*—now the tussle and the
　　furious maddening yells,
Now the corpses tumble curl'd upon the ground,
Cold, cold in death, for precious life of you,
Angry cloth I saw there leaping.)

12

Are you he who would assume a place to teach or be a poet
　　here in the States?
The place is august, the terms obdurate.

Who would assume to teach here may well prepare himself
　　body and mind,
He may well survey, ponder, arm, fortify, harden, make lithe
　　himself,
He shall surely be question'd beforehand by me with many
　　and stern questions.

Who are you indeed who would talk or sing to America?
Have you studied out the land, its idioms and men?
Have you learn'd the physiology, phrenology, politics, geo-
　　graphy, pride, freedom, friendship of the land? its sub-
　　stratums and objects?
Have you consider'd the organic compact of the first day of
　　the first year of Independence, sign'd by the Commis-
　　sioners, ratified by the States, and read by Washington
　　at the head of the army?
Have you possess'd yourself of the Federal Constitution?
Do you see who have left all feudal processes and poems
　　behind them, and assumed the poems and processes of
　　Democracy?

Are you faithful to things? do you teach what the land and
    sea, the bodies of men, womanhood, amativeness,
    heroic angers, teach?
Have you sped through fleeting customs, popularities?
Can you hold your hand against all seductions, follies, whirls,
    fierce contentions? are you very strong? are you really of
    the whole People?
Are you not of some coterie? some school or mere religion?
Are you done with reviews and criticisms of life? animating
    now to life itself?
Have you vivified yourself from the maternity of these States?
Have you too the old ever-fresh forbearance and impar-
    tiality?
Do you hold the like love for those hardening to maturity?
    for the last-born? little and big? and for the errant?

What is this you bring my America?
Is it uniform with my country?
Is it not something that has been better told or done before?
Have you not imported this or the spirit of it in some ship?
Is it not a mere tale? a rhyme? a prettiness?—is the good old
    cause in it?
Has it not dangled long at the heels of the poets, politicians,
    literats, of enemies' lands?
Does it not assume that what is notoriously gone is still here?
Does it answer universal needs? will it improve manners?
Does it sound with trumpet-voice the proud victory of the
    Union in that secession war?
Can your performance face the open fields and the seaside?
Will it absorb into me as I absorb food, air, to appear again
    in my strength, gait, face?
Have real employments contributed to it? original makers,
    not mere amanuenses?
Does it meet modern discoveries, calibres, facts, face to face?
What does it mean to American persons, progresses, cities?
    Chicago, Kanada, Arkansas?
Does it see behind the apparent custodians the real custodians
    standing, menacing, silent, the mechanics, Manhattan-
    ese, Western men, Southerners, significant alike in their
    apathy, and in the promptness of their love?

Does it see what finally befalls, and has always finally be-
    fallen, each temporizer, patcher, outsider, partialist,
    alarmist, infidel, who has ever ask'd any thing of
    America?
What mocking and scornful negligence?
The track strew'd with the dust of skeletons,
By the roadside others disdainfully toss'd.

13

Rhymes and rhymers pass away, poems distill'd from poems
    pass away,
The swarms of reflectors and the polite pass, and leave ashes,
Admirers, importers, obedient persons, make but the soil of
    literature,
America justifies itself, give it time, no disguise can deceive it
    or conceal from it, it is impassive enough,
Only toward the likes of itself will it advance to meet them,
If its poets appear it will in due time advance to meet them,
    there is no fear of mistake,
(The proof of a poet shall be sternly deferr'd till his country
    absorbs him as affectionately as he has absorb'd it.)

He masters whose spirit masters, he tastes sweetest who
    results sweetest in the long run,
The blood of the brawn beloved of time is unconstraint;
In the need of songs, philosophy, an appropriate native
    grand-opera, shipcraft, any craft,
He or she is greatest who contributes the greatest original
    practical example.

Already a nonchalant breed, silently emerging, appears on
    the streets,
People's lips salute only doers, lovers, satisfiers, positive
    knowers,
There will shortly be no more priests, I say their work is
    done,
Death is without emergencies here, but life is perpetual
    emergencies here,
Are your body, days, manners, superb? after death you shall
    be superb,

Justice, health, self-esteem, clear the way with irresistible
    power;
How dare you place any thing before a man?

14

Fall behind me States!
A man before all—myself, typical, before all.

Give me the pay I have served for,
Give to sing the songs of the great Idea, take all the rest,
I have loved the earth, sun, animals, I have despised riches,
I have given alms to every one that ask'd, stood up for the
    stupid and crazy, devoted my income and labor to
    others,
Hated tyrants, argued not concerning God, had patience and
    indulgence toward the people, taken off my hat to noth-
    ing known or unknown,
Gone freely with powerful uneducated persons and with the
    young, and with the mothers of families,
Read these leaves to myself in the open air, tried them by
    trees, stars, rivers,
Dismiss'd whatever insulted my own soul or defiled my
    body,
Claim'd nothing to myself which I have not carefully claim'd
    for others on the same terms,
Sped to the camps, and comrades found and accepted from
    every State,
(Upon this breast has many a dying soldier lean'd to breathe
    his last,
This arm, this hand, this voice, have nourish'd, rais'd,
    restored,
To life recalling many a prostrate form;)
I am willing to wait to be understood by the growth of the
    taste of myself,
Rejecting none, permitting all.

(Say O Mother, have I not to your thought been faith-
    ful?
Have I not through life kept you and yours before me?)

15

I swear I begin to see the meaning of these things,
It is not the earth, it is not America who is so great,
It is I who am great or to be great, it is You up there, or any
    one,
It is to walk rapidly through civilizations, governments,
    theories,
Through poems, pageants, shows, to form individuals.

Underneath all, individuals,
I swear nothing is good to me now that ignores individuals,
The American compact is altogether with individuals,
The only government is that which makes minute of indi-
    viduals,
The whole theory of the universe is directed unerringly to one
    single individual—namely to You.

(Mother! with subtle sense severe, with the naked sword in
    your hand,
I saw you at last refuse to treat but directly with individuals.)

16

Underneath all, Nativity,
I swear I will stand by my own nativity, pious or impious so
    be it;
I swear I am charm'd with nothing except nativity,
Men, women, cities, nations, are only beautiful from nativity.

Underneath all is the Expression of love for men and women,
(I swear I have seen enough of mean and impotent modes of
    expressing love for men and women,
After this day I take my own modes of expressing love for
    men and women.)

I swear I will have each quality of my race in myself,
(Talk as you like, he only suits these States whose manners
    favor the audacity and sublime turbulence of the States.)

Underneath the lessons of things, spirits, Nature, govern-
    ments, ownerships, I swear I perceive other lessons,

Underneath all to me is myself, to you yourself, (the same
monotonous old song.)

17

O I see flashing that this America is only you and me,
Its power, weapons, testimony, are you and me,
Its crimes, lies, thefts, defections, are you and me,
Its Congress is you and me, the officers, capitols, armies,
    ships, are you and me,
Its endless gestations of new States are you and me,
The war, (that war so bloody and grim, the war I will hence-
    forth forget), was you and me,
Natural and artificial are you and me,
Freedom, language, poems, employments, are you and me,
Past, present, future, are you and me.

I dare not shirk any part of myself,
Not any part of America good or bad,
Not to build for that which builds for mankind,
Not to balance ranks, complexions, creeds, and the sexes,
Not to justify science nor the march of equality,
Nor to feed the arrogant blood of the brawn belov'd of time.

I am for those that have never been master'd,
For men and women whose tempers have never been mas-
    ter'd,
For those whom laws, theories, conventions, can never
    master.

I am for those who walk abreast with the whole earth,
Who inaugurate one to inaugurate all.

I will not be outfaced by irrational things,
I will penetrate what it is in them that is sarcastic upon me,
I will make cities and civilizations defer to me,
This is what I have learnt from America—it is the amount,
    and it I teach again.

(Democracy, while weapons were everywhere aim'd at your
    breast,

I saw you serenely give birth to immortal children, saw in
    dreams your dilating form,
Saw you with spreading mantle covering the world.)

18

I will confront these shows of the day and night,
I will know if I am to be less than they,
I will see if I am not as majestic as they,
I will see if I am not as subtle and real as they,
I will see if I am to be less generous than they,
I will see if I have no meaning, while the houses and ships
    have meaning,
I will see if the fishes and birds are to be enough for them-
    selves, and I am not to be enough for myself.

I match my spirit against yours you orbs, growths, moun-
    tains, brutes,
Copious as you are I absorb you all in myself, and become
    the master myself,
America isolated yet embodying all, what is it finally except
    myself?
These States, what are they except myself?

I know now why the earth is gross, tantalizing, wicked, it is
    for my sake,
I take you specially to be mine, you terrible, rude forms.

(Mother, bend down, bend close to me your face,
I know not what these plots and wars and deferments are for,
I know not fruition's success, but I know that through war
    and crime your work goes on, and must yet go on.)

19

Thus by blue Ontario's shore,
While the winds fann'd me and the waves came trooping to-
    ward me,
I thrill'd with the power's pulsations, and the charm of my
    theme was upon me,
Till the tissues that held me parted their ties upon me.

And I saw the free souls of poets,
The loftiest bards of past ages strode before me,
Strange large men, long unwaked, undisclosed, were disclosed to me.

20

O my rapt verse, my call, mock me not!
Not for the bards of the past, not to invoke them have I launch'd you forth,
Not to call even those lofty bards here by Ontario's shores,
Have I sung so capricious and loud my savage song.

Bards for my own land only I invoke,
(For the war, the war is over, the field is clear'd,)
Till they strike up marches henceforth triumphant and onward,
To cheer O Mother your boundless expectant soul.

Bards of the great Idea! bards of the peaceful inventions! (for the war, the war is over!)
Yet bards of latent armies, a million soldiers waiting everready,
Bards with songs as from burning coals or the lightning's fork'd stripes!
Ample Ohio's, Kanada's bards—bards of California! inland bards—bards of the war!
You by my charm I invoke.
1856   1881

REVERSALS

LET that which stood in front go behind,
Let that which was behind advance to the front,
Let bigots, fools, unclean persons, offer new propositions,
Let the old propositions be postponed,
Let a man seek pleasure everywhere except in himself,
Let a woman seek happiness everywhere except in herself.
1856   1881

Autumn Rivulets

AS CONSEQUENT, Etc.

As consequent from store of summer rains,
Or wayward rivulets in autumn flowing,
Or many a herb-lined brook's reticulations,
Or subterranean sea-rills making for the sea,
Songs of continued years I sing.

Life's ever-modern rapids first, (soon, soon to blend,
With the old streams of death.)

Some threading Ohio's farm-fields or the woods,
Some down Colorado's cañons from sources of perpetual
    snow,
Some half-hid in Oregon, or away southward in Texas,
Some in the north finding their way to Erie, Niagara, Ottawa,
Some to Atlantica's bays, and so to the great salt brine.

In you whoe'er you are my book perusing,
In I myself, in all the world, these currents flowing,
All, all toward the mystic ocean tending.

Currents for starting a continent new,
Overtures sent to the solid out of the liquid,
Fusion of ocean and land, tender and pensive waves,
(Not safe and peaceful only, waves rous'd and ominous too,
Out of the depths the storm's abysmic waves, who knows
    whence?
Raging over the vast, with many a broken spar and tatter'd
    sail.)

Or from the sea of Time, collecting vasting all, I bring,
A windrow-drift of weeds and shells.

O little shells, so curious-convolute, so limpid-cold and
 voiceless,
Will you not little shells to the tympans of temples held,
Murmurs and echoes still call up, eternity's music faint and
 far,
Wafted inland, sent from Atlantica's rim, strains for the soul
 of the prairies,
Whisper'd reverberations, chords for the ear of the West
 joyously sounding,
Your tidings old, yet ever new and untranslatable,
Infinitesimals out of my life, and many a life,
(For not my life and yours alone I give—all, all I give,)
These waifs from the deep, cast high and dry,
Wash'd on America's shores?
1881   1881

THE RETURN OF THE HEROES

1

FOR the lands and for these passionate days and for myself,
Now I awhile retire to thee O soil of autumn fields,
Reclining on thy breast, giving myself to thee,
Answering the pulses of thy sane and equable heart,
Tuning a verse for thee.

O earth that hast no voice, confide to me a voice,
O harvest of my lands—O boundless summer growths,
O lavish brown parturient earth—O infinite teeming womb,
A song to narrate thee.

2

Ever upon this stage,
Is acted God's calm annual drama,
Gorgeous procession, songs of birds,
Sunrise that fullest feeds and freshens most the soul,
The heaving sea, the waves upon the shore, the musical,
 strong waves,
The woods, the stalwart trees, the slender, tapering trees,
The liliput countless armies of the grass,

The heat, the showers, the measureless pasturages,
The scenery of the snows, the winds' free orchestra,
The stretching light-hung roof of clouds, the clear cerulean
    and the silvery fringes,
The high dilating stars, the placid beckoning stars,
The moving flocks and herds, the plains and emerald mea-
    dows,
The shows of all the varied lands and all the growths and
    products.

3

Fecund America—to-day,
Thou art all over set in births and joys!
Thou groan'st with riches, thy wealth clothes thee as a
    swathing-garment,
Thou laughest loud with ache of great possessions,
A myriad-twining life like interlacing vines binds all thy vast
    demesne,
As some huge ship freighted to water's edge thou ridest into
    port,
As rain falls from the heaven and vapors rise from earth, so
    have the precious values fallen upon thee and risen out
    of thee;
Thou envy of the globe! thou miracle!
Thou, bathed, choked, swimming in plenty,
Thou lucky Mistress of the tranquil barns,
Thou Prairie Dame that sittest in the middle and lookest out
    upon thy world, and lookest East and lookest West,
Dispensatress, that by a word givest a thousand miles, a
    million farms, and missest nothing,
Thou all-acceptress—thou hospitable, (thou only art hospit-
    able as God is hospitable.)

4

When late I sang sad was my voice,
Sad were the shows around me with deafening noises of
    hatred and smoke of war;
In the midst of the conflict, the heroes, I stood,
Or pass'd with slow step through the wounded and dying.

But now I sing not war,
Nor the measur'd march of soldiers, nor the tents of camps,
Nor the regiments hastily coming up deploying in line of
    battle;
No more the sad, unnatural shows of war.

Ask'd room those flush'd immortal ranks, the first forth-
    stepping armies?
Ask room alas the ghastly ranks, the armies dread that
    follow'd.

(Pass, pass, ye proud brigades, with your tramping sinewy
    legs,
With your shoulders young and strong, with your knapsacks
    and your muskets;
How elate I stood and watch'd you, where starting off you
    march'd.

Pass—then rattle drums again,
For an army heaves in sight, O another gathering army,
Swarming, trailing on the rear, O you dread accruing army,
O you regiments so piteous, with your mortal diarrhœa, with
    your fever,
O my land's maim'd darlings, with the plenteous bloody
    bandage and the crutch,
Lo, your pallid army follows.)

5

But on these days of brightness,
On the far-stretching beauteous landscape, the roads and
    lanes, the high-piled farm-wagons, and the fruits and
    barns,
Should the dead intrude?

Ah the dead to me mar not, they fit well in Nature,
They fit very well in the landscape under the trees and grass,
And along the edge of the sky in the horizon's far margin.

Nor do I forget you Departed,
Nor in winter or summer my lost ones,

But most in the open air as now when my soul is rapt and at
   peace, like pleasing phantoms,
Your memories rising glide silently by me.

6

I saw the day the return of the heroes,
(Yet the heroes never surpass'd shall never return,
Them that day I saw not.)

I saw the interminable corps, I saw the processions of armies,
I saw them approaching, defiling by with divisions,
Streaming northward, their work done, camping awhile in
   clusters of mighty camps.

No holiday soldiers—youthful, yet veterans,
Worn, swart, handsome, strong, of the stock of homestead
   and workshop,
Harden'd of many a long campaign and sweaty march,
Inured on many a hard-fought bloody field.

A pause—the armies wait,
A million flush'd embattled conquerors wait,
The world too waits, then soft as breaking night and sure as
   dawn,
They melt, they disappear.

Exult O lands! victorious lands!
Not there your victory on those red shuddering fields,
But here and hence your victory.

Melt, melt away ye armies—disperse ye blue-clad soldiers,
Resolve ye back again, give up for good your deadly arms,
Other the arms the fields henceforth for you, or South or
   North,
With saner wars, sweet wars, life-giving wars.

7

Loud O my throat, and clear O soul!
The season of thanks and the voice of full-yielding,
The chant of joy and power for boundless fertility.

All till'd and untill'd fields expand before me,
I see the true arenas of my race, or first or last,
Man's innocent and strong arenas.

I see the heroes at other toils,
I see well-wielded in their hands the better weapons.

I see where the Mother of All,
With full-spanning eye gazes forth, dwells long,
And counts the varied gathering of the products.

Busy the far, the sunlit panorama,
Prairie, orchard, and yellow grain of the North,
Cotton and rice of the South and Louisianian cane,
Open unseeded fallows, rich fields of clover and timothy,
Kine and horses feeding, and droves of sheep and swine,
And many a stately river flowing and many a jocund brook,
And healthy uplands with herby-perfumed breezes,
And the good green grass, that delicate miracle the ever-
    recurring grass.

8

Toil on heroes! harvest the products!
Not alone on those warlike fields the Mother of All,
With dilated form and lambent eyes watch'd you.

Toil on heroes! toil well! handle the weapons well!
The Mother of All, yet here as ever she watches you.

Well-pleased America thou beholdest,
Over the fields of the West those crawling monsters,
The human-divine inventions, the labor-saving implements;
Beholdest moving in every direction imbued as with life the
    revolving hay-rakes,
The steam-power reaping-machines and the horse-power
    machines,
The engines, thrashers of grain and cleaners of grain, well
    separating the straw, the nimble work of the patent
    pitchfork,
Beholdest the newer saw-mill, the southern cotton-gin, and
    the rice-cleanser.

Beneath thy look O Maternal,
With these and else and with their own strong hands the
　　heroes harvest.

All gather and all harvest,
Yet but for thee O Powerful, not a scythe might swing as now
　　in security,
Not a maize-stalk dangle as now its silken tassels in peace.

Under thee only they harvest, even but a wisp of hay under
　　thy great face only,
Harvest the wheat of Ohio, Illinois, Wisconsin, every barbed
　　spear under thee,
Harvest the maize of Missouri, Kentucky, Tennessee, each
　　ear in its light-green sheath,
Gather the hay to its myriad mows in the odorous tranquil
　　barns,
Oats to their bins, the white potato, the buckwheat of Michi-
　　gan, to theirs;
Gather the cotton in Mississippi or Alabama, dig and hoard
　　the golden the sweet potato of Georgia and the Carolinas,
Clip the wool of California or Pennsylvania,
Cut the flax in the Middle States, or hemp or tobacco in the
　　Borders,
Pick the pea and the bean, or pull apples from the trees or
　　bunches of grapes from the vines,
Or aught that ripens in all these States or North or South,
Under the beaming sun and under thee.
1867　　　　　　　　　　　　　　　　　　　　　　　　1881

THERE WAS A CHILD WENT FORTH

THERE was a child went forth every day,
And the first object he look'd upon, that object he became,
And that object became part of him for the day or a certain
　　part of the day,
Or for many years or stretching cycles of years.

The early lilacs became part of this child,
And grass and white and red morning-glories, and white and
　　red clover, and the song of the phœbe-bird,

And the Third-month lambs and the sow's pink-faint litter,
and the mare's foal and the cow's calf,
And the noisy brood of the barnyard or by the mire of the
pond-side,
And the fish suspending themselves so curiously below there,
and the beautiful curious liquid,
And the water-plants with their graceful flat heads, all be-
came part of him.

The field-sprouts of Fourth-month and Fifth-month became
part of him,
Winter-grain sprouts and those of the light-yellow corn, and
the esculent roots of the garden,
And the apple-trees cover'd with blossoms and the fruit
afterward, and wood-berries, and the commonest weeds
by the road,
And the old drunkard staggering home from the outhouse of
the tavern whence he had lately risen,
And the schoolmistress that pass'd on her way to the school,
And the friendly boys that pass'd, and the quarrelsome boys,
And the tidy and fresh-cheek'd girls, and the barefoot negro
boy and girl,
And all the changes of city and country wherever he went.

His own parents, he that had father'd him and she that had
conceiv'd him in her womb and birth'd him,
They gave this child more of themselves than that,
They gave him afterward every day, they became part of him,

The mother at home quietly placing the dishes on the supper-
table,
The mother with mild words, clean her cap and gown, a
wholesome odor falling off her person and clothes as she
walks by,
The father, strong, self-sufficient, manly, mean, anger'd,
unjust,
The blow, the quick loud word, the tight bargain, the crafty
lure,
The family usages, the language, the company, the furniture,
the yearning and swelling heart,

Affection that will not be gainsay'd, the sense of what is real,
the thought if after all it should prove unreal,
The doubts of day-time and the doubts of night-time, the
curious whether and how,
Whether that which appears so is so, or is it all flashes and
specks?
Men and women crowding fast in the streets, if they are not
flashes and specks what are they?
The streets themselves and the façades of houses, and goods
in the windows,
Vehicles, teams, the heavy-plank'd wharves, the huge cross-
ing at the ferries,
The village on the highland seen from afar at sunset, the
river between,
Shadows, aureola and mist, the light falling on roofs and
gables of white or brown two miles off,
The schooner near by sleepily dropping down the tide, the
little boat slack-tow'd astern,
The hurrying tumbling waves, quick-broken crests, slap-
ping,
The strata of color'd clouds, the long bar of maroon-tint
away solitary by itself, the spread of purity it lies
motionless in,
The horizon's edge, the flying sea-crow, the fragrance of salt
marsh and shore mud,
These became part of that child who went forth every day,
and who now goes, and will always go forth every
day.

1855   1871

OLD IRELAND

FAR hence amid an isle of wondrous beauty,
Crouching over a grave an ancient sorrowful mother,
Once a queen, now lean and tatter'd seated on the ground,
Her old white hair drooping dishevel'd round her shoulders,
At her feet fallen an unused royal harp,
Long silent, she too long silent, mourning her shrouded hope
and heir,
Of all the earth her heart most full of sorrow because most
full of love.

Yet a word ancient mother,
You need crouch there no longer on the cold ground with
    forehead between your knees,
O you need not sit there veil'd in your old white hair so dis-
    hevel'd,
For know you the one you mourn is not in that grave,
It was an illusion, the son you love was not really dead,
The Lord is not dead, he is risen again young and strong in
    another country,
Even while you wept there by your fallen harp by the grave,
What you wept for was translated, pass'd from the grave,
The winds favor'd and the sea sail'd it,
And now with rosy and new blood,
Moves to-day in a new country.
1861   1867

THE CITY DEAD-HOUSE

By the city dead-house by the gate,
As idly sauntering wending my way from the clangor,
I curious pause, for lo, an outcast form, a poor dead prosti-
    tute brought,
Her corpse they deposit unclaim'd, it lies on the damp brick
    pavement,
The divine woman, her body, I see the body, I look on it
    alone,
That house once full of passion and beauty, all else I notice
    not,
Nor stillness so cold, nor running water from faucet, nor
    odors morbific impress me,
But the house alone—that wondrous house—that delicate
    fair house—that ruin!
That immortal house more than all the rows of dwellings
    ever built!
Or white-domed capitol with majestic figure surmounted, or
    all the old high-spired cathedrals,
That little house alone more than them all—poor, desperate
    house!
Fair, fearful wreck—tenement of a soul—itself a soul,
Unclaim'd, avoided house—take one breath from my tremu-
    lous lips,

Take one tear dropt aside as I go for thought of you,
Dead house of love—house of madness and sin, crumbled,
  crush'd,
House of life, erewhile talking and laughing—but ah, poor
  house, dead even then,
Months, years, an echoing, garnish'd house—but dead, dead,
  dead.
1867   1867

THIS COMPOST

1

SOMETHING startles me where I thought I was safest,
I withdraw from the still woods I loved,
I will not go now on the pastures to walk,
I will not strip the clothes from my body to meet my lover
  the sea,
I will not touch my flesh to the earth as to other flesh to
  renew me.

O how can it be that the ground itself does not sicken?
How can you be alive you growths of spring?
How can you furnish health you blood of herbs, roots,
  orchards, grain?
Are they not continually putting distemper'd corpses within
  you?
Is not every continent work'd over and over with sour dead?

Where have you disposed of their carcasses?
Those drunkards and gluttons of so many generations?
Where have you drawn off all the foul liquid and meat?
I do not see any of it upon you to-day, or perhaps I am de-
  ceiv'd,
I will run a furrow with my plough, I will press my spade
  through the sod and turn it up underneath,
I am sure I shall expose some of the foul meat.

2

Behold this compost! behold it well!
Perhaps every mite has once form'd part of a sick person—
  yet behold!
The grass of spring covers the prairies,

The bean bursts noiselessly through the mould in the garden,
The delicate spear of the onion pierces upward,
The apple-buds cluster together on the apple-branches,
The resurrection of the wheat appears with pale visage out of
its graves,
The tinge awakes over the willow-tree and the mulberry-tree,
The he-birds carol mornings and evenings while the she-birds
sit on their nests,
The young of poultry break through the hatch'd eggs,
The new-born of animals appear, the calf is dropt from the
cow, the colt from the mare,
Out of its little hill faithfully rise the potato's dark green
leaves,
Out of its hill rises the yellow maize-stalk, the lilacs bloom in
the door-yards,
The summer growth is innocent and disdainful above all
those strata of sour dead.

What chemistry!
That the winds are really not infectious,
That this is no cheat, this transparent green-wash of the sea
which is so amorous after me,
That it is safe to allow it to lick my naked body all over with
its tongues,
That it will not endanger me with the fevers that have de-
posited themselves in it,
That all is clean forever and forever,
That the cool drink from the well tastes so good,
That blackberries are so flavorous and juicy,
That the fruits of the apple-orchard and the orange-orchard,
that melons, grapes, peaches, plums, will none of them
poison me,
That when I recline on the grass I do not catch any disease,
Though probably every spear of grass rises out of what was
once a catching disease.

Now I am terrified at the Earth, it is that calm and patient,
It grows such sweet things out of such corruptions,
It turns harmless and stainless on its axis, with such endless
successions of diseas'd corpses,

It distills such exquisite winds out of such infused fetor,
It renews with such unwitting looks its prodigal, annual,
     sumptuous crops,
It gives such divine materials to men, and accepts such leav-
     ings from them at last.
1856   1881

TO A FOIL'D EUROPEAN REVOLUTIONAIRE

COURAGE yet, my brother or my sister!
Keep on—Liberty is to be subserv'd whatever occurs;
That is nothing that is quell'd by one or two failures, or any
     number of failures,
Or by the indifference or ingratitude of the people, or by any
     unfaithfulness,
Or the show of the tushes of power, soldiers, cannon, penal
     statutes.

What we believe in waits latent forever through all the con-
     tinents,
Invites no one, promises nothing, sits in calmness and light,
     is positive and composed, knows no discouragement,
Waiting patiently, waiting its time.

(Not songs of loyalty alone are these,
But songs of insurrection also,
For I am the sworn poet of every dauntless rebel the world
     over,
And he going with me leaves peace and routine behind him,
And stakes his life to be lost at any moment.)

The battle rages with many a loud alarm and frequent ad-
     vance and retreat,
The infidel triumphs, or supposes he triumphs,
The prison, scaffold, garrote, handcuffs, iron necklace and
     lead-balls do their work,
The named and unnamed heroes pass to other spheres,
The great speakers and writers are exiled, they lie sick in dis-
     tant lands,
The cause is asleep, the strongest throats are choked with
     their own blood,

The young men droop their eyelashes toward the ground
    when they meet;
But for all this Liberty has not gone out of the place, nor the
    infidel enter'd into full possession.

When Liberty goes out of a place it is not the first to go, nor
    the second or third to go,
It waits for all the rest to go, it is the last.

When there are no more memories of heroes and martyrs,
And when all life and all the souls of men and women are
    discharged from any part of the earth,
Then only shall liberty or the idea of liberty be discharged
    from that part of the earth,
And the infidel come into full possession.

Then courage European revolter, revoltress!
For till all ceases neither must you cease.

I do not know what you are for, (I do not know what I am
    for myself, nor what any thing is for,)
But I will search carefully for it even in being foil'd,
In defeat, poverty, misconception, imprisonment—for they
    too are great.

Did we think victory great?
So it is—but now it seems to me, when it cannot be help'd,
    that defeat is great,
And that death and dismay are great.
1856   1881

UNNAMED LANDS

NATIONS ten thousand years before these States, and many
    times ten thousand years before these States,
Garner'd clusters of ages that men and women like us grew
    up and travel'd their course and pass'd on,
What vast-built cities, what orderly republics, what pastoral
    tribes and nomads,
What histories, rulers, heroes, perhaps transcending all
    others,

What laws, customs, wealth, arts, traditions,
What sort of marriage, what costumes, what physiology and
    phrenology,
What of liberty and slavery among them, what they thought
    of death and the soul,
Who were witty and wise, who beautiful and poetic, who
    brutish and undevelop'd,
Not a mark, not a record remains—and yet all remains.

O I know that those men and women were not for nothing,
    any more than we are for nothing,
I know that they belong to the scheme of the world every bit
    as much as we now belong to it.

Afar they stand, yet near to me they stand,
Some with oval countenances learn'd and calm,
Some naked and savage, some like huge collections of in-
    sects,
Some in tents, herdsmen, patriarchs, tribes, horsemen,
Some prowling through woods, some living peaceably on
    farms, laboring, reaping, filling barns,
Some traversing paved avenues, amid temples, palaces, fac-
    tories, libraries, shows, courts, theatres, wonderful
    monuments.

Are those billions of men really gone?
Are those women of the old experience of the earth gone?
Do their lives, cities, arts, rest only with us?
Did they achieve nothing for good for themselves?

I believe of all those men and women that fill'd the unnamed
    lands, every one exists this hour here or elsewhere, in-
    visible to us,
In exact proportion to what he or she grew from in life, and
    out of what he or she did, felt, became, loved, sinn'd, in
    life.

I believe that was not the end of those nations or any person
    of them, any more than this shall be the end of my
    nation, or of me;

Of their languages, governments, marriage, literature, pro-
   ducts, games, wars, manners, crimes, prisons, slaves,
   heroes, poets,
I suspect their results curiously await in the yet unseen world,
   counterparts of what accrued to them in the seen world,
I suspect I shall meet them there,
I suspect I shall there find each old particular of those un-
   named lands.
1860   1881

SONG OF PRUDENCE

MANHATTAN's streets I saunter'd, pondering
On Time, Space, Reality—on such as these, and abreast with
   them Prudence.

The last explanation always remains to be made about prud-
   ence,
Little and large alike drop quietly aside from the prudence
   that suits immortality.

The soul is of itself,
All verges to it, all has reference to what ensues,
All that a person does, says, thinks, is of consequence,
Not a move can a man or woman make, that affects him or
   her in a day, month, any part of the direct lifetime, or
   the hour of death,
But the same affects him or her onward afterward through
   the indirect lifetime.

The indirect is just as much as the direct,
The spirit receives from the body just as much as it gives to
   the body, if not more.

Not one word or deed, not venereal sore, discoloration,
   privacy of the onanist,
Putridity of gluttons or rum-drinkers, peculation, cunning,
   betrayal, murder, seduction, prostitution,
But has results beyond death as really as before death.

Charity and personal force are the only investments worth
    any thing.

No specification is necessary, all that a male or female does,
    that is vigorous, benevolent, clean, is so much profit to
    him or her,
In the unshakable order of the universe and through the
    whole scope of it forever.

Who has been wise receives interest,
Savage, felon, President, judge, farmer, sailor, mechanic,
    literat, young, old, it is the same,
The interest will come round—all will come round.

Singly, wholly, to affect now, affected their time, will forever
    affect, all of the past and all of the present and all of the
    future,
All the brave actions of war and peace,
All help given to relatives, strangers, the poor, old, sorrow-
    ful, young children, widows, the sick, and to shunn'd
    persons,
All self-denial that stood steady and aloof on wrecks, and saw
    others fill the seats of the boats,
All offering of substance or life for the good old cause, or for
    a friend's sake, or opinion's sake,
All pains of enthusiasts scoff'd at by their neighbors,
All the limitless sweet love and precious suffering of mothers,
All honest men baffled in strifes recorded or unrecorded,
All the grandeur and good of ancient nations whose frag-
    ments we inherit,
All the good of the dozens of ancient nations unknown to us
    by name, date, location,
All that was ever manfully begun, whether it succeeded or no,
All suggestions of the divine mind of man or the divinity of
    his mouth, or the shaping of his great hands,
All that is well thought or said this day on any part of the
    globe, or on any of the wandering stars, or on any of the
    fix'd stars, by those there as we are here,
All that is henceforth to be thought or done by you whoever
    you are, or by any one,

These inure, have inured, shall inure, to the identities from
    which they sprang, or shall spring.

Did you guess any thing lived only its moment?
The world does not so exist, no parts palpable or impalpable
    so exist,
No consummation exists without being from some long pre-
    vious consummation, and that from some other,
Without the farthest conceivable one coming a bit nearer the
    beginning than any.

Whatever satisfies souls is true;
Prudence entirely satisfies the craving and glut of souls,
Itself only finally satisfies the soul,
The soul has that measureless pride which revolts from every
    lesson but its own.

Now I breathe the word of the prudence that walks abreast
    with time, space, reality,
That answers the pride which refuses every lesson but its
    own.

What is prudence is indivisible,
Declines to separate one part of life from every part,
Divides not the righteous from the unrighteous or the living
    from the dead,
Matches every thought or act by its correlative,
Knows no possible forgiveness or deputed atonement,
Knows that the young man who composedly peril'd his life
    and lost it has done exceedingly well for himself without
    doubt,
That he who never peril'd his life, but retains it to old age in
    riches and ease, has probably achiev'd nothing for him-
    self worth mentioning,
Knows that only that person has really learn'd who has
    learn'd to prefer results,
Who favors body and soul the same,
Who perceives the indirect assuredly following the direct,
Who in his spirit in any emergency whatever neither hurries
    nor avoids death.

1856   1881

THE SINGER IN THE PRISON

1

O sight of pity, shame and dole !
O fearful thought—a convict soul.

RANG the refrain along the hall, the prison,
Rose to the roof, the vaults of heaven above,
Pouring in floods of melody in tones so pensive sweet and
    strong the like whereof was never heard,
Reaching the far-off sentry and the armed guards, who
    ceas'd their pacing,
Making the hearer's pulses stop for ecstasy and awe.

2

The sun was low in the west one winter day,
When down a narrow aisle amid the thieves and outlaws of
    the land,
(There by the hundreds seated, sear-faced murderers, wily
    counterfeiters,
Gather'd to Sunday church in prison walls, the keepers
    round,
Plenteous, well-armed, watching with vigilant eyes,)
Calmly a lady walk'd holding a little innocent child by either
    hand,
Whom seating on their stools beside her on the platform,
She, first preluding with the instrument a low and musical
    prelude,
In voice surpassing all, sang forth a quaint old hymn.

      A soul confined by bars and bands,
      Cries, help! O help! and wrings her hands,
      Blinded her eyes, bleeding her breast,
      Nor pardon finds, nor balm of rest.

      Ceaseless she paces to and fro,
      O heart-sick days! O nights of woe!
      Nor hand of friend, nor loving face,
      Nor favor comes, nor word of grace.

It was not I that sinn'd the sin,
The ruthless body dragg'd me in;
Though long I strove courageously,
The body was too much for me.

Dear prison'd soul bear up a space,
For soon or late the certain grace;
To set thee free and bear thee home,
The heavenly pardoner death shall come.

Convict no more, nor shame, nor dole!
Depart—a God-enfranchis'd soul!

3

The singer ceas'd,
One glance swept from her clear calm eyes o'er all those up-
  turn'd faces,
Strange sea of prison faces, a thousand varied, crafty, brutal,
  seam'd and beauteous faces,
Then rising, passing back along the narrow aisle between
  them,
While her gown touch'd them rustling in the silence,
She vanish'd with her children in the dusk.

While upon all, convicts and armed keepers ere they
  stirr'd,
(Convict forgetting prison, keeper his loaded pistol,)
A hush and pause fell down a wondrous minute,
With deep half-stifled sobs and sound of bad men bow'd and
  moved to weeping,
And youth's convulsive breathings, memories of home,
The mother's voice in lullaby, the sister's care, the happy
  childhood,
The long-pent spirit rous'd to reminiscence;
A wondrous minute then—but after in the solitary night, to
  many, many there,
Years after, even in the hour of death, the sad refrain, the
  tune, the voice, the words,

Resumed, the large calm lady walks the narrow aisle,
The wailing melody again, the singer in the prison sings,

> *O sight of pity, shame and dole !*
> *O fearful thought—a convict soul.*

1869   1881

WARBLE FOR LILAC-TIME

WARBLE me now for joy of lilac-time, (returning in reminis-
  cence,)
Sort me O tongue and lips for Nature's sake, souvenirs of
  earliest summer,
Gather the welcome signs, (as children with pebbles or
  stringing shells,)
Put in April and May, the hylas croaking in the ponds, the
  elastic air,
Bees, butterflies, the sparrow with its simple notes,
Blue-bird and darting swallow, nor forget the high-hole
  flashing his golden wings,
The tranquil sunny haze, the clinging smoke, the vapor,
Shimmer of waters with fish in them, the cerulean above,
All that is jocund and sparkling, the brooks running,
The maple woods, the crisp February days and the sugar-
  making,
The robin where he hops, bright-eyed, brown-breasted,
With musical clear call at sunrise, and again at sunset,
Or flitting among the trees of the apple-orchard, building the
  nest of his mate,
The melted snow of March, the willow sending forth its
  yellow-green sprouts,
For spring-time is here! the summer is here! and what is this
  in it and from it?
Thou, soul, unloosen'd—the restlessness after I know not
  what;
Come, let us lag here no longer, let us be up and away!
O if one could but fly like a bird!
O to escape, to sail forth as in a ship!
To glide with thee O soul, o'er all, in all, as a ship o'er the
  waters;

Gathering these hints, the preludes, the blue sky, the grass,
    the morning drops of dew,
The lilac-scent, the bushes with dark green heart-shaped
    leaves,
Wood-violets, the little delicate pale blossoms called inno-
    cence,
Samples and sorts not for themselves alone, but for their
    atmosphere,
To grace the bush I love—to sing with the birds,
A warble for joy of lilac-time, returning in reminiscence.
1870   1881

OUTLINES FOR A TOMB

(*G. P., Buried 1870*)

1

WHAT may we chant, O thou within this tomb?
What tablets, outlines, hang for thee, O millionaire?
The life thou lived'st we know not,
But that thou walk'dst thy years in barter, 'mid the haunts of
    brokers,
Nor heroism thine, nor war, nor glory.

2

Silent, my soul,
With drooping lids, as waiting, ponder'd,
Turning from all the samples, monuments of heroes.

While through the interior vistas,
Noiseless uprose, phantasmic, (as by night Auroras of the
    north,)
Lambent tableaus, prophetic, bodiless scenes,
Spiritual projections.

In one, among the city streets a laborer's home appear'd,
After his day's work done, cleanly, sweet-air'd, the gaslight
    burning,
The carpet swept and a fire in the cheerful stove.

In one, the sacred parturition scene,
A happy painless mother birth'd a perfect child.

In one, at a bounteous morning meal,
Sat peaceful parents with contented sons.

In one, by twos and threes, young people,
Hundreds concentring, walk'd the paths and streets and
    roads,
Toward a tall-domed school.

In one a trio beautiful,
Grandmother, loving daughter, loving daughter's daughter,
    sat,
Chatting and sewing.

In one, along a suite of noble rooms,
'Mid plenteous books and journals, paintings on the walls,
    fine statuettes,
Were groups of friendly journeymen, mechanics young and
    old,
Reading, conversing.

All, all the shows of laboring life,
City and country, women's, men's and children's,
Their wants provided for, hued in the sun and tinged for once
    with joy,
Marriage, the street, the factory, farm, the house-room,
    lodging-room,
Labor and toil, the bath, gymnasium, playground, library,
    college,
The student, boy or girl, led forward to be taught,
The sick cared for, the shoeless shod, the orphan father'd and
    mother'd,
The hungry fed, the houseless housed;
(The intentions perfect and divine,
The workings, details, haply human.)

3

O thou within this tomb,
From thee such scenes, thou stintless, lavish giver,

Tallying the gifts of earth, large as the earth,
Thy name an earth, with mountains, fields and tides.

Nor by your streams alone, you rivers,
By you, your banks Connecticut,
By you and all your teeming life old Thames,
By you Potomac laving the ground Washington trod, by you
    Patapsco,
You Hudson, you endless Mississippi—nor you alone,
But to the high seas launch, my thought, his memory.
1870   1881

OUT FROM BEHIND THIS MASK

(*To Confront a Portrait*)

1

Out from behind this bending rough-cut mask,
These lights and shades, this drama of the whole,
This common curtain of the face contain'd in me for me, in
    you for you, in each for each,
(Tragedies, sorrows, laughter, tears—O heaven!
The passionate teeming plays this curtain hid!)
This glaze of God's serenest purest sky,
This film of Satan's seething pit,
This heart's geography's map, this limitless small continent,
    this soundless sea;
Out from the convolutions of this globe,
This subtler astronomic orb than sun or moon, than Jupiter,
    Venus, Mars,
This condensation of the universe, (nay here the only universe,
Here the idea, all in this mystic handful wrapt;)
These burin'd eyes, flashing to you to pass to future time,
To launch and spin through space revolving sideling, from
    these to emanate,
To you whoe'er you are—a look.

2

A traveler of thoughts and years, of peace and war,
Of youth long sped and middle age declining,

(As the first volume of a tale perused and laid away, and this
    the second,
Songs, ventures, speculations, presently to close,)
Lingering a moment here and now, to you I opposite turn,
As on the road or at some crevice door by chance, or open'd
    window,
Pausing, inclining, baring my head, you specially I greet,
To draw and clinch your soul for once inseparably with mine,
Then travel travel on.
1876   1881

VOCALISM

1

VOCALISM, measure, concentration, determination, and the
    divine power to speak words;
Are you full-lung'd and limber-lipp'd from long trial? from
    vigorous practice? from physique?
Do you move in these broad lands as broad as they?
Come duly to the divine power to speak words?
For only at last after many years, after chastity, friendship,
    procreation, prudence, and nakedness,
After treading ground and breasting river and lake,
After a loosen'd throat, after absorbing eras, temperaments,
    races, after knowledge, freedom, crimes,
After complete faith, after clarifyings, elevations, and re-
    moving obstructions,
After these and more, it is just possible there comes to a man,
    . a woman, the divine power to speak words;
Then toward that man or that woman swiftly hasten all—
    none refuse, all attend,
Armies, ships, antiquities, libraries, paintings, machines,
    cities, hate, despair, amity, pain, theft, murder, aspira-
    tion, form in close ranks,
They debouch as they are wanted to march obediently
    through the mouth of that man or that woman.

2

O what is it in me that makes me tremble so at voices?
Surely whoever speaks to me in the right voice, him or her I
    shall follow,

As the water follows the moon, silently, with fluid steps, any-
    where around the globe.

All waits for the right voices;
Where is the practis'd and perfect organ? where is the devel-
    op'd soul?
For I see every word utter'd thence has deeper, sweeter, new
    sounds, impossible on less terms.

I see brains and lips closed, tympans and temples unstruck,
Until that comes which has the quality to strike and to un-
    close,
Until that comes which has the quality to bring forth what
    lies slumbering forever ready in all words.
1860   1881

TO HIM THAT WAS CRUCIFIED

MY spirit to yours dear brother,
Do not mind because many sounding your name do not
    understand you,
I do not sound your name, but I understand you,
I specify you with joy O my comrade to salute you, and to
    salute those who are with you, before and since, and
    those to come also,
That we all labor together transmitting the same charge and
    succession,
We few equals indifferent of lands, indifferent of times,
We, enclosers of all continents, all castes, allowers of all
    theologies,
Compassionaters, perceivers, rapport of men,
We walk silent among disputes and assertions, but reject
    not the disputers nor any thing that is asserted,
We hear the bawling and din, we are reach'd at by divisions,
    jealousies, recriminations on every side,
They close peremptorily upon us to surround us, my com-
    rade,
Yet we walk unheld, free, the whole earth over, journeying
    up and down till we make our ineffaceable mark upon
    time and the diverse eras,

Till we saturate time and eras, that the men and women of
    races, ages to come, may prove brethren and lovers as
    we are.
1860   1881

YOU FELONS ON TRIAL IN COURTS

You felons on trial in courts,
You convicts in prison-cells, you sentenced assassins chain'd
    and hand-cuff'd with iron,
Who am I too that I am not on trial or in prison?
Me ruthless and devilish as any, that my wrists are not
    chain'd with iron, or my ankles with iron?

You prostitutes flaunting over the trottoirs or obscene in
    your rooms,
Who am I that I should call you more obscene than myself?

O culpable! I acknowledge—I exposé!
(O admirers, praise not me—compliment not me—you make
    me wince,
I see what you do not—I know what you do not.)

Inside these breast-bones I lie smutch'd and choked,
Beneath this face that appears so impassive hell's tides con-
    tinually run,
Lusts and wickedness are acceptable to me,
I walk with delinquents with passionate love,
I feel I am of them—I belong to those convicts and prosti-
    tutes myself,
And henceforth I will not deny them—for how can I deny
    myself?
1860   1867

LAWS FOR CREATIONS

Laws for creations,
For strong artists and leaders, for fresh broods of teachers
    and perfect literats for America,
For noble savans and coming musicians.

All must have reference to the ensemble of the world, and the
    compact truth of the world,
There shall be no subject too pronounced—all works shall
    illustrate the divine law of indirections.

What do you suppose creation is?
What do you suppose will satisfy the soul, except to walk
    free and own no superior?
What do you suppose I would intimate to you in a hundred
    ways, but that man or woman is as good as God?
And that there is no God any more divine than Yourself?
And that that is what the oldest and newest myths finally
    mean?
And that you or any one must approach creations through
    such laws?
1860   1871

TO A COMMON PROSTITUTE

BE composed—be at ease with me—I am Walt Whitman,
    liberal and lusty as Nature,
Not till the sun excludes you do I exclude you,
Not till the waters refuse to glisten for you and the leaves to
    rustle for you, do my words refuse to glisten and rustle
    for you.

My girl I appoint with you an appointment, and I charge you
    that you make preparation to be worthy to meet me,
And I charge you that you be patient and perfect till I come.

Till then I salute you with a significant look that you do not
    forget me.
1860   1860

I WAS LOOKING A LONG WHILE

I WAS looking a long while for Intentions,
For a clew to the history of the past for myself, and for these
    chants—and now I have found it,
It is not in those paged fables in the libraries, (them I neither
    accept nor reject,)

It is no more in the legends than in all else,
It is in the present—it is this earth to-day,
It is in Democracy—(the purport and aim of all the past,)
It is the life of one man or one woman to-day—the average
    man of to-day,
It is in languages, social customs, literatures, arts,
It is in the broad show of artificial things, ships, machinery,
    politics, creeds, modern improvements, and the inter-
    change of nations,
All for the modern—all for the average man of to-day.
1860   1881

THOUGHT

OF persons arrived at high positions, ceremonies, wealth,
    scholarships, and the like;
(To me all that those persons have arrived at sinks away
    from them, except as it results to their bodies and souls,
So that often to me they appear gaunt and naked,
And often to me each one mocks the others, and mocks him-
    self or herself,
And of each one the core of life, namely happiness, is full of
    the rotten excrement of maggots,
And often to me those men and women pass unwittingly the
    true realities of life, and go toward false realities,
And often to me they are alive after what custom has served
    them, but nothing more,
And often to me they are sad, hasty, unwaked sonnambules
    walking the dusk,)
1860   1871

MIRACLES

WHY, who makes much of a miracle?
As to me I know of nothing else but miracles,
Whether I walk the streets of Manhattan,
Or dart my sight over the roofs of houses toward the sky,
Or wade with naked feet along the beach just in the edge of
    the water,
Or stand under trees in the woods,

Or talk by day with any one I love, or sleep in the bed at night
    with any one I love,
Or sit at table at dinner with the rest,
Or look at strangers opposite me riding in the car,
Or watch honey-bees busy around the hive of a summer fore-
    noon,
Or animals feeding in the fields,
Or birds, or the wonderfulness of insects in the air,
Or the wonderfulness of the sundown, or of stars shining so
    quiet and bright,
Or the exquisite delicate thin curve of the new moon in
    spring;
These with the rest, one and all, are to me miracles,
The whole referring, yet each distinct and in its place.

To me every hour of the light and dark is a miracle,
Every cubic inch of space is a miracle,
Every square yard of the surface of the earth is spread with
    the same,
Every foot of the interior swarms with the same.

To me the sea is a continual miracle,
The fishes that swim—the rocks—the motion of the waves—
    the ships with men in them,
What stranger miracles are there?
1856   1881

SPARKLES FROM THE WHEEL

WHERE the city's ceaseless crowd moves on the livelong day,
Withdrawn I join a group of children watching, I pause
    aside with them.

By the curb toward the edge of the flagging,
A knife-grinder works at his wheel sharpening a great knife,
Bending over he carefully holds it to the stone, by foot and
    knee,
With measur'd tread he turns rapidly, as he presses with light
    but firm hand,
Forth issue then in copious golden jets,
Sparkles from the wheel.

The scene and all its belongings, how they seize and affect me,
The sad sharp-chinn'd old man with worn clothes and broad
    shoulder-band of leather,
Myself effusing and fluid, a phantom curiously floating, now
    here absorb'd and arrested,
The group, (an unminded point set in a vast surrounding,)
The attentive, quiet children, the loud, proud, restive base of
    the streets,
The low hoarse purr of the whirling stone, the light-press'd
    blade,
Diffusing, dropping, sideways-darting, in tiny showers of
    gold,
Sparkles from the wheel.

1871   1871

TO A PUPIL

Is reform needed? is it through you?
The greater the reform needed, the greater the Personality
    you need to accomplish it.

You! do you not see how it would serve to have eyes, blood,
    complexion, clean and sweet?
Do you not see how it would serve to have such a body and
    soul that when you enter the crowd an atmosphere of
    desire and command enters with you, and every one is
    impress'd with your Personality?

O the magnet! the flesh over and over!
Go, dear friend, if need be give up all else, and commence
    to-day to inure yourself to pluck, reality, self-esteem,
    definiteness, elevatedness,
Rest not till you rivet and publish yourself of your own Per-
    sonality.

1860   1860

UNFOLDED OUT OF THE FOLDS

Unfolded out of the folds of the woman man comes un-
    folded, and is always to come unfolded,
Unfolded only out of the superbest woman of the earth is to
    come the superbest man of the earth,

Unfolded out of the friendliest woman is to come the friend-
    liest man,
Unfolded only out of the perfect body of a woman can a man
    be form'd of perfect body,
Unfolded only out of the inimitable poems of woman can
    come the poems of man, (only thence have my poems
    come;)
Unfolded out of the strong and arrogant woman I love, only
    thence can appear the strong and arrogant man I love,
Unfolded by brawny embraces from the well-muscled woman
    I love, only thence come the brawny embraces of the
    man,
Unfolded out of the folds of the woman's brain come all the
    folds of the man's brain, duly obedient,
Unfolded out of the justice of the woman all justice is un-
    folded,
Unfolded out of the sympathy of the woman is all sympathy;
A man is a great thing upon the earth and through eternity,
    but every jot of the greatness of man is unfolded out of
    woman;
First the man is shaped in the woman, he can then be shaped
    in himself.

1856   1871

WHAT AM I AFTER ALL

WHAT am I after all but a child, pleas'd with the sound of my
    own name? repeating it over and over;
I stand apart to hear—it never tires me.

To you your name also;
Did you think there was nothing but two or three pronun-
    ciations in the sound of your name?

1860   1867

KOSMOS

WHO includes diversity and is Nature,
Who is the amplitude of the earth, and the coarseness and
    sexuality of the earth, and the great charity of the earth,
    and the equilibrium also,

Who has not look'd forth from the windows the eyes for
    nothing, or whose brain held audience with messengers
    for nothing,
Who contains believers and disbelievers, who is the most
    majestic lover,
Who holds duly his or her triune proportion of realism,
    spiritualism, and of the æsthetic or intellectual,
Who having consider'd the body finds all its organs and parts
    good,
Who, out of the theory of the earth and of his or her body
    understands by subtle analogies all other theories,
The theory of a city, a poem, and of the large politics of these
    States;
Who believes not only in our globe with its sun and moon,
    but in other globes with their suns and moons,
Who, constructing the house of himself or herself, not for a
    day but for all time, sees races, eras, dates, generations,
The past, the future, dwelling there, like space, inseparable
    together.
1860   1867

OTHERS MAY PRAISE WHAT THEY LIKE

OTHERS may praise what they like;
But I, from the banks of the running Missouri, praise nothing
    in art or aught else,
Till it has well inhaled the atmosphere of this river, also the
    western prairie-scent,
And exudes it all again.
1865   1881

WHO LEARNS MY LESSON COMPLETE?

WHO learns my lesson complete?
Boss, journeyman, apprentice, churchman and atheist,
The stupid and the wise thinker, parents and offspring, mer-
    chant, clerk, porter and customer,
Editor, author, artist, and schoolboy—draw nigh and com-
    mence;
It is no lesson—it lets down the bars to a good lesson,
And that to another, and every one to another still.

The great laws take and effuse without argument,
I am of the same style, for I am their friend,
I love them quits and quits, I do not halt and make salaams.

I lie abstracted and hear beautiful tales of things and the reasons of things,
They are so beautiful I nudge myself to listen.

I cannot say to any person what I hear—I cannot say it to myself—it is very wonderful.

It is no small matter, this round and delicious globe moving so exactly in its orbit for ever and ever, without one jolt or the untruth of a single second,
I do not think it was made in six days, nor in ten thousand years, nor ten billions of years,
Nor plann'd and built one thing after another as an architect plans and builds a house.

I do not think seventy years is the time of a man or woman,
Nor that seventy millions of years is the time of a man or woman,
Nor that years will ever stop the existence of me, or any one else.

Is it wonderful that I should be immortal? as every one is immortal;
I know it is wonderful, but my eyesight is equally wonderful, and how I was conceived in my mother's womb is equally wonderful,
And pass'd from a babe in the creeping trance of a couple of summers and winters to articulate and walk—all this is equally wonderful.

And that my soul embraces you this hour, and we affect each other without ever seeing each other, and never perhaps to see each other, is every bit as wonderful.

And that I can think such thoughts as these is just as wonderful,
And that I can remind you, and you think them and know them to be true, is just as wonderful.

And that the moon spins round the earth and on with the
    earth, is equally wonderful,
And that they balance themselves with the sun and stars is
    equally wonderful.
1855   1867

TESTS

ALL submit to them where they sit, inner, secure, unap-
    proachable to analysis in the soul,
Not traditions, not the outer authorities are the judges,
They are the judges of outer authorities and of all traditions,
They corroborate as they go only whatever corroborates
    themselves, and touches themselves;
For all that, they have it forever in themselves to corroborate
    far and near without one exception.
1860   1860

THE TORCH

ON my Northwest coast in the midst of the night a fisher-
    men's group stands watching,
Out on the lake that expands before them, others are spear-
    ing salmon,
The canoe, a dim shadowy thing, moves across the black water,
Bearing a torch ablaze at the prow.
1865   1867

O STAR OF FRANCE

1870–71

O STAR of France,
The brightness of thy hope and strength and fame,
Like some proud ship that led the fleet so long,
Beseems to-day a wreck driven by the gale, a mastless hulk,
And 'mid its teeming madden'd half-drown'd crowds,
Nor helm nor helmsman.

Dim smitten star,
Orb not of France alone, pale symbol of my soul, its dearest
    hopes,
The struggle and the daring, rage divine for liberty,

Of aspirations toward the far ideal, enthusiast's dreams of
    brotherhood,
Of terror to the tyrant and the priest.

Star crucified—by traitors sold,
Star panting o'er a land of death, heroic land,
Strange, passionate, mocking, frivolous land.

Miserable! yet for thy errors, vanities, sins, I will not now
    rebuke thee,
Thy unexampled woes and pangs have quell'd them all,
And left thee sacred.

In that amid thy many faults thou ever aimedst highly,
In that thou wouldst not really sell thyself however great the
    price,
In that thou surely wakedst weeping from thy drugg'd sleep,
In that alone among thy sisters thou, giantess, didst rend the
    ones that shamed thee,
In that thou couldst not, wouldst not, wear the usual chains,
This cross, thy livid face, thy pierced hands and feet,
The spear thrust in thy side.

O star! O ship of France, beat back and baffled long!
Bear up O smitten orb!   O ship continue on!

Sure as the ship of all, the Earth itself,
Product of deathly fire and turbulent chaos,
Forth from its spasms of fury and its poisons,
Issuing at last in perfect power and beauty,
Onward beneath the sun following its course,
So thee O ship of France!

Finish'd the days, the clouds dispel'd,
The travail o'er, the long-sought extrication,
When lo! reborn, high o'er the European world,
(In gladness answering thence, as face afar to face, reflecting
    ours Columbia,)
Again thy star O France, fair lustrous star,
In heavenly peace, clearer, more bright than ever,
Shall beam immortal.
1871   1881

THE OX-TAMER

In a far-away northern county in the placid pastoral region,
Lives my farmer friend, the theme of my recitative, a famous
tamer of oxen,
There they bring him the three-year-olds and the four-year-
olds to break them,
He will take the wildest steer in the world and break him and
tame him,
He will go fearless without any whip where the young bullock
chafes up and down the yard,
The bullock's head tosses restless high in the air with raging
eyes,
Yet see you! how soon his rage subsides—how soon this
tamer tames him;
See you! on the farms hereabouts a hundred oxen young and
old, and he is the man who has tamed them,
They all know him, all are affectionate to him;
See you! some are such beautiful animals, so lofty look-
ing;
Some are buff-color'd, some mottled, one has a white line
running along his back, some are brindled,
Some have wide flaring horns (a good sign)—see you! the
bright hides,
See, the two with stars on their foreheads—see, the round
bodies and broad backs,
How straight and square they stand on their legs—what fine
sagacious eyes!
How they watch their tamer—they wish him near them—
how they turn to look after him!
What yearning expression! how uneasy they are when he
moves away from them;
Now I marvel what it can be he appears to them, (books,
politics, poems, depart—all else departs,)
I confess I envy only his fascination—my silent, illiterate
friend,
Whom a hundred oxen love there in his life on farms,
In the northern country far, in the placid pastoral region.
1874   1881

AN OLD MAN'S THOUGHT OF SCHOOL

For the Inauguration of a Public School, Camden, New Jersey, 1874

AN old man's thought of school,
An old man gathering youthful memories and blooms that
    youth itself cannot.

Now only do I know you,
O fair auroral skies—O morning dew upon the grass!

And these I see, these sparkling eyes,
These stores of mystic meaning, these young lives,
Building, equipping like a fleet of ships, immortal ships,
Soon to sail out over the measureless seas,
On the soul's voyage.

Only a lot of boys and girls?
Only the tiresome spelling, writing, ciphering classes?
Only a public school?

Ah more, infinitely more;
(As George Fox rais'd his warning cry, "Is it this pile of
    brick and mortar, these dead floors, windows, rails, you
    call the church?
Why this is not the church at all—the church is living, ever
    living souls.")

And you America,
Cast you the real reckoning for your present?
The lights and shadows of your future, good or evil?
To girlhood, boyhood look, the teacher and the school.
1874   1881

WANDERING AT MORN

WANDERING at morn,
Emerging from the night from gloomy thoughts, thee in my
    thoughts,
Yearning for thee harmonious Union! thee, singing bird
    divine!

Thee coil'd in evil times my country, with craft and black
    dismay, with every meanness, treason thrust upon thee,
This common marvel I beheld—the parent thrush I watch'd
    feeding its young,
The singing thrush whose tones of joy and faith ecstatic,
Fail not to certify and cheer my soul.

There ponder'd, felt I,
If worms, snakes, loathsome grubs, may to sweet spiritual
    songs be turn'd,
If vermin so transposed, so used and bless'd may be,
Then may I trust in you, your fortunes, days, my country;
Who knows but these may be the lessons fit for you?
From these your future song may rise with joyous trills,
Destin'd to fill the world.

1873   1881

ITALIAN MUSIC IN DAKOTA

("*The Seventeenth—the finest Regimental Band I ever
heard.*")

THROUGH the soft evening air enwinding all,
Rocks, woods, fort, cannon, pacing sentries, endless wilds,
In dulcet streams, in flutes' and cornets' notes,
Electric, pensive, turbulent, artificial,
(Yet strangely fitting even here, meanings unknown before,
Subtler than ever, more harmony, as if born here, related
    here,
Not to the city's fresco'd rooms, not to the audience of the
    opera house,
Sounds, echoes, wandering strains, as really here at home,
Sonnambula's innocent love, trios with *Norma's* anguish,
And thy ecstatic chorus *Poliuto;*)
Ray'd in the limpid yellow slanting sundown,
Music, Italian music in Dakota.

While Nature, sovereign of this gnarl'd realm,
Lurking in hidden barbaric grim recesses,
Acknowledging rapport however far remov'd,

(As some old root or soil of earth its last-born flower or fruit,)
Listens well pleas'd.
1881   1881

WITH ALL THY GIFTS

WITH all thy gifts America,
Standing secure, rapidly tending, overlooking the world,
Power, wealth, extent, vouchsafed to thee—with these and
     like of these vouchsafed to thee,
What if one gift thou lackest? (the ultimate human problem
     never solving,)
The gift of perfect women fit for thee—what if that gift of
     gifts thou lackest?
The towering feminine of thee? the beauty, health, comple-
     tion, fit for thee?
The mothers fit for thee?
1876   1881

MY PICTURE-GALLERY

IN a little house keep I pictures suspended, it is not a fix'd
     house,
It is round, it is only a few inches from one side to the other;
Yet behold, it has room for all the shows of the world, all
     memories!
Here the tableaus of life, and here the groupings of death;
Here, do you know this? this is cicerone himself,
With finger rais'd he points to the prodigal pictures.
1880   1881

THE PRAIRIE STATES

A NEWER garden of creation, no primal solitude,
Dense, joyous, modern, populous millions, cities and farms,
With iron interlaced, composite, tied, many in one,
By all the world contributed—freedom's and law's and
     thrift's society,
The crown and teeming paradise, so far, of time's accumula-
     tions,
To justify the past.
1880   1881

Proud Music of the Storm

1

PROUD music of the storm,
Blast that careers so free, whistling across the prairies,
Strong hum of forest tree-tops—wind of the mountains,
Personified dim shapes—you hidden orchestras,
You serenades of phantoms with instruments alert,
Bending with Nature's rhythmus all the tongues of nations;
You chords left as by vast composers—you choruses,
You formless, free, religious dances—you from the Orient,
You undertone of rivers, roar of pouring cataracts,
You sounds from distant guns with galloping cavalry,
Echoes of camps with all the different bugle-calls,
Trooping tumultuous, fiiling the midnight late, bending me
    powerless,
Entering my lonesome slumber-chamber, why have you
    seiz'd me?

2

Come forward O my soul, and let the rest retire,
Listen, lose not, it is toward thee they tend,
Parting the midnight, entering my slumber-chamber,
For thee they sing and dance O soul.

A festival song,
The duet of the bridegroom and the bride, a marriage-
    march,
With lips of love, and hearts of lovers fill'd to the brim with
    love,
The red-flush'd cheeks and perfumes, the cortege swarming
    full of friendly faces young and old,
To flutes' clear notes and sounding harps' cantabile.

Now loud approaching drums,
Victoria! see'st thou in powder-smoke the banners torn but
    flying? the rout of the baffled?
Hearest those shouts of a conquering army?

(Ah soul, the sobs of women, the wounded groaning in
    agony,
The hiss and crackle of flames, the blacken'd ruins, the em-
    bers of cities,
The dirge and desolation of mankind.)

Now airs antique and mediæval fill me,
I see and hear old harpers with their harps at Welsh festivals,
I hear the minnesingers singing their lays of love,
I hear the minstrels, gleemen, troubadours, of the middle
    ages.

Now the great organ sounds,
Tremulous, while underneath, (as the hid footholds of the
    earth,
On which arising rest, and leaping forth depend,
All shapes of beauty, grace and strength, all hues we know,
Green blades of grass and warbling birds, children that gam-
    bol and play, the clouds of heaven above,)
The strong base stands, and its pulsations intermits not,
Bathing, supporting, merging all the rest, maternity of all the
    rest,
And with it every instrument in multitudes,
The players playing, all the world's musicians,
The solemn hymns and masses rousing adoration,
All passionate heart-chants, sorrowful appeals,
The measureless sweet vocalists of ages,
And for their solvent setting earth's own diapason,
Of winds and woods and mighty ocean waves,
A new composite orchestra, binder of years and climes, ten-
    fold renewer,
As of the far-back days the poets tell, the Paradiso,
The straying thence, the separation long, but now the wan-
    dering done,
The journey done, the journeyman come home,
And man and art with Nature fused again.

Tutti! for earth and heaven;
(The Almighty leader now for once has signal'd with his
    wand.)

The manly strophe of the husbands of the world,
And all the wives responding.

The tongues of violins,
(I think O tongues ye tell this heart, that cannot tell itself,
This brooding yearning heart, that cannot tell itself.)

3

Ah from a little child,
Thou knowest soul how to me all sounds became music,
My mother's voice in lullaby or hymn,
(The voice, O tender voices, memory's loving voices,
Last miracle of all, O dearest mother's, sister's, voices;)
The rain, the growing corn, the breeze among the long-
    leav'd corn,
The measur'd sea-surf beating on the sand,
The twittering bird, the hawk's sharp scream,
The wild-fowl's notes at night as flying low migrating north
    or south,
The psalm in the country church or mid the clustering trees,
    the open air camp-meeting,
The fiddler in the tavern, the glee, the long-strung sailor-
    song,
The lowing cattle, bleating sheep, the crowing cock at dawn.

All songs of current lands come sounding round me,
The German airs of friendship, wine and love,
Irish ballads, merry jigs and dances, English warbles,
Chansons of France, Scotch tunes, and o'er the rest,
Italia's peerless compositions.

Across the stage with pallor on her face, yet lurid passion,
Stalks Norma brandishing the dagger in her hand.

I see poor crazed Lucia's eyes' unnatural gleam,
Her hair down her back falls loose and dishevel'd.

I see where Ernani walking the bridal garden,
Amid the scent of night-roses, radiant, holding his bride by
    the hand,
Hears the infernal call, the death-pledge of the horn.

To crossing swords and gray hairs bared to heaven,
The clear electric base and baritone of the world,
The trombone duo, Libertad forever!

From Spanish chestnut trees' dense shade,
By old and heavy convent walls a wailing song,
Song of lost love, the torch of youth and life quench'd in
    despair,
Song of the dying swan, Fernando's heart is breaking.

Awaking from her woes at last retriev'd Amina sings,
Copious as stars and glad as morning light the torrents of her
    joy.

(The teeming lady comes,
The lustrous orb, Venus contralto, the blooming mother,
Sister of loftiest gods, Alboni's self I hear.)

4

I hear those odes, symphonies, operas,
I hear in the *William Tell* the music of an arous'd and angry
    people,
I hear Meyerbeer's *Huguenots*, the *Prophet*, or *Robert*,
Gounod's *Faust*, or Mozart's *Don Juan*.

I hear the dance-music of all nations,
The waltz, some delicious measure, lapsing, bathing me in bliss,
The bolero to tinkling guitars and clattering castanets.

I see religious dances old and new,
I hear the sound of the Hebrew lyre,
I see the crusaders marching bearing the cross on high, to the
    martial clang of cymbals,
I hear dervishes monotonously chanting, interspers'd with
    frantic shouts, as they spin around turning always to-
    wards Mecca,

I see the rapt religious dances of the Persians and the Arabs,
Again, at Eleusis, home of Ceres, I see the modern Greeks
    dancing,
I hear them clapping their hands as they bend their bodies,
I hear the metrical shuffling of their feet.

I see again the wild old Corybantian dance, the performers
    wounding each other,
I see the Roman youth to the shrill sound of flageolets throw-
    ing and catching their weapons,
As they fall on their knees and rise again.

I hear from the Mussulman mosque the muezzin calling,
I see the worshippers within, nor form nor sermon, argument
    nor word,
But silent, strange, devout, rais'd glowing heads, ecstatic
    faces.

I hear the Egyptian harp of many strings,
The primitive chants of the Nile boatmen,
The sacred imperial hymns of China,
To the delicate sounds of the king, (the stricken wood and
    stone,)
Or to Hindu flutes and the fretting twang of the vina,
A band of bayaderes.

5

Now Asia, Africa leave me, Europe seizing inflates me,
To organs huge and bands I hear as from vast concourses of
    voices,
Luther's strong hymn *Eine feste Burg ist unser Gott*,
Rossini's *Stabat Mater dolorosa*,
Or floating in some high cathedral dim with gorgeous color'd
    windows,
The passionate *Agnus Dei* or *Gloria in Excelsis*.

Composers! mighty maestros!
And you, sweet singers of old lands, soprani, tenori, bassi!
To you a new bard caroling in the West,
Obeisant sends his love.

(Such led to thee O soul,
All senses, shows and objects, lead to thee,
But now it seems to me sound leads o'er all the rest.)

I hear the annual singing of the children in St. Paul's cathedral,
Or, under the high roof of some colossal hall, the sym-
    phonies, oratorios of Beethoven, Handel, or Haydn,
The *Creation* in billows of godhood laves me.

Give me to hold all sounds, (I madly struggling cry,)
Fill me with all the voices of the universe,
Endow me with their throbbings, Nature's also,
The tempests, waters, winds, operas and chants, marches and
    dances,
Utter, pour in, for I would take them all!

6

Then I woke softly,
And pausing, questioning awhile the music of my dream,
And questioning all those reminiscences, the tempest in its
    fury,
And all the songs of sopranos and tenors,
And those rapt oriental dances of religious fervor,
And the sweet varied instruments, and the diapason of
    organs,
And all the artless plaints of love and grief and death,
I said to my silent curious soul out of the bed of the slumber-
    chamber,
Come, for I have found the clew I sought so long,
Let us go forth refresh'd amid the day,
Cheerfully tallying life, walking the world, the real,
Nourish'd henceforth by our celestial dream.

And I said, moreover,
Haply what thou hast heard O soul was not the sound of
    winds,
Nor dream of raging storm, nor sea-hawk's flapping wings
    nor harsh scream,
Nor vocalism of sun-bright Italy,

Nor German organ majestic, nor vast concourse of voices,
　　nor layers of harmonies,
Nor strophes of husbands and wives, nor sound of marching
　　soldiers,
Nor flutes, nor harps, nor the bugle-calls of camps,
But to a new rhythmus fitted for thee,
Poems bridging the way from Life to Death, vaguely wafted
　　in night air, uncaught, unwritten,
Which let us go forth in the bold day and write.
(1868)　　　　　　　　　　　　　　　　　　　1881

Passage to India

1

SINGING my days,
Singing the great achievements of the present,
Singing the strong light works of engineers,
Our modern wonders, (the antique ponderous Seven out-
　　vied,)
In the Old World the east the Suez canal,
The New by its mighty railroad spann'd,
The seas inlaid with eloquent gentle wires;
Yet first to sound, and ever sound, the cry with thee O soul,
The Past! the Past! the Past!

The Past—the dark unfathom'd retrospect!
The teeming gulf—the sleepers and the shadows!
The past—the infinite greatness of the past!
For what is the present after all but a growth out of the past?
(As a projectile form'd, impell'd, passing a certain line, still
　　keeps on,
So the present, utterly form'd, impell'd by the past.)

2

Passage O soul to India!
Eclaircise the myths Asiatic, the primitive fables.

Not you alone proud truths of the world,
Nor you alone ye facts of modern science,
But myths and fables of eld, Asia's, Africa's fables,
The far-darting beams of the spirit, the unloos'd dreams,
The deep diving bibles and legends,
The daring plots of the poets, the elder religions;
O you temples fairer than lilies pour'd over by the rising
    sun!
O you fables spurning the known, eluding the hold of the
    known, mounting to heaven!
You lofty and dazzling towers, pinnacled, red as roses, bur-
    nish'd with gold!
Towers of fables immortal fashion'd from mortal dreams!
You too I welcome and fully the same as the rest!
You too with joy I sing.

Passage to India!
Lo, soul, seest thou not God's purpose from the first?
The earth to be spann'd, connected by network,
The races, neighbors, to marry and be given in marriage,
The oceans to be cross'd, the distant brought near,
The lands to be welded together.

A worship new I sing,
You captains, voyagers, explorers, yours,
You engineers, you architects, machinists, yours,
You, not for trade or transportation only,
But in God's name, and for thy sake O soul.

3

Passage to India!
Lo soul for thee of tableaus twain,
I see in one the Suez canal initiated, open'd,
I see the procession of steamships, the Empress Eugenie's
    leading the van,
I mark from on deck the strange landscape, the pure sky, the
    level sand in the distance,
I pass swiftly the picturesque groups, the workmen gather'd,
The gigantic dredging machines.

In one again, different, (yet thine, all thine, O soul, the same,)
I see over my own continent the Pacific railroad surmounting
    every barrier,
I see continual trains of cars winding along the Platte carry-
    ing freight and passengers,
I hear the locomotives rushing and roaring, and the shrill
    steam-whistle,
I hear the echoes reverberate through the grandest scenery in
    the world,
I cross the Laramie plains, I note the rocks in grotesque
    shapes, the buttes,
I see the plentiful larkspur and wild onions, the barren,
    colorless, sage-deserts,
I see in glimpses afar or towering immediately above me the
    great mountains, I see the Wind river and the Wahsatch
    mountains,
I see the Monument mountain and the Eagle's Nest, I pass
    the Promontory, I ascend the Nevadas,
I scan the noble Elk mountain and wind around its base,
I see the Humboldt range, I thread the valley and cross the
    river,
I see the clear waters of lake Tahoe, I see forests of majestic
    pines,
Or crossing the great desert, the alkaline plains, I behold en-
    chanting mirages of waters and meadows,
Marking through these and after all, in duplicate slender
    lines,
Bridging the three or four thousand miles of land travel,
Tying the Eastern to the Western sea,
The road between Europe and Asia.

(Ah Genoese thy dream! thy dream!
Centuries after thou art laid in thy grave,
The shore thou foundest verifies thy dream.)

4

Passage to India!
Struggles of many a captain, tales of many a sailor dead,
Over my mood stealing and spreading they come,
Like clouds and cloudlets in the unreach'd sky.

Along all history, down the slopes,
As a rivulet running, sinking now, and now again to the sur-
    face rising,
A ceaseless thought, a varied train—lo, soul, to thee, thy
    sight, they rise,
The plans, the voyages again, the expeditions;
Again Vasco de Gama sails forth,
Again the knowledge gain'd, the mariner's compass,
Lands found and nations born, thou born America,
For purpose vast, man's long probation fill'd,
Thou rondure of the world at last accomplish'd.

5

O vast Rondure, swimming in space,
Cover'd all over with visible power and beauty,
Alternate light and day and the teeming spiritual darkness,
Unspeakable high processions of sun and moon and count-
    less stars above,
Below, the manifold grass and waters, animals, mountains,
    trees,
With inscrutable purpose, some hidden prophetic intention,
Now first it seems my thought begins to span thee.

Down from the gardens of Asia descending radiating,
Adam and Eve appear, then their myriad progeny after
    them,
Wandering, yearning, curious, with restless explorations,
With questionings, baffled, formless, feverish, with never-
    happy hearts,
With that sad incessant refrain, *Wherefore unsatisfied soul?*
    and *Whither O mocking life?*

Ah who shall soothe these feverish children?
Who justify these restless explorations?
Who speak the secret of impassive earth?
Who bind it to us? what is this separate Nature so unnatural?
What is this earth to our affections? (unloving earth, without
    a throb to answer ours,
Cold earth, the place of graves.)

Yet soul be sure the first intent remains, and shall be carried
    out,
Perhaps even now the time has arrived.

After the seas are all cross'd, (as they seem already cross'd,)
After the great captains and engineers have accomplish'd
    their work,
After the noble inventors, after the scientists, the chemist, the
    geologist, ethnologist,
Finally shall come the poet worthy that name,
The true son of God shall come singing his songs.

Then not your deeds only O voyagers, O scientists and in-
    ventors, shall be justified,
All these hearts as of fretted children shall be sooth'd,
All affection shall be fully responded to, the secret shall be
    told,
All these separations and gaps shall be taken up and hook'd
    and link'd together,
The whole earth, this cold, impassive, voiceless earth, shall
    be completely justified,
Trinitas divine shall be gloriously accomplish'd and com-
    pacted by the true son of God, the poet,
(He shall indeed pass the straits and conquer the mountains,
He shall double the cape of Good Hope to some purpose,)
Nature and Man shall be disjoin'd and diffused no more,
The true son of God shall absolutely fuse them.

6

Year at whose wide-flung door I sing!
Year of the purpose accomplish'd!
Year of the marriage of continents, climates and oceans!
(No mere doge of Venice now wedding the Adriatic,)
I see O year in you the vast terraqueous globe given and
    giving all,
Europe to Asia, Africa join'd, and they to the New World,
The lands, geographies, dancing before you, holding a festi-
    val garland,
As brides and bridegrooms hand in hand.

Passage to India!
Cooling airs from Caucasus, far, soothing cradle of man,
The river Euphrates flowing, the past lit up again.

Lo soul, the retrospect brought forward,
The old, most populous, wealthiest of earth's lands,
The streams of the Indus and the Ganges and their many
    affluents,
(I my shores of America walking to-day behold, resuming all,)
The tale of Alexander on his warlike marches suddenly dying,
On one side China and on the other side Persia and Arabia,
To the south the great seas and the bay of Bengal,
The flowing literatures, tremendous epics, religions, castes,
Old occult Brahma interminably far back, the tender and
    junior Buddha,
Central and southern empires and all their belongings, pos-
    sessors,
The wars of Tamerlane, the reign of Aurungzebe,
The traders, rulers, explorers, Moslems, Venetians, Byzan-
    tium, the Arabs, Portuguese,
The first travelers famous yet, Marco Polo, Batouta the Moor,
Doubts to be solv'd, the map incognita, blanks to be fill'd,
The foot of man unstay'd, the hands never at rest,
Thyself O soul that will not brook a challenge.

The mediæval navigators rise before me,
The world of 1492, with its awaken'd enterprise,
Something swelling in humanity now like the sap of the earth
    in spring,
The sunset splendor of chivalry declining.

And who art thou sad shade?
Gigantic, visionary, thyself a visionary,
With majestic limbs and pious beaming eyes,
Spreading around with every look of thine a golden world,
Enhuing it with gorgeous hues.

As the chief histrion,
Down to the footlights walks in some great scena,
Dominating the rest I see the Admiral himself,
(History's type of courage, action, faith,)

Behold him sail from Palos leading his little fleet,
His voyage behold, his return, his great fame,
His misfortunes, calumniators, behold him a prisoner,
    chain'd,
Behold his dejection, poverty, death.

(Curious in time I stand, noting the efforts of heroes,
Is the deferment long? bitter the slander, poverty, death?
Lies the seed unreck'd for centuries in the ground? lo, to
    God's due occasion,
Uprising in the night, it sprouts, blooms,
And fills the earth with use and beauty.)

7

Passage indeed O soul to primal thought,
Not lands and seas alone, thy own clear freshness,
The young maturity of brood and bloom,
To realms of budding bibles.

O soul, repressless, I with thee and thou with me,
Thy circumnavigation of the world begin,
Of man, the voyage of his mind's return,
To reason's early paradise,
Back, back to wisdom's birth, to innocent intuitions,
Again with fair creation.

8

O we can wait no longer,
We too take ship O soul,
Joyous we too launch out on trackless seas,
Fearless for unknown shores on waves of ecstasy to sail,
Amid the wafting winds, (thou pressing me to thee, I thee to
    me, O soul,)
Caroling free, singing our song of God,
Chanting our chant of pleasant exploration.

With laugh and many a kiss,
(Let others deprecate, let others weep for sin, remorse,
    humiliation,)
O soul thou pleasest me, I thee.

Ah more than any priest O soul we too believe in God,
But with the mystery of God we dare not dally.

O soul thou pleasest me, I thee,
Sailing these seas or on the hills, or waking in the night,
Thoughts, silent thoughts, of Time and Space and Death, like
    waters flowing,
Bear me indeed as through the regions infinite,
Whose air I breathe, whose ripples hear, lave me all over,
Bathe me O God in thee, mounting to thee,
I and my soul to range in range of thee.

O Thou transcendent,
Nameless, the fibre and the breath,
Light of the light, shedding forth universes, thou centre of
    them,
Thou mightier centre of the true, the good, the loving,
Thou moral, spiritual fountain—affection's source—thou
    reservoir,
(O pensive soul of me—O thirst unsatisfied—waitest not
    there?
Waitest not haply for us somewhere there the Comrade per-
    fect?)
Thou pulse—thou motive of the stars, suns, systems,
That, circling, move in order, safe, harmonious,
Athwart the shapeless vastnesses of space,
How should I think, how breathe a single breath, how speak,
    if, out of myself,
I could not launch, to those, superior universes?

Swiftly I shrivel at the thought of God,
At Nature and its wonders, Time and Space and Death,
But that I, turning, call to thee O soul, thou actual Me,
And lo, thou gently masterest the orbs,
Thou matest Time, smilest content at Death,
And fillest, swellest full the vastnesses of Space.

Greater than stars or suns,
Bounding O soul thou journeyest forth;
What love than thine and ours could wider amplify?
What aspirations, wishes, outvie thine and ours O soul?

What dreams of the ideal? what plans of purity, perfection,
    strength,
What cheerful willingness for others' sake to give up all?
For others' sake to suffer all?

Reckoning ahead O soul, when thou, the time achiev'd,
The seas all cross'd, weather'd the capes, the voyage done,
Surrounded, copest, frontest God, yieldest, the aim attain'd,
As fill'd with friendship, love complete, the Elder Brother
    found,
The Younger melts in fondness in his arms.

9

Passage to more than India!
Are thy wings plumed indeed for such far flights?
O soul, voyagest thou indeed on voyages like those?
Disportest thou on waters such as those?
Soundest below the Sanscrit and the Vedas?
Then have thy bent unleash'd.

Passage to you, your shores, ye aged fierce enigmas!
Passage to you, to mastership of you, ye strangling problems!
You, strew'd with the wrecks of skeletons, that, living, never
    reach'd you.

Passage to more than India!
O secret of the earth and sky!
Of you O waters of the sea! O winding creeks and rivers!
Of you O woods and fields! of you strong mountains of my
    land!
Of you O prairies! of you gray rocks!
O morning red! O clouds! O rain and snows!
O day and night, passage to you!
O sun and moon and all you stars! Sirius and Jupiter!
Passage to you!

Passage, immediate passage! the blood burns in my veins!
Away O soul! hoist instantly the anchor!
Cut the hawsers—haul out—shake out every sail!
Have we not stood here like trees in the ground long enough?

Have we not grovel'd here long enough, eating and drinking
    like mere brutes?
Have we not darken'd and dazed ourselves with books long
    enough?

Sail forth—steer for the deep waters only,
Reckless O soul, exploring, I with thee, and thou with me,
For we are bound where mariner has not yet dared to go,
And we will risk the ship, ourselves and all.

O my brave soul!
O farther farther sail!
O daring joy, but safe! are they not all the seas of God?
O farther, farther, farther sail!
(1868)   1871

Prayer of Columbus

A BATTER'D, wreck'd old man,
Thrown on this savage shore, far, far from home,
Pent by the sea and dark rebellious brows, twelve dreary
    months,
Sore, stiff with many toils, sicken'd and nigh to death,
I take my way along the island's edge,
Venting a heavy heart.

I am too full of woe!
Haply I may not live another day;
I cannot rest O God, I cannot eat or drink or sleep,
Till I put forth myself, my prayer, once more to Thee,
Breathe, bathe myself once more in Thee, commune with
    Thee,
Report myself once more to Thee.

Thou knowest my years entire, my life,
My long and crowded life of active work, not adoration
    merely;
Thou knowest the prayers and vigils of my youth,

Thou knowest my manhood's solemn and visionary medi-
    tations,
Thou knowest how before I commenced I devoted all to
    come to Thee,
Thou knowest I have in age ratified all those vows and
    strictly kept them,
Thou knowest I have not once lost nor faith nor ecstasy in
    Thee,
In shackles, prison'd, in disgrace, repining not,
Accepting all from Thee, as duly come from Thee.

All my emprises have been fill'd with Thee,
My speculations, plans, begun and carried on in thought of
    Thee,
Sailing the deep or journeying the land for Thee;
Intentions, purports, aspirations mine, leaving results to
    Thee.

O I am sure they really came from Thee,
The urge, the ardor, the unconquerable will,
The potent, felt, interior command, stronger than words,
A message from the Heavens whispering to me even in sleep,
These sped me on.

By me and these the work so far accomplish'd,
By me earth's elder cloy'd and stifled lands uncloy'd, un-
    loos'd,
By me the hemispheres rounded and tied, the unknown to the
    known.

The end I know not, it is all in Thee,
Or small or great I know not—haply what broad fields, what
    lands,
Haply the brutish measureless human undergrowth I know,
Transplanted there may rise to stature, knowledge worthy
    Thee,
Haply the swords I know may there indeed be turn'd to
    reaping-tools,
Haply the lifeless cross I know, Europe's dead cross, may
    bud and blossom there.

One effort more, my altar this bleak sand;
That Thou O God my life hast lighted,
With ray of light, steady, ineffable, vouchsafed of Thee,
Light rare untellable, lighting the very light,
Beyond all signs, descriptions, languages;
For that O God, be it my latest word, here on my knees,
Old, poor, and paralyzed, I thank Thee.

My terminus near,
The clouds already closing in upon me,
The voyage balk'd, the course disputed, lost,
I yield my ships to Thee.

My hands, my limbs grow nerveless,
My brain feels rack'd, bewilder'd,
Let the old timbers part, I will not part,
I will cling fast to Thee, O God, though the waves buffet me,
Thee, Thee at least I know.

Is it the prophet's thought I speak, or am I raving?
What do I know of life? what of myself?
I know not even my own work past or present,
Dim ever-shifting guesses of it spread before me,
Of newer better worlds, their mighty parturition,
Mocking, perplexing me.

And these things I see suddenly, what mean they?
As if some miracle, some hand divine unseal'd my eyes,
Shadowy vast shapes smile through the air and sky,
And on the distant waves sail countless ships,
And anthems in new tongues I hear saluting me.
1874   1881

The Sleepers

1

I WANDER all night in my vision,
Stepping with light feet, swiftly and noiselessly stepping and
    stopping,

Bending with open eyes over the shut eyes of sleepers,
Wandering and confused, lost to myself, ill-assorted, contradictory,
Pausing, gazing, bending, and stopping.

How solemn they look there, stretch'd and still,
How quiet they breathe, the little children in their cradles.

The wretched features of ennuyés, the white features of corpses, the livid faces of drunkards, the sick-gray faces of onanists,
The gash'd bodies on battle-fields, the insane in their strong-door'd rooms, the sacred idiots, the new-born emerging from gates, and the dying emerging from gates,
The night pervades them and infolds them.

The married couple sleep calmly in their bed, he with his palm on the hip of the wife, and she with her palm on the hip of the husband;
The sisters sleep lovingly side by side in their bed,
The men sleep lovingly side by side in theirs,
And the mother sleeps with her little child carefully wrapt.

The blind sleep, and the deaf and dumb sleep,
The prisoner sleeps well in the prison, the runaway son sleeps,
The murderer that is to be hung next day, how does he sleep?
And the murder'd person, how does he sleep?

The female that loves unrequited sleeps,
And the male that loves unrequited sleeps,
The head of the money-maker that plotted all day sleeps,
And the enraged and treacherous dispositions, all, all sleep.

I stand in the dark with drooping eyes by the worst-suffering and the most restless,
I pass my hands soothingly to and fro a few inches from them,
The restless sink in their beds, they fitfully sleep.

Now I pierce the darkness, new beings appear,
The earth recedes from me into the night,

I saw that it was beautiful, and I see that what is not the
    earth is beautiful.

I go from bedside to bedside, I sleep close with the other
    sleepers each in turn,
I dream in my dream all the dreams of the other dreamers,
And I become the other dreamers.

I am a dance—play up there! the fit is whirling me fast!

I am the ever-laughing—it is new moon and twilight,
I see the hiding of douceurs, I see nimble ghosts whichever
    way I look,
Cache and cache again deep in the ground and sea, and where
    it is neither ground nor sea.

Well do they do their jobs those journeymen divine,
Only from me can they hide nothing, and would not if they
    could,
I reckon I am their boss and they make me a pet besides,
And surround me and lead me and run ahead when I walk,
To lift their cunning covers to signify me with stretch'd arms,
    and resume the way;
Onward we move, a gay gang of blackguards! with mirth-
    shouting music and wild-flapping pennants of joy!

I am the actor, the actress, the voter, the politician,
The emigrant and the exile, the criminal that stood in the box,
He who has been famous and he who shall be famous after
    to-day,
The stammerer, the well-formed person, the wasted or feeble
    person.

I am she who adorn'd herself and folded her hair expectantly,
My truant lover has come, and it is dark.

Double yourself and receive me darkness,
Receive me and my lover too, he will not let me go without
    him.

I roll myself upon you as upon a bed, I resign myself to the
    dusk.

He whom I call answers me and takes the place of my lover,
He rises with me silently from the bed.

Darkness, you are gentler than my lover, his flesh was sweaty
    and panting,
I feel the hot moisture yet that he left me.

My hands are spread forth, I pass them in all directions,
I would sound up the shadowy shore to which you are jour-
    neying.

Be careful darkness! already what was it touch'd me?
I thought my lover had gone, else darkness and he are one,
I hear the heart-beat, I follow, I fade away.

2

I descend my western course, my sinews are flaccid,
Perfume and youth course through me and I am their wake.

It is my face yellow and wrinkled instead of the old woman's,
I sit low in a straw-bottom chair and carefully darn my
    grandson's stockings.

It is I too, the sleepless widow looking out on the winter
    midnight,
I see the sparkles of starshine on the icy and pallid earth.

A shroud I see and I am the shroud, I wrap a body and lie in
    the coffin,
It is dark here under ground, it is not evil or pain here, it is
    blank here, for reasons.

(It seems to me that every thing in the light and air ought to
    be happy,
Whoever is not in his coffin and the dark grave let him know
    he has enough.)

3

I see a beautiful gigantic swimmer swimming naked through
    the eddies of the sea,

His brown hair lies close and even to his head, he strikes out
with courageous arms, he urges himself with his legs,
I see his white body, I see his undaunted eyes,
I hate the swift-running eddies that would dash him head-
foremost on the rocks.

What are you doing you ruffianly red-trickled waves?
Will you kill the courageous giant? will you kill him in the
prime of his middle age?

Steady and long he struggles,
He is baffled, bang'd, bruis'd, he holds out while his strength
holds out,
The slapping eddies are spotted with his blood, they bear him
away, they roll him, swing him, turn him,
His beautiful body is borne in the circling eddies, it is con-
tinually bruis'd on rocks,
Swiftly and out of sight is borne the brave corpse.

4

I turn but do not extricate myself,
Confused, a past-reading, another, but with darkness yet.

The beach is cut by the razory ice-wind, the wreck-guns
sound,
The tempest lulls, the moon comes floundering through the
drifts.

I look where the ship helplessly heads end on, I hear the
burst as she strikes, I hear the howls of dismay, they
grow fainter and fainter.

I cannot aid with my wringing fingers,
I can but rush to the surf and let it drench me and freeze upon
me.

I search with the crowd, not one of the company is wash'd to
us alive,
In the morning I help pick up the dead and lay them in rows
in a barn.

5

Now of the older war-days, the defeat at Brooklyn,
Washington stands inside the lines, he stands on the in-
trench'd hills amid a crowd of officers,
His face is cold and damp, he cannot repress the weeping
drops,
He lifts the glass perpetually to his eyes, the color is blanch'd
from his cheeks,
He sees the slaughter of the southern braves confided to him
by their parents.

The same at last and at last when peace is declared,
He stands in the room of the old tavern, the well-belov'd
soldiers all pass through,
The officers speechless and slow draw near in their turns,
The chief encircles their necks with his arm and kisses them
on the cheek,
He kisses lightly the wet cheeks one after another, he shakes
hands and bids good-by to the army.

6

Now what my mother told me one day as we sat at dinner
together,
Of when she was a nearly grown girl living home with her
parents on the old homestead.

A red squaw came one breakfast-time to the old homestead,
On her back she carried a bundle of rushes for rush-bottom-
ing chairs,
Her hair, straight, shiny, coarse, black, profuse, half-en-
velop'd her face,
Her step was free and elastic, and her voice sounded ex-
quisitely as she spoke.

My mother looked in delight and amazement at the stranger,
She look'd at the freshness of her tall-borne face and full and
pliant limbs,
The more she look'd upon her she loved her,
Never before had she seen such wonderful beauty and purity,

She made her sit on a bench by the jamb of the fireplace, she
    cook'd food for her,
She had no work to give her, but she gave her remembrance
    and fondness.

The red squaw staid all the forenoon, and toward the middle
    of the afternoon she went away,
O my mother was loth to have her go away,
All the week she thought of her, she watch'd for her many a
    month,
She remember'd her many a winter and many a summer,
But the red squaw never came nor was heard of there again.

7

A show of the summer softness—a contact of something un-
    seen—an amour of the light and air,
I am jealous and overwhelm'd with friendliness,
And will go gallivant with the light and air myself.

O love and summer, you are in the dreams and in me,
Autumn and winter are in the dreams, the farmer goes with
    his thrift,
The droves and crops increase, the barns are well-fill'd.

Elements merge in the night, ships make tacks in the dreams,
The sailor sails, the exile returns home,
The fugitive returns unharm'd, the immigrant is back beyond
    months and years,
The poor Irishman lives in the simple house of his childhood
    with the well-known neighbors and faces,
They warmly welcome him, he is barefoot again, he forgets
    he is well off,
The Dutchman voyages home, and the Scotchman and
    Welshman voyage home, and the native of the Mediter-
    ranean voyages home,
To every port of England, France, Spain, enter well-fill'd
    ships,
The Swiss foots it toward his hills, the Prussian goes his way,
    the Hungarian his way, and the Pole his way,
The Swede returns, and the Dane and Norwegian return.

The homeward bound and the outward bound,
The beautiful lost swimmer, the ennuyé, the onanist, the
    female that loves unrequited, the money-maker,
The actor and actress, those through with their parts and
    those waiting to commence,
The affectionate boy, the husband and wife, the voter, the
    nominee that is chosen and the nominee that has fail'd,
The great already known and the great any time after to-day,
The stammerer, the sick, the perfect-form'd, the homely,
The criminal that stood in the box, the judge that sat and
    sentenced him, the fluent lawyers, the jury, the audience,
The laugher and weeper, the dancer, the midnight widow, the
    red squaw,
The consumptive, the erysipalite, the idiot, he that is wrong'd,
The antipodes, and every one between this and them in the
    dark,
I swear they are averaged now—one is no better than the other,
The night and sleep have liken'd them and restored them.

I swear they are all beautiful,
Every one that sleeps is beautiful, every thing in the dim light
    is beautiful,
The wildest and bloodiest is over, and all is peace.

Peace is always beautiful,
The myth of heaven indicates peace and night.

The myth of heaven indicates the soul,
The soul is always beautiful, it appears more or it appears
    less, it comes or it lags behind,
It comes from its embower'd garden and looks pleasantly on
    itself and encloses the world,
Perfect and clean the genitals previously jetting, and perfect
    and clean the womb cohering,
The head well-grown proportion'd and plumb, and the
    bowels and joints proportion'd and plumb.

The soul is always beautiful,
The universe is duly in order, every thing is in its place,
What has arrived is in its place and what waits shall be in its
    place,

The twisted skull waits, the watery or rotten blood waits,

The child of the glutton or venerealee waits long, and the child of the drunkard waits long, and the drunkard himself waits long,

The sleepers that lived and died wait, the far advanced are to go on in their turns, and the far behind are to come on in their turns,

The diverse shall be no less diverse, but they shall flow and unite—they unite now.

8

The sleepers are very beautiful as they lie unclothed,

They flow hand in hand over the whole earth from east to west as they lie unclothed,

The Asiatic and African are hand in hand, the European and American are hand in hand,

Learn'd and unlearn'd are hand in hand, and male and female are hand in hand,

The bare arm of the girl crosses the bare breast of her lover, they press close without lust, his lips press her neck,

The father holds his grown or ungrown son in his arms with measureless love, and the son holds the father in his arms with measureless love,

The white hair of the mother shines on the white wrist of the daughter,

The breath of the boy goes with the breath of the man, friend is inarm'd by friend,

The scholar kisses the teacher and the teacher kisses the scholar, the wrong'd is made right,

The call of the slave is one with the master's call, and the master salutes the slave,

The felon steps forth from the prison, the insane becomes sane, the suffering of sick persons is reliev'd,

The sweatings and fevers stop, the throat that was unsound is sound, the lungs of the consumptive are resumed, the poor distress'd head is free,

The joints of the rheumatic move as smoothly as ever, and smoother than ever,

Stiflings and passages open, the paralyzed become supple,

They swell'd and convuls'd and congested awake to them-
    selves in condition,
They pass the invigoration of the night and the chemistry of
    the night, and awake.

I too pass from the night,
I stay a while away O night, but I return to you again and
    love you.

Why should I be afraid to trust myself to you?
I am not afraid, I have been well brought forward by you,
I love the rich running day, but I do not desert her in whom I
    lay so long,
I know not how I came of you and I know not where I go
    with you, but I know I came well and shall go well.

I will stop only a time with the night, and rise betimes,
I will duly pass the day O my mother, and duly return to you.
1855   1881

TRANSPOSITIONS

LET the reformers descend from the stands where they are
    forever bawling—let an idiot or insane person appear on
    each of the stands;
Let judges and criminals be transposed—let the prison-
    keepers be put in prison—let those that were prisoners
    take the keys;
Let them that distrust birth and death lead the rest.
1856   1881

To Think of Time

1

To think of time—of all that retrospection,
To think of to-day, and the ages continued henceforward.

Have you guess'd you yourself would not continue?
Have you dreaded these earth-beetles?
Have you fear'd the future would be nothing to you?

Is to-day nothing? is the beginningless past nothing?
If the future is nothing they are just as surely nothing.

To think that the sun rose in the east—that men and women
    were flexible, real, alive—that every thing was alive,
To think that you and I did not see, feel, think, nor bear our
    part,
To think that we are now here and bear our part.

2

Not a day passes, not a minute or second without an ac-
    couchement,
Not a day passes, not a minute or second without a corpse.

The dull nights go over and the dull days also,
The soreness of lying so much in bed goes over,
The physician after long putting off gives the silent and ter-
    rible look for an answer,
The children come hurried and weeping, and the brothers
    and sisters are sent for,
Medicines stand unused on the shelf, (the camphor-smell has
    long pervaded the rooms,)
The faithful hand of the living does not desert the hand of the
    dying,
The twitching lips press lightly on the forehead of the dying,
The breath ceases and the pulse of the heart ceases,
The corpse stretches on the bed and the living look upon it,
It is palpable as the living are palpable.

The living look upon the corpse with their eyesight,
But without eyesight lingers a different living and looks
    curiously on the corpse.

3

To think the thought of death merged in the thought of
    materials,
To think of all these wonders of city and country, and others
    taking great interest in them, and we taking no interest
    in them.

To think how eager we are in building our houses,
To think others shall be just as eager, and we quite indifferent.

(I see one building the house that serves him a few years, or seventy or eighty years at most,
I see one building the house that serves him longer than that.)

Slow-moving and black lines creep over the whole earth—they never cease—they are the burial lines,
He that was President was buried, and he that is now President shall surely be buried.

4

A reminiscence of the vulgar fate,
A frequent sample of the life and death of workmen,
Each after his kind.

Cold dash of waves at the ferry-wharf, posh and ice in the river, half-frozen mud in the streets,
A gray discouraged sky overhead, the short last daylight of December,
A hearse and stages, the funeral of an old Broadway stage-driver, the cortege mostly drivers.

Steady the trot to the cemetery, duly rattles the death-bell,
The gate is pass'd, the new-dug grave is halted at, the living alight, the hearse uncloses,
The coffin is pass'd out, lower'd and settled, the whip is laid on the coffin, the earth is swiftly shovel'd in,
The mound above is flatted with the spades—silence,
A minute—no one moves or speaks—it is done,
He is decently put away—is there any thing more?

He was a good fellow, free-mouth'd, quick-temper'd, not bad-looking,
Ready with life or death for a friend, fond of women, gambled, ate hearty, drank hearty,
Had known what it was to be flush, grew low-spirited toward the last, sicken'd, was help'd by a contribution,
Died, aged forty-one years—and that was his funeral.

Thumb extended, finger uplifted, apron, cape, gloves, strap,
    wet-weather clothes, whip carefully chosen,
Boss, spotter, starter, hostler, somebody loafing on you, you
    loafing on somebody, headway, man before and man
    behind,
Good day's work, bad day's work, pet stock, mean stock,
    first out, last out, turning-in at night,
To think that these are so much and so nigh to other drivers,
    and he there takes no interest in them.

5

The markets, the government, the working-man's wages, to
    think what account they are through our nights and
    days,
To think that other working-men will make just as great
    account of them, yet we make little or no account.

The vulgar and the refined, what you call sin and what you
    call goodness, to think how wide a difference,
To think the difference will still continue to others, yet we lie
    beyond the difference.

To think how much pleasure there is,
Do you enjoy yourself in the city? or engaged in business? or
    planning a nomination and election? or with your wife
    and family?
Or with your mother and sisters? or in womanly housework?
    or the beautiful maternal cares?
These also flow onward to others, you and I flow onward,
But in due time you and I shall take less interest in them.

Your farm, profits, crops—to think how engross'd you are,
To think there will still be farms, profits, crops, yet for you of
    what avail?

6

What will be will be well, for what is is well,
To take interest is well, and not to take interest shall be well.

The domestic joys, the daily housework or business, the
    building of houses, are not phantasms, they have weight,
    form, location,
Farms, profits, crops, markets, wages, government, are none
    of them phantasms,
The difference between sin and goodness is no delusion,
The earth is not an echo, man and his life and all the things of
    his life are well-consider'd.

You are not thrown to the winds, you gather certainly and
    safely around yourself,
Yourself! yourself! yourself, for ever and ever!

7

It is not to diffuse you that you were born of your mother
    and father, it is to identify you,
It is not that you should be undecided, but that you should
    be decided,
Something long preparing and formless is arrived and form'd
    in you,
You are henceforth secure, whatever comes or goes.

The threads that were spun are gather'd, the weft crosses the
    warp, the pattern is systematic.

The preparations have every one been justified,
The orchestra have sufficiently tuned their instruments, the
    baton has given the signal.

The guest that was coming, he waited long, he is now housed,
He is one of those who are beautiful and happy, he is one of
    those that to look upon and be with is enough.

The law of the past cannot be eluded,
The law of the present and future cannot be eluded,
The law of the living cannot be eluded, it is eternal,
The law of promotion and transformation cannot be eluded,
The law of heroes and good-doers cannot be eluded,
The law of drunkards, informers, mean persons, not one iota
    thereof can be eluded.

8

Slow moving and black lines go ceaselessly over the earth,

Northerner goes carried and Southerner goes carried, and they on the Atlantic side and they on the Pacific,

And they between, and all through the Mississippi country, and all over the earth.

The great masters and kosmos are well as they go, the heroes and good-doers are well,

The known leaders and inventors and the rich owners and pious and distinguish'd may be well,

But there is more account than that, there is strict account of all.

The interminable hordes of the ignorant and wicked are not nothing,

The barbarians of Africa and Asia are not nothing,

The perpetual successions of shallow people are not nothing as they go.

Of and in all these things,

I have dream'd that we are not to be changed so much, nor the law of us changed,

I have dream'd that heroes and good-doers shall be under the present and past law,

And that murderers, drunkards, liars, shall be under the present and past law,

For I have dream'd that the law they are under now is enough.

And I have dream'd that the purpose and essence of the known life, the transient,

Is to form and decide identity for the unknown life, the permanent.

If all came but to ashes of dung,

If maggots and rats ended us, then Alarum! for we are betray'd,

Then indeed suspicion of death.

Do you suspect death? if I were to suspect death I should die
    now,
Do you think I could walk pleasantly and well-suited toward
    annihilation?

Pleasantly and well-suited I walk,
Whither I walk I cannot define, but I know it is good,
The whole universe indicates that it is good,
The past and the present indicate that it is good.

How beautiful and perfect are the animals!
How perfect the earth, and the minutest thing upon it!
What is called good is perfect, and what is called bad is just
    as perfect,
The vegetables and minerals are all perfect, and the impon-
    derable fluids perfect;
Slowly and surely they have pass'd on to this, and slowly and
    surely they yet pass on.

9

I swear I think now that every thing without exception has an
    eternal soul!
The trees have, rooted in the ground! the weeds of the sea
    have! the animals!

I swear I think there is nothing but immortality!
That the exquisite scheme is for it, and the nebulous float is
    for it, and the cohering is for it!
And all preparation is for it—and identity is for it—and life
    and materials are altogether for it!

1855   1881

Whispers of Heavenly Death

DAREST THOU NOW O SOUL

DAREST thou now O soul,
Walk out with me toward the unknown region,
Where neither ground is for the feet nor any path to follow?

No map there, nor guide,
Nor voice sounding, nor touch of human hand,
Nor face with blooming flesh, nor lips, nor eyes, are in that
    land.

I know it not O soul,
Nor dost thou, all is a blank before us,
All waits undream'd of in that region, that inaccessible land.

Till when the ties loosen,
All but the ties eternal, Time and Space,
Nor darkness, gravitation, sense, nor any bounds bounding
    us.

Then we burst forth, we float,
In Time and Space O soul, prepared for them,
Equal, equipt at last, (O joy! O fruit of all!) them to fulfil O
    soul.
1868   1881

WHISPERS OF HEAVENLY DEATH

WHISPERS of heavenly death murmur'd I hear,
Labial gossip of night, sibilant chorals,
Footsteps gently ascending, mystical breezes wafted soft and
    low,

Ripples of unseen rivers, tides of a current flowing, forever
    flowing,
(Or is it the plashing of tears? the measureless waters of
    human tears?)

I see, just see skyward, great cloud-masses,
Mournfully slowly they roll, silently swelling and mixing,
With at times a half-dimm'd sadden'd far-off star,
Appearing and disappearing.

(Some parturition rather, some solemn immortal birth;
On the frontiers to eyes impenetrable,
Some soul is passing over.)
1868   1871

CHANTING THE SQUARE DEIFIC

1

CHANTING the square deific, out of the One advancing, out of
    the sides,
Out of the old and new, out of the square entirely divine,
Solid, four-sided, (all the sides needed,) from this side Jeho-
    vah am I,
Old Brahm I, and I Saturnius am;
Not Time affects me—I am Time, old, modern as any,
Unpersuadable, relentless, executing righteous judgments,
As the Earth, the Father, the brown old Kronos, with laws,
Aged beyond computation, yet ever new, ever with those
    mighty laws rolling,
Relentless I forgive no man—whoever sins dies—I will have
    that man's life;
Therefore let none expect mercy—have the seasons, gravita-
    tion, the appointed days, mercy? no more have I,
But as the seasons and gravitation, and as all the appointed
    days that forgive not,
I dispense from this side judgments inexorable without the
    least remorse.

2

Consolator most mild, the promis'd one advancing,
With gentle hand extended, the mightier God am I,

Foretold by prophets and poets in their most rapt prophecies
    and poems,
From this side, lo! the Lord Christ gazes—lo! Hermes I—
    lo! mine is Hercules' face,
All sorrow, labor, suffering, I, tallying it, absorb in my-
    self,
Many times have I been rejected, taunted, put in prison, and
    crucified, and many times shall be again,
All the world have I given up for my dear brothers' and sis-
    ters' sake, for the soul's sake,
Wending my way through the homes of men, rich or poor,
    with the kiss of affection,
For I am affection, I am the cheer-bringing God, with hope
    and all-enclosing charity,
With indulgent words as to children, with fresh and sane
    words, mine only,
Young and strong I pass knowing well I am destin'd myself
    to an early death;
But my charity has no death—my wisdom dies not, neither
    early nor late,
And my sweet love bequeath'd here and elsewhere never
    dies.

3

Aloof, dissatisfied, plotting revolt,
Comrade of criminals, brother of slaves,
Crafty, despised, a drudge, ignorant,
With sudra face and worn brow, black, but in the depths of
    my heart, proud as any,
Lifted now and always against whoever scorning assumes to
    rule me,
Morose, full of guile, full of reminiscences, brooding, with
    many wiles,
(Though it was thought I was baffled and dispel'd, and my
    wiles done, but that will never be,)
Defiant, I, Satan, still live, still utter words, in new lands duly
    appearing, (and old ones also,)
Permanent here from my side, warlike, equal with any, real
    as any,
Nor time nor change shall ever change me or my words.

4

Santa Spirita, breather, life,
Beyond the light, lighter than light,
Beyond the flames of hell, joyous, leaping easily above hell,
Beyond Paradise, perfumed solely with mine own perfume,
Including all life on earth, touching, including God, includ-
    ing Saviour and Satan,
Ethereal, pervading all, (for without me what were all? what
    were God?)
Essence of forms, life of the real identities, permanent, posi-
    tive, (namely the unseen,)
Life of the great round world, the sun and stars, and of man,
    I, the general soul,
Here the square finishing, the solid, I the most solid,
Breathe my breath also through these songs.
1865–6

OF HIM I LOVE DAY AND NIGHT

Of him I love day and night I dream'd I heard he was dead,
And I dream'd I went where they had buried him I love, but
    he was not in that place,
And I dream'd I wander'd searching among burial-places to
    find him,
And I found that every place was a burial-place;
The houses full of life were equally full of death, (this house
    is now,)
The streets, the shipping, the places of amusement, the Chi-
    cago, Boston, Philadelphia, the Mannahatta, were as
    full of the dead as of the living,
And fuller, O vastly fuller of the dead than of the living;
And what I dream'd I will henceforth tell to every person and
    age,
And I stand henceforth bound to what I dream'd,
And now I am willing to disregard burial-places and dis-
    pense with them,
And if the memorials of the dead were put up indifferently
    everywhere, even in the room where I eat or sleep, I
    should be satisfied,

And if the corpse of any one I love, or if my own corpse, be
    duly render'd to powder and pour'd in the sea, I shall be
    satisfied,
Or if it be distributed to the winds I shall be satisfied.
1871   1871

YET, YET, YE DOWNCAST HOURS

YET, yet, ye downcast hours, I know ye also,
Weights of lead, how ye clog and cling at my ankles,
Earth to a chamber of mourning turns—I hear the o'er-
    weening, mocking voice,
Matter is conqueror—matter, triumphant only, continues on-
    ward.

Despairing cries float ceaselessly toward me,
The call of my nearest lover, putting forth, alarm'd, un-
    certain,
The sea I am quickly to sail, come tell me,
Come tell me where I am speeding, tell me my destination.

I understand your anguish, but I cannot help you,
I approach, hear, behold, the sad mouth, the look out of the
    eyes, your mute inquiry,
Whither I go from the bed I recline on, come tell me;
Old age, alarm'd, uncertain—a young woman's voice, ap-
    pealing to me for comfort;
A young man's voice, *Shall I not escape?*
1860   1871

AS IF A PHANTOM CARESS'D ME

As if a phantom caress'd me,
I thought I was not alone walking here by the shore;
But the one I thought was with me as now I walk by the
    shore, the one I loved that caress'd me,
As I lean and look through the glimmering light, that one has
    utterly disappear'd,
And those appear that are hateful to me and mock me.
1860   1867

ASSURANCES

I NEED no assurances, I am a man who is pre-occupied of his
    own soul;
I do not doubt that from under the feet and beside the hands
    and face I am cognizant of, are now looking faces I am
    not cognizant of, calm and actual faces,
I do not doubt but the majesty and beauty of the world are
    latent in any iota of the world,
I do not doubt I am limitless, and that the universes are
    limitless, in vain I try to think how limitless,
I do not doubt that the orbs and the systems of orbs play
    their swift sports through the air on purpose, and that I
    shall one day be eligible to do as much as they, and more
    than they,
I do not doubt that temporary affairs keep on and on mil-
    lions of years,
I do not doubt interiors have their interiors, and exteriors
    have their exteriors, and that the eyesight has another
    eyesight, and the hearing another hearing, and the voice
    another voice,
I do not doubt that the passionately-wept deaths of young
    men are provided for, and that the deaths of young
    women and the deaths of little children are provided for,
(Did you think Life was so well provided for, and Death, the
    purport of all Life, is not well provided for?)
I do not doubt that wrecks at sea, no matter what the horrors
    of them, no matter whose wife, child, husband, father,
    lover, has gone down, are provided for, to the minutest
    points,
I do not doubt that whatever can possibly happen anywhere
    at any time, is provided for in the inherences of things,
I do not think Life provides for all and for Time and Space,
    but I believe Heavenly Death provides for all.

1856   1871

QUICKSAND YEARS

QUICKSAND years that whirl me I know not whither,
Your schemes, politics, fail, lines give way, substances mock
    and elude me,

Only the theme I sing, the great and strong-possess'd soul,
eludes not,
One's-self must never give way—that is the final substance—
that out of all is sure,
Out of politics, triumphs, battles, life, what at last finally
remains?
When shows break up what but One's-Self is sure?
(1861–2)   1867

THAT MUSIC ALWAYS ROUND ME

THAT music always round me, unceasing, unbeginning, yet
long untaught I did not hear,
But now the chorus I hear and am elated,
A tenor, strong, ascending with power and health, with glad
notes of daybreak I hear,
A soprano at intervals sailing buoyantly over the tops of im-
mense waves,
A transparent base shuddering lusciously under and through
the universe,
The triumphant tutti, the funeral wailings with sweet flutes
and violins, all these I fill myself with,
I hear not the volumes of sound merely, I am moved by the
exquisite meanings,
I listen to the different voices winding in and out, striving,
contending with fiery vehemence to excel each other in
emotion;
I do not think the performers know themselves—but now I
think I begin to know them.
1860   1867

WHAT SHIP PUZZLED AT SEA

WHAT ship puzzled at sea, cons for the true reckoning?
Or coming in, to avoid the bars and follow the channel a
perfect pilot needs?
Here, sailor! here, ship! take aboard the most perfect pilot,
Whom, in a little boat, putting off and rowing, I hailing you
offer.
1860   1881

A NOISELESS PATIENT SPIDER

A NOISELESS patient spider,
I mark'd where on a little promontory it stood isolated,
Mark'd how to explore the vacant vast surrounding,
It launched forth filament, filament, filament, out of itself,
Ever unreeling them, ever tirelessly speeding them.

And you O my soul where you stand,
Surrounded, detached, in measureless oceans of space,
Ceaselessly musing, venturing, throwing, seeking the spheres
    to connect them,
Till the bridge you will need be form'd, till the ductile anchor
    hold,
Till the gossamer thread you fling catch somewhere, O my
    soul.
(1862–3)   1881

O LIVING ALWAYS, ALWAYS DYING

O LIVING always, always dying!
O the burials of me past and present,
O me while I stride ahead, material, visible, imperious as
    ever;
O me, what I was for years, now dead, (I lament not, I am
    content;)
O to disengage myself from those corpses of me, which I turn
    and look at where I cast them,
To pass on, (O living! always living!) and leave the corpses
    behind.
1860   1867

TO ONE SHORTLY TO DIE

FROM all the rest I single out you, having a message for you,
You are to die—let others tell you what they please, I cannot
    prevaricate,
I am exact and merciless, but I love you—there is no escape
    for you.

Softly I lay my right hand upon you, you just feel it,
I do not argue, I bend my head close and half envelop it,
I sit quietly by, I remain faithful,
I am more than nurse, more than parent or neighbor,
I absolve you from all except yourself spiritual bodily, that is
    eternal, you yourself will surely escape,
The corpse you will leave will be but excrementitious.

The sun bursts through in unlooked-for directions,
Strong thoughts fill you and confidence, you smile,
You forget you are sick, as I forget you are sick,
You do not see the medicines, you do not mind the weeping
    friends, I am with you,
I exclude others from you, there is nothing to be commiserated,
I do not commiserate, I congratulate you.
1860   1871

NIGHT ON THE PRAIRIES

NIGHT on the prairies,
The supper is over, the fire on the ground burns low,
The wearied emigrants sleep, wrapt in their blankets;
I walk by myself—I stand and look at the stars, which I think
    now I never realized before.

Now I absorb immortality and peace,
I admire death and test propositions.

How plenteous! how spiritual! how rèsumé!
The same old man and soul—the same old aspirations, and
    the same content.

I was thinking the day most splendid till I saw what the not-
    day exhibited,
I was thinking this globe enough till there sprang out so
    noiseless around me myriads of other globes.

Now while the great thoughts of space and eternity fill me I
    will measure myself by them,
And now touch'd with the lives of other globes arrived as far
    along as those of the earth,

Or waiting to arrive, or pass'd on farther than those of the
earth,
I henceforth no more ignore them than I ignore my own life,
Or the lives of the earth arrived as far as mine, or waiting to
arrive.

O I see now that life cannot exhibit all to me, as the day can-
not,
I see that I am to wait for what will be exhibited by death.
1860   1871

THOUGHT

As I sit with others at a great feast, suddenly while the music
is playing,
To my mind, (whence it comes I know not,) spectral in mist
of a wreck at sea,
Of certain ships, how they sail from port with flying streamers
and wafted kisses, and that is the last of them,
Of the solemn and murky mystery about the fate of the
President,
Of the flower of the marine science of fifty generations foun-
der'd off the Northeast coast and going down—of the
steamship Arctic going down,
Of the veil'd tableau—women gather'd together on deck,
pale, heroic, waiting the moment that draws so close—O
the moment!
A huge sob—a few bubbles—the white foam spirting up—
and then the women gone,
Sinking there while the passionless wet flows on—and I now
pondering, Are those women indeed gone?
Are souls drown'd and destroy'd so?
Is only matter triumphant?
1860   1871

THE LAST INVOCATION

At the last, tenderly,
From the walls of the powerful fortress'd house,
From the clasp of the knitted locks, from the keep of the
well-closed doors,
Let me be wafted.

Let me glide noiselessly forth;
With the key of softness unlock the locks—with a whisper,
Set ope the doors O soul.

Tenderly—be not impatient,
(Strong is your hold O mortal flesh,
Strong is your hold O love.)
1868   1871

AS I WATCH'D THE PLOUGHMAN PLOUGHING

As I watch'd the ploughman ploughing,
Or the sower sowing in the fields, or the harvester harvesting,
I saw there too, O life and death, your analogies;
(Life, life is the tillage, and Death is the harvest according.)
1871   1871

PENSIVE AND FALTERING

PENSIVE and faltering,
The words *the Dead* I write,
For living are the Dead,
(Haply the only living, only real,
And I the apparition, I the spectre.)
1868   1871

Thou Mother with Thy Equal Brood

1

Thou Mother with thy equal brood,
Thou varied chain of different States, yet one identity only,
A special song before I go I'd sing o'er all the rest,
For thee, the future.

I'd sow a seed for thee of endless Nationality,
I'd fashion thy ensemble including body and soul,
I'd show away ahead thy real Union, and how it may be
    accomplish'd.

The paths to the house I seek to make,
But leave to those to come the house itself.

Belief I sing, and preparation;
As Life and Nature are not great with reference to the pre-
    sent only,
But greater still from what is yet to come,
Out of that formula for thee I sing.

2

As a strong bird on pinions free,
Joyous, the amplest spaces heavenward cleaving,
Such be the thought I'd think of thee America,
Such be the recitative I'd bring for thee.

The conceits of the poets of other lands I'd bring thee not,
Nor the compliments that have served their turn so long,
Nor rhyme, nor the classics, nor perfume of foreign court or
    indoor library;

But an odor I'd bring as from forests of pine in Maine, or
    breath of an Illinois prairie,
With open airs of Virginia or Georgia or Tennessee, or from
    Texas uplands, or Florida's glades,
Or the Saguenay's black stream, or the wide blue spread of
        Huron,
With presentment of Yellowstone's scenes, or Yosemite,
And murmuring under, pervading all, I'd bring the rustling
    sea-sound,
That endlessly sounds from the two Great Seas of the world.

And for thy subtler sense subtler refrains dread Mother,
Preludes of intellect tallying these and thee, mind-formulas
    fitted for thee, real and sane and large as these and thee,
Thou! mounting higher, diving deeper than we knew, thou
    transcendental Union!
By thee fact to be justified, blended with thought,
Thought of man justified, blended with God,
Through thy idea, lo, the immortal reality!
Through thy reality, lo, the immortal ideal!

3

Brain of the New World, what a task is thine,
To formulate the Modern—out of the peerless grandeur of
    the modern,
Out of thyself, comprising science, to recast poems, churches,
    art,
(Recast, maybe discard them, end them—maybe their work
    is done, who knows?)
By vision, hand, conception, on the background of the
    mighty past, the dead,
To limn with absolute faith the mighty living present.

And yet thou living present brain, heir of the dead, the Old
    World brain,
Thou that lay folded like an unborn babe within its fold so
    long,
Thou carefully prepared by it so long—haply thou but un-
    foldest it, only maturest it.

It to eventuate in thee—the essence of the by-gone time con-
    tain'd in thee,
Its poems, churches, arts, unwitting to themselves, destined
    with reference to thee;
Thou but the apples, long, long, long a-growing,
The fruit of all the Old ripening to-day in thee.

4

Sail, sail thy best, ship of Democracy,
Of value is thy freight, 'tis not the Present only,
The Past is also stored in thee,
Thou holdest not the venture of thyself alone, not of the
    Western continent alone,
Earth's *résumé* entire floats on thy keel O ship, is steadied by
    thy spars,
With thee Time voyages in trust, the antecedent nations sink
    or swim with thee,
With all their ancient struggles, martyrs, heroes, epics, wars,
    thou bear'st the other continents,
Theirs, theirs as much as thine, the destination-port trium-
    phant;
Steer then with good strong hand and wary eye O helmsman,
    thou carriest great companions,
Venerable priestly Asia sails this day with thee,
And royal feudal Europe sails with thee.

5

Beautiful world of new superber birth that rises to my eyes,
Like a limitless golden cloud filling the western sky,
Emblem of general maternity lifted above all,
Sacred shape of the bearer of daughters and sons,
Out of thy teeming womb thy giant babes in ceaseless pro-
    cession issuing,
Acceding from such gestation, taking and giving continual
    strength and life,
World of the real—world of the twain in one,
World of the soul, born by the world of the real alone, led to
    identity, body, by it alone,

Yet in beginning only, incalculable masses of composite pre-
cious materials,

By history's cycles forwarded, by every nation, language,
hither sent,

Ready, collected here, a freer, vast, electric world, to be con-
structed here,

(The true New World, the world of orbic science, morals,
literatures to come,)

Thou wonder world yet undefined, unform'd, neither do I
define thee,

How can I pierce the impenetrable blank of the future?

I feel thy ominous greatness evil as well as good,

I watch thee advancing, absorbing the present, transcending
the past,

I see thy light lighting, and thy shadow shadowing, as if the
entire globe,

But I do not undertake to define thee, hardly to comprehend
thee,

I but thee name, thee prophesy, as now,

I merely thee ejaculate!

Thee in thy future,

Thee in thy only permanent life, career, thy own unloosen'd
mind, thy soaring spirit,

Thee as another equally needed sun, radiant, ablaze, swift-
moving, fructifying all,

Thee risen in potent cheerfulness and joy, in endless great
hilarity,

Scattering for good the cloud that hung so long, that weigh'd
so long upon the mind of man,

The doubt, suspicion, dread, of gradual, certain decadence of
man;

Thee in thy larger, saner brood of female, male—thee in
thy athletes, moral, spiritual, South, North, West,
East,

(To thy immortal breasts, Mother of All, thy every daughter,
son, endear'd alike, forever equal,)

Thee in thy own musicians, singers, artists, unborn yet, but
certain,

Thee in thy moral wealth and civilization, (until which thy
proudest material civilization must remain in vain,)

Thee in thy all-supplying, all-enclosing worship—thee in no
single bible, saviour, merely,
Thy saviours countless, latent within thyself, thy bibles in-
cessant within thyself, equal to any, divine as any,
(Thy soaring course thee formulating, not in thy two great
wars, nor in thy century's visible growth,
But far more in these leaves and chants, thy chants, great
Mother!)
Thee in an education grown of thee, in teachers, studies,
students, born of thee,
Thee in thy democratic fêtes en-masse, thy high original fes-
tivals, operas, lecturers, preachers,
Thee in thy ultimata, (the preparations only now completed,
the edifice on sure foundations tied,)
Thee in thy pinnacles, intellect, thought, thy topmost rational
joys, thy love and godlike aspiration,
In thy resplendent coming literati, thy full-lung'd orators,
thy sacerdotal bards, kosmic savans,
These! these in thee, (certain to come,) to-day I prophesy.

6

Land tolerating all, accepting all, not for the good alone, all
good for thee,
Land in the realms of God to be a realm unto thyself,
Under the rule of God to be a rule unto thyself.

(Lo, where arise three peerless stars,
To be thy natal stars my country, Ensemble, Evolution,
Freedom,
Set in the sky of Law.)

Land of unprecedented faith, God's faith,
Thy soil, thy very subsoil, all upheav'd,
The general inner earth so long so sedulously draped over,
now hence for what it is boldly laid bare,
Open'd by thee to heaven's light for benefit or bale.

Not for success alone,
Not to fair-sail unintermitted always,
The storm shall dash thy face, the murk of war and worse
than war shall cover thee all over,

(Wert capable of war, its tug and trials? be capable of peace,
    its trials,
For the tug and mortal strain of nations come at last in pros-
    perous peace, not war;)
In many a smiling mask death shall approach beguiling thee,
    thou in disease shalt swelter,
The livid cancer spread its hideous claws, clinging upon thy
    breasts, seeking to strike thee deep within,
Consumption of the worst, moral consumption, shall rouge
    thy face with hectic,
But thou shalt face thy fortunes, thy diseases, and surmount
    them all,
Whatever they are to-day and whatever through time they
    may be,
They each and all shall lift and pass away and cease from thee,
While thou, Time's spirals rounding, out of thyself, thyself
    still extricating, fusing,
Equable, natural, mystical Union thou, (the mortal with im-
    mortal blent,)
Shalt soar toward the fulfilment of the future, the spirit of
    the body and the mind,
The soul, its destinies.

The soul, its destinies, the real real,
(Purport of all these apparitions of the real;)
In thee America, the soul, its destinies,
Thou globe of globes! thou wonder nebulous!
By many a throe of heat and cold convuls'd, (by these thyself
    solidifying;)
Thou mental, moral orb—thou New, indeed new, Spiritual
    World!
The Present holds thee not—for such vast growth as thine,
For such unparallel'd flight as thine, such brood as thine,
The FUTURE only holds thee and can hold thee.
1872   1881

A PAUMANOK PICTURE

Two boats with nets lying off the sea-beach, quite still,
Ten fishermen waiting—they discover a thick school of moss-
    bonkers—they drop the join'd seine-ends in the water,

The boats separate and row off, each on its rounding course
    to the beach, enclosing the mossbonkers,
The net is drawn in by a windlass by those who stop ashore,
Some of the fishermen lounge in their boats, others stand
    ankle-deep in the water, pois'd on strong legs,
The boats partly drawn up, the water slapping against them,
Strew'd on the sand in heaps and windrows, well out from
    the water, the green-back'd spotted mossbonkers.

1881   1881

From Noon to Starry Night

THOU ORB ALOFT FULL-DAZZLING

Thou orb aloft full-dazzling! thou hot October noon!
Flooding with sheeny light the gray beach sand,
The sibilant near sea with vistas far and foam,
And tawny streaks and shades and spreading blue;
O sun of noon refulgent! my special word to thee.

Hear me illustrious!
Thy lover me, for always I have loved thee,
Even as basking babe, then happy boy alone by some wood
    edge, thy touching-distant beams enough,
Or man matured, or young or old, as now to thee I launch
    my invocation.

(Thou canst not with thy dumbness me deceive,
I know before the fitting man all Nature yields,
Though answering not in words, the skies, trees, hear his
    voice—and thou O sun,
As for thy throes, thy perturbations, sudden breaks and
    shafts of flame gigantic,
I understand them, I know those flames, those perturbations
    well.)

Thou that with fructifying heat and light,
O'er myriad farms, o'er lands and waters North and South,
O'er Mississippi's endless course, o'er Texas' grassy plains,
    Kanada's woods,
O'er all the globe that turns its face to thee shining in space,
Thou that impartially infoldest all, not only continents, seas,
Thou that to grapes and weeds and little wild flowers givest
    so liberally,

417

Shed, shed thyself on mine and me, with but a fleeting ray out
    of thy million millions,
Strike though these chants.

Nor only launch thy subtle dazzle and thy strength for these,
Prepare the later afternoon of me myself—prepare my
    lengthening shadows,
Prepare my starry nights.
1881   1881

FACES

1

SAUNTERING the pavement or riding the country by-road, lo,
    such faces!
Faces of friendship, precision, caution, sauvity, ideality,
The spiritual-prescient face, the always welcome common
    benevolent face,
The face of the singing of music, the grand faces of natural
    lawyers and judges broad at the back-top,
The faces of hunters and fishers bulged at the brows, the
    shaved blanch'd faces of orthodox citizens,
The pure, extravagant, yearning, questioning artist's face,
The ugly face of some beautiful soul, the handsome detested
    or despised face,
The sacred faces of infants, the illuminated face of the mother
    of many children,
The face of an amour, the face of veneration,
The face as of a dream, the face of an immobile rock,
The face withdrawn of its good and bad, a castrated face,
A wild hawk, his wings clipp'd by the clipper,
A stallion that yielded at last to the thongs and knife of the
    gelder.

Sauntering the pavement thus, or crossing the ceaseless ferry,
    faces and faces and faces,
I see them and complain not, and am content with all.

2

Do you suppose I could be content with all if I thought them
    their own finalè?

This now is too lamentable a face for a man,
Some abject louse asking leave to be, cringing for it,
Some milk-nosed maggot blessing what lets it wrig to its hole.

This face is a dog's snout sniffing for garbage,
Snakes nest in that mouth, I hear the sibilant threat.

This face is a haze more chill than the arctic sea,
Its sleepy and wabbling icebergs crunch as they go.

This is a face of bitter herbs, this an emetic, they need no
label,
And more of the drug-shelf, laudanum, caoutchouc, or hog's-
lard.

This face is an epilepsy, its wordless tongue gives out the
earthly cry,
Its veins down the neck distend, its eyes roll till they show
nothing but their whites,
Its teeth grit, the palms of the hands are cut by the turn'd-in
nails,
The man falls struggling and foaming to the ground, while he
speculates well.

This face is bitten by vermin and worms,
And this is some murderer's knife with a half-pull'd scabbard.

This face owes to the sexton his dismalest fee,
An unceasing death-bell tolls there.

3

Features of my equals would you trick me with your creas'd
and cadaverous march?
Well, you cannot trick me.

I see your rounded never-erased flow,
I see 'neath the rims of your haggard and mean disguises.

Splay and twist as you like, poke with the tangling fores of
fishes or rats,
You'll be unmuzzled, you certainly will.

I saw the face of the most smear'd and slobbering idiot they
    had at the asylum,
And I knew for my consolation what they knew not,
I knew of the agents that emptied and broke my brother,
The same wait to clear the rubbish from the fallen tenement,
And I shall look again in a score or two of ages,
And I shall meet the real landlord perfect and unharm'd,
    every inch as good as myself.

4

The Lord advances, and yet advances,
Always the shadow in front, always the reach'd hand bring-
    ing up the laggards.

Out of this face emerge banners and horses—O superb! I see
    what is coming,
I see the high pioneer-caps, see staves of runners clearing the
    way,
I hear victorious drums.

This face is a life-boat,
This is the face commanding and bearded, it asks no odds of
    the rest,
This face is flavor'd fruit ready for eating,
This face of a healthy honest boy is the programme of all good.

These faces bear testimony slumbering or awake,
They show their descent from the Master himself.

Off the word I have spoken I except not one—red, white,
    black, are all deific,
In each house is the ovum, it comes forth after a thousand
    years.

Spots or cracks at the windows do not disturb me,
Tall and sufficient stand behind and make signs to me,
I read the promise and patiently wait.

This is a full-grown lily's face,
She speaks to the limber-hipp'd man near the garden pickets,
Come here she blushingly cries, *Come nigh to me limber-
    hipp'd man,*

Stand at my side till I lean as high as I can upon you,
Fill me with albescent honey, bend down to me,
Rub to me with your chafing beard, rub to my breast and
* shoulders.*

5

The old face of the mother of many children,
Whist! I am fully content.

Lull'd and late is the smoke of the First-day morning,
It hangs low over the rows of trees by the fences,
It hangs thin by the sassafras and wild-cherry and cat-brier
  under them.

I saw the rich ladies in full dress at the soiree,
I heard what the singers were singing so long,
Heard who sprang in crimson youth from the white froth and
  the water-blue.

Behold a woman!
She looks out from her quaker cap, her face is clearer and
  more beautiful than the sky.

She sits in an armchair under the shaded porch of the farm-
  house,
The sun just shines on her old white head.

Her ample gown is of cream-hued linen,
Her grandsons raised the flax, and her grand-daughters spin
  it with the distaff and the wheel.

The melodious character of the earth,
The finish beyond which philosophy cannot go and does not
  wish to go,
The justified mother of men.
1855   1881

THE MYSTIC TRUMPETER

1

HARK, some wild trumpeter, some strange musician,
Hovering unseen in air, vibrates capricious tunes to-night.

I hear thee trumpeter, listening alert I catch thy notes,
Now pouring, whirling like a tempest round me,
Now low, subdued, now in the distance lost.

2

Come nearer bodiless one, haply in thee resounds
Some dead composer, haply thy pensive life
Was fill'd with aspirations high, unform'd ideals,
Waves, oceans musical, chaotically surging,
That now ecstatic ghost, close to me bending, thy cornet
     echoing, pealing,
Gives out to no one's ears but mine, but freely gives to mine,
That I may thee translate.

3

Blow trumpeter free and clear, I follow thee,
While at thy liquid prelude, glad, serene,
The fretting world, the streets, the noisy hours of day with-
     draw,
A holy calm descends like dew upon me,
I walk in cool refreshing night the walks of Paradise,
I scent the grass, the moist air and the roses;
Thy song expands my numb'd imbonded spirit, thou freest,
     launchest me,
Floating and basking upon heaven's lake.

4

Blow again trumpeter! and for my sensuous eyes,
Bring the old pageants, show the feudal world.

What charm thy music works! thou makest pass before me,
Ladies and cavaliers long dead, barons are in their castle halls,
     the troubadours are singing,
Arm'd knights go forth to redress wrongs, some in quest of
     the holy Graal;
I see the tournament, I see the contestants incased in heavy
     armor seated on stately champing horses,
I hear the shouts, the sounds of blows and smiting steel;

I see the Crusaders' tumultuous armies—hark, how the cym-
bals clang,
Lo, where the monks walk in advance, bearing the cross on
high.

5

Blow again trumpeter! and for thy theme,
Take now the enclosing theme of all, the solvent and the
setting,
Love, that is pulse of all, the sustenance and the pang,
The heart of man and woman all for love,
No other theme but love—knitting, enclosing, all-diffusing
love.

O how the immortal phantoms crowd around me!
I see the vast alembic ever working, I see and know the flames
that heat the world,
The glow, the blush, the beating hearts of lovers,
So blissful happy some, and some so silent, dark, and nigh to
death;
Love, that is all the earth to lovers—love, that mocks time
and space,
Love, that is day and night—love, that is sun and moon and
stars,
Love, that is crimson, sumptuous, sick with perfume,
No other words but words of love, no other thought but love.

6

Blow again trumpeter—conjure war's alarums.

Swift to thy spell a shuddering hum like distant thunder rolls,
Lo, where the arm'd men hasten—lo, mid the clouds of dust
the glint of bayonets,
I see the grime-faced cannoneers, I mark the rosy flash amid
the smoke, I hear the cracking of the guns;
Nor war alone—thy fearful music-song, wild prayer, brings
every sight of fear,
The deeds of ruthless brigands, rapine, murder—I hear the
cries for help!
I see ships foundering at sea, I behold on deck and below
deck the terrible tableaus.

7

O trumpeter, methinks I am myself the instrument thou
    playest,
Thou melt'st my heart, my brain—thou movest, drawest,
    changest them at will;
And now thy sullen notes send darkness through me,
Thou takest away all cheering light, all hope,
I see the enslaved, the overthrown, the hurt, the opprest of
    the whole earth,
I feel the measureless shame and humiliation of my race, it
    becomes all mine,
Mine too the revenges of humanity, the wrongs of ages,
    baffled feuds and hatreds,
Utter defeat upon me weighs—all lost—the foe victorious,
(Yet 'mid the ruins Pride colossal stands unshaken to the
    last,
Endurance, resolution to the last.)

8

Now trumpeter for thy close,
Vouchsafe a higher strain than any yet,
Sing to my soul, renew its languishing faith and hope,
Rouse up my slow belief, give me some vision of the future,
Give me for once its prophecy and joy.

O glad, exulting, culminating song!
A vigor more than earth's is in thy notes,
Marches of victory—man disenthral'd—the conqueror at
    last,
Hymns to the universal God from universal man—all joy!
A reborn race appears—a perfect world, all joy!
Women and men in wisdom innocence and health—all joy!
Riotous laughing bacchanals fill'd with joy!
War, sorrow, suffering gone—the rank earth purged—no-
    thing but joy left!
The ocean fill'd with joy—the atmosphere all joy!
Joy! joy! in freedom, worship, love! joy in the ecstasy of life!
Enough to merely be! enough to breathe!
Joy! joy! all over joy!
1872   1881

TO A LOCOMOTIVE IN WINTER

THEE for my recitative,

Thee in the driving storm even as now, the snow, the winter-
day declining,

Thee in thy panoply, thy measur'd dual throbbing and thy
beat convulsive,

Thy black cylindric body, golden brass and silvery steel,

Thy ponderous side-bars, parallel and connecting rods,
gyrating, shuttling at thy sides,

Thy metrical, now swelling pant and roar, now tapering in
the distance,

Thy great protruding head-light fix'd in front,

Thy long, pale, floating vapor-pennants, tinged with delicate
purple,

The dense and murky clouds out-belching from thy smoke-
stack,

Thy knitted frame, thy springs and valves, the tremulous
twinkle of thy wheels,

Thy train of cars behind, obedient, merrily following,

Through gale or calm, now swift, now slack, yet steadily
careering;

Type of the modern—emblem of motion and power—pulse
of the continent,

For once come serve the Muse and merge in verse, even as
here I see thee,

With storm and buffeting gusts of wind and falling snow,

By day thy warning ringing bell to sound its notes,

By night thy silent signal lamps to swing.

Fierce-throated beauty!

Roll through my chant with all thy lawless music, thy swing-
ing lamps at night,

Thy madly-whistled laughter, echoing, rumbling like an
earthquake, rousing all,

Law of thyself complete, thine own track firmly holding,

(No sweetness debonair of tearful harp or glib piano thine,)

Thy trills of shrieks by rocks and hills return'd,

Launch'd o'er the prairies wide, across the lakes,

To the free skies unpent and glad and strong.

1876   1881

O MAGNET-SOUTH

O MAGNET-SOUTH! O glistening perfumed South! my South!
O quick mettle, rich blood, impulse and love! good and evil!
    O all dear to me!
O dear to me my birth-things—all moving things and the
    trees where I was born—the grains, plants, rivers,
Dear to me my own slow sluggish rivers where they flow,
    distant, over flats of silvery sands or through swamps,
Dear to me the Roanoke, the Savannah, the Altamahaw, the
    Pedee, the Tombigbee, the Santee, the Coosa, and the
    Sabine,
O pensive, far away wandering, I return with my soul to
    haunt their banks again,
Again in Florida I float on transparent lakes, I float on the
    Okeechobee, I cross the hummock-land or through
    pleasant openings or dense forests,
I see the parrots in the woods, I see the papaw-tree and the
    blossoming titi;
Again, sailing in my coaster on deck, I coast off Georgia, I
    coast up the Carolinas,
I see where the live-oak is growing, I see where the yellow-
    pine, the scented bay-tree, the lemon and orange, the
    cypress, the graceful palmetto,
I pass rude sea-headlands and enter Pamlico sound through
    an inlet, and dart my vision inland;
O the cotton plant! the growing fields of rice, sugar, hemp!
The cactus guarded with thorns, the laurel-tree with large
    white flowers,
The range afar, the richness and barrenness, the old woods
    charged with mistletoe and trailing moss,
The piney odor and the gloom, the awful natural stillness,
    (here in these dense swamps the freebooter carries his
    gun, and the fugitive has his conceal'd hut;)
O the strange fascination of these half-known half-impass-
    able swamps, infested by reptiles, resounding with the
    bellow of the alligator, the sad noises of the night-owl
    and the wild-cat, and the whirr of the rattlesnake,
The mocking-bird, the American mimic, singing all the fore-
    noon, singing through the moon-lit night,

The humming-bird, the wild turkey, the raccoon, the opossum;
A Kentucky corn-field, the tall, graceful, long-leav'd corn,
slender, flapping, bright green, with tassels, with beauti-
ful ears each well-sheath'd in its husk;
O my heart! O tender and fierce pangs, I can stand them not,
I will depart;
O to be a Virginian where I grew up! O to be a Carolinian!
O longings irrepressible! O I will go back to old Tennessee
and never wander more.
1860   1881

MANNAHATTA

I was asking for something specific and perfect for my city,
Whereupon lo! upsprang the aboriginal name.

Now I see what there is in a name, a word, liquid, sane,
unruly, musical, self-sufficient,
I see that the word of my city is that word from of old,
Because I see that word nested in nests of water-bays, superb,
Rich, hemm'd thick all around with sailships and steamships,
an island sixteen miles long, solid-founded,
Numberless crowded streets, high growths of iron, slender,
strong, light, splendidly uprising toward clear skies,
Tides swift and ample, well-loved by me, toward sundown,
The flowing sea-currents, the little islands, larger adjoining
islands, the heights, the villas,
The countless masts, the white shore-steamers, the lighters,
the ferry-boats, the black sea-steamers well-model'd,
The down-town streets, the jobbers' houses of business, the
houses of business of the ship-merchants and money-
brokers, the river-streets,
Immigrants arriving, fifteen or twenty thousand in a week,
The carts hauling goods, the manly race of drivers of horses,
the brown-faced sailors,
The summer air, the bright sun shining, and the sailing clouds
aloft,
The winter snows, the sleigh-bells, the broken ice in the river,
passing along up or down with the flood-tide or ebb-tide,
The mechanics of the city, the masters, well-form'd, beauti-
ful-faced, looking you straight in the eyes,

Trottoirs throng'd, vehicles, Broadway, the women, the shops
and shows,
A million people—manners free and superb—open voices—
hospitality—the most courageous and friendly young
men,
City of hurried and sparkling waters! city of spires and masts!
City nested in bays! my city!
1860   1881

ALL IS TRUTH

O me, man of slack faith so long,
Standing aloof, denying portions so long,
Only aware to-day of compact all-diffused truth,
Discovering to-day there is no lie or form of lie, and can be
none, but grows as inevitably upon itself as the truth
does upon itself,
Or as any law of the earth or any natural production of the
earth does.

(This is curious and may not be realized immediately, but it
must be realized,
I feel in myself that I represent falsehoods equally with the rest,
And that the universe does.)

Where has fail'd a perfect return indifferent of lies or the truth?
Is it upon the ground, or in water or fire? or in the spirit of
man? or in the meat and blood?

Meditating among liars and retreating sternly into myself, I
see that there are really no liars or lies after all,
And that nothing fails its perfect return, and that what are
called lies are perfect returns,
And that each thing exactly represents itself and what has
preceded it,
And that the truth includes all, and is compact just as much
as space is compact,
And that there is no flaw or vacuum in the amount of the
truth—but that all is truth without exception;
And henceforth I will go celebrate any thing I see or am,
And sing and laugh and deny nothing.
1860   1871

A RIDDLE SONG

THAT which eludes this verse and any verse,
Unheard by sharpest ear, unform'd in clearest eye or cun-
      ningest mind,
Nor lore nor fame, nor happiness nor wealth,
And yet the pulse of every heart and life throughout the
      world incessantly,
Which you and I and all pursuing ever ever miss,
Open but still a secret, the real of the real, an illusion,
Costless, vouchsafed to each, yet never man the owner,
Which poets vainly seek to put in rhyme, historians in prose,
Which sculptor never chisel'd yet, not painter painted,
Which vocalist never sung, nor orator nor actor ever utter'd,
Invoking here and how I challenge for my song.

Indifferently, 'mid public, private haunts, in solitude,
Behind the mountain and the wood,
Companion of the city's busiest streets, through the assem-
      blage,
It and its radiations constantly glide.

In looks of fair unconscious babes,
Or strangely in the coffin'd dead,
Or show of breaking dawn or stars by night,
As some dissolving delicate film of dreams,
Hiding yet lingering.

Two little breaths of words comprising it,
Two words, yet all from first to last comprised in it.

How ardently for it!
How many ships have sail'd and sunk for it!
How many travelers started from their homes and ne'er
      return'd!
How much of genius boldly staked and lost for it!
What countless stores of beauty, love, ventur'd for it!
How all superbest deeds since Time began are traceable to it
      —and shall be to the end!
How all heroic martyrdoms to it!

How, justified by it, the horrors, evils, battles of the earth!
How the bright fascinating lambent flames of it, in every age
and land, have drawn men's eyes,
Rich as a sunset on the Norway coast, the sky, the islands,
and the cliffs,
Or midnight's silent glowing northern lights unreachable.

Haply God's riddle it, so vague and yet so certain,
The soul for it, and all the visible universe for it,
And heaven at last for it.
1881   1881

EXCELSIOR

WHO has gone farthest? for I would go farther,
And who has been just? for I would be the most just person
of the earth,
And who most cautious? for I would be more cautious,
And who has been happiest? O I think it is I—I think no one
was ever happier than I,
And who has lavish'd all? for I lavish constantly the best I
have,
And who proudest? for I think I have reason to be the
proudest son alive—for I am the son of the brawny and
tall-topt city,
And who has been bold and true? for I would be the boldest
and truest being of the universe,
And who benevolent? for I would show more benevolence
than all the rest,
And who has receiv'd the love of the most friends? for I
know what it is to receive the passionate love of many
friends,
And who possesses a perfect and enamour'd body? for I do
not believe any one possesses a more perfect or en-
amour'd body than mine,
And who thinks the amplest thoughts? for I would surround
those thoughts,
And who has made hymns fit for the earth? for I am mad
with devouring ecstasy to make joyous hymns for the
whole earth.
1856   1881

AH POVERTIES, WINCINGS, AND SULKY RETREATS

Aʜ poverties, wincings, and sulky retreats,
Ah you foes that in conflict have overcome me,
(For what is my life or any man's life but a conflict with foes,
the old, the incessant war?)
You degradations, you tussle with passions and appetites,
You smarts from dissatisfied friendships, (ah wounds the
sharpest of all!)
You toil of painful and choked articulations, you mean-
nesses,
You shallow tongue-talks at tables, (my tongue the shallow-
est of any;)
You broken resolutions, you racking angers, you smother'd
ennuis!
Ah think not you finally triumph, my real self has yet to come
forth,
It shall yet march forth o'ermastering, till all lies beneath me,
It shall yet stand up the soldier of ultimate victory.
1865–6   1881

THOUGHTS

Oғ public opinion,
Of a calm and cool fiat sooner or later, (how impassive! how
certain and final!)
Of the President with pale face asking secretly to himself,
What will the people say at last?
Of the frivolous Judge—of the corrupt Congressman,
Governor, Mayor—of such as these standing helpless
and exposed,
Of the mumbling and screaming priest, (soon, soon deserted,)
Of the lessening year by year of venerableness, and of the
dicta of officers, statutes, pulpits, schools,
Of the rising forever taller and stronger and broader of the
intuitions of men and women, and of Self-esteem and
Personality;
Of the true New World—of the Democracies resplendent en-
masse,
Of the conformity of politics, armies, navies, to them,

Of the shining sun by them—of the inherent light, greater
    than the rest,
Of the envelopment of all by them, and the effusion of all
    from them.
1860   1881

MEDIUMS

THEY shall arise in the States,
They shall report Nature, laws, physiology, and happiness,
They shall illustrate Democracy and the kosmos,
They shall be alimentive, amative, perceptive,
They shall be complete women and men, their pose brawny
    and supple, their drink water, their blood clean and clear,
They shall fully enjoy materialism and the sight of products,
    they shall enjoy the sight of the beef, lumber, bread-
    stuffs, of Chicago the great city,
They shall train themselves to go in public to become orators
    and oratresses,
Strong and sweet shall their tongues be, poems and materials
    of poems shall come from their lives, they shall be
    makers and finders,
Of them and of their works shall emerge divine conveyers, to
    convey gospels,
Characters, events, retrospections, shall be convey'd in gos-
    pels, trees, animals, waters, shall be convey'd,
Death, the future, the invisible faith, shall all be convey'd.
1860   1871

WEAVE IN, MY HARDY LIFE

WEAVE in, weave in, my hardy life,
Weave yet a soldier strong and full for great campaigns to
    come,
Weave in red blood, weave sinews in like ropes, the senses,
    sight weave in,
Weave lasting sure, weave day and night the weft, the warp,
    incessant weave, tire not,
(We know not what the use O life, nor know the aim, the end,
    nor really aught we know,
But know the work, the need goes on and shall go on, the
    death-envelop'd march of peace as well as war goes on,)

For great campaigns of peace the same the wiry threads to
　　weave,
We know not why or what, yet weave, forever weave.
1865　　　　　　　　　　　　　　　　　　　　1881

SPAIN, 1873–74

OUT of the murk of heaviest clouds,
Out of the feudal wrecks and heap'd-up skeletons of kings,
Out of that old entire European debris, the shatter'd mum-
　　meries,
Ruin'd cathedrals, crumble of palaces, tombs of priests,
Lo, Freedom's features fresh undimm'd look forth—the same
　　immortal face looks forth;
(A glimpse as of thy Mother's face Columbia,
A flash significant as of a sword,
Beaming towards thee.)

Nor think we forget thee maternal;
Lag'd'st thou so long? shall the clouds close again upon thee?
Ah, but thou hast thyself now appear'd to us—we know thee,
Thou hast given us a sure proof, the glimpse of thyself,
Thou waitest there as everywhere thy time.
1873　　　　　　　　　　　　　　　　　　　　1881

BY BROAD POTOMAC'S SHORE

BY broad Potomac's shore, again old tongue,
(Still uttering, still ejaculating, canst never cease this babble?)
Again old heart so gay, again to you, your sense, the full
　　flush spring returning,
Again the freshness and the odors, again Virginia's summer
　　sky, pellucid blue and silver,
Again the forenoon purple of the hills,
Again the deathless grass, so noiseless soft and green,
Again the blood-red roses blooming.

Perfume this book of mine O blood-red roses!
Lave subtly with your waters every line Potomac!
Give me of you O spring, before I close, to put between its
　　pages!
O forenoon purple of the hills, before I close, of you!
O deathless grass, of you!
1876　　　　　　　　　　　　　　　　　　　　1881

FROM FAR DAKOTA'S CAÑONS

June 25, 1876

FROM far Dakota's cañons,
Lands of the wild ravine, the dusky Sioux, the lonesome
    stretch, the silence,
Haply to-day a mournful wail, haply a trumpet-note for
    heroes.

The battle-bulletin,
The Indian ambuscade, the craft, the fatal environment,
The cavalry companies fighting to the last in sternest hero-
    ism,
In the midst of their little circle, with their slaughter'd horses
    for breastworks,
The fall of Custer and all his officers and men.

Continues yet the old, old legend of our race,
The loftiest of life upheld by death,
The ancient banner perfectly maintain'd,
O lesson opportune, O how I welcome thee!

As sitting in dark days,
Lone, sulky, through the time's thick murk looking in vain
    for light, for hope,
From unsuspected parts a fierce and momentary proof,
(The sun there at the centre though conceal'd,
Electric life forever at the centre,)
Breaks forth a lightning flash.

Thou of the tawny flowing hair in battle,
I erewhile saw, with erect head, pressing ever in front, bear-
    ing a bright sword in thy hand,
Now ending well in death the splendid fever of thy deeds,
(I bring no dirge for it or thee, I bring a glad triumphal
    sonnet,)
Desperate and glorious, aye in defeat most desperate, most
    glorious,
After thy many battles in which never yielding up a gun or a
    color,

Leaving behind thee a memory sweet to soldiers,
Thou yieldest up thyself.
1876   1881

OLD WAR-DREAMS

IN midnight sleep of many a face of anguish,
Of the look at first of the mortally wounded, (of that inde-
    scribable look,)
Of the dead on their backs with arms extended wide,
            I dream, I dream, I dream.

Of scenes of Nature, fields and mountains,
Of skies so beauteous after a storm, and at night the moon so
    unearthly bright,
Shining sweetly, shining down, where we dig the trenches and
    gather the heaps,
            I dream, I dream, I dream.

Long have they pass'd, faces and trenches and fields,
Where through the carnage I moved with a callous com-
    posure, or away from the fallen,
Onward I sped at the time—but now of their forms at night,
            I dream, I dream, I dream.
1865-6   1881

THICK-SPRINKLED BUNTING

THICK-SPRINKLED bunting! flag of stars!
Long yet your road, fateful flag—long yet your road, and
    lined with bloody death,
For the prize I see at issue at last is the world,
All its ships and shores I see interwoven with your threads
    greedy banner;
Dream'd again the flags of kings, highest borne, to flaunt
    unrival'd?
O hasten flag of man— O with sure and steady step, passing
    highest flags of kings,
Walk supreme to the heavens mighty symbol—run up above
    them all,
Flag of stars! thick-sprinkled bunting!
1865   1871

WHAT BEST I SEE IN THEE

To U. S. G. return'd from his World's Tour

WHAT best I see in thee,
Is not that where thou mov'st down history's great highways,
Ever undimm'd by time shoots warlike victory's dazzle,
Or that thou sat'st where Washington sat, ruling the land in
    peace,
Or thou the man whom feudal Europe fêted, venerable Asia
    swarm'd upon,
Who walk'd with kings with even pace the round world's
    promenade;
But that in foreign lands, in all thy walks with kings,
Those prairie sovereigns of the West, Kansas, Missouri,
    Illinois,
Ohio's, Indiana's millions, comrades, farmers, soldiers, all to
    the front,
Invisibly with thee walking with kings with even pace the
    round world's promenade,
Were all so justified.
(1879?)   1881

SPIRIT THAT FORM'D THIS SCENE

Written in Platte Cañon, Colorado

SPIRIT that form'd this scene,
These tumbled rock-piles grim and red,
These reckless heaven-ambitious peaks,
These gorges, turbulent-clear streams, this naked freshness,
These formless wild arrays, for reasons of their own,
I know thee, savage spirit—we have communed together,
Mine too such wild arrays, for reasons of their own;
Was't charged against my chants they had forgotten art?
To fuse within themselves its rules precise and delicatesse?
The lyrist's measur'd beat, the wrought-out temple's grace—
    column and polish'd arch forgot?
But thou that revelest here—spirit that form'd this scene,
They have remember'd thee.
1881   1881

AS I WALK THESE BROAD MAJESTIC DAYS

As I walk these broad majestic days of peace,
(For the war, the struggle of blood finish'd, wherein, O
terrific Ideal,
Against vast odds erewhile having gloriously won,
Now thou stridest on, yet perhaps in time toward denser wars,
Perhaps to engage in time in still more dreadful contests,
dangers,
Longer campaigns and crises, labors beyond all others,)
Around me I hear that eclat of the world, politics, produce,
The announcements of recognized things, science,
The approved growth of cities and the spread of inventions.

I see the ships, (they will last a few years,)
The vast factories with their foremen and workmen,
And hear the indorsement of all, and do not object to it.

But I too announce solid things,
Science, ships, politics, cities, factories, are not nothing,
Like a grand procession to music of distant bugles pouring,
triumphantly moving, and grander heaving in sight,
They stand for realities—all is as it should be.

Then my realities;
What else is so real as mine?
Libertad and the divine average, freedom to every slave on
the face of the earth,
The rapt promises and luminè of seers, the spiritual world,
these centuries-lasting songs,
And our visions, the visions of poets, the most solid an-
nouncements of any.
1860   1881

A CLEAR MIDNIGHT

THIS is thy hour O soul, thy free flight into the wordless,
Away from books, away from art, the day erased, the lesson
done,
Thee fully forth emerging, silent, gazing, pondering the
themes thou lovest best,
Night, sleep, death and the stars.
1881   1881

Songs of Parting

AS THE TIME DRAWS NIGH

As the time draws nigh glooming a cloud,
A dread beyond of I know not what darkens me.

I shall go forth,
I shall traverse the States awhile, but I cannot tell whither or
    how long,
Perhaps soon some day or night while I am singing my voice
    will suddenly cease.

O book, O chants! must all then amount to but this?
Must we barely arrive at this beginning of us?—and yet it is
    enough, O soul;
O soul, we have positively appear'd—that is enough.
1860   1871

YEARS OF THE MODERN

YEARS of the modern! years of the unperform'd!
Your horizon rises, I see it parting away for more august
    dramas,
I see not America only, not only Liberty's nation but other
    nations preparing,
I see tremendous entrances and exits, new combinations, the
    solidarity of races,
I see that force advancing with irresistible power on the
    world's stage,
(Have the old forces, the old wars, played their parts? are the
    acts suitable to them closed?)
I see Freedom, completely arm'd and victorious and very
    haughty, with Law on one side and Peace on the other,
A stupendous trio all issuing forth against the idea of caste;

438

What historic denouements are these we so rapidly approach?
I see men marching and countermarching by swift millions,
I see the frontiers and boundaries of the old aristocracies broken,
I see the landmarks of European kings removed,
I see this day the People beginning their landmarks, (all others give way;)
Never were such sharp questions ask'd as this day,
Never was average man, his soul, more energetic, more like a God,
Lo, how he urges and urges, leaving the masses no rest!
His daring foot is on land and sea everywhere, he colonizes the Pacific, the archipelagoes,
With the steamship, the electric telegraph, the newspaper, the wholesale engines of war,
With these and the world-spreading factories he interlinks all geography, all lands;
What whispers are these O lands, running ahead of you, passing under the seas?
Are all nations communing? is there going to be but one heart to the globe?
Is humanity forming en-masse? for lo, tyrants tremble, crowns grow dim,
The earth, restive, confronts a new era, perhaps a general divine war,
No one knows what will happen next, such portents fill the days and nights;
Years prophetical! the space ahead as I walk, as I vainly try to pierce it, is full of phantoms,
Unborn deeds, things soon to be, project their shapes around me,
This incredible rush and heat, this strange ecstatic fever of dreams O years!
Your dreams O years, how they penetrate through me! (I know not whether I sleep or wake;)
The perform'd America and Europe grow dim, retiring in shadow behind me,
The unperform'd, more gigantic than ever, advance, advance upon me.

1865   1881

ASHES OF SOLDIERS

Ashes of soldiers South or North,
As I muse retrospective murmuring a chant in thought,
The war resumes, again to my sense your shapes,
And again the advance of the armies.

Noiseless as mists and vapors,
From their graves in the trenches ascending,
From cemeteries all through Virginia and Tennessee,
From every point of the compass out of the countless graves,
In wafted clouds, in myriads large, or squads of twos or
        threes or single ones they come,
And silently gather round me.

Now sound no note O trumpeters,
Not at the head of my cavalry parading on spirited horses,
With sabres drawn and glistening, and carbines by their
        thighs, (ah my brave horsemen!
My handsome tan-faced horsemen! what life, what joy and
        pride,
With all the perils were yours.)

Nor you drummers, neither at reveillé at dawn,
Nor the long roll alarming the camp, nor even the muffled
        beat for a burial,
Nothing from you this time O drummers bearing my warli[1]
        drums.

But aside from these and the marts of wealth and the crowded
        promenade,
Admitting around me comrades close unseen by the rest and
        voiceless,
The slain elate and alive again, the dust and debris alive,
I chant this chant of my silent soul in the name of all dead
        soldiers.

Faces so pale with wondrous eyes, very dear, gather closer
        yet,
Draw close, but speak not.

Phantoms of countless lost,
Invisible to the rest henceforth become my companions,
Follow me ever—desert me not while I live.

Sweet are the blooming cheeks of the living—sweet are the
    musical voices sounding,
But sweet, ah sweet, are the dead with their silent eyes.

Dearest comrades, all is over and long gone,
But love is not over—and what love, O comrades
Perfume from battle-fields rising, up from the fœtor arising.

Perfume therefore my chant, O love, immortal love,
Give me to bathe the memories of all dead soldiers,
Shroud them, embalm them, cover them all over with tender
    pride.

Perfume all—make all wholesome,
Make these ashes to nourish and blossom,
O love, solve all, fructify all with the last chemistry.

Give me exhaustless, make me a fountain,
That I exhale love from me wherever I go like a moist
    perennial dew,
For the ashes of all dead soldiers South or North.
1865   1881

THOUGHTS

1

OF these years I sing,
How they pass and have pass'd through convuls'd pains, as
    through parturitions,
How America illustrates birth, muscular youth, the promise,
    the sure fulfilment, the absolute success, despite of
    people—illustrates evil as well as good,
The vehement struggle so fierce for unity in one's -self;
How many hold despairingly yet to the models departed,
    caste, myths, obedience, compulsion, and to infidelity,
How few see the arrived models, the athletes, the Western
    States, or see freedom or spirituality, or hold any faith
    in results,

(But I see the athletes, and I see the results of the war glorious
   and inevitable, and they again leading to other results.)

How the great cities appear—how the Democratic masses,
   turbulent, wilful, as I love them,
How the whirl, the contest, the wrestle of evil with good, the
   sounding and resounding, keep on and on,
How society waits unform'd, and is for a while between
   things ended and things begun,
How America is the continent of glories, and of the triumph
   of freedom and of the Democracies, and of the fruits of
   society, and of all that is begun,
And how the States are complete in themselves—and how all
   triumphs and glories are complete in themselves, to lead
   onward,
And how these of mine and of the States will in their turn be
   convuls'd, and serve other parturitions and transitions,
And how all people, sights, combinations, the democratic
   masses too, serve—and how every fact, and war itself,
   with all its horrors, serves,
And how now or at any time each serves the exquisite transi-
   tion of death.

2

Of seeds dropping into the ground, of births,
Of the steady concentration of America, inland, upward, to
   impregnable and swarming places,
Of what Indiana, Kentucky, Arkansas, and the rest, are to be,
Of what a few years will show there in Nebraska, Colorado,
   Nevada, and the rest,
(Or afar, mounting the Northern Pacific to Sitka or Aliaska,)
Of what the feuillage of America is the preparation for—and
   of what all sights, North, South, East and West, are,
Of this Union welded in blood, of the solemn price paid, of
   the unnamed lost ever present in my mind;
Of the temporary use of materials for identity's sake,
Of the present, passing, departing—of the growth of com-
   pleter men than any yet,
Of all sloping down there where the fresh free giver the
   mother, the Mississippi flows,

Of mighty inland cities yet unsurvey'd and unsuspected,
Of the new and good names, of the modern developments, of
   inalienable homesteads,
Of a free and original life there, of simple diet and clean and
   sweet blood,
Of litheness, majestic faces, clear eyes, and perfect physique
   there,
Of immense spiritual results future years far West, each side
   of the Anahuacs,
Of these songs, well understood there, (being made for that
   area,)
Of the native scorn of grossness and gain there,
(O it lurks in me night and day—what is gain after all to
   savageness and freedom?)
1860   1881

SONG AT SUNSET

SPLENDOR of ended day floating and filling me,
Hour prophetic, hour resuming the past,
Inflating my throat, you divine average,
You earth and life till the last ray gleams I sing.

Open mouth of my soul uttering gladness,
Eyes of my soul seeing perfection,
Natural life of me faithfully praising things,
Corroborating forever the triumph of things.

Illustrious every one!
Illustrious what we name space, sphere of unnumber'd
   spirits,
Illustrious the mystery of motion in all beings, even the
   tiniest insect,
Illustrious the attribute of speech, the senses, the body,
Illustrious the passing light—illustrious the pale reflection
   on the new moon in the western sky,
Illustrious whatever I see or hear or touch, to the last.

Good in all,
In the satisfaction and aplomb of animals,
In the annual return of the seasons,

In the hilarity of youth,
In the strength and flush of manhood,
In the grandeur and exquisiteness of old age,
In the superb vistas of death.

Wonderful to depart!
Wonderful to be here!
The heart, to jet the all-alike and innocent blood!
To breathe the air, how delicious!
To speak—to walk—to seize something by the hand!
To prepare for sleep, for bed, to look on my rose-color'd
flesh!
To be conscious of my body, so satisfied, so large!
To be this incredible God I am!
To have gone forth among other Gods, these men and
women I love.

Wonderful how I celebrate you and myself!
How my thoughts play subtly at the spectacles around!
How the clouds pass silently overhead!
How the earth darts on and on! and how the sun, moon,
stars, dart on and on!
How the water sports and sings! (surely it is alive!)
How the trees rise and stand up, with strong trunks, with
branches and leaves!
(Surely there is something more in each of the trees, some
living soul.)

O amazement of things—even the least particle!
O spirituality of things!
O strain musical flowing through ages and continents, now
reaching me and America!
I take your strong chords, intersperse them, and cheerfully
pass them forward.

I too carol the sun, usher'd or at noon, or as now, set-
ting,
I too throb to the brain and beauty of the earth and of all the
growths of the earth,
I too have felt the resistless call of myself.

As I steam'd down the Mississippi,
As I wander'd over the prairies,
As I have lived, as I have look'd through my windows my eyes,
As I went forth in the morning, as I beheld the light breaking
    in the east,
As I bathed on the beach of the Eastern Sea, and again on the
    beach of Western Sea,
As I roam'd the streets of inland Chicago, whatever streets I
    have roam'd,
Or cities or silent woods, or even amid the sights of war,
Wherever I have been I have charged myself with content-
    ment and triumph.

I sing to the last the equalities modern or old,
I sing the endless finalés of things,
I say Nature continues, glory continues,
I praise with electric voice,
For I do not see one imperfection in the universe,
And I do not see one cause or result lamentable at last in the
    universe.

O setting sun! though the time has come,
I still warble under you, if none else does, unmitigated adora-
    tion.
1860   1881

AS AT THY PORTALS ALSO DEATH

As at thy portals also death,
Entering thy sovereign, dim, illimitable grounds,
To memories of my mother, to the divine blending, maternity,
To her, buried and gone, yet buried not, gone not from me,
(I see again the calm benignant face fresh and beautiful still,
I sit by the form in the coffin,
I kiss and kiss convulsively again the sweet old lips, the
    cheeks, the closed eyes in the coffin;)
To her, the ideal woman, practical, spiritual, of all of earth,
    life, love, to me the best,
I grave a monumental line, before I go, amid these songs,
And set a tombstone here.
1881   1881

MY LEGACY

THE business man the acquirer vast,
After assiduous years surveying results, preparing for departure,
Devises houses and lands to his children, bequeaths stocks, goods, funds for a school or hospital,
Leaves money to certain companions to buy tokens, souvenirs of gems and gold.

But I, my life surveying, closing,
With nothing to show to devise from its idle years,
Nor houses nor lands, nor tokens of gems or gold for my friends,
Yet certain remembrances of the war for you, and after you,
And little souvenirs of camps and soldiers, with my love,
I bind together and bequeath in this bundle of songs.
1872   1881

PENSIVE ON HER DEAD GAZING

PENSIVE on her dead gazing I heard the Mother of All,
Desperate on the torn bodies, on the forms covering the battle-fields gazing,
(As the last gun ceased, but the scent of the powder-smoke linger'd,)
As she call'd to her earth with mournful voice while she stalk'd,
Absorb them well O my earth, she cried, I charge you lose not my sons, lose not an atom,
And you streams absorb them well, taking their dear blood,
And you local spots, and you airs that swim above lightly impalpable,
And all you essences of soil and growth, and you my rivers' depths,
And you mountain sides, and the woods where my dear children's blood trickling redden'd,
And you trees down in your roots to bequeath to all future trees,
My dead absorb or South or North—my young men's bodies absorb, and their precious precious blood,

Which holding in trust for me faithfully back again give me
    many a year hence,
In unseen essence and odor of surface and grass, centuries
    hence,
In blowing airs from the fields back again give me my dar-
    lings, give my immortal heroes,
Exhale me them centuries hence, breathe me their breath, let
    not an atom be lost,
O years and graves! O air and soil! O my dead, an aroma
    sweet!
Exhale them perennial sweet death, years, centuries hence.
1865   1881

CAMPS OF GREEN

NOT alone those camps of white, old comrades of the wars,
When as order'd forward, after a long march,
Footsore and weary, soon as the light lessens we halt for the
    night,
Some of us so fatigued carrying the gun and knapsack, drop-
    ping asleep in our tracks,
Others pitching the little tents, and the fires lit up begin to
    sparkle,
Outposts of pickets posted surrounding alert through the dark,
And a word provided for countersign, careful for safety,
Till to the call of the drummers at daybreak loudly beating
    the drums,
We rise up refresh'd, the night and sleep pass'd over, and
    resume our journey,
Or proceed to battle.

Lo, the camps of the tents of green,
Which the days of peace keep filling, and the days of war
    keep filling,
With a mystic army, (is it too order'd forward? is it too only
    halting awhile,
Till night and sleep pass over?)

Now in those camps of green, in their tents dotting the world,
In the parents, children, husbands, wives, in them, in the old
    and young,

Sleeping under the sunlight, sleeping under the moonlight,
    content and silent there at last,
Behold the mighty bivouac-field and waiting-camp of all,
Of the corps and generals all, and the President over the
    corps and generals all,
And of each of us O soldiers, and of each and all in the ranks
    we fought,
(There without hatred we all, all meet.)

For presently O soldiers, we too camp in our place in the
    bivouac-camps of green,
But we need not provide for outposts, nor word for the
    counter-sign,
Nor drummer to beat the morning drum.
1865   1881

THE SOBBING OF THE BELLS

(*Midnight, Sept.* 19–20, 1881)

THE sobbing of the bells, the sudden death-news everywhere,
The slumberers rouse, the rapport of the People,
(Full well they know that message in the darkness,
Full well return, respond within their breasts, their brains,
    the sad reverberations,)
The passionate toll and clang—city to city, joining, sounding,
    passing,
Those heart-beats of a Nation in the night.
1881   1881

AS THEY DRAW TO A CLOSE

As they draw to a close,
Of what underlies the precedent songs—of my aims in them,
Of the seed I have sought to plant in them,
Of joy, sweet joy, through many a year, in them,
(For them, for them have I lived. in them my work is done,)
Of many an aspiration fond, of many a dream and plan;
Through Space and Time fused in a chant, and the flowing
    eternal identity,
To Nature encompassing these, encompassing God—to the
    joyous, electric all,

To the sense of Death, and accepting exulting in Death in its
    turn the same as life,
The entrance of man to sing;
To compact you, ye parted, diverse lives,
To put rapport the mountains and rocks and streams,
And the winds of the north, and the forests of oak and pine,
With you O soul.
1871   1881

JOY, SHIPMATE, JOY!

JOY, shipmate, joy!
(Pleas'd to my soul at death I cry,)
Our life is closed, our life begins,
The long, long anchorage we leave,
The ship is clear at last, she leaps!
She swiftly courses from the shore,
Joy, shipmate, joy!
1871   1871

THE UNTOLD WANT

THE untold want by life and land ne'er granted,
Now voyager sail thou forth to seek and find.
1871   1871

PORTALS

WHAT are those of the known but to ascend and enter the
    Unknown?
And what are those of life but for Death?
1871   1871

THESE CAROLS

THESE carols sung to cheer my passage through the world I
    see,
For completion I dedicate to the Invisible World.
1871   1871

NOW FINALÈ TO THE SHORE

Now finalè to the shore,
Now land and life finalè and farewell,
Now Voyager depart, (much, much for thee is yet in store,)

Often enough hast thou adventur'd o'er the seas,
Cautiously cruising, studying the charts,
Duly again to port and hawser's tie returning;
But now obey thy cherish'd secret wish,
Embrace thy friends, leave all in order,
To port and hawser's tie no more returning,
Depart upon thy endless cruise old Sailor.
1871   1871

SO LONG!

To conclude, I announce what comes after me.

I remember I said before my leaves sprang at all,
I would raise my voice jocund and strong with reference to
    consummations.

When America does what was promis'd,
When through these States walk a hundred millions of superb
    persons,
When the rest part away for superb persons and contribute
    to them,
When breeds of the most perfect mothers denote America,
Then to me and mine our due fruition.

I have press'd through in my own right,
I have sung the body and the soul, war and peace have I sung,
    and the songs of life and death,
And the songs of birth, and shown that there are many
    births.

I have offer'd my style to every one, I have journey'd with
    confident step;
While my pleasure is yet at the full I whisper *So long!*
And take the young woman's hand and the young man's
    hand for the last time.

I announce natural persons to arise,
I announce justice triumphant,
I announce uncompromising liberty and equality,
I announce the justification of candor and the justification of
    pride.

I announce that the identity of these States is a single identity
only,

I announce the Union more and more compact, indissoluble,

I announce splendors and majesties to make all the previous
politics of the earth insignificant.

I announce adhesiveness, I say it shall be limitless, un-
loosen'd,

I say you shall yet find the friend you were looking for.

I announce a man or woman coming, perhaps you are the
one, (*So long!*)

I announce the great individual, fluid as Nature, chaste,
affectionate, compassionate, fully arm'd.

I announce a life that shall be copious, vehement, spiritual,
bold,

I announce an end that shall lightly and joyfully meet its
translation.

I announce myriads of youths, beautiful, gigantic, sweet-
blooded,

I announce a race of splendid and savage old men.

O thicker and faster—(*So long!*)

O crowding too close upon me,

I foresee too much, it means more than I thought,

It appears to me I am dying.

Hasten throat and sound your last,

Salute me—salute the days once more. Peal the old cry once
more.

Screaming electric, the atmosphere using,

At random glancing, each as I notice absorbing,

Swiftly on, but a little while alighting,

Curious envelop'd messages delivering,

Sparkles hot, seed ethereal down in the dirt dropping,

Myself unknowing, my commission obeying, to question it
never daring,

To ages and ages yet the growth of the seed leaving,

To troops out of the war arising, they the tasks I have set
    promulging,
To women certain whispers of myself bequeathing, their
    affection me more clearly explaining,
To young men my problems offering—no dallier I—I the
    muscle of their brains trying,
So I pass, a little time vocal, visible, contrary,
Afterward a melodious echo, passionately bent for, (death
    making me really undying,)
The best of me then when no longer visible, for toward that
    I have been incessantly preparing.

What is there more, that I lag and pause and crouch extended
    with unshut mouth?
Is there a single final farewell?

My songs cease, I abandon them,
From behind the screen where I hid I advance personally
    solely to you.

Camerado, this is no book,
Who touches this touches a man,
(Is it night? are we here together alone?)
It is I you hold and who holds you,
I spring from the pages into your arms—decease calls me
    forth.

O how your fingers drowse me,
Your breath falls around me like dew, your pulse lulls the
    tympans of my ears,
I feel immerged from head to foot,
Delicious, enough.

Enough O deed impromptu and secret,
Enough O gliding present—enough O summ'd-up past.

Dear friend whoever you are take this kiss,
I give it especially to you, do not forget me,
I feel like one who has done work for the day to retire awhile,
I receive now again of my many translations, from my ava-
    taras ascending, while others doubtless await me,

An unknown sphere more real than I dream'd, more direct,
    darts awakening rays about me, *So long !*
Remember my words, I may again return,
I love you, I depart from materials,
I am as one disembodied, triumphant, dead.
1860   1881

Sands at Seventy

[First Annex]

MANNAHATTA

My city's fit and noble name resumed,
Choice aboriginal name, with marvellous beauty, meaning,
*A rocky founded island—shores where ever gayly dash the
     coming, going, hurrying sea waves.*
1888   1888-9

PAUMANOK

SEA-BEAUTY! stretch'd and basking!
One side thy inland ocean laving, broad, with copious com-
     merce, steamers, sails,
And one the Atlantic's wind caressing, fierce or gentle—
     mighty hulls dark-gliding in the distance.
Isle of sweet brooks of drinking-water—healthy air and soil!
Isle of the salty shore and breeze and brine!
1888   1888-9

FROM MONTAUK POINT

I STAND as on some mighty eagle's beak,
Eastward the sea absorbing, viewing, (nothing but sea and
     sky,)
The tossing waves, the foam, the ships in the distance.
The wild unrest, the snowy, curling caps—that inbound urge
     and urge of waves,
Seeking the shores forever.
1888   1888-9

TO THOSE WHO'VE FAIL'D

To those who've fail'd, in aspiration vast,
To unnam'd soldiers fallen in front on the lead,

454

To calm, devoted engineers—to over-ardent travelers—to
    pilots on their ships,
To many a lofty song and picture without recognition—I'd
    rear a laurel-cover'd monument,
High, high above the rest—To all cut off before their time,
Possess'd by some strange spirit of fire,
Quench'd by an early death.
1888   1888–9

A CAROL CLOSING SIXTY-NINE

A CAROL closing sixty-nine—a *résumé*—a repetition,
My lines in joy and hope continuing on the same,
Of ye, O God, Life, Nature, Freedom, Poetry;
Of you, my Land—your rivers, prairies, States—you, mottled
    Flag I love,
Your aggregate retain'd entire—Of north, south, east and
    west, your items all;
Of me myself—the jocund heart yet beating in my breast,
The body wreck'd, old, poor and paralyzed—the strange
    inertia falling pall-like round me,
The burning fires down in my sluggish blood not yet extinct,
The undiminish'd faith—the groups of loving friends.
1888   1888–9

THE BRAVEST SOLDIERS

BRAVE, brave were the soldiers (high named to-day) who
    lived through the fight;
But the bravest press'd to the front and fell, unnamed, un-
    known.
1888   1888–9

A FONT OF TYPE

THIS latent mine—these unlaunch'd voices—passionate
    powers,
Wrath, argument, or praise, or comic leer, or prayer devout,
(Not nonpareil, brevier, bourgeois, long primer merely,)
These ocean waves arousable to fury and to death,
Or sooth'd to ease and sheeny sun and sleep,
Within the pallid slivers slumbering.
1888   1888–9

AS I SIT WRITING HERE

As I sit writing here, sick and grown old,
Not my least burden is that dulness of the years, querilities,
Ungracious glooms, aches, lethargy, constipation, whimper-
     ing *ennui*,
May filter in my daily songs.
1888   1888–9

MY CANARY BIRD

DID we count great, O soul, to penetrate the themes of
     mighty books,
Absorbing deep and full from thoughts, plays, speculations?
But now from thee to me, caged bird, to feel thy joyous
     warble,
Filling the air, the lonesome room, the long forenoon,
Is it not just as great, O soul?
1888   1888–9

QUERIES TO MY SEVENTIETH YEAR

APPROACHING, nearing, curious,
Thou dim, uncertain spectre—bringest thou life or death?
Strength, weakness, blindness, more paralysis and heavier?
Or placid skies and sun? Wilt stir the waters yet?
Or haply cut me short for good? Or leave me here as now,
Dull, parrot-like and old, with crack'd voice harping,
     screeching?
1888   1888–9

THE WALLABOUT MARTYRS

(*In Brooklyn, in an old vault, mark'd by no special recogni-
tion, lie huddled at this moment the undoubtedly authentic re-
mains of the stanchest and earliest Revolutionary patriots from
the British prison ships and prisons of the times of 1776–83, in
and around New York, and from all over Long Island; origin-
ally buried—many thousands of them—in trenches in the
Wallabout sands.*)

GREATER than memory of Achilles or Ulysses,
More, more by far to thee than tomb of Alexander,

Those cart loads of old charnel ashes, scales and splints of
  mouldy bones,
Once living men—once resolute courage, aspiration, strength,
The stepping stones to thee to-day and here, America.
1888   1888–9

THE FIRST DANDELION

SIMPLE and fresh and fair from winter's close emerging,
As if no artifice of fashion, business, politics, had ever been,
Forth from its sunny nook of shelter'd grass—innocent,
  golden, calm as the dawn,
The spring's first dandelion shows its trustful face.
1888   1888–9

AMERICA

CENTRE of equal daughters, equal sons,
All, all alike endear'd, grown, ungrown, young or old,
Strong, ample, fair, enduring, capable, rich,
Perennial with the Earth, with Freedom, Law and Love,
A grand, sane, towering, seated Mother,
Chair'd in the adamant of Time.
1888   1888–9

MEMORIES

How sweet the silent backward tracings!
The wanderings as in dreams—the meditation of old times
  resumed—their loves, joys, persons, voyages.
1888   1888–9

TO-DAY AND THEE

THE appointed winners in a long-stretch'd game;
The course of Time and nations—Egypt, India, Greece and
  Rome;
The past entire, with all its heroes, histories, arts, experi-
  ments,
Its store of songs, inventions, voyages, teachers, books,
Garner'd for now and thee—To think of it!
The heirdom all converged in thee!
1888   1888–9

AFTER THE DAZZLE OF DAY

AFTER the dazzle of day is gone,
Only the dark, dark night shows to my eyes the stars;
After the clangor of organ majestic, or chorus, or perfect
    band,
Silent, athwart my soul, moves the symphony true.
1888   1888–9

ABRAHAM LINCOLN, BORN FEB. 12, 1809

(*Publish'd Feb.* 12, 1888)

To-DAY, from each and all, a breath of prayer—a pulse of
    thought,
To memory of Him—to birth of Him.
1888   1888–9

OUT OF MAY'S SHOWS SELECTED

APPLE orchards, the trees all cover'd with blossoms;
Wheat fields carpeted far and near in vital emerald green;
The eternal, exhaustless freshness of each early morning;
The yellow, golden, transparent haze of the warm afternoon
    sun;
The aspiring lilac bushes with profuse purple or white
    flowers.
1888   1888–9

HALCYON DAYS

NOT from successful love alone,
Nor wealth, nor honor'd middle age, nor victories of politics
    or war;
But as life wanes, and all the turbulent passions calm,
As gorgeous, vapory, silent hues cover the evening sky,
As softness, fulness, rest, suffuse the frame, like fresher,
    balmier air,
As the days take on a mellower light, and the apple at last
    hangs really finish'd and indolent-ripe on the tree,
Then for the teeming quietest, happiest days of all!
The brooding and blissful halcyon days!
1888   1888–9

FANCIES AT NAVESINK

THE PILOT IN THE MIST

Steaming the northern rapids—(an old St. Lawrence re-
    miniscence,
A sudden memory-flash comes back, I know not why,
Here waiting for the sunrise, gazing from this hill;)*
Again 'tis just at morning—a heavy haze contends with day-
    break,
Again the trembling, laboring vessel veers me—I press
    through foam-dash'd rocks that almost touch me,
Again I mark where aft the small thin Indian helmsman
Looms in the mist, with brow elate and governing hand.

HAD I THE CHOICE

HAD I the choice to tally greatest bards,
To limn their portraits, stately, beautiful, and emulate at
    will,
Homer with all his wars and warriors—Hector, Achilles,
    Ajax,
Or Shakspere's woe-entangled Hamlet, Lear, Othello—
    Tennyson's fair ladies,
Metre or wit the best, or choice conceit to wield in perfect
    rhyme, delight of singers;
These, these, O sea, all these I'd gladly barter,
Would you the undulation of one wave, its trick to me trans-
    fer,
Or breathe one breath of yours upon my verse,
And leave its odor there,

YOU TIDES WITH CEASELESS SWELL

You tides with ceaseless swell! you power that does this
    work!
You unseen force, centripetal, centrifugal, through space's
    spread,
Rapport of sun, moon, earth, and all the constellations,

* Navesink—a sea-side mountain, lower entrance of New York Bay.

What are the messages by you from distant stars to us? what
   Sirius'? what Capella's?
What central heart—and you the pulse—vivifies all? what
   boundless aggregate of all?
What subtle indirection and significance in you? what clue to
   all in you? what fluid, vast identity,
Holding the universe with all its parts as one—as sailing in a
   ship?

LAST OF EBB, AND DAYLIGHT WANING

LAST of ebb, and daylight waning,
Scented sea-cool landward making, smells of sedge and salt
   incoming,
With many a half-caught voice sent up from the eddies,
Many a muffled confession—many a sob and whisper'd
   word,
As of speakers far or hid.

How they sweep down and out! how they mutter!
Poets unnamed—artists greatest of any, with cherish'd lost
   designs,
Love's unresponse—a chorus of age's complaints—hope's
   last words,
Some suicide's despairing cry, *Away to the boundless waste,
   and never again return.*

On to oblivion then!
On, on, and do your part, ye burying, ebbing tide!
On for your time, ye furious debouché!

AND YET NOT YOU ALONE

AND yet not you alone, twilight and burying ebb,
Nor you, ye lost designs alone—nor failures, aspirations;
I know, divine deceitful ones, your glamour's seeming;
Duly by you, from you, the tide and light again—duly the
   hinges turning,
Duly the needed discord-parts offsetting, blending,
Weaving from you, from Sleep, Night, Death itself,
The rhythmus of Birth eternal.

PROUDLY THE FLOOD COMES IN

PROUDLY the flood comes in, shouting, foaming, advancing,
Long it holds at the high, with bosom broad outswelling,
All throbs, dilates—the farms, woods, streets of cities—
    workmen at work,
Mainsails, topsails, jibs, appear in the offing—steamers'
    pennants of smoke—and under the forenoon sun,
Freighted with human lives, gaily the outward bound, gaily
    the inward bound,
Flaunting from many a spar the flag I love.

BY THAT LONG SCAN OF WAVES

By that long scan of waves, myself call'd back, resumed upon
    myself,
In every crest some undulating light or shade—some retro-
    spect,
Joys, travels, studies, silent panoramas—scenes, ephemeral,
The long past war, the battles, hospital sights, the wounded
    and the dead,
Myself through every by-gone phase—my idle youth—old
    age at hand,
My three-score years of life summ'd up, and more, and
    past,
By any grand ideal tried, intentionless, the whole a nothing,
And haply yet some drop within God's scheme's ensemble—
    some wave, or part of wave,
Like one of yours, ye multitudinous ocean.

THEN LAST OF ALL

THEN last of all, caught from these shores, this hill,
Of you O tides, the mystic human meaning:
Only by law of you, your swell and ebb, enclosing me the
    same,
The brain that shapes, the voice that chants this song.
1885   1888–9

ELECTION DAY, NOVEMBER, 1884

IF I should need to name, O Western World, your powerfulest
    scene and show,
'Twould not be you, Niagara—nor you, ye limitless prairies
    —nor your huge rifts of canyons, Colorado,
Nor you, Yosemite—nor Yellowstone, with all its spasmic
    geyser loops ascending to the skies, appearing and dis-
    appearing,
Nor Oregon's white cones—nor Huron's belt of mighty lakes
    —nor Mississippi's stream:
—This seething hemisphere's humanity, as now, I'd name—
    the still small voice vibrating—America's choosing day,
(The heart of it not in the chosen—the act itself the main, the
    quadrennial choosing,)
The stretch of North and South arous'd—sea-board and in-
    land—Texas to Maine—the Prairie States—Vermont,
    Virginia, California,
The final ballot-shower from East to West—the paradox and
    conflict,
The countless snow-flakes falling—(a swordless conflict,
Yet more than all Rome's wars of old, or modern Napo-
    leon's:) the peaceful choice of all,
Or good or ill humanity—welcoming the darker odds, the
    dross:
—Foams and ferments the wine? it serves to purify—while
    the heart pants, life glows:
These stormy gusts and winds waft precious ships,
Swell'd Washington's, Jefferson's, Lincoln's sails.
1884   1888-9

WITH HUSKY-HAUGHTY LIPS, O SEA!

WITH husky-haughty lips, O sea!
Where day and night I wend thy surf-beat shore,
Imaging to my sense thy varied strange suggestions,
(I see and plainly list thy talk and conference here,)
Thy troops of white-maned racers racing to the goal,
Thy ample, smiling face, dash'd with the sparkling dimples of
    the sun,
Thy brooding scowl and murk—thy unloos'd hurricanes,

Thy unsubduedness, caprices, wilfulness;
Great as thou art above the rest, thy many tears—a lack from
 all eternity in thy content,
(Naught but the greatest struggles, wrongs, defeats, could
 make thee greatest—no less could make thee,)
Thy lonely state—something thou ever seek'st and seek'st,
 yet never gain'st,
Surely some right withheld—some voice, in huge monoton-
 ous rage, of freedom-lover pent,
Some vast heart, like a planet's, chain'd and chafing in those
 breakers,
By lengthen'd swell, and spasm, and panting breath,
And rhythmic rasping of thy sands and waves,
And serpent hiss, and savage peals of laughter,
And undertones of distant lion roar,
(Sounding, appealing to the sky's deaf ear—but now, rapport
 for once,
A phantom in the night thy confidant for once,)
The first and last confession of the globe,
Outsurging, muttering from thy soul's abysms,
The tale of cosmic elemental passion,
Thou tellest to a kindred soul.
(1883)   1888-9

DEATH OF GENERAL GRANT

As one by one withdraw the lofty actors,
From that great play on history's stage eterne,
That lurid, partial act of war and peace—of old and new
 contending,
Fought out through wrath, fears, dark dismays, and many a
 long suspense;
All past—and since, in countless graves receding, mellowing,
Victor's and vanquish'd—Lincoln's and Lee's—now thou
 with them,
Man of the mighty days—and equal to the days!
Thou from the prairies!—tangled and many-vein'd and hard
 has been thy part,
To admiration has it been enacted!
1885   1888-9

RED JACKET (FROM ALOFT)

(*Impromptu on Buffalo City's monument to, and re-burial of
the old Iroquois orator, October* 9, 1884)

UPON this scene, this show,
Yielded to-day by fashion, learning, wealth,
(Nor in caprice alone—some grains of deepest meaning,)
Haply, aloft, (who knows?) from distant sky-clouds' blended
     shapes,
As some old tree, or rock or cliff, thrill'd with its soul,
Product of Nature's sun, stars, earth direct—a towering
     human form,
In hunting-shirt of film, arm'd with the rifle, a half-ironical
     smile curving its phantom lips,
Like one of Ossian's ghosts looks down.
(1884)   1888-9

WASHINGTON'S MONUMENT, FEBRUARY, 1885

AH, not this marble, dead and cold:
Far from its base and shaft expanding—the round zones
     circling, comprehending,
Thou, Washington, art all the world's, the continents' entire
     —not yours alone, America,
Europe's as well, in every part, castle of lord or laborer's
     cot,
Or frozen North, or sultry South—the African's—the Arab's
     in his tent,
Old Asia's there with venerable smile, seated amid her
     ruins;
(Greets the antique the hero new? 'tis but the same—the heir
     legitimate, continued ever,
The indomitable heart and arm—proofs of the never-broken
     line,
Courage, alertness, patience, faith, the same—e'en in defeat
     defeated not, the same:)
Wherever sails a ship, or house is built on land, or day or
     night,
Through teeming cities' streets, indoors or out, factories or
     farms,

Now, or to come, or past—where patriot wills existed or
    exist,
Wherever Freedom, pois'd by Toleration, sway'd by Law,
Stands or is rising thy true monument.
(1885?)   1888–9

OF THAT BLITHE THROAT OF THINE

(*More than eighty-three degrees north—about a good day's
steaming distance to the Pole by one of our fast oceaners in
clear water—Greely the explorer heard the song of a single
snow-bird merrily sounding over the desolation.*)

OF that blithe throat of thine from arctic bleak and blank,
I'll mind the lesson, solitary bird—let me too welcome chill-
    ing drifts,
E'en the profoundest chill, as now—a torpid pulse, a brain
    unnerv'd,
Old age land-lock'd within its winter bay—(cold, cold, O
    cold!)
These snowy hairs, my feeble arm, my frozen feet,
For them thy faith, thy rule I take, and grave it to the last;
Not summer's zones alone—not chants of youth, or south's
    warm tides alone,
But held by sluggish floes, pack'd in the northern ice, the
    cumulus of years,
These with gay heart I also sing.
(1884)   1888–9

BROADWAY

WHAT hurrying human tides, or day or night!
What passions, winnings, losses, ardors, swim thy waters!
What whirls of evil, bliss and sorrow, stem thee!
What curious questioning glances—glints of love!
Leer, envy, scorn, contempt, hope, aspiration!
Thou portal—thou arena—thou of the myriad long-drawn
    lines and groups!
(Could but thy flagstones, curbs, façades, tell their inimitable
    tales;
Thy windows rich, and huge hotels—thy side-walks wide;)

Thou of the endless sliding, mincing, shuffling feet!
Thou, like the parti-colored world itself—like infinite, teem-
    ing, mocking life!
Thou visor'd, vast, unspeakable show and lesson!
1888   1888–9

TO GET THE FINAL LILT OF SONGS

To get the final lilt of songs,
To penetrate the inmost lore of poets—to know the mighty
    ones,
Job, Homer, Eschylus, Dante, Shakspere, Tennyson, Emer-
    son;
To diagnose the shifting-delicate tints of love and pride and
    doubt—to truly understand,
To encompass these, the last keen faculty and entrance-
    price,
Old age, and what it brings from all its past experiences.
1888   1888–9

OLD SALT KOSSABONE

FAR back, related on my mother's side,
Old Salt Kossabone, I'll tell you how he died:
(Had been a sailor all his life—was nearly 90—lived with his
    married grandchild, Jenny;
House on a hill, with view of bay at hand, and distant cape,
    and stretch to open sea;
The last of afternoons, the evening hours, for many a year his
    regular custom,
In his great arm chair by the window seated,
(Sometimes, indeed, through half the day,)
Watching the coming, going of the vessels, he mutters to
    himself—And now the close of all:
One struggling outbound brig, one day, baffled for long—
    cross-tides and much wrong going,
At last at nightfall strikes the breeze aright, her whole luck
    veering,
And swiftly bending round the cape, the darkness proudly
    entering, cleaving, as he watches,

"She's free—she's on her destination"—these the last words
  —when Jenny came, he sat there dead,
Dutch Kossabone, Old Salt, related on my mother's side, far
  back.
1888   1888–9

THE DEAD TENOR

As down the stage again,
With Spanish hat and plumes, and gait inimitable,
Back from the fading lessons of the past, I'd call, I'd tell and
  own,
How much from thee! the revelation of the singing voice
  from thee!
(So firm—so liquid soft—again that tremulous, manly timbre!
The perfect singing voice—deepest of all to me the lesson—
  trial and test of all :)
How through those strains distill'd—how the rapt ears, the
  soul of me, absorbing
Fernando's heart, *Manrico's* passionate call, *Ernani's*, sweet
  Gennaro's,
I fold thenceforth, or seek to fold, within my chants trans-
  muting,
Freedom's and Love's and Faith's unloos'd cantabile,
(As perfume's, color's, sunlight's correlation :)
From these, for these, with these, a hurried line, dead tenor,
A wafted autumn leaf, dropt in the closing grave, the
  shovel'd earth,
To memory of thee.
1884   1888–9

CONTINUITIES

(From a talk I had lately with a German spiritualist)

NOTHING is ever really lost, or can be lost,
No birth, identity, form—no object of the world,
Nor life, nor force, nor any visible thing;
Appearance must not foil, nor shifted sphere confuse thy
  brain.
Ample are time and space—ample the fields of Nature.
The body, sluggish, aged, cold—the embers left from earlier
  fires,

The light in the eye grown dim, shall duly flame again;
The sun now low in the west rises for mornings and for noons
      continual;
To frozen clods ever the spring's invisible law returns,
With grass and flowers and summer fruits and corn.
1888   1888–9

YONNONDIO

(The sense of the word is lament for the aborigines. *It is an
    Iroquois term; and has been used for a personal name.)*

A SONG, a poem of itself—the word itself a dirge,
Amid the wilds, the rocks, the storm and wintry night,
To me such misty, strange tableaux the syllables calling up;
Yonnondio—I see, far in the west or north, a limitless ravine,
      with plains and mountains dark,
I see swarms of stalwart chieftains, medicine-men, and war-
      riors,
As flitting by like clouds of ghosts, they pass and are gone in
      the twilight,
(Race of the woods, the landscapes free, and the falls!
No picture, poem, statement, passing them to the future:)
Yonnondio! Yonnondio!—unlimn'd they disappear;
To-day gives place, and fades—the cities, farms, factories
      fade;
A muffled sonorous sound, a wailing word is borne through
      the air for a moment,
Then blank and gone and still, and utterly lost.
1887   1888–9

LIFE

EVER the undiscouraged, resolute, struggling soul of man;
(Have former armies fail'd? then we send fresh armies—and
      fresh again;)
Ever the grappled mystery of all earth's ages old or new;
Ever the eager eyes, hurrahs, the welcome-clapping hands,
      the loud applause;
Ever the soul dissatisfied, curious, unconvinced at last;
Struggling to-day the same—battling the same.
1888   1888–9

"GOING SOMEWHERE"

MY science-friend, my noblest woman-friend,
(Now buried in an English grave—and this a memory-leaf
· for her dear sake,)
Ended our talk—"The sum, concluding all we know of old
or modern learning, intuitions deep,
"Of all Geologies—Histories—of all Astronomy—of Evolu-
tion, Metaphysics all,
"Is, that we all are onward, onward, speeding slowly, surely
bettering,
"Life, life an endless march, an endless army, (no halt, but it
is duly over,)
"The world, the race, the soul—in space and time the uni-
verses,
"All bound as is befitting each—all surely going some-
where."

1887   1888-9

SMALL THE THEME OF MY CHANT

(*From the* 1867 *edition* "*L. of G.*")

SMALL the theme of my Chant, yet the greatest—namely,
One's-Self—a simple, separate person. That, for the use
of the New World, I sing,
Man's physiology complete, from top to toe, I sing. Not
physiognomy alone, nor brain alone, is worthy for the
Muse;—I say the Form complete is worthier far. The
Female equally with the Male, I sing.
Nor cease at the theme of One's-Self. I speak the word of the
modern, the word En-Masse.
My Days I sing, and the Lands—with interstice I knew of
hapless War.
(O friend, whoe'er you are, at last arriving hither to com-
mence, I feel through every leaf the pressure of your
hand, which I return.
And thus upon our journey, footing the road, and more than
once, and link'd together let us go.)

1867   1888-9

TRUE CONQUERORS

OLD farmers, travelers, workmen (no matter how crippled or
    bent,)
Old sailors, out of many a perilous voyage, storm and wreck,
Old soldiers from campaigns, with all their wounds, defeats
    and scars;
Enough that they've survived at all—long life's unflinching
    ones!
Forth from their struggles, trials, fights, to have emerged at
    all—in that alone,
True conquerors o'er all the rest.
1888   1888–9

THE UNITED STATES TO OLD WORLD CRITICS

HERE first the duties of to-day, the lessons of the concrete,
Wealth, order, travel, shelter, products, plenty;
As of the building of some varied, vast, perpetual edifice,
Whence to arise inevitable in time, the towering roofs, the
    lamps,
The solid-planted spires tall shooting to the stars.
1888   1888–9

THE CALMING THOUGHT OF ALL

THAT coursing on, whate'er men's speculations,
Amid the changing schools, theologies, philosophies,
Amid the bawling presentations new and old,
The round earth's silent vital laws, facts, modes continue.
1888   1888–9

THANKS IN OLD AGE

THANKS in old age—thanks ere I go,
For health, the midday sun, the impalpable air—for life,
    mere life,
For precious ever-lingering memories, (of you my mother
    dear—you father—you, brothers, sisters, friends,)
For all my days—not those of peace alone—the days of war
    the same,

For gentle words, caresses, gifts from foreign lands,
For shelter, wine and meat—for sweet appreciation,
(You distant, dim unknown—or young or old—countless,
    unspecified, readers belov'd,
We never met, and ne'er shall meet—and yet our souls em-
    brace, long, close and long;)
For beings, groups, love, deeds, words, books—for colors,
    forms,
For all the brave strong men—devoted, hardy men—who've
    forward sprung in freedom's help, all years, all lands,
For braver, stronger, more devoted men—(a special laurel
    ere I go, to life's war's chosen ones,
The cannoneers of song and thought—the great artillerists—
    the foremost leaders, captains of the soul:)
As soldier from an ended war return'd—As traveler out of
    myriads, to the long procession retrospective,
Thanks—joyful thanks!—a soldier's, traveler's thanks.
1888   1888-9

LIFE AND DEATH

The two old, simple problems ever intertwined,
Close home, elusive, present, baffled, grappled.
By each successive age insoluble, pass'd on,
To ours to-day—and we pass on the same.
1888   1888-9

THE VOICE OF THE RAIN

And who art thou? said I to the soft-falling shower,
Which, strange to tell, gave me an answer, as here translated:
I am the Poem of Earth, said the voice of the rain,
Eternal I rise impalpable out of the land and the bottomless
    sea,
Upward to heaven, whence, vaguely form'd, altogether
    changed, and yet the same,
I descend to lave the drouths, atomies, dust-layers of the
    globe,
And all that in them without me were seeds only, latent, un-
    born;

And forever, by day and night, I give back life to my own
    origin and make pure and beautify it;
(For song, issuing from its birth-place, after fulfilment, wan-
    dering,
Reck'd or unreck'd, duly with love returns.)
(1885)   1888–9

SOON SHALL THE WINTER'S FOIL BE HERE

Soon shall the winter's foil be here;
Soon shall these icy ligatures unbind and melt—A little
    while,
And air, soil, wave, suffused shall be in softness, bloom and
    growth—a thousand forms shall rise
From these dead clods and chills as from low burial graves.
Thine eyes, ears—all thy best attributes—all that takes cog-
    nizance of natural beauty,
Shall wake and fill. Thou shalt perceive the simple shows,
    the delicate miracles of earth,
Dandelions, clover, the emerald grass, the early scents and
    flowers,
The arbutus under foot, the willow's yellow-green, the blos-
    soming plum and cherry;
With these the robin, lark and thrush, singing their songs—
    the flitting bluebird;
For such the scenes the annual play brings on.
1888   1888–9

WHILE NOT THE PAST FORGETTING

(*Publish'd May* 30, 1888)

While not the past forgetting,
To-day, at least, contention sunk entire—peace, brotherhood
    uprisen;
For sign reciprocal our Northern, Southern hands,
Lay on the graves of all dead soldiers, North or South,
(Nor for the past alone—for meanings to the future,)
Wreaths of roses and branches of palm.
1888   1888–9

THE DYING VETERAN

(A Long Island incident—early part of the nineteenth century)

AMID these days of order, ease, prosperity,
Amid the current songs of beauty, peace, decorum,
I cast a reminiscence—(likely 'twill offend you,
I heard it in my boyhood;)—More than a generation since,
A queer old savage man, a fighter under Washington himself,
(Large, brave, cleanly, hot-blooded, no talker, rather spiri-
      tualistic,
Had fought in the ranks—fought well—had been all through
      the Revolutionary war,)
Lay dying—sons, daughters, church-deacons, lovingly tend-
      ing him,
Sharping their sense, their ears, towards his murmuring,
      half-caught words:
"Let me return again to my war-days,
To the sights and scenes—to forming the line of battle,
To the scouts ahead reconnoitering,
To the cannons, the grim artillery,
To the galloping aids, carrying orders,
To the wounded, the fallen, the heat, the suspense,
The perfume strong, the smoke, the deafening noise;
Away with your life of peace!—your joys of peace!
Give me my old wild battle-life again!"
(1887)   1888–9

STRONGER LESSONS

HAVE you learn'd lessons only of those who admired you,
      and were tender with you, and stood aside for you?
Have you not learn'd great lessons from those who reject
      you, and brace themselves against you? or who treat you
      with contempt, or dispute the passage with you?
1888   1888–9

A PRAIRIE SUNSET

SHOT gold, maroon and violet, dazzling silver, emerald, fawn,
The earth's whole amplitude and Nature's multiform power
      consign'd for once to colors;

The light, the general air possess'd by them—colors till now
  unknown,
No limit, confine—not the Western sky alone—the high
  meridian—North, South, all,
Pure luminous color fighting the silent shadows to the last.
1888   1888-9

TWENTY YEARS

Down on the ancient wharf, the sand, I sit, with a new-
  comer chatting:
He shipp'd as green-hand boy, and sail'd away, (took some
  sudden, vehement notion;)
Since, twenty years and more have circled round and round,
While he the globe was circling round and round,—and now
  returns:
How changed the place—all the old land-marks gone—the
  parents dead;
(Yes, he comes back *to lay in port for good—to settle*—has a
  well-fill'd purse—no spot will do but this;)
The little boat that scull'd him from the sloop, now held in
  leash I see,
I hear the slapping waves, the restless keel, the rocking in the
  sand,
I see the sailor kit, the canvas bag, the great box bound with
  brass,
I scan the face all berry-brown and bearded—the stout-
  strong frame,
Dress'd in its russet suit of good Scotch cloth:
(Then what the told-out story of those twenty years? What
  of the future?)
(1887)   1888-9

ORANGE BUDS BY MAIL FROM FLORIDA

(*Voltaire closed a famous argument by claiming that a ship
of war and the grand opera were proofs enough of civilization's
and France's progress, in his day.*)

A lesser proof than old Voltaire's, yet greater,
Proof of this present time, and thee, thy broad expanse,
  America,

To my plain Northern hut, in outside clouds and snow,
Brought safely for a thousand miles o'er land and tide,
Some three days since on their own soil live-sprouting,
Now here their sweetness through my room unfolding,
A bunch of orange buds by mail from Florida.
1888   1888–9

TWILIGHT

THE soft voluptuous opiate shades,
The sun just gone, the eager light dispell'd—(I too will soon
    be gone, dispell'd,)
A haze—nirwana—rest and night—oblivion.
(1887)   1888–9

YOU LINGERING SPARSE LEAVES OF ME

YOU lingering sparse leaves of me on winter-nearing
    boughs,
And I some well-shorn tree of field or orchard-row;
You tokens diminute and lorn—(not now the flush of May,
    or July clover-bloom—no grain of August now;)
You pallid banner-staves—you pennants valueless—you
    overstay'd of time,
Yet my soul-dearest leaves confirming all the rest,
The faithfulest—hardiest—last.
1887   1888–9

NOT MEAGRE, LATENT BOUGHS ALONE

NOT meagre, latent boughs alone, O songs! (scaly and bare,
    like eagles' talons,)
But haply for some sunny day (who knows?) some future
    spring, some summer—bursting forth,
To verdant leaves, or sheltering shade—to nourishing
    fruit,
Apples and grapes—the stalwart limbs of trees emerging—
    the fresh, free, open air,
And love and faith, like scented roses blooming.
1887   1888–9

THE DEAD EMPEROR

(*Publish'd March* 10, 1888)

To-day, with bending head and eyes, thou, too, Columbia,
Less for the mighty crown laid low in sorrow—less for the
    Emperor,
Thy true condolence breathest, sendest out o'er many a salt
    sea mile,
Mourning a good old man—a faithful shepherd, patriot.
1888   1888–9

AS THE GREEK'S SIGNAL FLAME

(*For Whittier's eightieth birthday, December* 17, 1887)

As the Greek's signal flame, by antique records told,
Rose from the hill-top, like applause and glory,
Welcoming in fame some special veteran, hero,
With rosy tinge reddening the land he'd served,
So I aloft from Mannahatta's ship-fringed shore,
Lift high a kindled brand for thee, Old Poet.
1887   1888–9

THE DISMANTLED SHIP

In some unused lagoon, some nameless bay,
On sluggish, lonesome waters, anchor'd near the shore,
An old, dismasted, gray and batter'd ship, disabled, done,
After free voyages to all the seas of earth, haul'd up at last
    and hawser'd tight,
Lies rusting, mouldering.
1888   1888–9

NOW PRECEDENT SONGS, FAREWELL

Now precedent songs, farewell—by every name farewell,
(Trains of a staggering line in many a strange procession,
    waggons,
From ups and downs—with intervals—from elder years,
    mid-age, or youth,)
"In Cabin'd Ships", or "Thee Old Cause" or "Poets to
    Come"

Or "Paumanok", "Song of Myself", "Calamus", or "Adam",
Or "Beat! Beat! Drums!" or "To the Leaven'd Soil they
    Trod,"
Or "Captain! My Captain!" "Kosmos", "Quicksand Years",
    or "Thoughts",
"Thou Mother with thy Equal Brood", and many, many
    more unspecified,
From fibre heart of mine—from throat and tongue—(My
    life's hot pulsing blood,
The personal urge and form for me—not merely paper, auto-
    matic type and ink,)
Each song of mine—each utterance in the past—having its
    long, long history,
Of life or death, or soldier's wound, of country's loss or
    safety,
(O heaven! what flash and started endless train of all! com-
    pared indeed to that!
What wretched shred e'en at the best of all!)
1888   1888–9

AN EVENING LULL

AFTER a week of physical anguish,
Unrest and pain, and feverish heat,
Toward the ending day a calm and lull comes on,
Three hours of peace and soothing rest of brain.*
1888   1888–9

OLD AGE'S LAMBENT PEAKS

THE touch of flame—the illuminating fire—the loftiest look
    at last,
O'er city, passion, sea—o'er prairie, mountain, wood—the
    earth itself;
The airy, different, changing hues of all, in falling twilight,
Objects and groups, bearings, faces, reminiscences;

* The two songs on pages 476-477 ["Now Precedent Songs, Farewell"
and "an Evening Lull"] are eked out during an afternoon, June, 1888,
in my seventieth year, at a critical spell of illness. Of course no reader
and probably no human being at any time will ever have such phases of
emotional and solemn action as these involve to me. I feel in them an
end and close of all.

The calmer sight—the golden setting, clear and broad :
So much i' the atmosphere, the points of view, the situations
    whence we scan,
Bro't out by them alone—so much (perhaps the best) un-
    reck'd before ;
The lights indeed from them—old age's lambent peaks.
1888   1889

AFTER THE SUPPER AND TALK

AFTER the supper and talk—after the day is done,
As a friend from friends his final withdrawal prolonging,
Good-bye and Good-bye with emotional lips repeating,
(So hard for his hand to release those hands—no more will
    they meet,
No more for communion of sorrow and joy, of old and
    young,
A far-stretching journey awaits him, to return no more,)
Shunning, postponing severance—seeking to ward off the
    last word ever so little,
E'en at the exit-door turning—charges superfluous calling
    back—e'en as he descends the steps,
Something to eke out a minute additional—shadows of
    nightfall deepening,
Farewells, messages lessening—dimmer the forthgoer's vis-
    age and form,
Soon to be lost for aye in the darkness—loth, O so loth to
    depart!
Garrulous to the very last.
1887   1888–9

Good-bye My Fancy

(Second Annex)

SAIL OUT FOR GOOD, EIDÓLON YACHT!

HEAVE the anchor short!
Raise main-sail and jib—steer forth,
O little white-hull'd sloop, now speed on really deep
waters,
(I will not call it our concluding voyage,
But outset and sure entrance to the truest, best, maturest;)
Depart, depart from solid earth—no more returning to these
shores,
Now on for aye our infinite free venture wending,
Spurning all yet tried ports, seas, hawsers, densities, gravi-
tation,
Sail out for good, eidólon yacht of me!
1891   1891–2

LINGERING LAST DROPS

AND whence and why come you?

We know not whence, (was the answer,)
We only know that we drift here with the rest,
That we linger'd and lagg'd—but were wafted at last, and are
now here,
To make the passing shower's concluding drops,
1891   1891–2

479

GOOD-BYE MY FANCY

GOOD-BYE* my fancy—(I had a word to say,
But 'tis not quite the time—The best of any man's word or say,
Is when its proper place arrives—and for its meaning,
I keep mine till the last.)
1891   1891–2

ON, ON THE SAME, YE JOCUND TWAIN!

ON, on the same, ye jocund twain!
My life and recitative, containing birth, youth, mid-age years,
Fitful as motley-tongues of flame, inseparably twined and
　　　merged in one—combining all,
My single soul—aims, confirmations, failures, joys—Nor
　　　single soul alone,
I chant my nation's crucial stage, (America's, haply human-
　　　ity's)—the trial great, the victory great,
A strange *eclaircissement* of all the masses past, the eastern
　　　world, the ancient, medieval,
Here, here from wanderings, strayings, lessons, wars, defeats
　　　—here at the west a voice triumphant—justifying all,
A gladsome pealing cry—a song for once of utmost pride and
　　　satisfaction;
I chant from it the common bulk, the general average horde,
　　　(the best no sooner than the worst)—And now I chant
　　　old age,
(My verses, written first for forenoon life, and for the sum-
　　　mer's, autumn's spread,
I pass to snow-white hairs the same, and give to pulses win-
　　　ter-cool'd the same;)
As here in careless trill, I and my recitatives, with faith and
　　　love,

* Behind a Good-bye there lurks much of the salutation of another
beginning—to me, Development, Continuity, Immortality, Transfor-
mation, are the chiefest life-meanings of Nature and Humanity, and
are the *sine qua non* of all facts, and each fact.
　　Why do folks dwell so fondly on the last words, advice, appearance,
of the departing? Those last words are not samples of the best, which
involve vitality at its full, and balance, and perfect control and scope.
But they are valuable beyond measure to confirm and endorse the
varied train, facts, theories and faith of the whole preceding life.

Wafting to other work, to unknown songs, conditions,
On, on, ye jocund twain! continue on the same!
1891   1891-2

MY 71ST YEAR

AFTER surmounting three-score and ten,
With all their chances, changes, losses, sorrows,
My parents' deaths, the vagaries of my life, the many tearing
    passions of me, the war of '63 and '4,
As some old broken soldier, after a long, hot, wearying
    march, or haply after battle,
To-day at twilight, hobbling, answering company roll-call,
    Here, with vital voice,
Reporting yet, saluting yet the Officer over all.
1889   1891-2

APPARITIONS

A VAGUE mist hanging 'round half the pages:
(Sometimes how strange and clear to the soul,
That all these solid things are indeed but apparitions, con-
    cepts, non-realities.)
1891   1891-2

THE PALLID WREATH

SOMEHOW I cannot let it go yet, funeral though it is,
Let it remain back there on its nail suspended,
With pink, blue, yellow, all blanch'd, and the white now gray
    and ashy,
One wither'd rose put years ago for thee, dear friend;
But I do not forget thee. Hast thou then faded?
Is the odor exhaled? Are the colors, vitalities, dead?
No, while memories subtly play—the past vivid as ever;
For but last night I woke, and in that spectral ring saw
    thee,
Thy smile, eyes, face, calm, silent, loving as ever;
So let the wreath hang still awhile within my eye-reach,
It is not yet dead to me, nor even pallid.
1891   1891-2

AN ENDED DAY

THE soothing sanity and blitheness of completion,
The pomp and hurried contest-glare and rush are done;
Now triumph! transformation! jubilate!*
1891   1891-2

OLD AGE'S SHIP & CRAFTY DEATH'S

FROM east and west across the horizon's edge,
Two mighty masterful vessels sailers steal upon us:
But we'll make race a-time upon the seas—a battle-contest
    yet! bear lively there!
(Our joys of strife and derring-do to the last!)
Put on the old ship all her power to-day!
Crowd top-sail, top-gallant and royal studding-sails,
Out challenge and defiance—flags and flaunting pennants
    added,
As we take to the open! take to the deepest, freest waters.
1890   1891-2

* NOTE.—*Summer country life.*—*Several years.*—In my rambles and explorations I found a woody place near the creek, where for some reason the birds in happy mood seem'd to resort in unusual numbers. Especially at the beginning of the day, and again at the ending, I was sure to get there the most copious bird-concerts. I repair'd there frequently at sunrise——and also at sunset, or just before. . . . Once the question arose in me: Which is the best singing, the first or the latter-most? The first always exhilarated, and perhaps seem'd more joyous and stronger; but I always felt the sunset or late afternoon sounds more penetrating and sweeter—seem'd to touch the soul—often the evening thrushes, two or three of them, responding and perhaps blending. Though I miss'd some of the mornings, I found myself getting to be quite strictly punctual at the evening utterances.

ANOTHER NOTE.—"He went out with the tide and the sunset," was a phrase I heard from a surgeon describing an old sailor's death under peculiarly gentle conditions.
During the Secession War, 1863 and '4, visiting the Army Hospitals around Washington, I form'd the habit, and continued it to the end, whenever the ebb or flood tide began the latter part of the day, of punctually visiting those at that time populous wards of suffering men. Somehow (or I thought so) the effect of the hour was palpable. The badly wounded would get some ease, and would like to talk a little, or be talk'd to. Intellectual and emotional natures would be at their best: Deaths were always easier; medicines seem'd to have better effect when given then, and a lulling atmosphere would pervade the wards.
Similar influences, similar circumstances and hours, day-close, after great battles, even with all their horrors. I had more than once the same experience on the fields cover'd with fallen or dead.

TO THE PENDING YEAR

HAVE I no weapon-word for thee—some message brief and
    fierce?
(Have I fought out and done indeed the battle?) Is there no
    shot left,
For all thy affectations, lisps, scorns, manifold silliness?
Nor for myself—my own rebellious self in thee?

Down, down, proud gorge!—though choking thee;
Thy bearded throat and high-borne forehead to the gutter;
Crouch low thy neck to eleemosynary gifts.
(1889)   1891-2

SHAKSPERE-BACON'S CIPHER

I DOUBT it not—then more, far more;
In each old song bequeath'd—in every noble page or text,
(Different—something unreck'd before—some unsuspected
    author,)
In every object, mountain, tree, and star—in every birth and
    life,
As part of each—evolv'd from each—meaning, behind the
    ostent,
A mystic cipher waits infolded.
1891   1891-2

LONG, LONG HENCE

AFTER a long, long course, hundreds of years, denials,
Accumulations, rous'd love and joy and thought,
Hopes, wishes, aspirations, ponderings, victories, myriads of
    readers,
Coating, compassing, covering—after ages' and ages' en-
    crustations,
Then only may these songs reach fruition.
1891   1891-2

BRAVO, PARIS EXPOSITION!

ADD to your show, before you close it, France,
With all the rest, visible, concrete, temples, towers, goods,
    machines and ores,
Our sentiment wafted from many million heart-throbs,
    ethereal but solid,

(We grand-sons and great-grand-sons do not forget your
    grand-sires,)
From fifty Nations and nebulous Nations, compacted, sent
    oversea to-day,
America's applause, love, memories and good-will.
1889   1891–2

INTERPOLATION SOUNDS

(*General Philip Sheridan was buried at the Cathedral,
Washington, D.C., August*, 1888, *with all the pomp, music, and
ceremonies of the Roman Catholic service*.)

OVER and through the burial chant,
Organ and solemn service, sermon, bending priests,
To me come interpolation sounds not in the show—plainly
    to me, crowding up the aisle and from the window,
Of sudden battle's hurry and harsh noises—war's grim game
    to sight and ear in earnest;
The scout call'd up and forward—the general mounted and
    his aids around him—the new-brought word—the in-
    stantaneous order issued;
The rifle crack—the cannon thud—the rushing forth of men
    from their tents;   ,
The clank of cavalry—the strange celerity of forming ranks
    —the slender bugle note;
The sound of horses' hoofs departing—saddles, arms, ac-
    coutrements.*
1888   1891–2

---

* NOTE.—CAMDEN. N.J., August 7, 1888.—Walt Whitman asks the
New York Herald "to add his tribute to Sheridan":
"In the grand constellation of five or six names. under Lincoln's
Presidency, that history will bear for ages in her firmament as marking
the last life-throbs of secession, and beaming on its dying gasps,
Sheridan's will be bright. One consideration rising out of the now dead
soldier's example as it passes my mind, is worth taking notice of. If the
war had continued any long time these States, in my opinion, would
have shown and proved the most conclusive military talents ever
evinced by any nation on earth. That they possess'd a rank and file
ahead of all other known in points of quality and limitlessness of num-
ber are easily admitted. But we have, too, the eligibility of organizing,
handling and officering equal to the other. These two, with modern
arms, transportation and inventive American genius, would make the
United States, with earnestness. not only able to stand the whole
world. but conquer that world united against us."

TO THE SUNSET BREEZE

AH, whispering, something again, unseen,
Where late this heated day thou enterest at my window, door,
Thou, laving, tempering all, cool-freshing, gently vitalizing
Me, old, alone, sick, weak-down, melted-worn with sweat;
Thou, nestling, folding close and firm yet soft, companion
    better than talk, book, art,
(Thou hast, O Nature! elements! utterance to my heart be-
    yond the rest—and this is of them,)
So sweet thy primitive taste to breathe within—thy soothing
    fingers on my face and hands,
Thou, messenger-magical strange bringer to body and spirit
    of me,
(Distances balk'd—occult medicines penetrating me from
    head to foot,)
I feel the sky, the prairies vast—I feel the mighty northern
    lakes,
I feel the ocean and the forest—somehow I feel the globe
    itself swift-swimming in space;
Thou blown from lips so loved, now gone—haply from end-
    less store, God-sent,
(For thou art spiritual, Godly, most of all known to my
    sense,)
Minister to speak to me, here and now, what word has never
    told, and cannot tell,
Art thou not universal concrete's distillation? Law's, all
    Astronomy's last refinement?
Hast thou no soul? Can I not know, identify thee?
1890   1891–2

OLD CHANTS

AN ancient song, reciting, ending,
Once gazing toward thee, Mother of All,
Musing, seeking themes fitted for thee,
Accept for me, thou saidst, *the elder ballads*,
And name for me before thou goest each ancient poet.

(Of many debts incalculable,
Haply our New World's chiefest debt is to old poems.)

Ever so far back, preluding thee, America,
Old chants, Egyptian priests, and those of Ethiopia,
The Hindu epics, the Grecian, Chinese, Persian,
The Biblic books and prophets, and deep idyls of the Nazarene,
The Iliad, Odyssey, plots, doings, wanderings of Eneas,
Hesiod, Eschylus, Sophocles, Merlin, Arthur,
The Cid, Roland at Roncesvalles, the Nibelungen,
The troubadours, minstrels, minnesingers, skalds,
Chaucer, Dante, flocks of singing birds,
The Border Minstrelsy, the bye-gone ballads, feudal tales,
    essays, plays,
Shakspere, Schiller, Walter Scott, Tennyson,
As some vast wondrous weird dream-presences,
The great shadowy groups gathering around,
Darting their mighty masterful eyes forward at thee,
Thou! with as now thy bending neck and head, with cour-
    teous hand and word, ascending,
Thou! pausing a moment, drooping thine eyes upon them,
    blent with their music,
Well pleased, accepting all, curiously prepared for by them,
Thou enterest at thy entrance porch.
1891   1891–2

A CHRISTMAS GREETING

(From a Northern Star-Group to a Southern, 1889–90)

WELCOME, Brazilian brother—thy ample place is ready;
A loving hand—a smile from the north—a sunny instant hail!
(Let the future care for itself, where it reveals its troubles,
    impedimentas,
Ours, ours the present throe, the democratic aim, the accept-
    ance and the faith;)
To thee to-day our reaching arm, our turning neck—to thee
    from us the expectant eye,
Thou cluster free! thou brilliant lustrous one! thou, learning
    well,
The true lesson of a nation's light in the sky,
(More shining than the Cross, more than the Crown,)
The height to be superb humanity.
(1889)   1891–2

SOUNDS OF THE WINTER

SOUNDS of the winter too,
Sunshine upon the mountains—many a distant strain
From cheery railroad train—from nearer field, barn, house,
The whispering air—even the mute crops, garner'd apples,
   corn,
Children's and women's tones—rhythm of many a farmer
   and of flail,
An old man's garrulous lips among the rest, *Think not we
   give out yet,*
Forth from these snowy hairs we keep up yet the lilt.
1891   1891-2

A TWILIGHT SONG

As I sit in twilight late alone by the flickering oak-flame,
Musing on long-pass'd war-scenes—of the countless buried
   unknown soldiers,
Of the vacant names, as unindented air's and sea's—the un-
   return'd,
The brief truce after battle, with grim burial-squads, and the
   deep-fill'd trenches
Of gather'd dead from all America, North, South, East,
   West, whence they came up,
From wooded Maine, New-England's farms, from fertile
   Pennsylvania, Illinois, Ohio,
From the measureless West, Virginia, the South, the Caro-
   linas, Texas,
(Even here in my room-shadows and half-lights in the noise-
   less flickering flames,
Again I see the stalwart ranks on-filing, rising—I hear the
   rhythmic tramp of the armies;)
You million unwrit names all, all—you dark bequest from all
   the war,
A special verse for you—a flash of duty long neglected—your
   mystic roll strangely gather'd here,
Each name recall'd by me from out the darkness and death's
   ashes,
Henceforth to be, deep, deep within my heart recording, for
   many a future year,

Your mystic roll entire of unknown names, or North or
    South,
Embalm'd with love in this twilight song.
1890   1891-2

WHEN THE FULL-GROWN POET CAME

WHEN the full-grown poet came,
Out spake pleased Nature (the round impassive globe, with
    all its shows of day and night,) saying, *He is mine;*
But out spake too the Soul of man, proud, jealous and unre-
    conciled, *Nay, he is mine alone;*
—Then the full-grown poet stood between the two, and took
    each by the hand;
And to-day and ever so stands, as blender, uniter, tightly
    holding hands,
Which he will never release until he reconciles the two,
And wholly and joyously blends them.
1891   1891-2

OSCEOLA

   (*When I was nearly grown to manhood in Brooklyn, New
York (middle of* 1838), *I met one of the return'd U.S. Marines
from Fort Moultrie, S. C., and had long talks with him—
learn'd the occurrence below described—death of Osceola. The
latter was a young, brave, leading Seminole, in the Florida war
of that time—was surrender'd to our troops, imprison'd, and
literally died of "a broken heart", at Fort Moultrie. He
sicken'd of his confinement—the doctor and officers made
every allowance and kindness possible for him; then the close.*)

WHEN his hour for death had come,
He slowly rais'd himself from the bed on the floor,
Drew on his war-dress, shirt, leggings, and girdled the belt
    around his waist,
Call'd for vermilion paint (his looking-glass was held before
    him,)
Painted half his face and neck, his wrists, and back-hands,
Put the scalp-knife carefully in his belt—then lying down,
    resting a moment,

Rose again, half sitting, smiled, gave in silence his extended
    hand to each and all,
Sank faintly low to the floor (tightly grasping the tomahawk
    handle,)
Fix'd his look on wife and little children—the last :
(And here a line in memory of his name and death.)
1890   1891–2

A VOICE FROM DEATH

(*The Johnstown, Penn., cataclysm, May* 31, 1889)

A voice from Death, solemn and strange, in all his sweep and
    power,
With sudden, indescribable blow—towns drown'd—human-
    ity by thousands slain,
The vaunted work of thrift, goods, dwellings, forge, street,
    iron bridge,
Dash'd pell-mell by the blow—yet usher'd life continuing on,
(Amid the rest, amid the rushing, whirling, wild debris,
A suffering woman saved—a baby safely born!)
Although I come and unannounc'd, in horror and in pang,
In pouring flood and fire, and wholesale elemental crash,
    (this voice so solemn, strange,)
I too a minister of Deity.

Yea, Death, we bow our faces, veil our eyes to thee,
We mourn the old, the young untimely drawn to thee,
The fair, the strong, the good, the capable,
The household wreck'd, the husband and the wife, the en-
    gulf'd forger in his forge,
The corpses in the whelming waters and the mud,
The gather'd thousands to their funeral mounds, and thou-
    sands never found or gather'd.

Then after burying, mourning the dead,
(Faithful to them found or unfound, forgetting not, bearing
    the past, here new musing,)
A day—a passing moment or an hour—America itself bends
    low,
Silent, resign'd, submissive.

War, death, cataclysm like this, America,
Take deep to thy proud prosperous heart.

E'en as I chant, lo! out of death, and out of ooze and slime,
The blossoms rapidly blooming, sympathy, help, love,
From West and East, from South and North and over sea,
Its hot-spurr'd hearts and hands humanity to human aid
 moves on;
And from within a thought and lesson yet.

Thou ever-darting Globe! through Space and Air!
Thou waters that encompass us!
Thou that in all the life and death of us, in action or in sleep!
Thou laws invisible that permeate them and all,
Thou that in all, and over all, and through and under all,
 incessant!
Thou! thou! the vital, universal, giant force resistless, sleep-
 less, calm,
Holding Humanity as in thy open hand, as some ephemeral
 toy,
How ill to e'er forget thee!

For I too have forgotten,
(Wrapt in these little potencies of progress, politics, culture,
 wealth, inventions, civilization,)
Have lost my recognition of your silent ever-swaying power,
 ye mighty, elemental throes,
In which and upon which we float, and every one of us is
 buoy'd.

1889   1891-2

A PERSIAN LESSON

FOR his o'erarching and last lesson the greybeard sufi,
In the fresh scent of the morning in the open air,
On the slope of a teeming Persian rose-garden,
Under the ancient chestnut-tree wide spreading its branches,
Spoke to the young priests and students.

Finally my children, to envelop each word, each part of the
 rest,
Allah is all, all, all—is immanent in every life and object,

May-be at many and many-a-more removes—yet Allah,
    Allah, Allah is there.

"Has the estray wander'd far? Is the reason-why strangely
    hidden?
Would you sound below the restless ocean of the entire world?
Would you know the dissatisfaction? the urge and spur of
    every life;
The something never still'd—never entirely gone? the invis-
    ible need of every seed?

"It is the central urge in every atom,
(Often unconscious, often evil, downfallen,)
To return to its divine source and origin, however distant,
Latent the same in subject and in object, without one excep-
    tion."

1891   1891–2

THE COMMONPLACE

The commonplace I sing;
How cheap is health! how cheap nobility!
Abstinence, no falsehood, no gluttony, lust;
The open air I sing, freedom, toleration,
(Take here the mainest lesson—less from books—less from
    the schools,)
The common day and night—the common earth and waters,
Your farm—your work, trade, occupation,
The democratic wisdom underneath, like solid ground for all.

1891   1891–2

"THE ROUNDED CATALOGUE DIVINE COMPLETE"

(*Sunday —— — ——. —Went this forenoon to church. A
college professor, Rev. Dr. ——, gave us a fine sermon, during
which I caught the above words; but the minister included in his
"rounded catalogue" letter and spirit, only the esthetic things,
and entirely ignored what I name in the following:*)

The devilish and the dark, the dying and diseas'd,
The countless (nineteen-twentieths) low and evil, crude and
    savage,

The crazed, prisoners in jail, the horrible, rank, malig-
    nant,
Venom and filth, serpents, the ravenous sharks, liars, the
    dissolute;
(What is the part the wicked and the loathsome bear within
    earth's orbic scheme?)
Newts, crawling things in slime and mud, poisons,
The barren soil, the evil men, the slag and hideous rot.
1891   1891–2

MIRAGES

*(Noted verbatim after a supper-talk out doors in Nevada with
two old miners)*

MORE experiences and sights, stranger, than you'd think
    for;
Times again, now mostly just after sunrise or before sun-
    set,
Sometimes in spring, oftener in autumn, perfectly clear
    weather, in plain sight,
Camps far or near, the crowded streets of cities and the shop-
    fronts,
(Account for it or not—credit or not—it is all true,
And my mate there could tell you the like—we have often
    confab'd about it,)
People and scenes, animals, trees, colors and lines, plain as
    could be,
Farms and dooryards of home, paths border'd with box,
    lilacs in corners,
Weddings in churches, thanksgiving dinners, returns of long-
    absent sons,
Glum funerals, the crape-veil'd mother and the daughters,
Trials in courts, jury and judge, the accused in the box,
Contestants, battles, crowds, bridges, wharves,
Now and then mark'd faces of sorrow or joy,
(I could pick them out this moment if I saw them again,)
Show'd to me just aloft to the right in the sky-edge,
Or plainly there to the left on the hill-tops.
1891   1891–2

L. OF G.'S PURPORT

NOT to exclude or demarcate, or pick out evils from their
    formidable masses (even to expose them,)
But add, fuse, complete, extend—and celebrate the immortal
    and the good.

Haughty this song, its words and scope,
To span vast realms of space and time,
Evolution—the cumulative—growths and generations.

Begun in ripen'd youth and steadily pursued,
Wandering, peering, dallying with all—war, peace, day and
    night absorbing,
Never even for one brief hour abandoning my task,
I end it here in sickness, poverty, and old age.

I sing of life, yet mind me well of death:
To-day shadowy Death dogs my steps, my seated shape, and
    has for years—
Draws sometimes close to me, as face to face.
1891   1891–2

THE UNEXPRESS'D

How dare one say it?
After the cycles, poems, singers, plays,
Vaunted Ionia's, India's—Homer, Shakspere—the long, long
    times, thick dotted roads, areas,
The shining clusters and the Milky Ways of stars—Nature's
    pulses reap'd,
All retrospective passions, heroes, war, love, adoration,
All ages' plummets dropt to their utmost depths,
All human lives, throats, wishes, brains—all experiences'
    utterance;
After the countless songs, or long or short, all tongues, all
    lands,
Still something not yet told in poesy's voice or print— some-
    thing lacking,
(Who knows? the best yet unexpress'd and lacking.)
1891   1891–2

GRAND IS THE SEEN

GRAND is the seen, the light, to me—grand are the sky and
stars,
Grand is the earth, and grand are lasting time and space,
And grand their laws, so multiform, puzzling, evolutionary;
But grander far the unseen soul of me, comprehending, en-
dowing all those,
Lighting the light, the sky and stars, delving the earth, sailing
the sea,
(What were all those, indeed, without thee, unseen soul? of
what amount without thee?)
More evolutionary, vast, puzzling, O my soul!
More multiform far—more lasting thou than they.
1891   1891-2

UNSEEN BUDS

UNSEEN buds, infinite, hidden well,
Under the snow and ice, under the darkness, in every square
or cubic inch,
Germinal, exquisite, in delicate lace, microscopic, unborn,
Like babes in wombs, latent, folded, compact, sleeping;
Billions of billions, and trillions of trillions of them waiting,
(On earth and in the sea—the universe—the stars there in the
heavens,)
Urging slowly, surely forward, forming endless,
And waiting ever more, forever more behind.
1891   1891-2

GOOD-BYE MY FANCY!

GOOD-BYE my Fancy!
Farewell dear mate, dear love!
I'm going away, I know not where,
Or to what fortune, or whether I may ever see you again,
So Good-bye my Fancy.

Now for my last—let me look back a moment;
The slower fainter ticking of the clock is in me,
Exit, nightfall, and soon the heart-thud stopping.

Long have we lived, joy'd, caress'd together;
Delightful!—now separation—Good-bye my Fancy.

Yet let me not be too hasty,
Long indeed have we lived, slept, filter'd, become really
    blended into one;
Then if we die we die together, (yes, we'll remain one,)
If we go anywhere we'll go together to meet what happens,
May-be we'll be better off and blither, and learn something,
May-be it is yourself now really ushering me to the true songs,
    (who knows?)
May-be it is you the mortal knob really undoing, turning—
    so now finally,
Good-bye—and hail! my Fancy.
1891   1891–2

Old Age Echoes

(*Posthumous Additions*)

TO SOAR IN FREEDOM AND IN FULLNESS
OF POWER

I HAVE not so much emulated the birds that musically sing,
I have abandon'd myself to flights, broad circles.
The hawk, the seagull, have far more possess'd me than the
      canary or mocking-bird,
I have not felt to warble and trill, however sweetly,
I have felt to soar in freedom and in the fullness of power,
      joy, volition.
1897   1897

THEN SHALL PERCEIVE

IN softness, languor, bloom, and growth,
Thine eyes, ears, all thy sense—thy loftiest attribute—all that
      takes cognizance of beauty,
Shall rouse and fill—then shall perceive!
1897   1897

THE FEW DROPS KNOWN

OF heroes, history, grand events, premises, myths, poems,
The few drops known must stand for oceans of the un-
      known,
On this beautiful and thick peopl'd earth, here and there a
      little specimen put on record,
A little of Greeks and Romans, a few Hebrew canticles, a few
      death odors as from graves, from Egypt—
What are they to the long and copious retrospect of anti-
      quity?
1897   1897

ONE THOUGHT EVER AT THE FORE

ONE thought ever at the fore—
That in the Divine Ship, the World, breasting Time and
    Space,
All Peoples of the globe together sail, sail the same voyage,
    are bound to the same destination.
1897   1897

WHILE BEHIND ALL FIRM AND ERECT

WHILE behind all, firm and erect as ever,
Undismay'd amid the rapids—amid the irresistible and
    deadly urge,
Stands a helmsman, with brow elate and strong hand.
1897   1897

A KISS TO THE BRIDE

Marriage of Nelly Grant, May 21, 1874

SACRED, blithesome, undenied,
With benisons from East and West,
And salutations North and South,
Through me indeed to-day a million hearts and hands,
Wafting a million loves, a million soulfelt prayers;
—Tender and true remain the arm that shields thee!
Fair winds always fill the ship's sails that sail thee!
Clear sun by day, and light stars at night, beam on thee!
Dear girl—through me the ancient privilege too,
For the New World, through me, the old, old wedding greeting,
O youth and health! O sweet Missouri rose! O bonny bride!
Yield thy red cheeks, thy lips, to-day,
Unto a Nation's loving kiss.
1874   1897

NAY, TELL ME NOT TO-DAY THE PUBLISH'D SHAME

Winter of 1873, *Congress in Session*

NAY, tell me not to-day the publish'd shame,
Read not to-day the journal's crowded page,
The merciless reports still branding forehead after forehead,
The guilty column following guilty column.

To-day to me the tale refusing,
Turning from it—from the white capitol turning,
Far from these swelling domes, topt with statues,
More endless, jubilant, vital visions rise
Unpublish'd, unreported.

Through all your quiet ways, or North or South, you Equal
     States, you honest farms,
Your million untold manly healthy lives, or East or West,
     city or country,
Your noiseless mothers, sisters, wives, unconscious of their
     good,
Your mass of homes nor poor nor rich, in visions rise—(even
     your excellent poverties,)
Your self-distilling, never-ceasing virtues, self-denials, graces,
Your endless base of deep integrities within, timid but cer-
     tain,
Your blessings steadily bestow'd, sure as the light, and still,
(Plunging to these as a determin'd diver down the deep
     hidden waters,)
These, these to-day I brood upon—all else refusing, these
     will I con,
To-day to these give audience.
1873   1897

SUPPLEMENT HOURS

Sane, random, negligent hours,
Sane, easy, culminating hours,
After the flush, the Indian summer, of my life,
Away from Books—away from Art—the lesson learn'd,
     pass'd o'er,
Soothing, bathing, merging all—the sane, magnetic,
Now for the day and night themselves—the open air,
Now for the fields, the seasons, insects, trees—the rain and
     snow,
Where wild bees flitting hum,
Or August mulleins grow, or winter's snowflakes fall,
Or stars in the skies roll round—
The silent sun and stars.
1897   1897

OF MANY A SMUTCH'D DEED REMINISCENT

FULL of wickedness, I—of many a smutch'd deed reminis-
cent—of worse deeds capable,
Yet I look composedly upon nature, drink day and night the
joys of life, and await death with perfect equanimity.
Because of my tender and boundless love for him I love and
because of his boundless love for me.

1897   1897

TO BE AT ALL

(*Cf. Stanza* 27, "Song of Myself," *p.* 53)

To be at all—what is better than that?
I think if there were nothing more developed, the clam in its
callous shell in the sand were august enough.
I am not in any callous shell;
I am cased with supple conductors, all over,
They take every object by the hand, and lead it within me;
They are thousands, each one with his entry to himself;
They are always watching with their little eyes, from my head
to my feet;
One no more than a point lets in and out of me such bliss and
magnitude,
I think I could lift the girder of the house away if it lay be-
tween me and whatever I wanted.

1855   1897

DEATH'S VALLEY

To accompany a picture; by request. "The Valley of the
Shadow of Death," from the painting by George Inness

NAY, do not dream, designer dark,
Thou hast portray'd or hit thy theme entire;
I, hoverer of late by this dark valley, by its confines, having
glimpses of it,
Here enter lists with thee, claiming my right to make a sym-
bol too.

For I have seen many wounded soldiers die,
After dread suffering—have seen their lives pass off with
　　smiles;
And I have watch'd the death-hours of the old; and seen the
　　infant die;
The rich with all his nurses and his doctors;
And then the poor, in meagreness and poverty;
And I myself for long, O Death, have breath'd my every
　　breath
Amid the nearness and the silent thought of thee.
And out of these and thee,
I make a scene, a song (not fear of thee,
Nor gloom's ravines, nor bleak, nor dark—for I do not fear
　　thee,
Nor celebrate the struggle, or contortion, or hard-tied knot),
Of the broad blessed light and perfect air, with meadows,
　　rippling tides, and trees and flowers and grass,
And the low hum of living breeze—and in the midst God's
　　beautiful eternal right hand,
Thee, holiest minister of Heaven—thee, envoy, usherer,
　　guide at last of all,
Rich, florid, loosener of the stricture-knot call'd life,
Sweet, peaceful, welcome Death.
1892   1897

ON THE SAME PICTURE

Intended for first stanza of "Death's Valley"

Aye, well I know 'tis ghastly to descend that valley:
Preachers, musicians, poets, painters, always render it,
Philosophs exploit—the battlefield, the ship at sea, the myriad
　　beds, all lands,
All, all the past have enter'd, the ancientest humanity we
　　know,
Syria's, India's, Egypt's, Greece's, Rome's;
Till now for us under our very eyes spreading the same to-
　　day,
Grim, ready, the same to-day, for entrance, yours and mine,
Here, here 'tis limn'd.
1892   1897

A THOUGHT OF COLUMBUS

THE mystery of mysteries, the crude and hurried ceaseless
  flame, spontaneous, bearing on itself.
The bubble and the huge, round, concrete orb!
A breath of Deity, as thence the bulging universe unfolding!
The many issuing cycles from their precedent minute!
The eras of the soul incepting in an hour,
Haply the widest, farthest evolutions of the world and
  man.

Thousands and thousands of miles hence, and now four
  centuries back,
A mortal impulse thrilling its brain cell,
Reck'd or unreck'd, the birth can no longer be postpon'd:
A phantom of the moment, mystic, stalking, sudden,
Only a silent thought, yet toppling down of more than walls
  of brass or stone.
(A flutter at the darkness' edge as if old Time's and Space's
  secret near revealing.)
A thought! a definite thought works out in shape.
Four hundred years roll on.
The rapid cumulus—trade, navigation, war, peace, demo-
  cracy, roll on;
The restless armies and the fleets of time following their
  leader—the old camps of ages pitch'd in newer, larger
  areas,
The tangl'd, long-deferr'd, éclaircissement of human life and
  hopes boldly begins untying,
As here to-day up-grows the Western World.

(An added word yet to my song, far Discoverer, as ne'er
  before sent back to son of earth—
If still thou hearest, hear me,
Voicing as now—lands, races, arts, bravas to thee,
O'er the long backward path to thee—one vast consensus
  north, south, east, west,
Soul plaudits! acclamation! reverent echoes!
One manifold, huge memory to thee! oceans and lands!
The modern world to thee and thought of thee!)
(1891)   1897

Uncollected and Rejected Poems

AMBITION

One day an obscure youth, a wanderer,
Known but to few, lay musing with himself
About the chances of his future life.
In that youth's heart, there dwelt the coal Ambition,
Burning and glowing; and he asked himself,
"Shall I, in time to come, be great and famed?"
Now soon an answer wild and mystical
Seemed to sound forth from out the depths of air;
And to the gazer's eye appeared a shape
Like one as of a cloud—and thus it spoke:

"O, many a panting, noble heart
    Cherishes in its deep recess
The hope to win renown o'er earth
    From Glory's prized caress.

"And some will win that envied goal,
    And have their deeds known far and wide;
And some—by far the most—will sink
    Down in oblivion's tide.

"But *thou*, who visions bright dost cull
    From the imagination's store,
With dreams, such as the youthful dream
    Of grandeur, love, and power,

"Fanciest that thou shalt build a name
    And come to have the nations know
What conscious might dwells in the brain
    That throbs beneath that brow?

"And see thick countless ranks of men
    Fix upon *thee* their reverent gaze—

And listen to the plaudits loud
    To *thee* that thousands raise?

"Weak, childish soul! the very place
    That pride has made for folly's rest;
What thoughts, with vanity all rife,
    Fill up thy heaving breast!

"At night, go view the solemn stars
    Those wheeling worlds through time the same—
How puny seem the widest power,
    The proudest mortal name!

"Think too, that all, lowly and rich,
    Dull idiot mind and teeming sense,
Alike must sleep the endless sleep,
    A hundred seasons hence.

"So, frail one, never more repine,
    Though thou livest on obscure, unknown;
Though after death unsought may be
    Thy markless resting stone."

And as these accents dropped in the youth's ears,
He felt him sick at heart; for many a month
His fancy had amused and charmed itself
With lofty aspirations, visions fair
Of what he *might be.* And it pierced him sore
To have his airy castles thus dashed down.

1842

BLOOD-MONEY

"Guilty of the body and the blood of Christ"

1

OF olden time, when it came to pass
That the beautiful god, Jesus, should finish his work on earth
Then went Judas, and sold the divine youth,
And took pay for his body.

Curs'd was the deed, even before the sweat of the clutching
    hand grew dry;
And darkness frown'd upon the seller of the like of God,
Where, as though earth lifted her breast to throw him from
    her, and heaven refused him,
He hung in the air, self-slaughter'd.

The cycles, with their long shadows, have stalk'd silently
    forward,
Since those ancient days—many a pouch enwrapping mean-
    while
Its fee, like that paid for the son of Mary.

And still goes one, saying,
"What will ye give me, and I will deliver this man unto
    you?"
And they make the covenant, and pay the pieces of silver.

2

Look forth, deliverer,
Look forth, first-born of the dead,
Over the tree-tops of Paradise;
See thyself in yet continued bonds,
Toilsome and poor, thou bear'st man's form again,
Thou art reviled, scourged, put into prison,
Hunted from the arrogant equality of the rest;
With staves and swords throng the willing servants of
    authority,
Again they surround thee, mad with devilish spite;
Toward thee stretch the hands of a multitude, like vultures'
    talons,
The meanest spit in thy face, they smite thee with their
    palms;
Bruised, bloody, and pinion'd is thy body,
More sorrowful than death is thy soul.

Witness of anguish, brother of slaves,
Not with thy price closed the price of thine image:
And still Iscariot plies his trade.
1850

RESURGEMUS

SUDDENLY, out of its stale and drowsy air, the air of slaves,
Like lightning Europe le'pt forth,
Sombre, superb and terrible,
As Ahimoth, brother of Death.
God, 'twas delicious!
That brief, tight, glorious grip
Upon the throats of kings.
You liars paid to defile the People,

Mark you now:
Not for numberless agonies, murders, lusts,
For court thieving in its manifold mean forms,
Worming from his simplicity the poor man's wages;
For many a promise sworn by royal lips
And broken, and laughed at in the breaking;
Then, in their power, not for all these,
Did a blow fall in personal revenge,
Or a hair draggle in blood:
The People scorned the ferocity of kings.

But the sweetness of mercy brewed bitter destruction,
And frightened rulers come back:
Each comes in state, with his train,
Hangman, priest, and tax-gatherer,
Soldier, lawyer, and sycophant;
As appalling procession of locusts,
And the king struts grandly again.

Yet behind all, lo, a Shape
Vague as the night, draped interminably,
Head, front and form, in scarlet folds,
Whose face and eyes none may see,
Out of its robes only this,
The red robes, lifted by the arm,
One finger pointed high over the top,
Like the head of a snake appears.

Meanwhile, corpses lie in new-made graves,
Bloody corpses of young men;
The rope of the gibbet hangs heavily,

The bullets of tyrants are flying,
The creatures of power laugh aloud:
And all these things bear fruits, and they are good.

Those corpses of young men,
Those martyrs that hang from the gibbets,
Those hearts pierced by the grey lead,
Cold and motionless as they seem,
Live elsewhere with undying vitality;
They live in other young men, O, kings,
They live in brothers, again ready to defy you;
They were purified by death,
They were taught and exalted.
Not a grave of those slaughtered ones,
But is growing its seed of freedom,
In its turn to bear seed,
Which the winds shall carry afar and resow,
And the rain nourish.
Not a disembodied spirit
Can the weapon of tyrants let loose,
But it shall stalk invisibly over the earth,
Whispering, counselling, cautioning.

Liberty, let others despair of thee,
But I will never despair of thee:
Is the house shut? Is the master away?
Nevertheless, be ready, be not weary of watching,
He will surely return; his messengers come anon.
1850

GREAT ARE THE MYTHS

1

GREAT are the myths—I too delight in them;
Great are Adam and Eve—I too look back and accept them;
Great the risen and fallen nations, and their poets, women,
    sages, inventors, rulers, warriors, and priests.

Great is Liberty! great is Equality! I am their follower;
Helmsmen of nations, choose your craft! where you sail, I sail,
I weather it out with you, or sink with you.

Great is Youth—equally great is Old Age—great are the Day
   and Night;
Great is Wealth—great is Poverty—great is Expression—
   great is Silence.

Youth, large, lusty, loving—Youth, full of grace, force, fas-
   cination!
Do you know that Old Age may come after you, with equal
   grace, force, fascination?

Day, full-blown and splendid—Day of the immense sun,
   action, ambition, laughter,
The Night follows close, with millions of suns, and sleep, and
   restoring darkness.

Wealth, with the flush hand, fine clothes, hospitality;
But then the Soul's wealth, which is candor, knowledge,
   pride, enfolding love;
(Who goes for men and women showing Poverty richer than
   wealth?)

Expression of speech! in what is written or said, forget not
   that Silence is also expressive,
That anguish as hot as the hottest, and contempt as cold as
   the coldest, may be without words.

2

Great is the Earth, and the way it became what it is;
Do you imagine it has stopt at this? the increase aban-
   don'd?
Understand then that it goes as far onward from this, as this
   is from the times when it lay in covering waters and
   gases, before man had appear'd.

Great is the quality of Truth in man;
The quality of truth in man supports itself through all
   changes,
It is inevitably in the man—he and it are in love, and never
   leave each other.

The truth in man is no dictum, it is vital as eyesight;
If there be any Soul, there is truth—if there be man or woman
    there is truth—if there be physical or moral, there is
    truth;
If there be equilibrium or volition, there is truth—if there be
    things at all upon the earth, there is truth.

O truth of the earth! I am determin'd to press my way to-
    ward you;
Sound your voice! I scale mountains, or dive in the sea after
    you.

3

Great is Language—it is the mightiest of the sciences,
It is the fulness, color, form, diversity of the earth, and of
    men and women, and of all qualities and processes;
It is greater than wealth—it is greater than buildings, ships,
    religions, paintings, music.

Great is the English speech—what speech is so great as the
    English?
Great is the English brood—what brood has so vast a des-
    tiny as the English?
It is the mother of the brood that must rule the earth with the
    new rule;
The new rule shall rule as the Soul rules, and as the love,
    justice, equality in the Soul rule.

Great is Law—great are the few old land-marks of the law,
They are the same in all times, and shall not be disturb'd.

4

Great is Justice!
Justice is not settled by legislators and laws—it is in the Soul;
It cannot be varied by statutes, any more than love, pride,
    the attraction of gravity, can;
It is immutable—it does not depend on majorities—majori-
    ties or what not, come at last before the same passion-
    less and exact tribunal.

For justice are the grand natural lawyers, and perfect judges
—it is in their Souls;
It is well assorted—they have not studied for nothing—the
great includes the less;
They rule on the highest grounds—they oversee all eras,
states, administrations.

The perfect judge fears nothing—he could go front to front
before God;
Before the perfect judge all shall stand back—life and death
shall stand back—heaven and hell shall stand back.

5

Great is Life, real and mystical, wherever and whoever;
Great is Death—sure as life holds all parts together, Death
holds all parts together.

Has Life much purport?—Ah, Death has the greatest pur-
port.
1855

POEM OF REMEMBRANCE FOR A GIRL OR A BOY OF THESE STATES

You just maturing youth! You male or female!
Remember the organic compact of These States,
Remember the pledge of the Old Thirteen thenceforward to
the rights, life, liberty, equality of man,
Remember what was promulged by the founders, ratified by
The States, signed in black and white by the Commis-
sioners, and read by Washington at the head of the
army,
Remember the purposes of the founders,—Remember Wash-
ington;
Remember the copious humanity streaming from every
direction toward America;
Remember the hospitality that belongs to nations and men;
(Cursed be nation, woman, man, without hospitality!)
Remember, government is to subserve individuals,

Not any, not the President, is to have one jot more than you
  or me,
Not any habitan of America is to have one jot less than you
  or me.

Anticipate when the thirty or fifty millions, are to become the
  hundred or two hundred millions, of equal freemen and
  freewomen, amicably joined.

Recall ages—One age is but a part—ages are but a part;
Recall the angers, bickerings, delusions, superstitions, of the
  idea of caste,
Recall the bloody cruelties and crimes.

Anticipate the best women;
I say an unnumbered new race of hardy and well-defined
  women are to spread through all These States,
I say a girl fit for These States must be free, capable, daunt-
  less, just the same as a boy.

Anticipate your own life—retract with merciless power,
Shirk nothing—retract in time—Do you see those errors,
  diseases, weaknesses, lies, thefts?
Do you see that lost character?—Do you see decay, con-
  sumption, rum-drinking, dropsy, fever, mortal cancer or
  inflammation?
Do you see death, and the approach of death?
1856

THINK OF THE SOUL

THINK of the Soul;
I swear to you that body of yours gives proportions to your
  Soul somehow to live in other spheres;
I do not know how, but I know it is so.

Think of loving and being loved;
I swear to you, whoever you are, you can interfuse yourself
  with such things that everybody that sees you shall look
  longingly upon you.

Think of the past;
I warn you that in a little while others will find their past in
    you and your times.

The race is never separated—nor man nor woman escapes;
All is inextricable—things, spirits, Nature, nations, you too
    —from precedents you come.

Recall the ever-welcome defiers, (The mothers precede them;)
Recall the sages, poets, saviors, inventors, lawgivers, of the
    earth;
Recall Christ, brother of rejected persons—brother of slaves,
    felons, idiots, and of insane and diseas'd persons.

Think of the time when you were not yet born;
Think of times you stood at the side of the dying;
Think of the time when your own body will be dying.

Think of spiritual results,
Sure as the earth swims through the heavens, does every one
    of its objects pass into spiritual results.

Think of manhood, and you to be a man;
Do you count manhood, and the sweet of manhood, no-
    thing?

Think of womanhood, and you to be a woman;
The creation is womanhood;
Have I not said that womanhood involves all?
Have I not told how the universe has nothing better than the
    best womanhood?
1856

RESPONDEZ!

RESPONDEZ! Respondez!
(The war is completed—the price is paid—the title is settled
    beyond recall;)
Let every one answer! let those who sleep be waked! let none
    evade!
Must we still go on with our affections and sneaking?

Let me bring this to a close—I pronounce openly for a new
    distribution of roles;

Let that which stood in front go behind! and let that which
    was behind advance to the front and speak;

Let murderers, bigots, fools, unclean persons, offer new pro-
    positions!

Let the old propositions be postponed!

Let faces and theories be turn'd inside out! let meanings be
    freely criminal, as well as results!

Let there be no suggestion above the suggestion of drud-
    gery!

Let none be pointed toward his destination! (Say! do you
    know your destination?)

Let men and women be mock'd with bodies and mock'd with
    Souls!

Let the love that waits in them, wait! let it die, or pass still-
    born to other spheres!

Let the sympathy that waits in every man, wait! or let it also
    pass, a dwarf, to other spheres!

Let contradictions prevail! let one thing contradict another!
    and let one line of my poems contradict another!

Let the people sprawl with yearning, aimless hands! let their
    tongues be broken! let their eyes be discouraged! let
    none descend into their hearts with the fresh luscious-
    ness of love!

(Stifled, O days! O lands! in every public and private cor-
    ruption!

Smother'd in thievery, impotence, shamelessness, mountain-
    high;

Brazen effrontery, scheming, rolling like ocean's waves
    around and upon you, O my days! my lands!

For not even those thunderstorms, nor fiercest lightnings of
    the war, have purified the atmosphere;)

—Let the theory of America still be management, caste, com-
    parison! (Say! what other theory would you?)

Let them that distrust birth and death still lead the rest! (Say!
    why shall they not lead you?)

Let the crust of hell be neared and trod on! let the days be
    darker than the nights! let slumber bring less slumber
    than waking time brings!

Let the world never appear to him or her for whom it was all made!

Let the heart of the young man still exile itself from the heart of the old man! and let the heart of the old man be exiled from that of the young man!

Let the sun and moon go! let scenery take the applause of the audience! let there be apathy under the stars!

Let freedom prove no man's inalienable right! every one who can tyrannize, let him tyrannize to his satisfaction!

Let none but infidels be countenanced!

Let the eminence of meanness, treachery, sarcasm, hate, greed, indecency, impotence, lust, be taken for granted above all! let writers, judges, governments, households, religions, philosophies, take such for granted above all!

Let the worst men beget children out of the worst women!

Let the priest still play at immortality!

Let death be inaugurated!

Let nothing remain but the ashes of teachers, artists, moralists, lawyers, and learn'd and polite persons!

Let him who is without my poems be assassinated!

Let the cow, the horse, the camel, the garden-bee—let the mud-fish, the lobster, the mussel, eel, the sting-ray, and the grunting pig-fish—let these, and the like of these, be put on a perfect equality with man and woman!

Let churches accommodate serpents, vermin, and the corpses of those who have died of the most filthy of diseases!

Let marriage slip down among fools, and be for none but fools!

Let men among themselves talk and think forever obscenely of women! and let women among themselves talk and think obscenely of men!

Let us all, without missing one, be exposed in public, naked, monthly, at the peril of our lives! let our bodies be freely handled and examined by whoever chooses!

Let nothing but copies at second hand be permitted to exist upon the earth!

Let the earth desert God, nor let there ever henceforth be mention'd the name of God!

Let there be no God!

Let there be money, business, imports, exports, custom, authority, precedents, pallor, dyspepsia, smut, ignorance, unbelief!

Let judges and criminals be transposed! let the prison-keepers be put in prison! let those that were prisoners take the keys! (Say! why might they not just as well be transposed?)

Let the slaves be masters! let the masters become slaves!

Let the reformers descend from the stands where they are forever bawling! let an idiot or insane person appear on each of the stands!

Let the Asiatic, the African, the European, the American, and the Australian, go armed against the murderous stealthiness of each other! let them sleep armed! let none believe in good will!

Let there be no unfashionable wisdom! let such be scorn'd and derided off from the earth!

Let a floating cloud in the sky—let a wave of the sea—let growing mint, spinach, onions, tomatoes—let these be exhibited as shows, at a great price for admission!

Let all the men of These States stand aside for a few smouchers! let the few seize on what they choose! let the rest gawk, giggle, starve, obey!

Let shadows be furnish'd with genitals! let substances be deprived of their genitals!

Let there be wealthy and immense cities—but still through any of them, not a single poet, savior, knower, lover!

Let the infidels of These States laugh all faith away!

If one man be found who has faith, let the rest set upon him!

Let them affright faith! let them destroy the power of breeding faith!

Let the she-harlots and the he-harlots be prudent! let them dance on, while seeming lasts! (O seeming! seeming! seeming!)

Let the preachers recite creeds! let them still teach only what they have been taught!

Let insanity still have charge of sanity!

Let books take the place of trees, animals, rivers, clouds!

Let the daub'd portraits of heroes supersede heroes!

Let the manhood of man never take steps after itself!

Let it take steps after eunuchs, and after consumptive and
    genteel persons!
Let the white person again tread the black person under his
    heel! (Say! which is trodden under heel, after all?)
Let the reflections of the things of the world be studied in
    mirrors! let the things themselves still continue un-
    studied!
Let a man seek pleasure everywhere except in himself!
Let a woman seek happiness everywhere except in herself!
(What real happiness have you had one single hour through
    your whole life?)
Let the limited years of life do nothing for the limitless years
    of death! (What do you suppose death will do, then?)
1856

APOSTROPH

O MATER! O fils!
O brood continental!
O flowers of the prairies!
O space boundless! O hum of mighty products!
O you teeming cities! O so invincible, turbulent, proud!
O race of the future! O women!
O fathers! O you men of passion and the storm!
O native power only! O beauty!
O yourself! O God! O divine average!
O you bearded roughs! O bards! O all those slumberers!
O arouse! the dawn-bird's throat sounds shrill! Do you not
    hear the cock crowing?
O, as I walk'd the beach, I heard the mournful notes fore-
    boding a tempest—the low, oft-repeated shriek of the
    diver, the long-lived loon;
O I heard, and yet hear, angry thunder;—O you sailors! O
    ships! make quick preparation!
O from his masterful sweep, the warning cry of the eagle!
(Give way there, all! It is useless! Give up your spoils;)
O sarcasms! Propositions! (O if the whole world should
    prove indeed a sham, a sell!)
O I believe there is nothing real but America and freedom!
O to sternly reject all except Democracy!
O imperator! O who dare confront you and me?

O to promulgate our own! O to build for that which build
for mankind!

O feuillage! O North! O the slope drained by the Mexican
sea!

O all, all inseparable—ages, ages, ages!

O a curse on him that would dissever this Union for any
reason whatever!

O climate, labors! O good and evil! O death!

O you strong with iron and wood! O Personality!

O the village or place which has the greatest man or woman!
even if it be only a few ragged huts;

O the city where women walk in public processions in the
streets, the same as the men;

O a wan and terrible emblem, by me adopted!

O shapes arising! shapes of the future centuries!

O muscle and pluck forever for me!

O workmen and workwomen forever for me!

O farmers and sailors! O drivers of horses forever for me!

O I will make the new bardic list of trades and tools!

O you coarse and wilful! I love you!

O South! O longings for my dear home! O soft and sunny
airs!

O pensive! O I must return where the palm grows and the
mocking bird sings, or else I die!

O equality! O organic compacts! I am come to be your born
poet!

O whirl, contest, sounding and resounding! I am your poet,
because I am part of you;

O days by-gone! Enthusiasts! Antecedents!

O vast preparations for These States! O years!

O what is now being sent forward thousands of years to
come!

O mediums! O to teach! to convey the invisible faith!

To promulge real things! to journey through all The States!

O creation! O to-day! O laws! O unmitigated adoration!

O for mightier broods of orators, artists, and singers!

O for native songs! carpenter's, boatman's, ploughman's
songs! shoemaker's songs!

O haughtiest growth of time! O free and extatic!

O what I, here, preparing, warble for!

O you hastening light! O the sun of the world will ascend,
   dazzling, and take his height—and you too will ascend;
O so amazing and so broad! up there resplendent, darting
   and burning;
O prophetic! O vision staggered with weight of light! with
   pouring glories!
O copious! O hitherto unequalled!
O Libertad! O compact! O union impossible to dissever!
O my Soul! O lips becoming tremulous, powerless!
O centuries, centuries yet ahead!
O voices of greater orators! I pause—I listen for you!
O you States! Cities! defiant of all outside authority! I
   spring at once into your arms! you I most love!
O you grand Presidentiads! I wait for you!
New history! New heroes! I project you!
Visions of poets! only you really last! O sweep on! sweep on!
O Death! O you striding there! O I cannot yet!
O heights! O infinitely too swift and dizzy yet!
O purged lumine! you threaten me more than I can stand!
O present! I return while yet I may to you!
O poets to come, I depend upon you!
1860

O SUN OF REAL PEACE

O sun of real peace! O hastening light!
O free and extatic! O what I here, preparing, warble for!
O the sun of the world will ascend, dazzling, and take his
   height—and you too, O my Ideal will surely ascend!
O so amazing and broad—up there resplendent, darting and
   burning!
O vision prophetic, stagger'd with weight of light! with pour-
   ing glories!
O lips of my soul, already becoming powerless!
O ample and grand Presidentiads! Now the war, the war is
   over!
New history! new heroes! I project you!
Visions of poets! only you really last! sweep on! sweep on!
O heights too swift and dizzy yet!
O purged and luminous! you threaten me more than I can
   stand!

(I must not venture—the ground under my feet menaces me
    —it will not support me:
O future too immense,)—O present, I return, while yet I may,
    to you.
1860

[SO FAR AND SO FAR, AND ON TOWARD
THE END]

So far, and so far, and on toward the end,
Singing what is sung in this book, from the irresistible im-
    pulses of me;
But whether I continue beyond this book, to maturity,
Whether I shall dart forth the true rays, the ones that wait
    unfired,
(Did you think the sun was shining its brightest?
No—it has not yet fully risen;)
Whether I shall complete what is here started,
Whether I shall attain my own height, to justify these, yet
    unfinished,
Whether I shall make THE POEM OF THE NEW WORLD, trans-
    cending all others—depends, rich persons, upon you,
Depends, whoever you are now filling the current Presiden-
    tiad, upon you,
Upon you, Governor, Mayor, Congressman,
And you, contemporary America.
1860

IN THE NEW GARDEN, IN ALL THE PARTS

IN the new garden, in all the parts,
In cities now, modern, I wander,
Though the second or third result, or still further, primitive
    yet,
Days, places, indifferent—though various, the same,
Time, Paradise, the Mannahatta, the prairies, finding me un-
    changed,
Death indifferent—Is it that I lived long since? Was I buried
    very long ago?
For all that, I may now be watching you here, this moment;

For the future, with determined will, I seek—the woman of
 the future,
You, born years, centuries after me, I seek.
1860

[STATES!]

STATES!
Were you looking to be held together by the lawyers?
By an agreement on a paper? Or by arms?

Away!
I arrive, bringing these, beyond all the forces of courts and
 arms,
These! to hold you together as firmly as the earth itself is
 held together.

The old breath of life, ever new,
Here! I pass it by contact to you, America.

O mother! have you done much for me?
Behold, there shall from me be much done for you.

There shall from me be a new friendship—It shall be called
 after my name,
It shall circulate through The States, indifferent of place,
It shall twist and intertwist them through and around each
 other—Compact shall they be, showing new signs,
Affection shall solve every one of the problems of freedom,
Those who love each other shall be invincible,
They shall finally make America completely victorious, in
 my name.

One from Massachusetts shall be a comrade to a Missourian,
One from Maine or Vermont, and a Carolinian and an Ore-
 gonese, shall be friends triune, more precious to each
 other than all the riches of the earth.

To Michigan shall be wafted perfume from Florida,
To the Mannahatta from Cuba or Mexico,
Not the perfume of flowers, but sweeter, and wafted beyond
 death.

No danger shall balk Columbia's lovers,
If need be, a thousand shall sternly immolate themselves for
one,
The Kanuck shall be willing to lay down his life for the Kan-
sian, and the Kansian for the Kanuck, on due need.

It shall be customary in all directions, in the houses and
streets, to see manly affection,
The departing brother or friend shall salute the remaining
brother or friend with a kiss.

There shall be innovations,
There shall be countless linked hands—namely, the North-
easterner's, and the Northwesterner's, and the South-
westerner's, and those of the interior, and all their
brood,
These shall be masters of the world under a new power,
They shall laugh to scorn the attacks of all the remainder of
the world.

The most dauntless and rude shall touch face to face lightly,
The dependence of Liberty shall be lovers,
The continuance of Equality shall be comrades.

These shall tie and band stronger than hoops of iron,
I, extatic, O partners! O lands! henceforth with the love of
lovers tie you.
1860

[LONG I THOUGHT THAT KNOWLEDGE]

LONG I thought that knowledge alone would suffice me—O if
I could but obtain knowledge!
Then my lands engrossed me—Lands of the prairies, Ohio's
land, the southern savannas, engrossed me—For them I
would live—I would be their orator;
Then I met the examples of old and new heroes—I heard of
warriors, sailors, and all dauntless persons—And it
seemed to me that I too had it in me to be as dauntless
as any—and would be so;

And then, to enclose all, it came to me to strike up the songs
of the New World—And then I believed my life must be
spent in singing;

But now take notice, land of the prairies, land of the south
savannas, Ohio's land,

Take notice, you Kanuck woods—and you Lake Huron—
and all that with you roll toward Niagara—and you
Niagara also,

And you, Californian mountains—That you each and all find
somebody else to be your singer of songs,

For I can be your singer of songs no longer—One who loves
me is jealous of me, and withdraws me from all but love,

With the rest I dispense—I sever from what I thought would
suffice me, for it does not—it is now empty and tasteless
to me,

I heed knowledge, and the grandeur of The States, and the
example of heroes, no more,

I am indifferent to my own songs—I will go with him I love,

It is to be enough for us that we are together—We never
separate again.

1860

[HOURS CONTINUING LONG, SORE AND HEAVY-HEARTED]

HOURS continuing long, sore and heavy-hearted,

Hours of the dusk, when I withdraw to a lonesome and un-
frequented spot, seating myself, leaning my face in my
hands;

Hours sleepless, deep in the night, when I go forth, speeding
swiftly the country roads, or through the city streets, or
pacing miles and miles, stifling plaintive cries;

Hours discouraged, distracted—for the one I cannot content
myself without, soon I saw him content himself without
me;

Hours when I am forgotten, (O weeks and months are pass-
ing, but I believe I am never to forget!)

Sullen and suffering hours! (I am ashamed—but it is useless
—I am what I am;)

Hours of my torment—I wonder if other men ever have the
like, out of the like feelings?

Is there even one other like me—distracted—his friend, his
    lover, lost to him?
Is he too as I am now? Does he still rise in the morning, de-
    jected, thinking who is lost to him? and at night, awak-
    ing, think who is lost?
Does he too harbor his friendship silent and endless? harbor
    his anguish and passion?
Does some stray reminder, or the casual mention of a name,
    bring the fit back upon him, taciturn and deprest?
Does he see himself reflected in me? In these hours, does he
    see the face of his hours reflected?
1860

[WHO IS NOW READING THIS?]

Who is now reading this?

May-be one is now reading this who knows some wrong-
    doing of my past life,
Or may-be a stranger is reading this who has secretly loved me,
Or may-be one who meets all my grand assumptions and
    egotisms with derision,
Or may-be one who is puzzled at me.

As if I were not puzzled at myself!
Or as if I never deride myself! (O conscience-struck! O self-
    convicted!)
Or as if I do not secretly love strangers! (O tenderly, a long
    time, and never avow it;)
Or as if I did not see, perfectly well, interior in myself, the
    stuff of wrong-doing,
Or as if it could cease transpiring from me until it must cease.
1860

TO YOU

Let us twain walk aside from the rest;
Now we are together privately, do you discard ceremony,
Come! vouchsafe to me what has yet been vouchsafed to
    none—Tell me the whole story,
Tell me what you would not tell your brother, wife, husband,
    or physician.
1860

[OF THE VISAGES OF THINGS]

OF the visages of things—And of piercing through to the accepted hells beneath;

Of ugliness—To me there is just as much in it as there is in beauty—And now the ugliness of human beings is acceptable to me;

Of detected persons—To me, detected persons are not, in any respect, worse than undetected persons—and are not in any respect worse than I am myself;

Of criminals—To me, any judge, or any juror, is equally criminal—and any reputable person is also—and the President is also.

1860

SAYS

1

I SAY whatever tastes sweet to the most perfect person, that is finally right.

2

I SAY nourish a great intellect, a great brain;
If I have said anything to the contrary, I hereby retract it.

3

I SAY man shall not hold property in man;
I say the least developed person on earth is just as important and sacred to himself or herself, as the most developed person is to himself or herself.

4

I SAY where liberty draws not the blood out of slavery, there slavery draws the blood out of liberty,
I say the word of the good old cause in These States, and resound it hence over the world.

5

I SAY the human shape or face is so great, it must never be made ridiculous;
I say for ornaments nothing outre can be allowed,

And that anything is most beautiful without ornament,
And that exaggerations will be sternly revenged in your own
    physiology, and in other persons' physiology also;
And I say that clean-shaped children can be jetted and con-
    ceived only where natural forms prevail in public, and
    the human face and form are never caricatured;
And I say that genius need never more be turned to romances,
(For facts properly told, how mean appear all romances.)

6

I say the word of lands fearing nothing—I will have no other
    land;
I say discuss all and expose all—I am for every topic openly;
I say there can be no salvation for These States without inno-
    vators—without free tongues, and ears willing to hear
    the tongues;
And I announce as a glory of These States, that they respect-
    fully listen to propositions, reforms, fresh views and
    doctrines, from successions of men and women,
Each age with its own growth.

7

I have said many times that materials and the Soul are great,
    and that all depends on physique;
Now I reverse what I said, and affirm that all depends on the
    æsthetic or intellectual,
And that criticism is great—and that refinement is greatest of
    all;
And I affirm now that the mind governs—and that all de-
    pends on the mind.

8

With one man or woman—(no matter which one—I even
    pick out the lowest,)
With him or her I now illustrate the whole law;
I say that every right, in politics or what-not, shall be elig-
    ible to that one man or woman, on the same terms as
    any.

1860

DEBRIS

HE is wisest who has the most caution,
He only wins who goes far enough.

ANY thing is as good as established, when that is established
   that will produce and continue it.

WHAT General has a good army in himself, has a good army;
He happy in himself, or she happy in herself, is happy,
But I tell you you cannot be happy by others, any more than
   you can beget or conceive a child by others.

ONE sweeps by, attended by an immense train,
All emblematic of peace—not a soldier or menial among
   them.

ONE sweeps by, old, with black eyes, and profuse white hair,
He has the simple magnificence of health and strength,
His face strikes as with flashes of lightning whoever it turns
   toward.

THREE old men slowly pass, followed by three others, and
   they by three others,
They are beautiful—the one in the middle of each group
   holds his companions by the hand,
As they walk, they give out perfume wherever they walk.

WHAT weeping face is that looking from the window?
Why does it stream those sorrowful tears?
Is it for some burial place, vast and dry?
Is it to wet the soil of graves?

I WILL take an egg out of the robin's nest in the orchard,
I will take a branch of gooseberries from the old bush in the
   garden, and go and preach to the world;
You shall see I will not meet a single heretic or scorner,
You shall see how I stump clergymen, and confound them,
You shall see me showing a scarlet tomato, and a white
   pebble from the beach.

BEHAVIOR—fresh, native, copious, each one for himself or
   herself,
Nature and the Soul expressed—America and freedom ex-
   pressed—in it the finest art,
In it pride, cleanliness, sympathy, to have their chance,
In it physique, intellect, faith—in it just as much as to man-
   age an army or a city, or to write a book—perhaps more,
The youth, the laboring person, the poor person, rivalling all
   the rest—perhaps outdoing the rest,
The effects of the universe no greater than its;
For there is nothing in the whole universe that can be more
   effective than a man's or a woman's daily behavior can
   be,
In any position, in any one of These States.

I THOUGHT I was not alone, walking here by the shore,
But the one I thought was with me, as now I walk by the
   shore,
As I lean and look through the glimmering light—that one
   has utterly disappeared,
And those appear that perplex me.
1860

THOUGHT

OF what I write from myself—As if that were not the resumé;
Of Histories—As if such, however complete, were not less
   complete than the preceding poems;
As if those shreds, the records of nations, could possibly be
   as lasting as the preceding poems;
As if here were not the amount of all nations, and of all the
   lives of heroes.
1860

SOLID, IRONICAL, ROLLING ORB

SOLID, ironical, rolling orb!
Master of all, and matter of fact!—at last I accept your
   terms;
Bringing to practical, vulgar tests, of all my ideal dreams,
And of me, as lover and hero.
1865

BATHED IN WAR'S PERFUME

BATHED in war's perfume—delicate flag!
(Should the days needing armies, needing fleets, come again,)
O to hear you call the sailors and the soldiers! flag like a
    beautiful woman!
O to hear the tramp, tramp, of a million answering men! O
    the ships they arm with joy!
O to see you leap and beckon from the tall masts of ships!
O to see you peering down on the sailors on the decks!
Flag like the eyes of women.
1865

NOT MY ENEMIES EVER INVADE ME

NOT my enemies ever invade me—no harm to my pride from
    them I fear;
But the lovers I recklessly love—lo! how they master me!
Lo! me, ever open and helpless, bereft of my strength!
Utterly abject, grovelling on the ground before them.
1865–6

THIS DAY, O SOUL

THIS day, O Soul, I give you a wondrous mirror;
Long in the dark, in tarnish and cloud it lay—But the cloud
    has pass'd, and the tarnish gone;
. . . Behold, O Soul! it is now a clean and bright mirror,
Faithfully showing you all the things of the world.
1865–6

LESSONS

THERE are who teach only the sweet lessons of peace and safety;
But I teach lessons of war and death to those I love,
That they readily meet invasions, when they come.
1871

ONE SONG, AMERICA, BEFORE I GO

ONE song, America, before I go,
I'd sing, o'er all the rest, with trumpet sound,
For thee—the Future.

I'd sow a seed for thee of endless Nationality;
I'd fashion thy Ensemble, including Body, and Soul;
I'd show, away ahead, the real Union, and how it may be
    accomplish'd.

(The paths to the House I seek to make,
But leave to those to come, the House itself.)

Belief I sing—and Preparation;
As Life and Nature are not great with reference to the Pre-
    sent only,
But greater still from what is to come,
Out of that formula for Thee I sing.
1872

AFTER AN INTERVAL

(*Nov.* 22, 1875, *midnight—Saturn and Mars in conjunction*)

AFTER an interval, reading, here in the midnight,
With the great stars looking on—all the stars of Orion looking,
And the silent Pleiades—and the duo looking of Saturn and
    ruddy Mars;
Pondering, reading my own songs, after a long interval,
    (sorrow and death familiar now,)
Ere closing the book, what pride! what joy! to find them,
Standing so well the test of death and night!
And the duo of Saturn and Mars!
1875

THE BEAUTY OF THE SHIP

WHEN, staunchly entering port,
After long ventures, hauling up, worn and old,
Battered by sea and wind, torn by many a fight,
With the original sails all gone, replaced, or mended,
I only saw, at last, the beauty of the Ship.
1876

TWO RIVULETS

Two Rivulets side by side,
Two blended, parallel, strolling tides,
Companions, travelers, gossiping as they journey.

For the Eternal Ocean bound,
These ripples, passing surges, streams of Death and Life,
Object and Subject hurrying, whirling by,
The Real and Ideal,

Alternate ebb and flow the Days and Nights,
(Strands of a Trio twining, Present, Future, Past.)

In You, whoe'er you are, my book perusing,
In I myself—in all the World—these ripples flow,
All, all, toward the mystic Ocean tending.

(O yearnful waves! the kisses of your lips!
Your breast so broad, with open arms, O firm, expanded
    shore!)
1876

OR FROM THAT SEA OF TIME

1

Or, from that Sea of Time,
Spray, blown by the wind—a double winrow-drift of weeds
    and shells;
(O little shells, so curious-convolute! so limpid-cold and
    voiceless!
Yet will you not, to the tympans of temples held,
Murmurs and echoes still bring up—Eternity's music, faint
    and far,
Wafted inland, sent from Atlantica's rim—strains for the
    Soul of the Prairies,
Whisper'd reverberations—chords for the ear of the West,
    joyously sounding
Your tidings old, yet ever new and untranslatable;)
Infinitesimals out of my life, and many a life,
(For not my life and years alone I give—all, all I give;)
These thoughts and Songs—waifs from the deep—here, cast
    high and dry,
Wash'd on America's shores.

2

Currents of starting a Continent new,
Overtures sent to the solid out of the liquid,

Fusion of ocean and land—tender and pensive waves,
(Not safe and peaceful only—waves rous'd and ominous too.

Out of the depths, the storm's abysms—who knows whence?
    Death's waves,
Raging over the vast, with many a broken spar and tatter'd
    sail.)
1876

FROM MY LAST YEARS

FROM my last years, last thoughts I here bequeath,
Scatter'd and dropt, in seeds, and wafted to the West,
Through moisture of Ohio, prairie soil of Illinois—through
    Colorado, California air,
For Time to germinate fully.
1876

IN FORMER SONGS

IN former songs Pride have I sung, and Love, and passionate,
    joyful Life,
But here I twine the strands of Patriotism and Death.

And now, Life, Pride, Love, Patriotism and Death,
To you, O FREEDOM, purport of all!
(You that elude me most—refusing to be caught in songs of
    mine,)
I offer all to you.

2

'Tis not for nothing, Death,
I sound out you, and words of you, with daring tone—em-
    bodying you,
In my new Democratic chants—keeping you for a close,
For last impregnable retreat—a citadel and tower,
For my last stand—my pealing, final cry.
1876

Notes

ABBREVIATIONS

The following abbreviations have been used:

Barrus for *Whitman and Burroughs Comrades*, 1931, Clara Barrus.

Bucke for *Walt Whitman*, 1883, Richard Maurice Bucke, M.D.

Comp. Prose for *Complete Prose*, 1907, Walt Whitman.

Donaldson for *Walt Whitman the Man*, 1896, Thomas Donaldson.

Furness for *Walt Whitman's Workshop*, 1928, Clifton Joseph Furness.

Glicksberg for *Walt Whitman and the Civil War*, 1933, Charles I. Glicksberg.

Harned for *The Letters of Anne Gilchrist and Walt Whitman*, 1918, ed. Thomas B. Harned.

Holloway for *Whitman*; *An Interpretation in Narrative*, 1926, Emory Holloway.

In Re for *In Re Walt Whitman*, 1893, eds. Horace L. Traubel, Richard Maurice Bucke, Thomas B. Harned.

Kennedy for *Reminiscences of Walt Whitman*, 1896, William Sloane Kennedy.

N. and F. for *Notes and Fragments Left by Walt Whitman*, 1899, ed. by Dr. Richard Maurice Bucke.

Perry for *Walt Whitman*, 1906, Bliss Perry.

Saunders for *Whitman Music List*, 1926, compiled and privately published by Henry S. Saunders.

S.D.C. for *Specimen Days—Collect*, 1907, Walt Whitman.

Traubel for *With Walt Whitman in Camden*, 1915, Horace Traubel.

U.P.P. for *Uncollected Poetry and Prose of Walt Whitman*, 1914, ed. Emory Holloway.

Notes

"*Come, Said My Soul*" (motto). Various drafts of this poem, first published in "A Christmas Garland", Christmas *Graphic*, 1874, are to be found in *The Conservator*, June 1896, the Putnam edition of Whitman's *Complete Writings*, 1902, X, p. 131 ff., and in U.P.P., II, p. 56.

"*One's Self I Sing*" (p. 3). Cf. "Small the Theme of my Chant" (p. 469).

"*Eidólons*" (p. 6). For an explanation of Whitman's use of this word see Kennedy, pp. 140-141, and Carleton Noyes, *An Approach to Walt Whitman*, p. 166. Frank Harris quotes Whitman as saying that the poem was "returned by Scribner's with a 'very insulting and contemptuous letter'". (*Contemporary Portraits*, Third Series, p. 221.)

"*To the States*" (p. 10). Title in the 1860 Edition, "Walt Whitman's Caution".

"*To a Certain Cantatrice*" (p. 10). Addressed to Marietta Alboni, according to Isaac Hull Platt. (*Walt Whitman*, p. 15.)

"*Starting from Paumanok*" (p. 14). Whitman was fond of the old Indian name for Long Island and sometimes used it as a *nom de plume*, e.g. U.P.P., I, p. 247. In "Brooklyniana" he gives the meaning as "The island with its breast long drawn out, and laid against the sea". (U.P.P., II, p. 274.)

p. 18, ll. 9-10: "*It may be*", etc. Cf. "Ambition" (p. 502).

"*Song of Myself*" (p. 26). First printed with a title, "A Poem of Walt Whitman, An American", in 1860.

p. 29, l. 8: "*show me to a cent*" substituted for "show to me a cent" in 1888 edition. (See Traubel, II, p. 324.)

p. 30, ll. 9-12: These lines were on the list of passages Osgood asked to be expurgated if he should continue the publication of *Leaves of Grass* in 1880. (Bucke, p. 149.)

p. 31, l. 11: "*Tuckahoe*"—a native of Virginia, the inhabitants of the poor lands of which state were supposed to live on tuckahoe, an underground fungus-sclerotium (*Standard Dictionary*). "*Cuff*" —short for Cuffy, a local nickname for a negro.

p. 33, ll. 14 ff.: "*the heavy omnibus*", etc. Cf. pp. 563 ff.

p. 36, l. 15: "*shuffle and break-down*", a form of negro dance.

p. 39, l. 7: "*The jour printer with gray head*", etc. A line probably suggested by William Hartshorne, the old printer who taught Whitman to set type. (U.P.P., I, p. 234 n.: II, pp. 245-249, 294.)

p. 41, l. 4: "*the fourth of Seventh-month*", a form of expression appearing in Whitman's early editions which reflects the Quaker influences of his childhood.

p. 49, ll. 14-23: "*And of the threads*", etc. These lines were also on the Osgood list of expurgations demanded.

p. 50, ll. 9-18: "*You my rich blood . . . it shall be you*". These lines were also on the Osgood list. (Bucke, p. 149.)

p. 53, l. 18: "*To be in any form*", etc. Cf. "To Be At All" (p. 499).

p. 54, ll. 1-23: "*Is this then a touch? . . . too much for me*". This passage was also on the Osgood list of recommended expurgations. The original manuscript of this passage is to be seen in U.P.P., II, pp. 72-73.

p. 55, ll. 20 ff.: "*I believe a leaf of grass*", etc. The original manuscript version of this passage is to be found in U.P.P., I, p. 70.

p. 57, ll. 23 ff.: "*My ties and ballasts leave me*", etc. Cf. U.P.P., II, p. 66. "*I am afoot with my vision*". Cf. *The Sleepers* (p. 383) and Holloway, pp. 123 ff.

p. 59, l. 6: "*Swims with her calf*". Originally "her calves", but altered when Whitman discovered that the whale usually has but one calf. See J. Johnston and J. W. Wallace, *Visits to Walt Whitman in* 1890-1891, p. 46.

p. 62, ll. 15-16: "*I turn the bridegroom out of bed*", etc. These lines were on the Osgood list of expurgations demanded.

p. 62, ll. 19 ff.: "*I understand the large hearts of heroes*", etc. According to Dr. R. M. Bucke this passage describes an actual shipwreck. ("Notes on the Text of Leaves of Grass", *Conservator*, VIII, p. 40.)

p. 64, ll. 20 ff.: "*Now I tell what I knew in Texas*", etc. Though Whitman may have been in Texas on some unidentified journey, this anecdote came from his reading rather than his personal experience. As editor of the Brooklyn *Eagle*, he had published, on March 11, 1846, an excerpt entitled "Fanning's Men, or The Massacre at Goliad", which he had found in *Blackwood's*. The original article was based in part on *A Campaign in Texas*, by Von H. Ehrenberg, Leipzig, 1845.

p. 66, ll. 1 ff.: "*Would you hear of an old-time sea-fight?*" etc. According to Dr. Bucke this passage describes the engagement between the *Bon Homme Richard*, John Paul Jones, commander, and the *Serapis*, Richard Pearson, commander, in the North Sea, September 23, 1779. (*Conservator*, VII, p. 88.)

p. 69, l. 12: "*Eleves*". For Whitman's attitude toward the incorporation of foreign words into English speech, see his article "America's Mightiest Inheritance", *New York Dissected*, pp. 55-65.

p. 70, ll. 21-22: "*On women*", etc. Cf. "*To the Garden the World*" (p. 86). These lines were included in the Osgood list.

p. 70, ll. 23 ff.: "*To any one dying*", etc. The original manuscript version of this passage is to be seen in U.P.P., II, p. 69.

p. 74, ll. 16 ff.: "*I do not despise you priests*", etc. For a very early employment of the device used in this passage see *Sun-Down Papers—No.* 8, p. 542. Albert Mordell (*Erotic Motive in Literature*, p. 240) thinks this passage may have been suggested by George Sand's *Consuelo*, a book of which Whitman was very fond. A fictional use of the method is made by Jack London in *The Star Rover*.

p. 79, ll. 10 ff.: "*I have no chair*", etc. For the original prose version of this passage see U.P.P., II, p. 66.

"*Children of Adam*" (pp. 86-105). For Whitman's statements concerning his purpose in writing this group of poems see "A Memorandum at a Venture" (p. 804) and "Boston Common— More of Emerson" (p. 797). Whitman said to Traubel in March, 1888: " 'Children of Adam' stumps the worst and the best: I have even tried hard to see if it might not as I grow older or experience new moods stump me: I have even almost deliberately tried to retreat. But it would not do. When I tried to take these pieces out of the scheme the whole scheme came down about my ears." (Traubel, I, p. 3.) Cf. Letter XXXVIII (p. 948).

"*From Pent-up Aching Rivers*" (p. 86):

p. 86, ll. 15-16: "*From my own voice*", etc. and
p. 87, l. 12; p. 88, l. 19: "*The female form approaching*", etc. These lines were on the Osgood list.

"*I Sing the Body Electric*" (p. 88).

p. 91, l. 15–p. 92, l. 3: "*Mad filaments*", etc. These lines were on the Osgood list.

p. 93, l. 13: During his visit to New Orleans in 1848 Whitman had an opportunity to observe the slave auctions in the basement of the old St. Louis Hotel. Advertisements of these auctions were carried in the daily *Crescent*, on which he worked.

p. 95, l. 17–p. 96, l. 10: "*Hips, lip-sockets . . . meat of the body.*" Osgood included these lines in his list.

"*A Woman Waits for Me*" (p. 96). The entire poem was on the Osgood list.

"*Spontaneous Me*" (p. 98, l. 17–p. 100, l. 10). "This poem . . . where it may". This passage was on the Osgood list.

"*Out of the Rolling Ocean the Crowd*" (p. 101). All that is known of the romantic attachment celebrated in this poem is given in U.P.P., I, lviii, n. 15. This poem has been set to music by Weda Cook Addicks, but the song has not been published.

"*Once I Pass'd through a Populous City*" (p. 104). This poem, often cited in support of the theory that Whitman had a love-affair in New Orleans, is shown in the original manuscript (U.P.P., II, p. 102) to have been addressed to a man. Mr. H. B. Binns mentions Whitman's "express desire that the poem be regarded merely in its universal application" (*A Life of Walt Whitman*, p. 51); since it was not published until 1860, it is possible to argue that, in his desire to celebrate the permanence of human affection as contrasted with other experiences, Whitman chose from his own memories, first, his memory of a "Calamus" relationship, and substituted later a reminiscence of some "Children of Adam" experience, both being equally suitable as illustrations, but the latter more likely to prove poetically effective. As bearing upon this interpretation, compare "Fast-Anchor'd Eternal O Love", published in the same edition as this poem (1860); it contained, until they were dropped from the 1881 edition, two lines whose phraseology is so similar to that of "Once I Pass'd through a Populous City" as to suggest the possibility of a common origin in Whitman's experience:

> "Singing what, to the Soul, entirely redeemed her, the faithful
> one, the prostitute, who detained me when I went to the city;
> Singing the song of prostitutes."

"*I Heard You Solemn-Sweet Pipes of the Organ*" (p. 104). I am indebted to Mr. Ralph Adimari for information concerning the first publication of this poem. Apparently it does not refer, as did "Out of the Rolling Ocean the Crowd", to Whitman's Washington inamorata, for it was first published in the New York *Leader*, October 12, 1861, as follows:

LITTLE BELLS LAST NIGHT

War-suggesting trumpets, I heard you;
And you I heard beating, you chorus of small and large drums;
You round-lipp'd cannons!—you I heard, thunder-cracking, saluting the frigate from France;
I heard you, solemn-sweet pipes of the organ, as last Sunday morn I pass'd the church;
Winds of Autumn!—as I walk'd the woods at dusk, I heard your long-stretch'd sighs, up above, so mournful;
I heard the perfect Italian tenor, singing at the opera; I heard the soprano in the midst of the quartet singing;
Lady! you, too, I heard, as with white arms in your parlor, you play'd for me delicious music on the harp;
Heart of my love!—you, too, I heard, murmuring low, through one of the wrists around my head—
Heard the pulse of you, when all was still, ringing little bells last night under my ear.

"*Calamus*" (pp. 106-125). Cf. Letter LI (p. 964), Letter CLVII (p. 1052), and Letter CLXI, n. (p. 1054). This group of poems has long been the subject of conflicting interpretation, which Whitman's own comments have not always helped to clarify. Some writers see in them plain evidence that Whitman was simply a Uranian. (See Eduard Bertz, *Walt Whitman Ein Charakterbild* and other writings; W. W. Rivers, *Walt Whitman's Anomaly*; Ludwig Lewisohn, *Expression in America*; and Edgar Lee Masters, *Whitman*.) Others, like George Rice Carpenter (*Walt Whitman*), and Leon Bazalgette (*Walt Whitman*) interpret these poems of comradeship purely in their spiritual sense. No evidence has ever been made public which would convict Whitman of homosexual practices, and to classify him psychologically as a simple Uranian raises difficulties in the interpretation of the "Children of Adam" poems, their counterpart, which are as outspoken on the subject of the attraction between man and woman. Havelock Ellis indicates his view, always worthy of respect, by including Whitman in his *Intermediate Sex*. Jean Catel (*Walt Whitman, La Naissance du Poète*) seeks to reconcile the two expressions given to the affectionate nature of Whitman by a theory of autoeroticism, a kind of narcissism which employed others, of either sex, as mirrors in whom he could admire himself. The poems which follow certainly contain some esoteric elements, but this is not the place to analyse them. Suffice it to say that it is difficult to believe that any very simple explanation can fit all the facts.

"*In Paths Untrodden*" (p. 106). A part of an early manuscript of this poem is to be found in the Camden Edition of Whitman's *Complete Writings*, III, p. 137.

"*These I Singing in Spring*" (p. 111, l. 11): "*a live-oak*". Cf. "I Saw in Louisiana a Live-Oak Growing" (p. 118).

"*I Saw in Louisiana a Live-Oak Growing*" (p. 118). An early draft of this poem is published in *Complete Writings*, III, p. 140.

"*Here the Frailest Leaves of Me*" (p. 121). This poem was set to music as a song (unpublished) by Nicolas Dority. (Henry S. Saunders in his privately published *Whitman Music List*, 1926. To this I am indebted for most of the notes on Whitman music.)

"*Sometimes with One I Love*" (p. 124). Set to music in an unpublished song by Nicolas Dority.

"*That Shadow My Likeness*" (p. 125). An early manuscript version of this poem is to be found in U.P.P., II, p. 91.

"*Salut au Monde!*" (p. 126). Cf. "Excelsior" (p. 430), also "Sun-Down Papers—No. 8" (p. 542), and *Pictures, An Unpublished Poem of Walt Whitman*, New York and London, 1927. For a description of this poem as presented in a musical festival at the Neighborhood Playhouse in New York in April, 1922, with pantomime and choral music by Charles T. Griffes and Edmund Rickett, see New York *Sun*, April 24, 1922. There was a revival of this festival in 1936 under the direction of Blanche Yurka, as a Federal Theater Project.

p. 130, l. 12: "*the full limb'd Bacchus*". Moncure Conway reports seeing a picture of Bacchus in Whitman's room when he visited him in Brooklyn. (*Fortnightly Review*, October 1866.)

"*Song of the Open Road*" (p. 136). William Sloane Kennedy is probably right in suggesting (*Conservator*, February 1907) that a hint for this poem may have been found by Whitman in George Sand's *Consuelo*, Chapter III: "What is more beautiful than a road? It is the symbol and the image of an active and varied life," etc. Whitman's unbounded enthusiasm for George Sand, and for this novel in particular, is well known. John Burroughs suggested that the idea of the poem might have come from Thoreau's essay on "Walking". (*Life and Letters of John Burroughs*, vol. II, p. 102.)

p. 140, ll. 21 ff.: "*Why are there trees*", etc. Cf. "I Saw in Louisiana a Live-Oak Growing" (p. 118).

p. 144, ll. 11-14: "*To see no possession*", etc. Cf. Emerson's 'Monadnoc".

p. 146, ll. 13-16: "*Let the paper remain on the desk*", etc. Cf. "Beat! Beat! Drums!" (p. 259).

"*Crossing Brooklyn Ferry*" (p. 147). Cf. "To Think of Time" (p. 392).

p. 148, ll. 11 ff.: "*I too many and many a time*". For a contemporary description of one of the many experiences out of which this poem confessedly grew see "Letters from Paumanok—No. 3", U.P.P., I, pp. 255-256.

p. 150, ll. 11-26: "*I am he who knew*", etc. Cf. "Of Many a Smutch'd Deed Reminiscent" (p. 499).

"*Song of the Answerer*" (p. 153). Cf. Emerson's essay, "The Poet".

p. 156, l. 13: "*The singers do not beget*", etc. Cf. "To the Garden the World" (p. 86).

"*Our Old Feuillage*" (p. 158). This poem, though substituting thumbnail descriptions of "catalogues", is a sort of "Salut au Monde" limited to the national horizon.

"*A Song of Joys*" (p. 163). Edward Hungerford seeks to trace each of the joys celebrated in this poem to a phrenological attribute. ("Walt Whitman and His Chart of Bumps", *American Literature*, January 1931.)

p. 166, ll. 16 ff.: "*O the whaleman's joys*", etc. This passage may well have been suggested by *Moby Dick* (1851).

"*Song of the Exposition*" (p. 181). Cf. "After All, Not to Create Only". The poem was read at the opening of the annual exhibition of the American Institute in New York, September 7, 1881. It was widely published at the time in the New York and Boston newspapers. (Camden Edition of Whitman's *Complete Writings*, X, p. 180.) The manuscript of this poem is said to have been sold in London in 1921 for $1500 (New York *Times*, February 6, 1921). For a discussion of Whitman's methods of turning the occasion to account see "Whitman as His Own Press Agent" (Emory Holloway), *American Mercury*, December 1929.

The poem was published in a second edition by Roberts Bros., Boston, in 1871, which contained a description of the occasion, probably written by Whitman himself for the *Washington Chronicle*. (See Kennedy, *The Fight of a Book for the World*, p. 196.)

"Song of the Redwood-Tree" (p. 191). Published in *Harper's Magazine*, February 1874; price paid, $100 (Kennedy, p. 16).

"Song of the Universal" (p. 209). First published in the *New Republic*, Camden, New Jersey, June 20, 1874. Read as a commencement poem at Tuft's College, June 17, 1874. (See *Two Rivulets*, "Centennial Songs", p. 15.)

"Pioneers! O Pioneers!" (p. 211). The title of this poem was borrowed by Willa Cather for one of her novels.

"France" (p. 217). Cf. "To a Foil'd European Revolutionaire" (p. 338), "O Star of France" (p. 360), "Spain, 1873-74" (p. 433), and "Resurgemus" (p. 505).

"Year of Meteors" (p. 220).

p. 220, ll. 20 ff.: *"I would sing how an old man"*, etc. The reference is to John Brown, executed in 1859 for inciting slaves to rebellion.

p. 221, l. 6: *"young prince of England"*, the Prince of Wales (Edward VII).

"A Broadway Pageant" (p. 224). This poem was occasioned by the reception given to the Japanese Embassy in June 1860.

p. 227, l. 6: *"her eldest son"*, the Prince of Wales. Cf. "Year of Meteors" (p. 221).

"Out of the Cradle Endlessly Rocking" (p. 228). Originally published as "A Child's Reminiscence" in the New York *Saturday Press*, December 24, 1859. The poem was perhaps written about 1858 (see Bucke, p. 29). For a full discussion of its first appearance and reception see Thomas Olive Mabott and Rollo G. Silver, *A Child's Reminiscence*.

p. 228, l. 2: *"The Mocking Bird's Throat."* As to whether Whitman was at fault in placing the mocking bird on Long Island, it may be noted that J. P. Giraud, Jr., says that the gray mocking bird sometimes was seen there in the mating season at the period to which Whitman's poem refers. (*The Birds of Long Island*, New York, 1843, p. 82.)

p. 229, ll. 7 ff.: *"Shine! shine! shine!"* etc. The exalted music of this poem has been highly commended, and many passages of it, especially these lines, have been set to music by Stanley Addicks, W. W. Gilchrist, Arthur Hartmann, Marshall Kernochan, A. H. Ryder and Frank O. Warner.

"*As I Ebb'd with the Ocean of Life*" (p. 234). First published in the *Atlantic Monthly*, April 1860, as "Bardic Symbols".

"*Tears*" (p. 237). Set to music, 1905, by C. V. Stanford, Opus 97, No. 5.

"*To the Man-of-War Bird*" (p. 237). Published in the *Athenæum*, April 1, 1876.

"*Aboard at the Ship's Helm*" (p. 238). Set to music in an unpublished song by Phillip Dalmas.

"*Song for All Seas, All Ships*" (p. 241). Published in the New York *Daily Graphic*, April 4, 1873, under the title, "Sea Captains, Young or Old".

"*Patroling Barnegat*" (p. 242). Published in the *American*, June 1880 (Vol. X, p. 179) and republished in *Harper's Monthly*, April 1881. Set to music by Eugene Bonner.
The Barnegat Shoals are off the shore of New Jersey at the Barnegat Inlet and Long Beach.

"*After the Sea-Ship*" (p. 243). First published under the title "In the Wake Following", New York *Daily Graphic*, Christmas Number, 1874.

"*A Boston Ballad*" (p. 244). The occasion of this poem was the arrest of Anthony Burns in Boston and his rendition to slavery, on May 24, 1854, despite an attempt to free him led by T. W. Higginson. According to William Sloane Kennedy, Whitman intended to drop this poem, but was persuaded to retain it by John T. Trowbridge. (*The Fight of a Book for the World*, p. 175.)

"*Europe, the 72d and 73d Years of These States*" (p. 246). Whitman's chronology dates from the Declaration of Independence (1776), so that he refers to the years 1848 and 1849. The poem, one of his earliest in free verse, was published as "Resurgemus" in the New York *Tribune*, June 21, 1850. For a collection of the poems in the two versions, and the growth of Whitman's characteristic verse form, see U.P.P., I, pp. 27-30. The occasion was, of course, the abortive popular movements in Italy, Hungary, France and Germany, in these years. Compare "To a Foil'd European Revolutionaire" (p. 338), "O Star of France" (p. 360), "Spain, 1873-74" (p. 433), and "Resurgemus" (p. 505).

"*To a President*" (p. 251). The poem is apparently addressed to President Buchanan. Cf. poem entitled, "To the States" (p. 255).

"*The Dalliance of the Eagles*" (p. 252). First published in *Cope's Tobacco Plant*, November 1880. This poem was included in the Osgood list of expurgations (Bucke, p. 149). This poem seems to have been based on a description given to the poet by John Burroughs. (Barrus, p. 170.)

"*Roaming in Thought*" (p. 252). Cf. "Carlyle from American Points of View" (p. 780).

"*To the States*" (p. 255). Cf. "To a President" (p. 251).

"*Drum-Taps*" (p. 256). Apparently this group of poems, or some of them, was in manuscript as early as March 1863. (*Wound Dresser*, p. 61; also see pp. 163, 164, 188.)

"*Eighteen Sixty-One*" (p. 258). Cf. Letter VI (p. 887). Although Whitman in 1861 and 1862 was supporting himself by doing hack work for the Brooklyn *Standard* and the New York *Leader*, much of which had no reference to the war, it is unfair to assume that he was not profoundly moved by it from the start. (See U.P.P., I, LVII, 2, 222 ff., Glicksberg, and the note following.)

"*Beat! Beat! Drums!*" (p. 259). A manuscript letter dated October 1, 1861, offered this poem for $20, to James Russell Lowell, then editor of the *Atlantic Monthly* (Bayard Wyman collection). But the poem was actually published in *Harper's Weekly*, September 28, 1861, and copied in the New York *Leader* on the same date, where the third line from the end concluded with the exhortation, "Recruit! Recruit!" It seems clear that the poem, like Bryant's "Our Country's Call", which appeared in the New York *Ledger* on November 2, and Whittier's "The Summons", in the *Leader*, July 27, was written in an effort to counteract the moral effect of the defeat at Bull Run on July 21. See "Battle of Bull Run", and "The Stupor Passes" (pp. 620-624). For information concerning the original version of this poem, the editor is indebted to Mr. Ralph Adimari.

This poem was set to music by Coleridge-Taylor, Opus 45, No. 6.

"*Song of the Banner at Daybreak*" (p. 260). This is the only poem of Whitman's cast in dramatic form.

"*The Centenarian's Story*" (p. 270). According to Whitman's literary executors, Traubel, Bucke and Harned (Camden Edition, I, p. xix) the poet had a great uncle, the son of Nehemiah Whitman, his great grandfather, who "was a lieutenant in Col. Josiah Smith's regiment of the American Army. He participated in the disastrous battle of Brooklyn and there lost his life. In the 'Centennarian' story will be found some informal account of this portentious event". As editor of the *Eagle*, Whitman urged the creation of Washington Park (Fort Greene), wrote a patriotic ode about the patriots buried there (U.P.P., I, pp. 22-23), and gave considerable space to it in his "Brooklyniana" (U.P.P., II, pp. 242-246). Cf. also "The Sleepers", § 5 (p. 388).

"*Cavalry Crossing a Ford*" (p. 275). This poem has been set to music by Tillie White.

"*By the Bivouac's Fitful Flame*" (p. 276). This poem was set to music by Harvey Gaul.

"*Come Up from the Fields Father*" (p. 277). Manuscripts in the Bayard Wyman collection seem to identify this poem with the case of Oscar Cunningham, mentioned in one of Whitman's letters to his mother (p. 944). Whitman wrote such a letter to Cunningham's sister when he died in June 1864.

"*A March in the Ranks, Hard Pres't, and the Road Unknown*" (p. 280). For an early manuscript version of this incident see Glicksberg, pp. 123-125.

"*Dirge for Two Veterans*" (p. 288). This poem was set to music by F. L. Ritter, Opus 13.

"*The Artilleryman's Vision*" (p. 291). Cf. "The Sleepers", § 5 (p. 388).

"*Ethiopia Saluting the Colors*" (p. 292). Set to music by Coleridge-Taylor, Opus 51, and by Charles Wood.

"*World Take Good Notice*" (p. 293). A longer manuscript version of this poem was printed in *facsimile* by J. H. Johnston, a friend of the poet, in the *Century Magazine*, February 1911, Vol. 59, p. 532, as follows:

"Rise, lurid stars, woolly white no more;
Change, angry cloth—weft of the silver stars no more;
Orbs blushing scarlet—thirty four stars, red as flame,
On the blue bunting this day we sew.

World take good notice, silver stars have vanished;
Orbs now of scarlet—now mortal coals all aglow
Dots of molten iron, wakeful and ominous,
On the blue bunting henceforth appear."

"*O Tan-Faced Prairie-Boy*" (p. 293). This poem was set to music by Weda Cook Addicks.

"*Look Down Fair Moon*" (p. 294). This poem was set to music by Phillip Dalmas.

"*Reconciliation*" (p. 294). This poem was set to music by Phillip Dalmas.

"*As I Lay with My Head in Your Lap Camerado*" (p. 295). In William Rossetti's selected edition of Whitman's poems the title of this poem was "Questionable".

"*Memories of President Lincoln*" (p. 300). The relationship of Whitman and Lincoln is the subject of an entire volume by William E. Barton, an unsympathetic study, the occasional inaccuracies of which are pointed out by Charles I. Glicksberg in his *Walt Whitman and the Civil War*. For Whitman's contemporary references to Lincoln, see pp. 644, 651, 959; his memorial lecture on Lincoln is given on pp. 752-762.

Abraham Lincoln was shot in Ford's theater in Washington, Good Friday night, April 14, 1865, and died the next morning, After the funeral in Washington, the funeral train passed through Maryland, Pennsylvania, New Jersey, New York, Ohio, Indiana, to Springfield, Illinois, where the body was buried in the Oak Ridge Cemetery. Whitman makes use of this fact in his poem. An article in the *Atlantic Monthly*, June 1865, declared: "Along the line of more than 1500 miles his remains were borne, as it were, through continued lines of the people; and the number of mourners and the sincerity and unanimity of grief was such as never before attended the obsequies of a human being. So that the terrible catastrophe of his end hardly struck more awe than the majestic sorrow of the people."

p. 305, l. 25–p. 306, l. 24 : *"Come Lovely and Soothing Death"*, etc. In the 1876 Edition this passage was called "Death Carol". This poem was set to music by W. H. Neidlinge and by Nicolas Douty : the "Death Carol" passage by Stanley Addicks.

"O Captain! My Captain!" (p. 308). First published in New York *Saturday Press*, November 4, 1865. The poem has been set to music by Weda Cook Addicks, Frank Butcher, H. H. Huss, E. S. Kelley, Charles F. Manning, Cyril Scott, Donald Nicholas Tweedy and Charles Wood.

Although this is perhaps Whitman's best-known poem, it is so atypical that he at times resented the fact that its popularity tended to obscure his more individual work. Horace Traubel gives (II, pp. 332-333), with partial *facsimile* reproduction, an early manuscript version which varies considerably from the one printed :

MY CAPTAIN

The mortal voyage over, the gales and tempests done,
The ship that bears me nears her home the prize I sought is won,
The port is close, the bells I hear, the people all exulting,
While (As) steady sails and enters straight my wondrous veteran
    vessel ;
But O heart! heart! heart! leave you not the little spot,
Where on the deck my Captain lies—sleeping pale and dead.

O Captain! dearest Captain! get up and hear the bells ;
Get up and see the flying flags, and see the splendid sun,
For you it is the cities shout—for you the shores are crowded ;
For you the red-rose garlands, and electric eyes of women ;
O Captain! O my father! My arm I push beneath you ;
It is some dream that on the deck you slumber pale and dead.

My captain does not answer, his lips are closed and still,
My father does not feel my arm—he has no pulse nor will ;
But his ship, his ship, is anchor'd safe, the fearful trip is done,
The wondrous ship, the ship divine, its mighty object won,
And our cities walk in triumph—but O heart, heart, you stay,
Where on the deck my captain lies sleeping cold   dead.

And cities shout and thunder—but my heart.

And all career in triumph wide—but I with gentle tread,
Walk the deck my captain lies, sleeping cold and dead.

My captain does not answer, his lips are closed and still,
My father does not feel my arm, he has no pulse nor will,
But his ship, his ship is anchor'd safe—the fearful trip is done,
The wondrous ship, the well-tried ship, its proudest object won;
And my lands career in triumph—but I with gentle tread
Walk the spot my captain lies sleeping pale and dead.

"*By Blue Ontario's Shore*" (p. 310). Parts of this poem have been taken from the prose Preface to the 1855 Edition, others were composed for the 1856 Edition, and several passages, including §§ 1, 7, and 20, and parts of 14, 17, and 18, were added in 1867. A few lines were added in 1871.

p. 313, ll. 10-11: "*Attracting it body and soul . . . merits and demerits*". Included in the Osgood list of expurgations.

p. 315, ll. 3-4: "*Slavery—the murderous, treacherous conspiracy*", etc. Cf. "The Eighteenth Presidency" (p. 586), also composed in 1856.

p. 317, l. 5: "*He judges not . . . a helpless thing*". Cf. "To a Common Prostitute" (p. 353).

pp. 318-320, § 12: Compare "Democratic Vistas" (pp. 657-722, *passim*), and "Poetry To-Day in America". (Comp. Prose, p. 281.)

"*Reversals*" (p. 325). This is only a fragment of a poem called "Poem of the Proposition of Nakedness" in the 1856 edition, and "Respondez!" in 1867 and 1871 editions. The original poem appears on p. 511.

"*The Return of the Heroes*" (p. 327). First published in *Galaxy*, in September 1867, under the title, "A Carol of Harvest".

"*There Was a Child Went Forth*" (p. 332). Though this poem with its description of Whitman's father and mother is obviously more or less autobiographical, yet Traubel records (II, p. 228): "People have often asked him the meaning of the poem There was a Child Went Forth and he has always made the same answer: 'What is the meaning? I wonder what? I wonder what?' Once he said to Bonsall: 'Harry, maybe it has no meaning.' "

p. 333, l. 16: "*The mother at home*", etc. Cf. "The Sleepers" (p. 383), and "Faces" (p. 418).

p. 334, l. 13: "*These became part of that child*", etc. Cf. Tennyson's "Ulysses": "I am a part of all that I have met."

"*Old Ireland*" (p. 334). First published in the New York *Leader* November 2, 1861. The editor is indebted to Mr. Ralph Adimari for information about its first publication. Originally the last two lines read:

"And now with rosy and new blood, again among the nations of the earth,

Moves to-day, an armed man, in a new country."

Like "Beat! Beat! Drums!" this was published not long after the defeat at Bull Run and may have been intended also to stimulate recruiting among the Irish.

"*The City Dead-House*" (p. 335). Cf. "To A Common Prostitute" (p. 353).

"*To a Foil'd European Revolutionaire*" (p. 338). Cf. "Europe" (p. 246), "O Star of France" (p. 360), and "Spain" (p. 433).

"*Song of Prudence*" (p. 341). Parts of this poem are taken from the Preface to the 1855 edition. It is apparently indebted somewhat to Emerson's essay on "Prudence". Cf. also "Song of the Rolling Earth" (p. 203).

"*The Singer in the Prison*" (p. 344). First published in the *Saturday Evening Visitor*, December 1869, with the subtitle, "A Christmas Incident". Sidney H. Morse, when sculpturing Whitman, was told that this poem was based on a personal observation. As Morse recalled it, the singer was Parepa Rosa singing to the convicts in a prison in New York. (*In Re.*, p. 370.)

"*Warble for Lilac-time*" (p. 346). Published in *Galaxy*, May 1870.

"*Outlines for a Tomb*" (p. 347). Originally published in *Galaxy*, 1870, with the title, "Brother of All, With Generous Hand". The poem was a tribute to George Peabody, who gave large sums for science, for the education of the negro, and for improving living conditions among the poor in London. Though he died in London, November 14, 1869, he was buried in Massachusetts, February 1870. In "Two Rivulets", above the title appeared the following inscription:

☞ "To any Hospital or School-Founder, or Public Beneficiary, anywhere."

"*Out from Behind this Mask*" (p. 349). In "Two Rivulets" appeared under the title this explanatory note: "To confront My Portrait, illustrating 'the Wound Dresser', in *Leaves of Grass*."

"*To A Common Prostitute*" (p. 353). This poem was on the Osgood list, notwithstanding the fact that Whitman said, "It is nothing but the beautiful little idyl of the New Testament concerning the woman taken in adultery." (See Kennedy, pp. 125-127.)

"*Unfolded Out of the Folds*" (p. 356). It is not clear why Whitman did not include this poem in the "Children of Adam" group, where it would seem to belong.

p. 357, ll. 6-7: "*Unfolded out of the strong . . . embraces of the man.*" These two lines were on the Osgood list of expurgations.

"*Kosmos*" (p. 357). Cf. "Walt Whitman, a kosmos", etc., p. 48, l. 21.

"*O Star of France*" (p. 360). First published in *Galaxy*, June

1871. The occasion of this poem was the defeat of France in the Franco-Prussian War.

"*The Ox-Tamer*" (p. 362). First published in the New York *Daily Graphic*, Christmas Number, 1874.

"*An Old Man's Thought of School*" (p. 363). Recited by the author at the Cooper Public School in Camden and published in the New York *Daily Graphic*, November 3, 1874.

"*Wandering at Morn*" (p. 363). First published as "The Singing Thrush" in the New York *Daily Graphic*, March 15, 1873.

"*Italian Music in Dakota*" (p. 364). Cf. "Proud Music of the Storm" (p. 366), "The Mystic Trumpeter" (p. 421), "Plays and Operas Too" (p. 564), "Old Actors, Singers, Shows, Etc., in New York" (p. 875), "The Opera" (*New York Dissected*, pp. 18-23), and Louise Pound "Walt Whitman and Italian Music" (*American Mercury*, September 1925).

"*My Picture-Gallery*" (p. 365). First published in the *American*, October 1880. For a long manuscript out of which this short poem grew, see *Pictures, An Unpublished Poem of Walt Whitman* (Emory Holloway, editor), New York and London, 1927. Cf. also N. and F., pp. 77, 177.

"*The Prairie States*" (p. 365). A *facsimile* manuscript of this poem was printed in the catalogue of the Saltus Sale at the Anderson Galleries (1922), and in the *Art Autograph*, March 16, 1880. It is said to have been published on behalf of the Irish Famine Fund.

"*Proud Music of the Storm*" (p. 366). First published in the *Atlantic Monthly*, February 1869, but written some months earlier. For this poem Whitman received $100. (See Traubel, II, 21-23.) The poem was offered to the *Atlantic* through Whitman's friend, Ralph Waldo Emerson (Letter LXVIII, p. 981). Cf. For other Whitman compositions on music, see note on "Italian Music in Dakota" (p. 364).

"*Passage to India*" (p. 372). This poem was rejected by Bret Harte when submitted to the *Overland Monthly* in April 1870. It was first printed as a thin booklet in 1871 (copyright 1870), but parts of it had been written earlier. Section 5 was printed from a manuscript by the Brooklyn *Eagle*, October 26, 1911, where the date of composition is said to be about 1848. This, however, seems to be a mistake, for Traubel gives a letter to James T. Fields, offering it to the *Atlantic* on January 20, 1869, and it appeared in the London *Fortnightly Review* in April of that year. Another passage apparently intended for a separate poem is that in § 8, beginning, "O soul thou pleasest me", and ending with the section. Mr. Oscar Lion of New York owns this manuscript.

The occasion of the poem was the completion of the Suez Canal and the Pacific Railroad. Of the poem Whitman said, "There's more of me, the essential ultimate me, in that than in any of the poems ... the burden of it is evolution—the one thing escaping the other—the unfolding of cosmic purposes." (Traubel, I, pp. 156-157.)

"*Prayer of Columbus*" (p. 381). First published in *Harper's Magazine*, March 1874, where it was accompanied by the following explanatory note:

"It was near the close of his indomitable and pious life—on his last voyage when nearly 70 years of age—that Columbus, to save his two remaining ships from foundering in the Caribbean Sea in a terrible storm, had to run them ashore on the Island of Jamaica where, laid up for a long and miserable year—1503—he was taken very sick, had several relapses, his men revolted, and death seem'd daily imminent; though he was eventually rescued, and sent home to Spain to die, unrecognized, neglected and in want. ... It is only ask'd, as preparation and atmosphere for the following lines, that the bare authentic facts be recall'd and realized, and nothing contributed by the fancy. See, the Antillean Island, with its florid skies and rich foliage and scenery, the waves beating the solitary sands, and the hulls of the ships in the distance. See, the figure of the great Admiral, walking the beach, as a stage, in this sublimest tragedy—for what tragedy, what poem, so piteous and majestic as the real scene?—and hear him uttering—as his mystical and religious soul surely utter'd, the ideas following—perhaps, in their equivalents, the very words." (Inclusive Edition, *Leaves*, p. 682.)

Whitman wrote to Pete Doyle concerning this poem: "I am told that I have colored it with thoughts of myself—very likely." (*Calamus*, p. 145.)

"*The Sleepers*" (p. 383). Though on the surface this poem is an attempt to picture the mind in sleep (see Bucke, p. 171), it serves also as a key to Whitman's poetic method (see Holloway, pp. 123 ff.).

p. 384, l. 9: "*he with his palm ... of the husband*". These phrases were on the Osgood list of expurgations.

p. 387, §4: The reference here is to the *Mexico*, wrecked off Hempstead, Long Island, in 1840. (See "Paumanok, and my Life on it as Child and Young Man." (p. 538).

p. 390, ll. 21-22: "*Perfect and clean ... and plumb*". These lines were on the Osgood list of expurgations.

"*Transpositions*" (p. 392). Part of the much longer poem "Respondez!" from the 1856 edition (p. 511).

"*To think of Time*" (p. 392). Cf. "Crossing Brooklyn Ferry" (p. 147).

"*Darest Thou Now O Soul*" (p. 399). First published in the *Broadway Magazine* (London), October 1868. This poem has been set to music by Rutland Boughton, G. W. Chadwick, Harper Seed and Eva Ruth Spalding.

"*Whispers of Heavenly Death*" (p. 399). First published in *Broadway Magazine* (London), October 1868

"*Chanting the Square Deific*" (p. 400). To Daniel G. Brinton, Whitman commented on this poem as follows: "It would be hard to give the idea mathematical expression: the idea of spiritual equity—of spiritual substance: the four-square entity—the north, south, east, west of the constituted universe (even the soul universe)—the four sides as sustaining the universe (the supernatural something): this is not the poem, but the idea back of the poem or below the poem. I am lame enough trying to explain it in other words—the idea seems to fit its own words better than mine. You see, at the time the poem wrote itself: now I am trying to write it." (Traubel, I, p. 156.) See also Leon Howard, "A Critique of Whitman's Transcendentalism" (*Modern Language Notes*, January 1931).

"*That Music Always Round Me*" (p. 405). Cf. "The Mystic Trumpeter" (p. 421), and "Proud Music of the Storm" (p. 366).

"*Quicksand Years*" (p. 404). For manuscript versions of this poem differing from the text, see Glicksberg, pp. 125-126.

"*A Noiseless Patient Spider*" (p. 406). First published in *Broadway Magazine* (London), October 1868. For an early manuscript of this poem, see U.P.P., II, p. 93.

"*The Last Invocation*" (p. 408). First published in the *Broadway Magazine* (London), October 1868. Originally without title, this poem is sometimes called "The Imprisoned Soul" (*Oxford Book of English Verse*). This poem was set to music by Eugene Bonner, Frank Bridge, Ada Weigle Powers and Eva Ruth Spalding.

"*Pensive and Flattering*" (p. 409). First published in *Broadway Magazine* (London), October 1868.

"*Thou mother with Thy Equal Brood*" (p. 410). This poem was read by Whitman before the United Literary Societies of Dartmouth College at commencement on Wednesday, June 26, 1872 (*Calamus*, p. 96). For an account of the circumstances connected with this occasional poem, see Perry, pp. 203-210, and Harold W. Blodgett, "Walt Whitman's Dartmouth Visit". (*Dartmouth Alumni Magazine*, February 1933.)

"*A Paumanok Picture*" (p. 415). Cf. "Paumanok, and my Life on it as Child and Young Man" (p. 538).

"*Faces*" (p. 418). For a counterpart of this poem, see "Street Yarn". (*New York Dissected*, pp. 128-132.)

p. 420, ll. 1-6: "*I saw the face*", etc. This passage Whitman said, was suggested by his brother Eddie, who was mentally defective.

p. 421, § 5: This is commonly interpreted as a description of Whitman's Quaker grandmother, Amy Williams Van Velsor.

p. 420, l. 25-p. 421, l. 3: "*She speaks . . . my breast and shoulders*". This passage was on the Osgood list of expurgations.

"*The Mystic Trumpeter*" (p. 421). First published in the *Kansas Magazine*, February 1872. Cf. "Proud Music of the Storm" (p. 366), "Italian Music in Dakota", and "That Music Always Round Me" (p. 405). Many years ago the present editor examined a manuscript, then in the collection of Mr. W. R. Benjamin, which indicated that one Julius Bing supplied Whitman with notes on classical music when he was writing this poem.

"*Mannahatta*" (p. 427). Whitman was fond of referring to Manhattan in this way in his poetry, and in compliment to him his brother Jefferson named a daughter Mannahatta.

"*A Riddle Song*" (p. 429). Whitman never gave the key to this riddle, but Dr. Bucke suggested that it is "good cause" of "old cause" (Traubel, II, 228); Kennedy offers "the Ideal" (*The Fight of a Book for the World*, p. 188). In the Bayard Wyman collection is a printed proof of the poem which omits lines 2-10, 29, and makes many changes in punctuation. Apparently it was published in the first number of *Sunnyside Press* in the spring of 1880 (see Barrus, p. 191).

"*Excelsior*" (p. 430). Whitman was an admirer of Longfellow, and may have borrowed the title from him. Cf. "Ambition" (p. 502).

"*Ah Poverties, Wincings, and Sulky Retreats*" (p. 431). Cf. "Crossing Brooklyn Ferry", § 6 (p. 150).

"*Weave in, My Hearty Life*" (p. 432). To show the metrical regularity of this poem, William Sloane Kennedy has arranged it in conventional form. (Kennedy, p. 167.)

"*Spain, 1873-74*" (p. 433). First published without the date and the title in the New York *Daily Graphic*, March 24, 1873, with the signature, "Washington, March 23, 1873, Walt Whitman".

"*From Far Dakota's Cañons*" (p. 434). First published as "A Death-Sonnet for Custer", in the New York *Tribune*, July 10, 1876. Cf. "Custer's Last Rally" (p. 793).

"*What Best I See In Thee*" (p. 436). President Grant returned from his world tour in the fall of 1879. Cf. "Death of General Grant" (p. 463), and "The Silent General" (p. 767).

"*Spirit that Form'd This Scene*" (p. 436). First published in the *Critic*, September 10, 1881.

"*A Clear Midnight*" (p. 437). Set to music by Eugene Bonner, F. S. Converse, Phillip Dalmas, W. H. Pommer, Ada Weigle Powers, Lynnel Reed, and Eva Ruth Spalding.

"*Years of the Modern*" (p. 438). Though first published in 1865 (in *Drum-Taps*), parts of this poem were written in prose form in 1856. (Cf. "The Eighteenth Presidency", pp. 586-602.)

"*As at Thy Portals also Death*" (p. 445). Whitman's mother died, May 23, 1873.

"*The Artilleryman's Vision*" (p. 291). Cf. "The Dying Veteran" (p. 473), and "The Sleepers", § 5 (p. 388).

"*The Sobbing of the Bells*" (p. 448). This tribute to President Garfield, whom Whitman had known personally (Traubel, I, p. 324), written at the Hotel Bulfinch in Boston (Kennedy, p. 3), was first published in the Boston *Daily Globe*, September 27, 1881. A *facsimile* reproduction of the manuscript is to be found in Bucke, facing p. 54. Whitman once expressed a doubt about the propriety of retaining the poem because it borrows a line from Poe's "The Bells" for its title. (Traubel, III, p. 129.)

"*So Long*" (p. 450). First appearing in the 1860 edition, this poem was always kept at the end of *Leaves of Grass* (though the Annexes in late editions came after it).

"*Mannahatta*" (p. 454). First published in New York *Herald*, February 27, 1888. Whitman has another poem with the same title (p. 427).

"*Paumanok*" (p. 454). First published in New York *Herald*, February 29, 1888.

"*From Montauk Point*" (p. 454). First published in New York *Herald*, March 1, 1888.

"*A Carol Closing Sixty-nine*" (p. 455). First published in New York *Herald*, May 21, 1888. Whitman had offered this poem to *Lippincott's Magazine*, but when it did not appear in the June issue, he withdrew it and sent it to the *Herald* in order that it might appear near his birthday (Traubel, I, p. 179). A *Critic* paragraph taking note of his approaching birthday, declared that "the number of those who greatly admire his writings, though without thinking them the be-all and the end-all of American poetry, and who feel for his personality a heartfelt and growing affection has increased in proportion as his work and the story of his career have become better known". (*Critic*, May 25, 1889.)

"*The Bravest Soldiers*" (p. 455). First published in New York *Herald*, March 18, 1888.

"*A Font of Type*" (p. 455). In John Russell Young's *Men and Memories* (Vol. I, p. 107) the original version of this poem is given as follows:

"O latent mine! O unlaunched voices!
    passionate powers, all eligible.
Wrath, argument, praise, or comic leer, or
    prayer devout, or love's caress,
(Not nonpareil, brevier, bourgeois, long primer, merely),
Shores, oceans, roused to fury and to death,
Or soothed to ease and sheeny sun, and sleep,
With these pallid slivers, waiting.

"*As I Sit Writing Here*" (p. 456). First published in New York *Herald*, May 14, 1888.

"*My Canary Bird*" (p. 456). First published in New York *Herald*, March 2, 1888.

"*Queries to My Seventieth Year*" (p. 456). First published in New York *Herald*, May 2, 1888.

"*The Wallabout Martyrs*" (p. 456). First published in New York *Herald*, March 16, 1888. Cf. "The Centenarian's Story" (p. 270).

"*The First Dandelion*" (p. 457). First published in New York *Herald*, March 12, 1888. It appeared, ironically, on the morning of New York's greatest blizzard, and was parodied in the press.

"*America*" (p. 457). First published in New York *Herald*, February 11, 1888.

"*To-day and Thee*" (p. 457). First published in New York *Herald*, April 23, 1888.

"*After the Dazzle of Day*" (p. 458). First published in New York *Herald*, February 3, 1888.

"*Out of May's Shows Selected*" (p. 458). First published in New York *Herald*, May 10, 1888.

"*Halcyon Days*" (p. 458). First published in New York *Herald*, January 29, 1888.

"*Fancies at Navesink*" (p. 459). All these poems except the fifth were published in *Nineteenth Century Magazine*, August 1885, after having been declined by Mr. H. M. Alden for *Harper's Magazine*. (Traubel, I, p. 61.)

"*Election Day, November 1884*" (p. 462). This poem was first published in the *Philadelphia Press*, October 26, 1884, using a part of the first line for a title. *Diary in Canada* (p. 73) contains the following explanatory note:

PRESIDENTIAL ELECTION. *Oct.* 31, '84

The political parties are trying—but mostly in vain—to get up some fervor of excitement on the pending Presidential election. It comes off next Tuesday. There is no question at issue of any importance. I cannot "enthuse" at all. I think of the elections of '30 and '20. Then there was something to arouse a fellow. But I like well the *fact* of all these national elections—have written a little poem about it (to order)—published in a Philadelphia daily of 26th instant. [The candidates in '84 were Blaine and Cleveland; the issues, tariff and Chinese exclusion. Blaine was defeated, owing to Conkling's defection.]

"*With Husky-Haughty Lips, O Sea!*" (p. 462). First published in *Harper's Magazine*, March 1884. Fifty dollars was paid for the poem on November 30, 1883 (Traubel, II, p. 220). The poem was written at Ocean Grove, New Jersey, where Whitman was visiting with John Burroughs, September 26–October 1, 1883 (Traubel, I, p. 406).

"*Death of General Grant*" (p. 463). Cf. "What Best I See in Thee" (p. 436), and "The Silent General" (p. 767). First published in the *Critic*, August 15, 1885, as "Grant". In a printed proofsheet the first line was used as a title and a second section was added as follows:

"And still shall be;—resume again, thou hero heart!
Strengthen to firmest day, O rosy dawn of hope!

Thou dirge I started first, to joyful shout reversed!—
    and thou, O grave,

Wait long and long."

"*Red Jacket (from Aloft)*" (p. 464). First published in the *Philadelphia Press*, October 10, 1884. (Rollo G. Silver, "Thirty-one Letters of Walt Whitman", *American Literature*, January 1937, p. 430.)

"*Washington's Monument, February, 1885*" (p. 464). Probably first printed in *Philadelphia Press*, February 22, 1885.

"*Of that Blythe Throat of Thine*" (p. 465). First published in *Harper's Monthly*, January 1885. The price paid was $30. (Traubel, II, p. 218-219.)

"*Broadway*" (p. 465). First published in New York *Herald*, April 10, 1888. Cf. "Broadway". (*New York Dissected*, pp. 119-124.)

"*To Get the Final Lilt of Songs*" (p. 466). First published in New York *Herald*, April 16, 1888, after having been rejected by the *Cosmopolitan*. (Traubel, I, p. 37.)

"*Old Salt Kossabone*" (p. 466). First published in New York *Herald*, February 25, 1888.

"*Continuities*" (p. 467). First published in New York *Herald*, March 20, 1888.

"*Yonnondio*" (p. 468): First published in the *Critic*, November 26, 1887. For a discussion of the meaning of the Indian word, see Traubel, II, p. 269. A *Critic* correspondent, who signed his letter "Etymologist", said Whitman had been misinformed—that the Hurons and Iroquois used it to mean "Beautiful Mountain", and applied it to the Canadian Governor, Montmagny, whose name had been incorrectly explained to them. (*Critic*, December 17, 1887.)

"*Life*" (p. 468): First published in New York *Herald*, April 5, 1888.

"*Going Somewhere*" (p. 469): First published in *Lippincott's Magazine*, November 1887. This elegiac poem was a tribute to Mrs. Anne Gilchrist. For the story of her friendship with the poet, see Harned; also Letters LXXV (p. 987), LXXXVIII (p. 998), XCVI (p. 1005), CIV (p. 1012), CVII (p. 1016), CXXIV (p. 1029), CXXVIII (p. 1032), CXXXI (p. 1035), CXL (p. 1042), and

CLXIV (p. 1045). The manuscript of this poem is reproduced in *facsimile* in Thomas Donaldson, *Walt Whitman, the Man*, facing p. 74.

"*Small the Theme of My Chant*" (p. 469): Cf. "One's Self I Sing" (p. 3).

"*True Conquerors*" (p. 470): First published in New York *Herald*, February 15, 1888.

"*The United States to Old World Critics*" (p. 470). First published in New York *Herald*, May 27, 1888.

"*The Calming Thought of All*" (p. 470). First published in New York *Herald*, May 27, 1888.

"*Life and Death*" (p. 471). First published in New York *Herald*, May 23, 1888.

"*Soon shall the Winter's Foil be Here*" (p. 472). First published in New York *Herald*, February 21, 1888.

"*The Dying Veteran*" (p. 473). Cf. "The Artilleryman's Vision" (p. 291). Whitman wrote to Kennedy, "A New York newspaper syndicate (S. S. McClure, Tribune Building) vehemently solicited and gave me $25 (far more than it is worth)." (Kennedy, p. 55.)

"*A Prairie Sunset*" (p. 473). First published in New York *Herald*, March 9, 1888.

"*Twenty Years*" (p. 474). First published in *Magazine of Art* (in England, July 1888; in America, August 1888), with a line drawing. The poem had been requested by M. H. Spielmann, editor of the magazine, on November 30, 1887. (Traubel, II, p. 232-233.)

"*Orange Buds by Mail from Florida*" (p. 474). First published in New York *Herald*, March 19, 1888.

"*Twilight*" (p. 475). First published in the *Century Magazine*, December 1887. The price paid was $10 (Kennedy, p. 55). The word "oblivion" in the poem called forth numerous protests from Whitman readers as being inconsistent with his philosophy. For his self defense, see Traubel, I, pp. 140-141.

"*You Lingering Sparse Leaves of Me*" (p. 475). First published in *Lippincott's Magazine*, November 1887.

"*Not Meager Latent Boughs Alone*" (p. 475). First published in *Lippincott's Magazine*, November 1887.

"*The Dead Emperor*" (p. 476). First published in New York *Herald*, March 10, 1888, where it is dated March 9. The poem was written at the request of the *Herald*. Concerning the criticism it aroused among Whitman's democratic and liberal friends, he said: "You know, I include Kings, Queens, Emperors, Nobles, Barons, and the aristocracy generally, in my net—excluding nobody and nothing human—and this does not seem to be relished by these narrow-minded folks." (J. Johnston and J. W. Wallace, *Visits to Walt Whitman in* 1890-1891, 1917, p. 50.)

"*As the Greek's Signal Flame*" (p. 476). First published in the New York *Herald*, December 15, 1887, with the heading, "Walt Whitman's Praise". In the *Herald* version, between lines 1 and 2, appears the line, "(Tally of many hard strain'd battle struggle, year—triumphant only at the last.)" Although Whittier is said to have thrown into the fire the complimentary copy of the first edition which Whitman sent him (Perry, 1908, p. 100), the poets admired each other personally, and Whitman at his seventy-second birthday dinner drank a toast to the Quaker poet, "a noble old man". (*In Re*, p. 297.)

"*The Dismantled Ship*" (p. 476). First published in New York *Herald*, February 23, 1888. Whitman said to Traubel: "Yes, it was suggested by the picture in Harned's parlor: that's me—that's my old hulk—was laid up at last: no good anymore—no good"— pausing—"a fellow might get melancholy seeing himself in such a mirror—but I guess we can see through as well as in the mirrors when the test comes!" (Traubel, I, p. 390.) Mr. Harned gave to the present editor a similar account of the origin of this poem.

"*An Evening Lull*" (p. 477). For a discussion concerning the poem, between Whitman, Traubel, and Bucke, see Traubel, I, pp. 354, 472-491.

"*Old Age's Lambent Peaks*" (p. 477). First published in the *Century*, September 1888.

"*After the Supper and Talk*" (p. 478). First published in *Lippincott's Magazine*, 1887. The manuscript of this poem is reproduced in *facsimile* in the *Complete Writings* (1902), Vol. II, facing p. 322.

"*Second Annex*" (*Good-Bye My Fancy*) (p. 479). In Whitman's final edition this group of poems had the following preface:

"Had I not better withhold (in this old age and paralysis of me) such little tags and fringe-dots (maybe specks, stains), as follow a long dusty journey, and witness it afterward? I have probably not been enough afraid of careless touches, from the first—and am not now—nor of parrot-like repetitions—nor platitudes and the commonplace. Perhaps I am too democratic for such avoidances. Besides, is not the verse-field, as originally plann'd by my theory, now sufficiently illustrated—and full time for me to silently retire? —(indeed amid no loud call or market for my sort of poetic utterance).

In answer, or rather defiance, to that kind of well-put interrogation, here comes this little cluster, and conclusion of my preceding clusters. Though not at all clear that, as here collated, it is worth printing (certainly I have nothing fresh to write)—I while away the hours of my 72d year—hours of forced confinement in my den— by putting in shape this small old age collation:

Last droplets of and after spontaneous rain,
From many limpid distillations and past showers;
(Will they germinate anything? mere exhalations as they all are
    —the land's and sea's—America's;
Will they filter to any deep emotion? any heart and brain?

However that may be, I feel like improving to-day's opportunity
and wind up. During the last two years I have sent out, in the lulls
of illness and exhaustion, certain chirps—lingering-dying ones
probably (undoubtedly)—which I may as well gather and put in
fair type while able to see correctly—(for my eyes plainly warn me
they are dimming, and my brain more and more palpably neglects
or refuses, month after month, even slight tasks or revisions).

In fact, here I am these current years 1890 and '91, (each succes-
sive fortnight getting stiffer and stuck deeper) much like some
hard-cased dilapidated grim ancient shell-fish or time-bang'd
conch (no legs, utterly non-locomotive) cast up high and dry on the
shore-sands, helpless to move anywhere—nothing left but behave
myself quiet, and while away the days yet assign'd, and discover if
there is anything for the said grim and time-bang'd conch to be got
at last out of inherited good spirits and primal buoyant centre-
pulses down there deep somewhere within his gray-blurr'd old
shell. . . . (Reader, you must allow a little fun here—for one reason
there are too many of the following poemets about death, &c., and
for another the passing hours (July 5, 1890) are so sunny-fine. And
old as I am I feel to-day almost a part of some frolicsome wave,
or for sporting yet like a kid or kitten—probably a streak of
physical adjustment and perfection here and now. I believe I have
it in me perennially anyhow.)

Then behind all, the deep down consolation (it is a glum one, but
I dare not be sorry for the fact of it in the past, nor refrain from
dwelling, even vaunting here at the end) that this late-years palsied
old shorn and shell-fish condition of me is the indubitable out-
come and growth, now near for 20 years along, of too over-zealous,
over-continued bodily and emotional excitement and action
through the times of 1862, '3, '4, and '5, visiting and waiting on
wounded and sick army volunteers, both sides, in campaigns or
contests, or after them, or in hospitals or fields south of Washing-
ton City, or in that place and elsewhere—those hot, sad, wrenching
times—the army volunteers, all States—or North or South—the
wounded, suffering, dying—the exhausting, sweating summers,
marches, battles, carnage—those trenches hurriedly heap'd by the
corpse-thousands, mainly unknown—Will the America of the
future—will this vast rich Union ever realize what itself cost, back
there after all?—those hecatombs of battle-deaths—Those times
of which, O far-off reader, this whole book is indeed finally but a
reminiscent memorial from thence by me to you?"

"*Sail Out for Good, Eidólon Yacht*" (p. 479). First published in
Lippincott's Magazine, March 1881.

"*On, on the Same, Ye Jocund Twain!*" (p. 480). Whitman is

quoted as saying that this poem was rejected by the *Century Magazine* as being merely personal. (Frank Harris, *Contemporary Portraits*, Third Series, p. 221.)

"*My 71st Year*" (p. 481). First published in the *Century Magazine*, November 1889.

"*The Pallid Wreath*" (p. 481). First published in the *Critic*, January 10, 1891.

"*Old Age's Ship & Crafty Death's*" (p. 482). First published in the *Century Magazine*, February 1890.

"*To the Pending Year*" (p. 483). First published in the *Critic*, with the title, "To the Year 1889", January 5, 1889.

"*Bravo, Paris Exposition!*" (p. 483). First published in *Harper's Weekly*, September 28, 1889.

"*Interpolation Sounds*" (p. 484). First published in New York *Herald*, August 12, 1888, without title. Whitman was chagrined that this poem, written in "ten minutes or so", was displayed so prominently in the paper. (Traubel, II, p. 125.)

"*To the Sun-set Breeze*" (p. 485). First published in *Lippincott's Magazine*, December 1890; previously rejected by *Harper's*. (Frank Harris, *Contemporary Portraits*, Third Series, p. 221.)

"*Old Chants*" (p. 485). First published in *Truth*, New York, March 19, 1891. Cf. "With Antecedents" (p. 222); also "Preparatory Reading and Thought". (N. and F., pp. 75-149.)

"*Sounds of the Winter*" (p. 487). First published in *Lippincott's Magazine*, March 1891.

"*A Twilight Song*" (p. 487). First published in the *Century Magazine*, May 1890.

"*When the Full-Grown Poet Came*" (p. 488). Cf. "Passage to India", § 5 (p. 375).

"*Osceola*" (p. 488). First published in *Munson's Illustrated World*, April 1890.

"*A Voice from Death*" (p. 489). First published in New York *World*, June 7, 1889.

"*The Commonplace*" (p. 491). First published, in *facsimile*, in *Munson's Illustrated World*, March 1891. (Rollo G. Silver, *American Literature*, January 1937, p. 435.)

"*The Unexpressed*" (p. 493). First published in *Lippincott's Magazine*, March 1891. A Whitman manuscript, on display in the Whitman Exhibition at the New York Public Library in 1925, indicates that the poem had been offered to *Harper's*, October 18, 1890.

"*Grand is the Seen*" (p. 494). A manuscript showing several variations was published in the *Conservator*, January 1897:

"Grand is the seen, the light—grand are the sky & stars.
  Grand is the earth, & grand are time & space,

> And grand their laws so multiform, so evolutionary, puzzling,
> lasting;
> Then grander is one's unseen soul, endowing comprehending
> those—
> Lighting the light, the sky & stars, sailing the sea, delving the
> earth,
> More multiform—more puzzling than they, more evolutionary
> vast & lasting."

"*A Kiss to the Bride*" (p. 497). Cf. Letter CXXVIII, n. (p. 1032).

"*Nay, Tell Me Not To-day the Published Shame*" (p. 497). First published in New York *Daily Graphic*, March 5, 1873.

"*Of Many a Smutch'd Deed Reminiscent*" (p. 499). Cf. "Ah Poverties, Wincings and Sulky Retreats" (p. 431), and "Crossing Brooklyn Ferry, § 6 (p. 150). The manuscript of this poem appears in N. and F., p. 39. Probably it was first published after the poet's death. Other "Old Age Echoes" may belong in the same category such as the first five poems in the group and "Supplement Hours".

"*Death's Valley*" (p. 499). First published in *Harper's Magazine*, April 1892.

"*A Thought of Columbus*" (p. 501). A *facsimile* of the manuscript of this, Whitman's last deliberate composition, was published in *Once a Week*, July 9, 1892. Cf. "Prayer of Columbus" (p. 381).

EARLY POEMS

"*Ambition*" (p. 502). First published in *Brother Jonathan*, January 29, 1842. The poem is an elaboration of "Fame's Vanity", published in the *Long Island Democrat*, October 23, 1839. Both poems were reprinted in U.P.P. (I, pp. 4-5, 19-20). A comparison of them shows gradual improvement in verse composition. Cf. "A Backward Glance O'er Travel'd Roads" (p. 858).

"*Blood-Money*" (p. 503). This poem, almost the first that Whitman published in free verse, appeared in Horace Greeley's New York *Tribune*, Supplement, March 22, 1850. It was inspired, like Whittier's "Ichabod", by Webster's speech conciliating the slave states, on the 7th of March, and by the Fugitive Slave Law.

"*Resurgemus*" (p. 505). First published in the New York *Daily Tribune*, June 21, 1850. Cf. "Europe, The 72d and 73d Years of These States" (p. 246). A comparison of the two versions is made in U.P.P., I, pp. xci, 27-30.

DISTRIBUTORS
for the Wordsworth Poetry Library

AUSTRALIA, BRUNEI, MALAYSIA & SINGAPORE

Reed Editions
22 Salmon Street
Port Melbourne
Vic 3207
Australia
Tel: (03) 646 6716
Fax: (03) 646 6925

GREAT BRITAIN & IRELAND

Wordsworth Editions Ltd
Cumberland House
Crib Street
Ware
Hertfordshire SG12 9ET

HOLLAND & BELGIUM

Uitgeverij en Boekhandel
Van Gennup BV, Spuistraat 283
1012 VR Amsterdam, Holland

INDIA

Om Book Service
1690 First Floor
Nai Sarak, Delhi - 110006
Tel: 3279823/3265303
Fax: 3278091

ITALY

Magis Books
Piazza della Vittoria 1/C
42100 Reggio Emilia
Tel: 0522-452303
Fax: 0522-452845

NEW ZEALAND

Whitcoulls Limited
Private Bag 92098, Auckland

SOUTHERN AFRICA

Struik Book Distributors (Pty) Ltd
Graph Avenue
Montague Gardens
7441
P O Box 193
Maitland
7405
South Africa
Tel: (021) 551-5900
Fax: (021) 551-1124

USA, CANADA & MEXICO

Universal Sales & Marketing
230 Fifth Avenue
Suite 1212
New York, NY 10001 USA
Tel: 212-481-3500
Fax: 212-481-3534